The Temple Architecture of India

Main ceiling, Mahavira temple,
Kumbhariya (Gujarat), *c* 1062 (**15.11**).

THE TEMPLE ARCHITECTURE OF INDIA

Adam Hardy

WILEY
wiley.com

To Fiona, Duncan and Benedict

Acknowledgements

For their photographs I would like to thank Rick Asher, Fiona Buckee, Anne Casile, Julia Hegewald, Adrian Smythies and especially Gerard Foekema, whose many wonderful pictures have made this book more beautiful. Geoffrey Samuel made helpful suggestions and MA Dhaky was generous as ever with his knowledge. I am very grateful to Shital Soni for help with maps and figures. Thanks to my parents for first awakening and sharing my interest in Indian art, and to my wife and sons for their love and patience.

Picture credits: all images are courtesy of the author unless otherwise stated.

Published in Great Britain in 2007 by John Wiley & Sons Ltd

Copyright © 2007
John Wiley & Sons Ltd, The Atrium, Southern Gate, Chichester,
West Sussex PO19 8SQ, England
Telephone +44 (0) 1243 779777

Email (for orders and customer service enquiries): cs-books@wiley.co.uk
Visit our Home Page on www.wiley.com

Anniversary Logo Design: Richard Pacifico

All Rights Reserved. No part of this publication may be reproduced, stored in a retrieval system or transmitted in any form or by any means, electronic, mechanical, photocopying, recording, scanning or otherwise, except under the terms of the Copyright, Designs and Patents Act 1988 or under the terms of a licence issued by the Copyright Licensing Agency Ltd, 90 Tottenham Court Road, London W1T 4LP, UK, without the permission in writing of the Publisher. Requests to the Publisher should be addressed to the Permissions Department, John Wiley & Sons Ltd, The Atrium, Southern Gate, Chichester, West Sussex PO19 8SQ, England, or emailed to permreq@wiley.co.uk, or faxed to +44 (0) 1243 770620.

Designations used by companies to distinguish their products are often claimed as trademarks. All brand names and product names used in this book are trade names, service marks, trademarks or registered trademarks of their respective owners. The Publisher is not associated with any product or vendor mentioned in this book.

This publication is designed to provide accurate and authoritative information in regard to the subject matter covered. It is sold on the understanding that the Publisher is not engaged in rendering professional services. If professional advice or other expert assistance is required, the services of a competent professional should be sought.

Other Wiley Editorial Offices:

John Wiley & Sons Inc, 111 River Street, Hoboken, NJ 07030, USA

Jossey-Bass, 989 Market Street, San Francisco, CA 94103-1741, USA

Wiley-VCH Verlag GmbH, Boschstr. 12, D-69469 Weinheim, Germany

John Wiley & Sons Australia Ltd, 42 McDougall Street, Milton, Queensland 4064, Australia

John Wiley & Sons (Asia) Pte Ltd, 2 Clementi Loop #02-01, Jin Xing Distripark, Singapore 129809

John Wiley & Sons Canada Ltd, 6045 Freemont Blvd, Mississauga, Ontario, L5R 4J3

Wiley also publishes its books in a variety of electronic formats. Some content that appears in print may not be available in electronic books.

Executive Commissioning Editor: Helen Castle
Project Editor: Miriam Swift
Publishing Assistant: Calver Lezama

ISBN 978-0-470-02827-8

Page design and layouts by Artmedia Press, London
Printed and bound by Conti Tipocolor, Italy

This book is printed on acid-free paper responsibly manufactured from sustainable forestry in which at least two trees are planted for each one used for paper production.

Contents

6		Maps
8	Part 1	CONTEXT AND CONCEPTS
10	1	Introduction
22	2	Centres of Power
36	3	Temple, Body and Movement
44	4	The Emanating Universe
56	5	Placing the Gods
62	6	The Architect and Unfolding Traditions
72	Part 2	PRECURSORS
74	7	Early Indian Architecture
82	8	Later Rock-Cut Architecture
88	Part 3	TEMPLE DESIGN
90	9	Plans and Spaces
106	10	Nagara Shrines
124	11	Dravida Shrines
136	12	Geometry
144	13	Mouldings
148	14	Pillars
156	15	Ceilings
160	16	Gavakshas
166	Part 4	A BRIEF HISTORY OF NAGARA TEMPLES
168	17	Early Nagara Temples
174	18	Latina and Related Valabhi Temples
182	19	Shekhari Temples
188	20	Bhumija Temples
192	21	Temples of Eastern India
204	Part 5	A BRIEF HISTORY OF DRAVIDA TEMPLES
206	22	Early Dravida Temples
210	23	The Great 8th-Century Dravida Temples
216	24	Temples of the Cholas and Their Contemporaries
222	25	The Karnata Dravida Tradition Continued
232	Part 6	LEGACY
234	26	What Happened Afterwards
242	27	What Next?
244		Glossary and Bibliography
246		Index

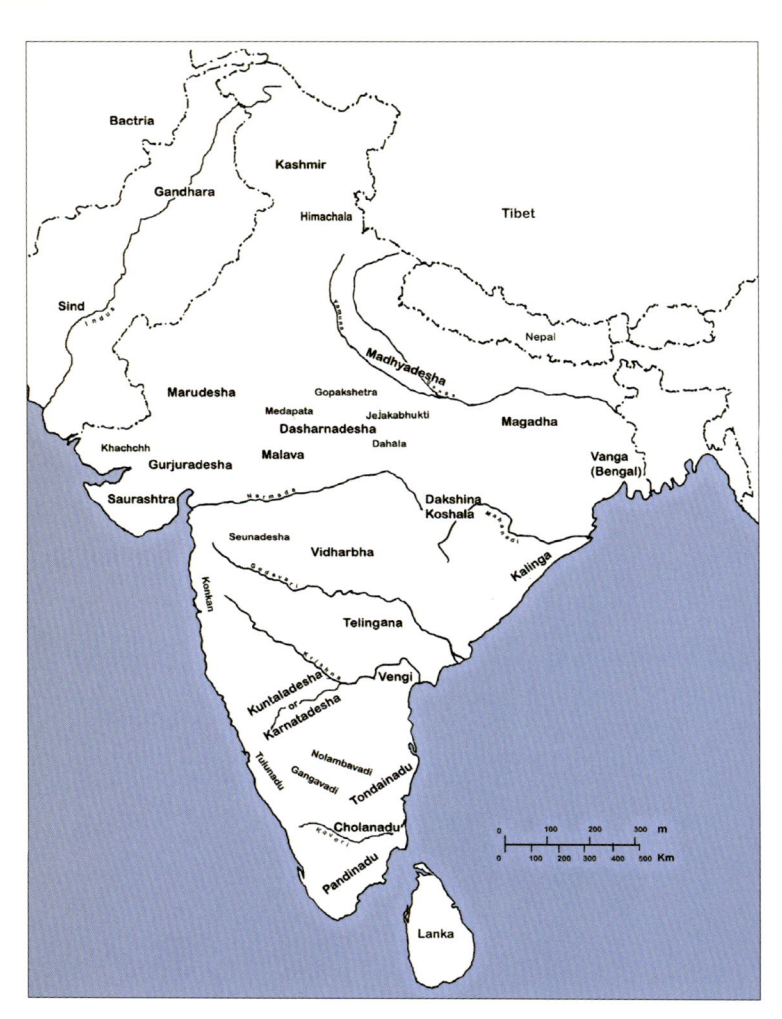

Top left Map 1. Map of India with names of ancient and medieval kingdoms.

Top right Map 2. Map of India showing modern states.

Right Map 3. Selected Buddhist sites and rock-cut cave temples, c 300 BC–AD 800 (see Chapters 7 and 8).

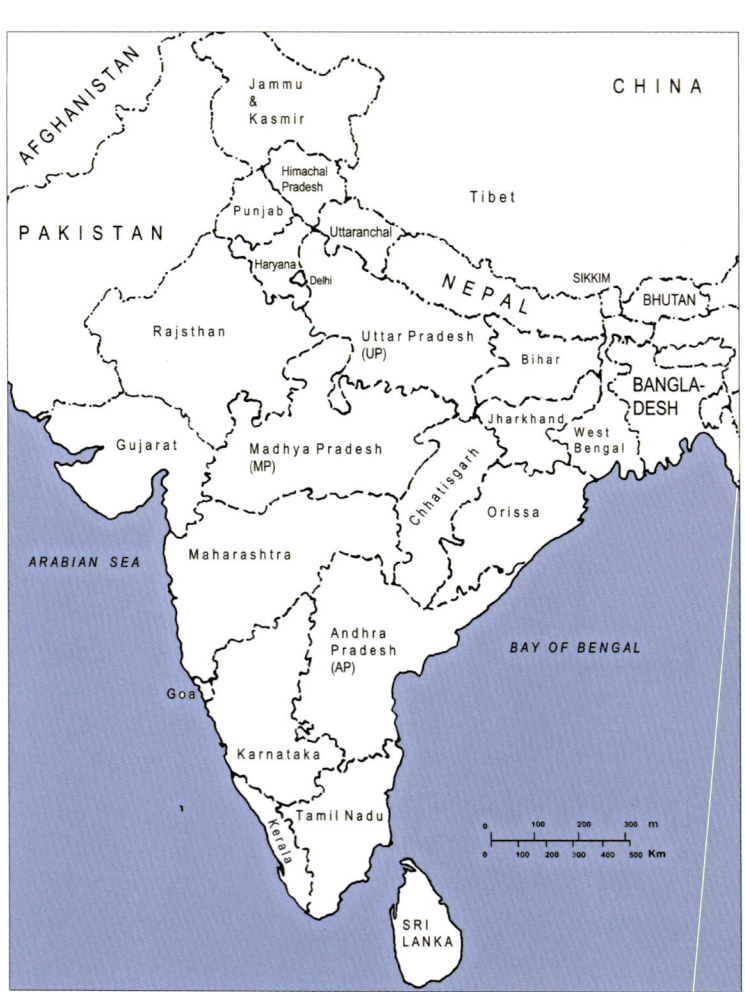

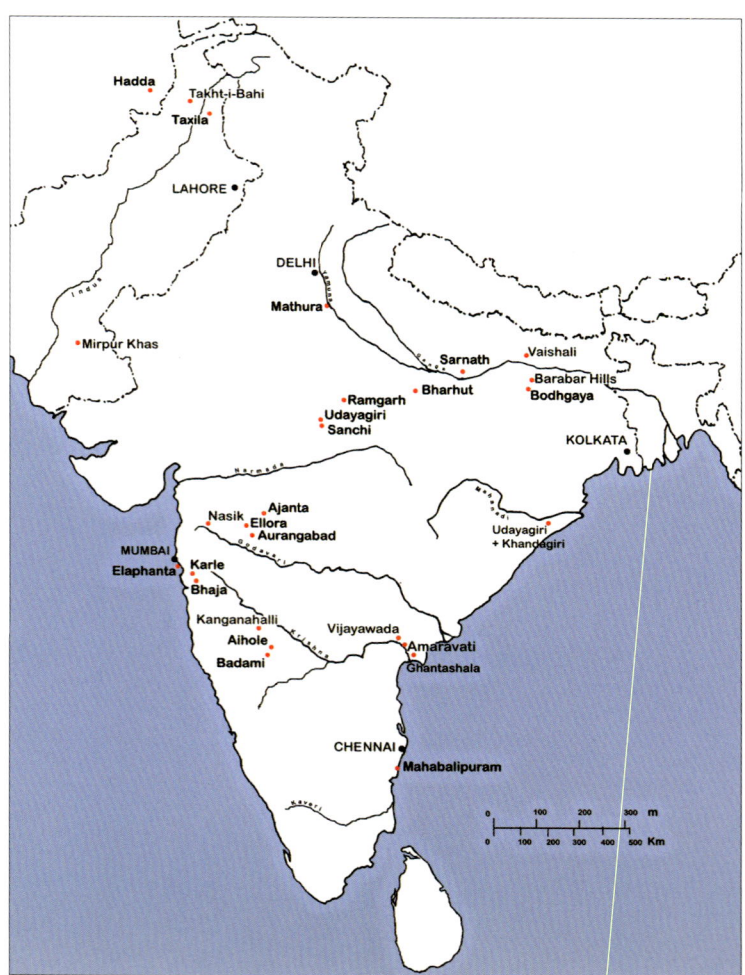

6 THE TEMPLE ARCHITECTURE OF INDIA

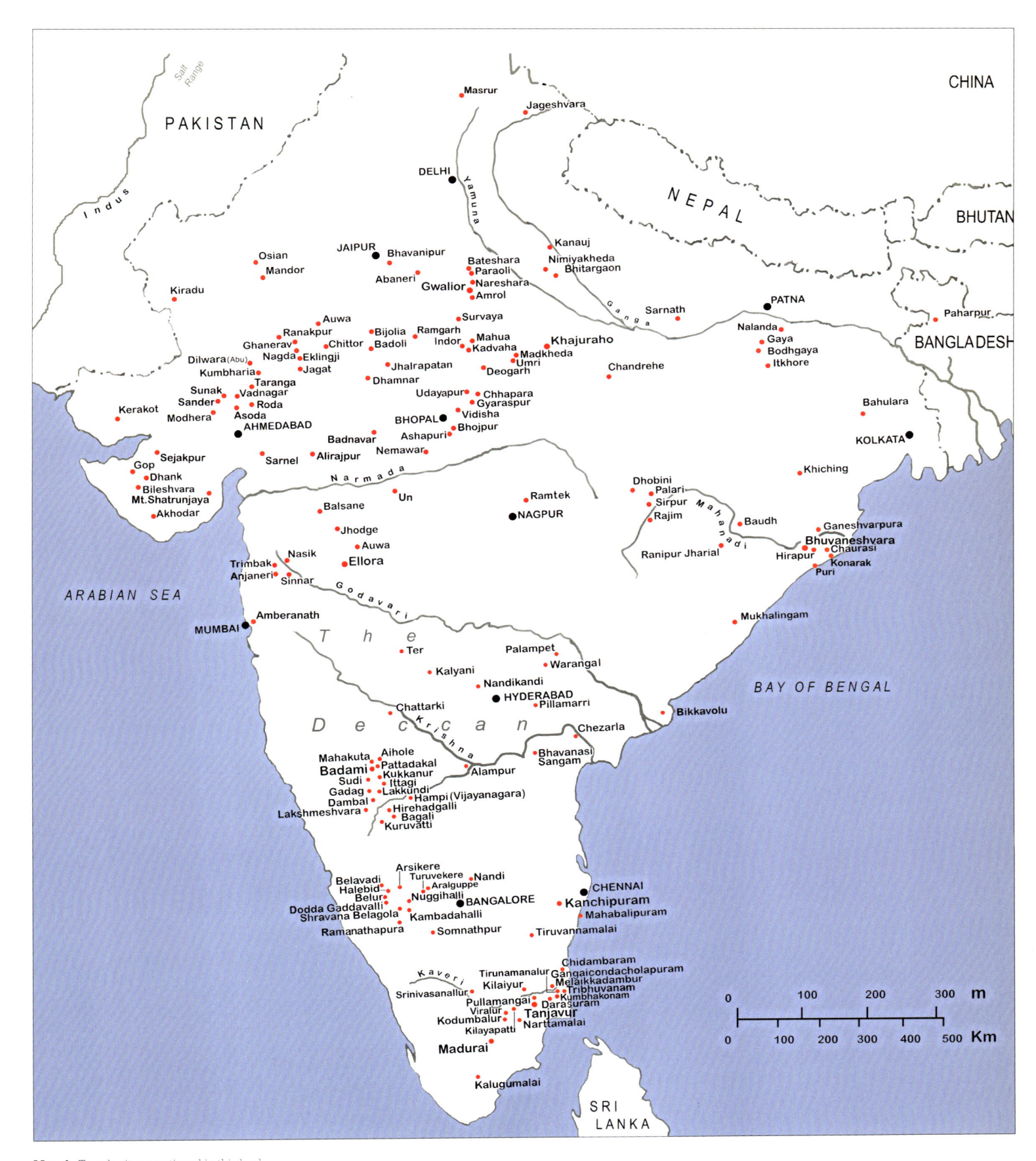

Map 4. Temple sites mentioned in this book.

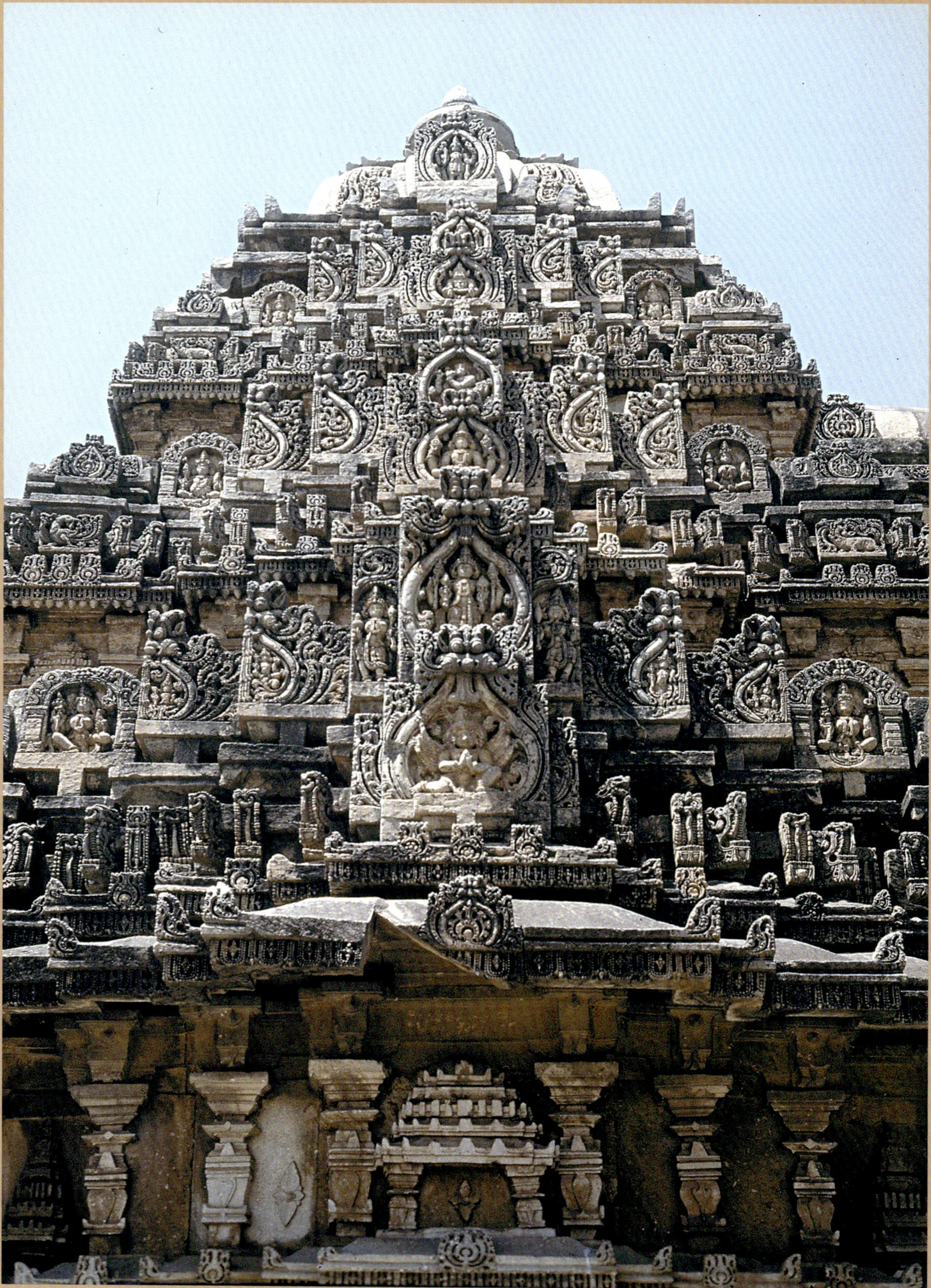

PART 1   CONTEXT AND CONCEPTS

    1   Introduction
    2   Centres of Power
    3   Temple, Body and Movement
    4   The Emanating Universe
    5   Placing the Gods
    6   The Architect and Unfolding Traditions

South-east *vimana* of the Vira-Narayana temple, Belavadi (Karnataka) (**3.15**).
Photo © Gerard Foekema

1 INTRODUCTION

A is for Aedicule

'There is a kind of play common to nearly every child; it is to get under a piece of furniture or some extemporized shelter of his own and to exclaim that he is in a "house". ... This kind of play has much to do with the aesthetics of architecture.'[1] So opens John Summerson's essay 'Heavenly Mansions' in which he interprets Gothic architecture – niches, openings, pinnacles, the pointed arch itself and the whole bay system – in terms of the aedicule. Aedicule, from the Latin *aedicula* (diminutive of *aedes*), means 'little building', and the term is applied both to a miniature shrine and to a representation of a shrine in architectural ornament; for example, in western classical architecture, the pedimented frame of a niche or a doorway, so familiar that it is rarely thought of as a temple-image.

Noting how aedicules combine cosiness and ceremony, Summerson continues, 'I am not going to trace back the history of the aedicule, but I suspect it is practically as old as architecture itself, and as widespread. The incidence of the aedicule in some Indian architecture, for instance, is very striking.'[2] In a footnote he cites James Fergusson's observation, in his pioneering work of 1876, that 'everywhere ... in India, architectural decoration is made up of small models of large buildings'.[3] Although Fergusson did not elaborate on this insight, subsequent writers on the architecture of Indian temples have not failed to notice the miniature buildings adorning them, often using the term 'aedicule' or 'aedicula' for a niche in a temple wall or a pavilion perched in its tower. However, the particular aedicules that they see are only part of the story, missing the whole storey. As one who remembers having a house (a palace, actually) under the table, it was some time after my first trip to India that it gradually became clear to me that aedicules are not just ornaments, but the basic units from which most Indian temple architecture is composed. A temple design is conceived as containing numerous smaller temples or shrines, arranged hierarchically at various scales, embedded within the whole or within one another. Once this simple concept is understood, other things fall into place. As Summerson found for Gothic, 'The aedicule unlocks door after door'.[4]

Before aedicules come shrines, houses for gods. It is impossible to know when the worship of a deity embodied in a sculpted image, and housed in a shrine, was first practised in India. This mode of worship could, conceivably, have been prevalent in the ancient civilisation of the Indus Valley (4th–2nd millennium BC). It was not, however, the official practice of the petty kingdoms dominated by the Aryans in northern India in the early centuries of the 1st millennium BC. This centred on sacrificial ritual around an altar, performed by Brahmin (or Brahman) priests. Such was the early orthodox form, sometimes referred to as Brahminism, of the vast confluence of beliefs and practices which we now know as Hinduism. Various heterodox groups, challenging the Brahminic emphasis on sacrifice and the caste system, arose around the middle of the 1st millennium BC. From among such groups two lasting religions emerged, Buddhism and Jainism. Both held that enlightenment and liberation from the cycle of death and rebirth could be attained only

1.1 Badami (Karnataka), capital of the Early Chalukya dynasty: view from the 6th-century cave temples. On the rocks opposite (left to right) are the Malegitti Shivalaya, the Lower Shivalaya and Upper Shivalaya, all of the 7th century; below, near the tank, is the 11th-century Yellama Gudi.

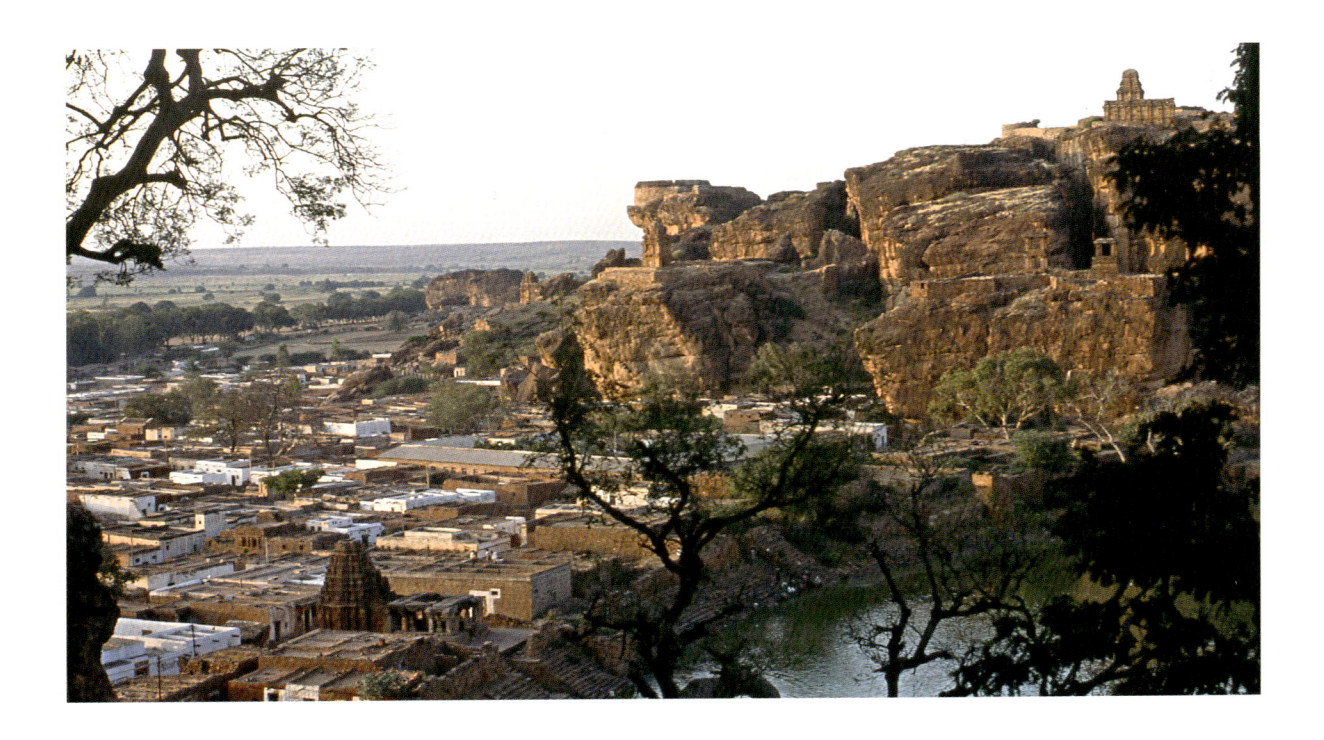

through one's own efforts, Jainism prescribing strict asceticism, Buddhism teaching the path of moderation and the practice of meditation. Both religions developed through monasticism, and both attracted support from the affluent merchant classes. A century or two (depending on which theory about his dates is followed) after Siddhartha Gautama, the historical Buddha, the spread of Buddhism, and of masonry structures erected in its service, was spurred by support of the Maurya emperor Ashoka (c 268–233 BC). It is to Buddhism that we owe the earliest monumental architecture still more or less intact in South Asia, consisting of mounded reliquaries or *stupas*, monasteries and rock-cut sanctuaries. Neither Buddhism nor Jainism, in their earlier years, advocated the use of religious images, or shrines to house them. In the early centuries AD, devotional worship through sculpted images increased in popularity among various cults which grew and merged into later forms of Hinduism, becoming the dominant form of religion under the Gupta dynasty (320–c 550). This required monumental temples in which to enshrine the divine embodiment. The inner sanctum of a shrine would shelter the main deity, most often Vishnu or Shiva. A growing pantheon, seen as the entourage or as the manifestations of the central god, was housed in the temple walls, especially outside, requiring aedicules to frame their images, or at least to evoke their presence. Buddhist practices, by the Gupta period, also entailed the use of images.

Though originally atheistic, by this time Buddhism in India had developed into forms known as the Mahayana ('Greater Vehicle'), more pantheistic, more accessible to the laity and more devotional in attitude. Images of the Buddha needed to be enshrined, along with those of past and future incarnations of the Buddha, and those of saints (Bodhisattvas). To serve this end, while retaining its own building types, Buddhist architecture was tending towards aedicularity earlier even than emergent Hindu temple architecture. Analogous trends can be seen in Jainism. Having begun, like Buddhism, as an atheistic philosophy, Jainism developed a pantheon of its great teachers (Tirthankaras), who populated its heavens alongside some of the Hindu gods and throngs of celestial beings. Jain temples, therefore, came to require a profusion of images installed in aedicular architecture; and, for a given region and period, Jain temple architecture is distinguishable from Hindu temple architecture mainly by its iconography, and to some extent its layout.

From the Guptas onwards the ruling elites of Indian kingdoms were mainly Vaishnava or Shaiva (worshippers of Vishnu or Shiva), ie Hindu; but, as well as endowing Hindu temples, they often supported Buddhist and Jain institutions. By the 10th century, however, through a combination of assimilation and suppression, Buddhism had died out in most of the subcontinent. Jainism remained a relatively small but significant force in many regions, but Hinduism predominated. Throughout the 'early medieval period' (c 6th–13th centuries), the core period for this book, Hindu temple construction took place on a scale comparable to the building of churches and cathedrals in medieval Europe. The foundation and endowment of temples played a central role in the development of state and society. Temples became social and educational centres, and important economic institutions – landowners, employers, moneylenders and dispensers of charity. They were a canvas for the visual arts, a stage for the performing arts. By the end of this period the great temple complexes in south India could have hundreds of employees, from priests and administrators to masons, dancers, cooks and potters.

The architecture of medieval Indian temples, with its aedicular components, grows from an earlier tradition of timber construction, known to us through early Buddhist stone structures dating from the 1st century BC onwards. Monastic remains and worship halls, built of

1.2 Temple complex at Mahakuta, near Badami, showing the Sangameshvara (left) and Mahakuteshvara temples. Both belonging to the second half of the 7th century they are, respectively, Nagara (Latina mode) and Dravida shrines. Photo © Gerard Foekema

1.3 Bhutanatha temple, Badami, *c* 730: view from north-east.
Photo © Gerard Foekema

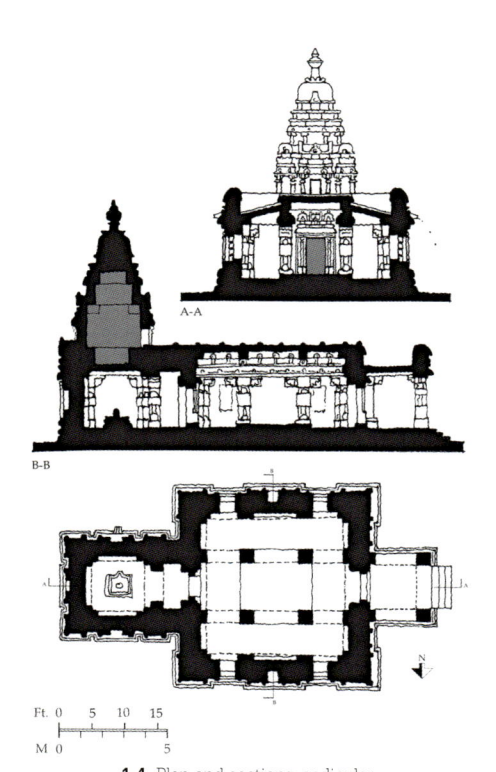

1.4 Plan and sections: aedicular components of the *vimana*.
After George Mitchell

masonry or carved in solid rock, preserve the shapes and details of structures made of wood and roofed in thatch (see Chapter 7). A greater variety of such structures is depicted in relief carvings. Certain basic building types with distinctive roof forms stand out, which were clearly in common use for both secular and sacred purposes. These types, transformed into masonry, are the basis for the simpler forms of image-housing shrine, which in turn are reflected in the early range of aedicules from which more complex temples are composed.

The two great classical languages of Indian temple architecture, the northern Nagara and southern Dravida (**1.2**), draw on this common legacy. They were formed and became differentiated during the 6th and 7th centuries; though concentrated in what is now India, they spread, between them, throughout most of the subcontinent. These are the 'styles' that Fergusson identified as Indo-Aryan and Dravidian, giving them racial labels in typically Victorian fashion, Nagara (literally 'of the city') and Dravida being terms since brought to light by textual scholarship. Nagara and Dravida may be called 'styles', but they cover vast areas and time spans, so the term 'Nagara style' is no more illuminating than, say, 'Doric style'; and 'style' is needed to designate the character sensed in the work of a regional or local school. They have been called 'orders', but their defining features are not columns and entablatures, but aedicules. They can be called 'modes', but 'mode' is needed for the distinct temple shapes that arise in the Nagara traditions, entailing distinct ways of combining the parts. They can be called 'types', but their variations are almost endless; and 'type' is needed to identify a specific design that becomes a standard one. So, in a relaxed sense and without wishing to force a sustained linguistic analogy, 'languages' seems a suitable term, in that each is a system providing a 'vocabulary', a kit of parts, along with a 'grammar' which regulates the ways of putting the parts together. The principal parts are the aedicules, for which the Nagara and the Dravida furnish their respective ranges.

This book is about the nature of these two architectural languages, how they ask to be looked at, their origins and development, the traditions which created them and the ways in which they might be understood as relating to the broader currents of South Asian history and culture (see Chapters 2 and 4). Its scope is not only Hindu temples: as already pointed out, the roots of this architecture can be traced in Buddhist monuments, themselves part of a broader tradition; and these languages, once established, are present in later Buddhist works and countless Jain temples. However, the book does not include the wooden temples with pitched roofs from the rainy regions of Kerala and the Himalayan foothills. Kashmir developed its own kind of stone temple, not covered here except in passing, and the scope does not extend to the distinct traditions which developed, under the influence of both Nagara and Dravida architecture, in South-east Asia. From around the 14th century, Islamic rule in much of India resulted both in disruption of earlier traditions and infusion of new forms into temple designs: this phenomenon is only touched on (see Chapter 26). Nor can the book encompass the shrines of villages and roadsides, those made of twigs on hilltops or of mud in the roots of trees, albeit these are as much temples as the grandest ones. This study is concerned with the two predominant monumental systems of the heyday of temple building in India. It briefly traces their tenuous survival since that period (see Chapter 26), fuelled by periodic revival up to the present day, when we find Nagara and Dravida temples erected by South Asian communities across the world as the epitome of traditional Hindu and also (in the case of Nagara) Jain architecture.

Indian temple architecture, then, is essentially an architecture of imagery. Stone or brick is articulated in terms of forms derived from timber construction, abstracted to create an expressive language. In terms of structure, it is a matter of heavy, piled up masonry, beams and corbelling, rather than arches and true domes; imagery and expression are chiefly in the sculpted exterior. Expression of structure, of load and support, is simply not an issue in this universe of weightless, interpenetrating, heavenly volumes; still less the expression of material or construction. Plastered, limewashed, painted, effulgent with glowing colours, temples of jewels floated in ether. Bound up with this representational character are the horizontal mouldings projecting from the piled up courses. These are conceived not as borders, divisions or elaborations, as generally in western classical architecture, but as things in themselves. Banded in rhythmic sequences, each moulding is a particular kind of entity, most of them with representational origins (a *kapota* cornice as a thatched eaves, etc). It is from this bed of strata that the aedicules are bodied forth. The aedicules, along with the mouldings from which they project, become increasingly abstract, but awareness is never lost of the innumerable little god-shelters within the divine palace.

Two relatively simple examples can be used as an illustration at this point. First, the Bhutanatha temple (**1.3**, **1.4**, **1.5**) stands on a promontory built out into the tank at Badami, the Early Chalukya capital (**1.1**). It is

1.5 Aedicular components of the *vimana*.

1.6 Vamana shrine in Sas-Bahu (mother-in-law/daughter-in-law) complex, Nagda, Rajasthan, *c* 975: a Nagara temple of the Shekhari mode, Type 1 (see Chapter 10).
Photo © Gerard Foekema

INTRODUCTION 15

1.7 A Type 1 Shekhari shrine (**a**) as it appears; (**b**) showing embedded aedicules; (**c**) showing aedicules emerging centrifugally.

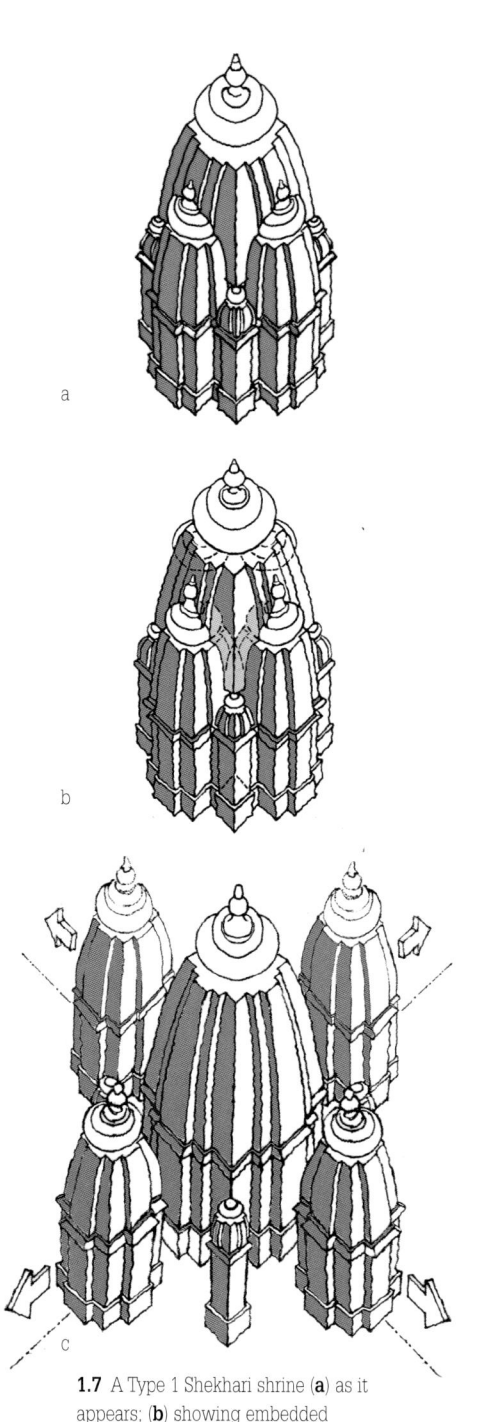

a Dravida temple of the early 8th century, of modest dimensions (the shrine exterior measures about 5 metres square and 13 metres high) and, having lost the paintwork that it must have had, rather plain. The shrine itself (*vimana*) has the Dravida pyramidal outline – here with three tiers (*talas*), and contains the dark, cuboid sanctum (*garbha-griha*) which houses the principal image of the deity, all centralised, symmetrical and organised around the cardinal axes. In front of the shrine is an intimate hall (*mandapa*) fronted by a porch (now joined to a later, open *mandapa*, with steps down to the water).

The usual way to describe the shrine (*vimana*) would be to say that the lower tiers support horizontal bands or 'cloisters' (*haras*) of pavilions based on timber prototypes; the pavilions at the corners being square, domed ones (*kutas*), the central pavilions being rectangular and barrel-roofed (*shalas*). Then the crowning element – looking just at the pavilion at the top in isolation – would be described as a large *kuta*, the pairing of pilasters under the *kutas* and *shalas* might be noted, and so on. This kind of description misses the two-storey nature of the aedicules, which represent ancient and well-established, two-storey shrine-types. In fact, the top tier – that is, the large *kuta* together with the conceptual storey below it – is the simple kind of shrine called an *alpa vimana*, while the lower tiers are composed of embedded *kuta* aedicules at the corners (narrow versions of crowning *alpa vimana*) and embedded *shala* aedicules in the centre. This is a perception of the whole which hangs together, shows a meaningful relationship between the parts, and can be instantly grasped and quickly described.

A second example is the Vamana shrine in the Sas-Bahu temple complex at Nagda, Rajasthan, *c* 975 (**1.6**). This is the most basic form of the Shekhari mode of Nagara architecture (**1.7**), a proliferation of the Latina with its single, curved spire (*shikhara*). Here the aedicules or 'aedicular components' have become less obviously representational than in our earlier, Dravida example. The Latina form has become the basic aedicule, forming both the central element and the smaller versions which project along the cardinal axes. At each corner is a pillar (*stambha*) crowned by a small Latina *shikhara*, together forming a component called a *kuta-stambha*. Projection of the embedded elements begins to express a dynamism which, in more complex Shekhari temples, creates a cosmos of emerging, expanding and proliferating forms (**3.9**; cf **1.8**). One of the doors which the aedicule opens lets out a stream of further aedicules, one after another. Again, if you do not see the aedicular composition, missing the vertical connections by mentally decapitating the temple, and missing the embeddedness by looking at the imagery as

16 THE TEMPLE ARCHITECTURE OF INDIA

surface decoration, then coherence will be lost, your description will be long-winded and the unfolding of the universe will pass you by.

Heaven or Unfolding Cosmos?
Scholarship has associated several meanings with Hindu temples: house of god, heavenly palace or city of god, body of god, mountain, cosmos. Sacred buildings from many cultures have, of course, been interpreted as images of the universe. Following the work of the psychologist CG Jung and its popularisation, it is commonplace to see buildings with 'mandala' plans, such as Buddhist *stupas* and Hindu temples, centralised and with cross axes, as symbols of psychic as well as cosmic balance, floating up from the collective unconscious. The work of Mircea Eliade, historian of comparative religion, uncovering widespread creation myths and corresponding rituals focused on a vertical world axis linking earth to heaven, has helped to add a dimension of time, of recurrent cosmogenesis (birth of the universe), to the imagery of a centralised cosmos.[5] In relation to Hindu temples, the 'unfolding cosmos' idea owes much to Stella Kramrisch and her interpretation of the outward multiplicity of gods and creatures in the temple walls as manifestations of a transcendent unity enshrined within.[6] Salvation, in this scheme, is the release (*moksha*) of union with the Absolute.

A paper by Phyllis Granoff questions this interpretation, noting that often the placement of sculpted deities in the walls (see Chapter 5) has no such logic, and arguing that actual temples and temple cities accord better with the voluptuous descriptions of heaven found in the Puranas, as well as in Jain and Buddhist texts.[7] In these varied visions, the heavenly city is bounded by rivers, girdled round with layered walls and palaces, hung with garlands, courtyard succeeding courtyard, radiant and golden, of jewels ever more precious, until the inner chamber of the great god or goddess is reached, within their palace floating in the skies. The city is teeming with gods, with people, with people gone to heaven and looking like gods, with beautiful girls and all kinds of creatures, thronging to visit the great god or goddess (**1.8**, **1.9**). All are enjoying sensuous delights, making love everywhere; all are fleshy and young.

The city of Vishnu 'has countless worlds in it, made of pure consciousness' and thus, 'like the medieval temple itself, is an intricately self-replicating structure'.[8] This observation, as indeed the recognition that heaven's concentric courtyards of jewelled palaces are like a temple, is all the more accurate if temples are understood as entirely aedicular. But so, too, is the idea of the temple as an unfolding cosmos: once the aedicules are perceived, so are their dynamic

1.8 Stele at Parel, near Mumbai, *c* 6th century, with emerging and proliferating manifestations of Shiva. The idea is immediately communicated because human bodies are familiar forms; to see such dynamism in temple architecture one first has to recognise the aedicules of which it is composed.
Photo © Gerard Foekema

INTRODUCTION **17**

relationships. Granoff concedes, if somewhat belatedly, that both interpretations can be valid.

With no philosophical position other than that the reader should choose their own, I can only affirm, like Galileo, that it does move – whichever mode of salvation one might aspire to. If I might claim a contribution to the theory of the Hindu temple as unfolding cosmos, it would be in showing *how* it happens architecturally; or, at least, whether or not it is anything to do with the cosmos, that the unfolding can be seen. It can be seen in two respects: in the centrifugal emergence and growth expressed in the architectural forms of temples (see Chapter 3) and in the cumulative evolution of these forms through the course of architectural traditions (see Chapter 6).

This, That and The Other

In her introduction to a volume on concepts of time, Kapila Vatsyayan refers to a paper of mine which is included:

> While art historians will no doubt debate the structural analysis of Dr. Adam Hardy ... there will be little disagreement with his cautiously stated conclusion that 'the dynamic formal structure of Indian temples shows irresistible analogies with certain metaphysical ideas recurrent in Indian thought: of the manifestation in transient, finite multiplicity of a timeless, limitless, undifferentiated yet all pervading unity; of the identity of this oceanic infinitude with the all-containing infinitesimal point; of finite things as fleeting transmutations of the infinite, momentarily differentiated, then sinking back into unity, in unending cycles of growth and decay'. This is true not only of Indian architecture, but of all forms of Indian art.[9]

With that endorsement from the Indian goddess of holistic thinking, I could probably just say 'this is what Indian architecture means', and get on with enjoying it. However, marked by a further decade or so in academe, I am even more cautious about Indian Thought and Art, but convinced as ever that the architecture of Indian temples has this kind of structure: well, not always, but at least, in the medieval period, in a lot of places a lot of the time.

Some 20 or 30 years ago it was a fashionable sport among academics, not least among architectural historians, to hunt out those who sought broad patterns among the different branches of a culture or a period, or traced coherent tendencies through time. Such people were labelled

1.9 Durga temple, Aihole (Karnataka), *c* 700: pillar with loving couple. In the porch beyond, celestial pavilions bridge the overdoor and run in courtyards around blind clerestories.
Photo © Gerard Foekema

'Hegelian', evoking the philosopher Karl Popper's *The Poverty of Historicism*, which had shown how grand schemes, forced onto history, obscure the rich variety of accident, detail and human motivation. Since then, via Post-Modernism's 'distrust of totalising discourses', the same bogeyman in the latest garb is usually called 'essentialism'. To posit a reified essence, after all, is to deny human agency in the negotiation and contestation of roles, identities and power relations in the social arena.

All this is true; so caution is a virtue when patterns jump out of architectural forms, linking them to perennial ideas and evolving in a characteristic way through the course of traditions. Clearly, there is a risk of committing determinism and unleashing a Spirit. The danger is all the greater when the topic is the Orient: we may be liable to essentialise the East as a feminine, irrational Other, in need of control by manly westerners. Even if we are innocent of such old-fashioned colonialism, the continuing post-colonialist critique warns that we may be perpetuating the Eurocentric canon by inscribing the 'other' into its grand narrative; moreover, we are reminded that even to speak of the 'other' may be impossible, and indeed the 'other' may not be able to speak of itself, since the language and framework for speaking of it belong to the colonisers. The temptation is to give up talking about buildings and join the critics, but some of us need to provide them with something to 'problematise'.

Faced with post-colonialism, all one can do is try to know the other, live with it (would Greek or Gothic really be more familiar bedfellows these days?) and attempt sincerely to explain it in what seem to be its own terms. Faced with possible accusations of essentialism and determinism, one must bear in mind human actions, while not ignoring general tendencies; point out analogies, but not pretend to know what causes what; find the patterns, but not let them dominate everything – valuing each event for its own sake, while not denying what it unwittingly led to; give place to what does not fit the patterns, remembering that the patterns which jump out may not be the only ones. It is worthwhile trying to paint the whole landscape, alive to the broad shapes which emerge, but cherishing the other passages, and not brushing out the happy accidents. Critical Holism, perhaps, or humility before an even greater whole.

A lightning historiography is needed here, in case anyone thinks that a general book like this comes from nowhere.[10]

James Fergusson (1808–86) made the first modern overview of Indian architecture and the documentation of Indian historic monuments by the Archaeological Survey of India followed (on the architectural side) in his wake. Comparing the Hoysaleshvara temple at Halebid (**1.10**) with the Parthenon, he wrote that:

> they form the two opposite poles – the alpha and omega of architectural design; but they are the best examples of their class, and between these two extremes lie the whole range of the art. The Parthenon is the best example we know of pure refined intellectual power applied to the production of architectural design ... The Halebid temple is the opposite of all this. It is regular, but with a studied variety of outline in plan, and even greater variety in detail. All the pillars of the Parthenon are identical, while no two facets of the Indian temple are the same; every convolution of every scroll is different. No two canopies in the whole building are alike, and every part exhibits a joyous exuberance of fancy scorning every mechanical restraint. All that is wild in human faith or warm in human feeling is found portrayed on these walls; but of pure intellect there is little – less than there is of human feeling in the Parthenon.[11]

1.10 Hoysaleshvara temple, Halebid (Karnataka), mid-12th century, looking towards one of the twin sanctums: 'all that is wild in human faith or warm in human feeling is found portrayed on these walls' (Fergusson).
Photo © Gerard Foekema

This account of Halebid is sympathetic, endowing it with changefulness beyond even Ruskin's Gothic; yet, in the light of the post-colonial critique of the Orientalist discourse it shouts out to be branded a classic case of feminising and irrationalising the Other. To put Fergusson in perspective, however, it is enough to quote one of the tweeded buffers back at the Royal Institute of British Architects, who declared: 'there is little in Hindu architecture of any intellectual interest; and some of the structures indulgently figured by Fergusson in his work on "Indian and Eastern Architecture" are really little better than monstrosities, unworthy of the name of architecture'.[12] Banister Fletcher meanwhile, though admitting that Indian architecture might not look as ugly if one were used to it, consigned it to the 'non-historical styles'.[13]

During the first half of the 20th century, an idealistic attitude to India and her spirituality is epitomised, in relation to art, by Stella Kramrisch (1898–1993) and, especially, by Ananda Coomaraswamy (1877–1947). For Coomaraswamy, with his Platonic/Vedantic vision of Indian art as a particular embodiment of the universal Perennial Philosophy, traditional art reflects transcendent archetypes, a divinely revealed, 'adequate' and intrinsic symbol, representing 'things that cannot be seen except by the intellect'.[14] 'Pure intellect' is not banished from India in this scheme, here meaning the supra-individual *buddhi*. Unashamedly essentialist by definition, this school of thought lives on. A more recent proponent contends that a traditional artistic style is perpetuated by 'the power of the spirit that animates it and by nothing else'.[15] This will solve all our methodological issues in one go, if only we can be so sure.

In the 19th century, early Buddhist art was generally considered as the highpoint from which Indian art declined. Then the Gupta era became the classic pinnacle, then the medieval era became respectable, and now more PhDs deal with things more recent because everything old has been done. A great amount of scholarship on Indian temple architecture has appeared in the past 40 years – documentation, detailed monographs and general surveys. MA Dhaky and Krishna Deva have led the analysis of canonical texts and their correlation with actual temples from their respective regional traditions, bringing to light much indigenous architectural terminology (used here, but sparingly and without diacritical marks, for the general reader's sake). Dhaky has been the mainstay of the monumental project undertaken by the American Institute of Indian Studies, brought together in its *Encyclopaedia of Indian Temple Architecture*. This, together with the institute's photographic archive (much of it at last online[16]), illustrates hundreds of sites, many previously undocumented. The *Encyclopaedia* includes authoritative dating of monuments, which I largely follow here. Yet there still seems to be room for an overview like this one, one that tries to show how to look at Indian temples, and perhaps thereby conveys a sense of how they were designed.

Notes

1. John Summerson, 'Heavenly Mansions: an Interpretation of Gothic' in his *Heavenly Mansions and Other Essays on Architecture* (London: Cresset Press, 1949), pp 1–28 (p 1).
2. Ibid, p 3.
3. James Fergusson, *A History of Indian and Eastern Architecture* (London: John Murray, 1876), p 285.
4. Summerson, 'Heavenly Mansions', p 18.
5. Eg in Mircea Eliade, *Myths, Dreams and Mysteries: The Encounter between Contemporary Faith and Archaic Realities*, trans P Mairet (London: Harvill Press, 1960).
6. Stella Kramrisch, *The Hindu Temple* (Calcutta: University of Calcutta, 1946).
7. Phyllis Granoff, 'Heaven on Earth: Temples and Temple Cities of Medieval India' in Dick van der Meij (ed), *India and Beyond: Aspects of Literature, Meaning, Ritual and Thought* (London: Routledge & Kegan Paul, 1977), pp 170–93.
8. Ibid, p 180.
9. Kapila Vatsyayan (ed.), *Concepts of Time, Ancient and Modern* (New Delhi: IGNCA, 1996), p xxix; Adam Hardy, 'Time in Indian Temple Architecture', pp 354–72.
10. For a general historiography see Pramod Chandra, 'The Study of Indian Temple Architecture' in P Chandra (ed), *Studies in Indian Temple Architecture* (New Delhi: AIIS, 1975), pp 1–39.
11. James Fegusson, *A History of Indian and Eastern Architecture* (London: John Murray, 1876; 1910 edn), pp 448–9.
12. H Heathcote Statham, *A Short Critical History of Architecture* (London: Batsford, 1912), p 348.
13. Banister Fletcher, *A History of Architecture on the Comparative Method*, 5th edn (London: Batsford, 1905), p 604.
14. 'Why Exhibit Works of Art?' in *Christian and Oriental Philosophy of Art* (New York: Dover, 1956), p 11.
15. Titus Burckhardt, *Sacred Art in East and West* (London: Perennial Books, 1967), p 8.
16. http://dsal.uchicago.edu/images/aiis/

2   CENTRES OF POWER

In a paper on 'The Feudal Mind', RC Sharma, protagonist of the feudal interpretation of medieval Indian society, notes that hierarchies of sculpted gods descending from one large central one to many small ones are 'in tune with the pyramidal social structure in which the number of peasants is much larger than that of the landlords', and that, in pyramidal temples, 'tiers, which were meant for decoration, fit in with the tiers that arise from a land grant society'.[1] These observations are undeniably true, yet banal. Once the design of temples is understood in terms of a hierarchy of interpenetrating aedicules, analogies with social structures, and even with the ways these seem to have evolved, become much more compelling.

Temple architecture reflects society, but not in a predetermined way. European feudal society was hierarchical, as were its sacred buildings, but they were not pyramidal. Trees are hierarchical. The aim of this chapter is to try to paint a historical background – or ground – to Indian temple architecture, while letting the congruencies or structural resemblances emerge, without forcing them. Chapter 4 will try to do something similar for religion and philosophy.

Ancient Kingdoms and Empires
By the beginning of the 1st millennium BC the Aryan tribes, formerly nomadic pastoralists who had migrated from Central Asia during the previous millennium, were becoming settled agriculturalists in the Gangetic Basin of northern India. Small states formed, at first governed by tribal councils, but increasingly by chiefs or kings whose legitimacy was established through sacrificial rituals. Society became stratified into four estates or *varnas* ('colours'), which later provided a general framework for the more complex structure of castes (*jatis*). The *varnas* comprised the Brahmins (priests), Kshatriyas (warrior nobles), Vaishyas (traders and free peasants) and Shudras (slaves and labourers from the indigenous population).

The hierarchical social order on earth was reflected in the Purusha Sukta or 'Hymn of Man' (*c* early 1st millennium BC), one of the later additions to the Rig Veda, a work which expressed the idea that creation and cosmic order come about through a sacrifice, conceiving of this order in terms of the human body. In this hymn, the gods create the universe through the sacrifice and dismemberment of a cosmic giant or primal man, *Purusha*: 'His mouth became the Brahmin; his arms were made into the Warrior, his thighs the People, and from his feet the Servants were born.'[2] The Vedic sacrifices performed by rulers, through the mediation of Brahmin priests, were understood not as mere reflections of a cosmic sacrifice, but as something of the same kind – real, effective, momentous actions which created a social and moral world, inseparable from the natural one. Vedic ritual was eventually overshadowed by temple worship, and to some degree subsumed into it: the term *yajamana*, performer of a sacrifice, came to designate the founder of a temple.

Around 500 BC, the small tribal states extending across northern India were swallowing one another to form larger ones, paving the way for empires. For a while the Persian empire touched the north-west frontier of the subcontinent, and the Greeks arrived there for the first time, briefly, under Alexander, from 327 to 325 BC. Then, propelled probably by the introduction of iron and certainly by the use of war elephants rather than horse-drawn chariots, the Mauryan empire (late 4th to early 2nd century BC) spread from Magadha (southern Bihar) northwards to what is now Afghanistan and southwards through the Deccan. The Maurya emperor Ashoka (c 268–233 BC) used Buddhism (founded a century or two earlier) and its quest for enlightenment as a moral and integrating force, famously proclaiming a message of law and tolerance through far-flung rock-cut edicts. Cities expanded during this period, linked by long-distance trade routes for spices and luxury items; this process continued, aided by healthy trade with the Roman world, under the later 'ancient' empires – that of the Kushanas (1st–3rd century AD), stretching from the Khyber to Mathura (south of Delhi), and the Shatavahana empire (1st century BC to 1st century AD) in the Deccan. Architectural remains from these empires are overwhelmingly Buddhist, but the Vedic tradition of the Brahmins flourished, as did Jainism, and various theistic cults emerged, forbears of later Hinduism (see Chapter 4).

2.1 The 5th-century mural paintings at Ajanta (Maharashtra) suggest that life was refined and cosmopolitan at the court of the Guptas and of their allies the Vakatakas, patrons of the Ajanta caves. This one, in Cave 17, tells the story of the Buddha's previous incarnation as Prince Vessantra, sent from court because of his excessive generosity. Photo © Gerard Foekema

The Gupta era (c AD 320–550) is called classical because of its standards in literature and the arts, and the establishment of classical Sanskrit (descended from Vedic Sanskrit) as the language of high culture and lingua franca of the elite. Around the time of Chandragupta II (c AD 376–415) 'India was perhaps the happiest and most civilized region of the world'.[3] The Gupta period was pivotal in that it was the last of the ancient empires, while setting the model in many domains for the medieval period which followed. Gupta rulers revived the old Brahminic rituals of kingship; they were themselves Vaishnavas (followers of Vishnu), while supporting other cults. Buddhist monasteries flourished, sometimes playing a vital role in the state as repositories of knowledge about irrigation.[4] The period saw the consolidation of the Hindu pantheon[5] that is still familiar, and its characterisation in myth and sculpture. Hindu temples appeared, both rock-cut cave temples and structural shrines.

The Gupta heartland was Magadha, the former Maurya stronghold, and the extent of Gupta influence across the map of India was similar to that of the earlier empire, if account is taken of their allies, the Vakataka dynasty, who ruled the whole central and northern Deccan, sharing the same cultural realm (**2.1**). Gupta emperors could claim to be universal rulers (*chakravartins*); returning from conquest of the four quarters (*digvijaya*), they could confirm their overlordship through performance of the Vedic horse sacrifice (*ashvamedha*). But their empire did not have the centralised administration that earlier empires are thought to have had. They directly controlled a core area stretching westwards from Magadha through the Gangetic Basin; beyond were the realms of border kings who paid tribute to the Guptas, but who otherwise ruled their own territories.[6] This multi-centric structure prefigured the medieval pattern.

Multi-centricity is a premise of Kautilya's Artha Shastra, the great treatise on statecraft. This is traditionally ascribed to the Maurya period, although parts are certainly later, and the situation that it depicts – of many competing kingdoms – seems more relevant both to earlier and to later periods. The Artha Shastra explains relationships of power in terms of a 'circle of kings' (*rajamandala*): a ruler should conceive of himself at the centre of concentric circles, his natural rivals surrounding him, his natural allies surrounding them, then more rivals, and so on dying away. This web will reconfigure itself according to which king is focused on. As in the game of chess, invented in ancient India, it is as well to imagine things from one's opponent's perspective.

24 THE TEMPLE ARCHITECTURE OF INDIA

The Early Medieval Period

After the Guptas we move swiftly into the age of 'temple Hinduism', the core period for this book. For historians this is the early medieval period. Broadly, it covers the whole of our core period, ending, in the north, with the establishment of the Delhi Sultanate in 1206, and through most of the remainder of India with Muslim conquests over the ensuing two centuries. This does not leave much late medieval before the beginnings of early modern; and it should be noted that Islamic rulers initially adopted feudal structures similar to those of their predecessors. For our purposes, they put an end to the core period by building mosques instead of temples. The great age of medieval temples can thus be defined as roughly from AD 600 to 1300. This is no more a static and uniform period in political and social history than in the history of temple architecture: both lead to a marked complexity around the 10th to 11th centuries, and perhaps to a certain ossification in the 12th.

Early in the period, new and enduring regional centres of power emerged in the east, the Deccan and the south, as well as the north; the regional languages and regional cultures developed and flourished. In the early 7th century the northern heartland shifted westwards to the Ganga-Yamuna (Ganges-Jumna) Doab, where Harsha (reigned 606–47) ruled over a large but relatively decentralised empire from Kanauj. Meanwhile, new regional centres were forming in eastern India (Bengal), the Deccan (centred on northern Karnataka/Maharashtra) and the far south (Tamil Nadu), where the ancient Tamil culture underwent Sanskritic influence. Particular dynasties would rise to prominence from their respective core areas within the regions, enforcing subservience among their neighbours (often defeated and reinstated), who would pay

2.2 All the company of heaven: ceiling structure at Padhaoli (Paraoli) (MP), 10th century. A *mandapa* is the audience hall of the deity.

tribute from their land revenues to the central power. The size of his circle of tributary princes (*samantachakra*) was a measure of a ruler's prestige. At times, rulers could greatly extend control beyond their regions, but the balance of power was such that this was never for long: 'interregional warfare was mostly aimed at the control of intermediate regions or simply at the acquisition of goods'.[7]

The pattern is increasingly multi-centric, crystallising around dominant main centres, from which the structure shades away towards vague peripheries. Dominance is always temporary, and the main centres shift. Historians agree about the multi-centricity, but explain and evaluate it differently. For colonialist and nationalist historians, for whom large and centralised empires were a good thing, the proliferation and fragmentation of states in early medieval India was generally seen as a descent into decadence, illumined only by the dying afterglow of the classical age. The light shed, from the 1950s onwards, by Indian Marxist-inspired historians applying the model of feudalism to medieval India, was more penetrating. According to their analysis, the contraction of long-distance trade led to the decline of cities, of artisanal production, of a money economy and centralised taxation. Kings had to resort to land grants to support religious foundations and to reward secular officers. State power was fragmented as the class of landed intermediaries grew, and through sub-infeudation the process of fragmentation continued lower down the scale. This school also reminds us, in case it were needed, that it was the peasants whose work made everything possible, and who got the worst deal; to which there is really no answer, except that, if society has to be a dungheap, maybe it is better to grow flowers on it.

More positive views of decentralised, polycentric power have emerged recently, often describing medieval Indian power structures in remarkably aedicular terms, and using imagery of embeddedness and overlap. The continuity that was believed to exist between the early medieval Indian political realm and the broader universe has been brought out through the concept of a Hindu 'chain of being': 'The whole world consisted of overlapping and intersecting life-spaces constituted as masteries and lordships', power descending through the hierarchy of gods and cosmic principles, continuing down through that of humans.[8] The theory of the segmentary state, developed specifically in relation to 11th-century Tamil Nadu,[9] stresses the relative autonomy of local groupings, especially where they are understood as ritually rather than politically subordinate to the king. Relationships within the parts of the pyramidal structure tended to replicate those within the whole, socio-political groupings embedded in each other, from the level of the village up to that of the kingdom. A related account suggests that someone visiting medieval southern India and looking for the centre would find that 'no single center exists ... the state has no real boundaries. Instead he would gradually become aware of a varied, shifting series of centers of different kinds and functions, connected with various interlocking networks.' Only eventually would he 'find himself directed to the courts of the dynastic kings'.[10]

Other recent studies have similarly criticised or refined the feudalist model, while not necessarily abandoning the term 'feudal'.[11] It has been pointed out that, while ancient cities in northern India did decline, new cities and towns appeared across India in formerly peripheral regions, in conjunction with the extension of agriculture. The formation of new states went hand in hand with this development, and was not merely a matter of fragmentation.

Crucial to this process was the integration of tribal areas. This could take place through gradual expansion from a nuclear area or, equally, tribal chieftains could themselves seek integration into the central structure for the sake of local rule. Many of the Rajput lineages of northern India were established in this way. The proliferation of new castes during this period is partly explicable in terms of the incorporation of tribal groups into Hindu society. Meanwhile, local deities were incorporated into the growing Hindu pantheon. If their locality rose in importance, they could be identified with a great god or (more often) the great Goddess. Deities remained rooted to their respective places in the landscape. A village deity would become attached to a god of the broader locality, and so on up to the level of the kingdom, all radiating power through their respective domains, according to their places in a pyramid of gods which reflected the hierarchy of lordships in society.[12]

Temple building progressed in parallel with the incorporation of local deities; it was not imposed on virgin territory, but integrated into a landscape already humming with numinous presence. In the 7th and 8th centuries, temples tended to be concentrated in royal temple complexes in or near a capital, with shrines scattered at sacred spots in the surrounding countryside. In the centuries that followed, temple construction, together with agriculture, advanced outwards from the core areas, and every village had a temple.

The medieval system could not be constructed on an ideology of exclusively Vedic ritual. Two modes of religiosity transformed the nature of Hinduism; both had popular appeal, and both were potentially subversive of caste and gender divisions, though neither ultimately disturbed the social hierarchy. One of these strands was Tantra (see

Chapter 4), with its sexual and esoteric rituals. The other, fed by Tamil traditions of the far south, was Bhakti, the attitude of emotional attachment and devotion to a personal deity, expressed through acts of worship (*puja*). Temples, where gods became manifest, were places for seeing the god (*darshan*) and *puja*.

Whether or not Brahmins were initially inimical to Tantra and Bhakti, they eventually accepted them and assimilated them into new systems. As the spiritual and intellectual elite, Brahmins played a central part in the 'expansion of state society',[13] their role always symbiotic with that of royalty. Inscriptions (usually engraved on copper plates) record vastly more donations of villages with attendant land, tax free, to groups of Brahmins than to feudatories or state officials. Around a capital, Brahmin settlements provided the state with administrative and ideological specialists[14] and may have created a kind of 'demilitarised zone', since any potential usurper hoping to maintain legitimacy would have to respect them. Towards the periphery, however, Brahmins would civilise the natives by imparting religious teaching and agricultural know-how.[15] Where a tribal clan or other group required recognition as kings, they would patronise Brahmins who, in return, would provide them with divine ancestry.[16]

Temple, Polity and Patronage
Monumental temples are bound up with the institution of kingship. A king was a mediator between the human and divine worlds, and royal temples were a special case of royal giving (*dana*), bringing prosperity to the community and religious merit to the giver. Typically, a dynasty would show allegiance to a particular god, usually Shiva or Vishnu, but also support temples and monasteries of other cults and religions. While the continuity between early sacrificial ritual and later rituals of temple foundation should not be exaggerated, they share the character of constitutive acts, seen as creating social order and wellbeing. In this way, temples were as practical as the dams and irrigation projects also undertaken by rulers.[17]

However, most patronage of temples, along with donation of land to sustain them, was not directly by kings. Apart from the royal family and officials such as ministers and generals, temples were increasingly founded and supported by mercantile and artisanal guilds. Inscriptions show that all kinds of people gave to temples; they might donate a field or a water tank, or fund a perpetual lamp, or give two sheep to supply milk to make ghee to keep a lamp burning.[18] Thereby they might acquire merit or remission of sins, approach release (*moksha*), book themselves into heaven for several millennia, or merely participate in emanated lordship. But temple patronage remained above all a courtly affair, and temple ceremony was unmistakably courtly: gods were treated like kings – woken, bathed, dressed, fed, visited, taken around in processions. Propelled by people's fervent desire to make gods and goddesses happy, the performing arts developed and flourished in pursuit of their entertainment.

For one class of temple, royal involvement and the centrality of the temple in the political order, are not in question. During the 8th century several dynasties were able, following a conquest of the four quarters, to declare themselves paramount overlords of wide regions and even, after distant campaigns and rather more theoretically, of the whole of India. Several great temples survive which were built as the preeminent shrines of these empires. In the south and the Deccan, imperial temples of this phase can be seen at Kanchipuram, Pattadakal and Ellora (see Chapter 23). We do not know what equivalent monuments in the north may have been lost, for example at Kanauj, the prestigious capital of the Gurjara Pratiharas, but the rock-cut temple at Masrur (**2.3**) may belong to this class,[19] along with the now lost temple of the Kashmiri king Lalitaditya.

2.3 Crown imperial: monolithic temple, Masrur (Himachal Pradesh), *c* late 8th century. Photo © Gerard Foekema

Most of the 8th-century paramount kings were devoted to Shiva, and their imperial temples are dedicated accordingly. Lalitaditya followed the Pancharatra cult of Vishnu, the sequentially emanatory theology of which is discussed in Chapter 4. Taking Lalitaditya's temple as a paradigm for 8th-century imperial temples, Ronald Inden has argued that it was 'an integral part of the paramount king's efforts to fashion a new chain of being, one that stretched out below him on earth and reached up into the heavens above. It was not only an icon of the Pancaratra conception of a chain of being, it was itself an integral link in that chain of being as it was actualised by the overlord of the earth.'[20] The new temple mountain became a new centre of the universe, and the 'cosmomoral order' that was being forged would be most clearly manifest on ceremonial occasions, through the strict hierarchy of permitted access applied to the graded spaces approaching the centre, from the excluded masses outside, through the assembled householders and courtiers and courtesans, past the drummers and the dancers to the king, and the Brahmin intermediaries tending the inner sanctum, and upwards through the ranks of gods to heaven.

Given the inextricable connection between a monarch and his royal temple, the inverted funnel through which power flowed down to him, it is not surprising that temple desecration became an act with which to set the seal on a conquest. Often this meant carrying home the principal idol, or it could be a matter of destroying the main shrine or even the entire temple. Later temple destruction by Muslims was largely a continuation of this tradition, rather than iconoclasm.

That desecration was not an inevitable outcome of conquest is illustrated by the action of Chalukya king Vikramaditya ('Son of Valour') II after his victory over the Pallavas in 742. Vikramaditya marvelled at the great temple of Rajasimheshvara ('Lord [Shiva] of Rajasimha or Lion King') at Kanchipuram, also known as the Kailasanatha ('Lord of Mount Kailasa', Shiva's Himalayan abode) (**9.23**, **11.8**, **23.2**). Rather than knocking it down or carrying off the god's image, his gesture was pious and magnanimous: an inscription at Kanchipuram records how he

> determined to root out the Pallavas, by nature hostile, who had dimmed the splendour of his ancestors. Going with great speed into Udaka province, he slew in battle the Pallava named Nandi-Potavarma who came against him, captured his defiant lotus-mouthed trumpet, his drum called 'Roar of the Sea', his chariot, his standard, immense and celebrated elephants, clusters of rubies, which by their radiance dispelled all darkness; and

entering Kanchipuram ... acquired the great merit of covering with gold Rajasimeshvara, and other Devakala [deities] sculpted in stone, which Narasimha Pota-Varma, the protector of indigent Brahmins ... had made.[21]

To celebrate their husband's victory, Vikramaditya's queens Lokamahadevi and Trailokamahadavi founded a pair of imperial temples at Pattadakal ('Coronation stone') (**9.3**, **23.5–23.6**). Originally called the Lokeshvara and Trailokeshvara, temple of the Lord (Shiva) of Lokamahadevi and Trailokamahadavi respectively, they are now known as the Virupaksha and Mallikarjuna temples. One of dancing girls of the Virupaksha, bless her, donated a horse chariot and an elephant chariot.[22]

The cosmic scale of being and the grandiloquent claims found in inscriptions are not, in the 8th century, translated into grandiose temples. The twin giants at Pattadakal were built to rival the Kailasanatha in size; but to put their monumentality in perspective, the Kailasanatha is about 20 metres high, the Virupaksha (the larger of the pair) 18 metres. My house is half the height of the Virupaksha, the church down the road certainly higher, and the block of flats further on is twice the height. These temples are not vast, but they have a greater architectural intensity than my house, greater even than the church and infinitely greater than the block of flats. Heaven comes to earth in these stones: dwarves tumble at one's feet, lions leap and elephants tussle at eye level, and you can almost touch the feet of the gods.

Nevertheless, while the number of temple foundations greatly increased, the size of the 8th-century imperial temples was rarely exceeded before the 11th century, when architectural megalomania finally arrived in a second wave of imperial temples. The Cholas in Tamil Nadu followed a tradition of building small, exquisite granite shrines. In *c* 1003 the Chola monarch Rajaraja I founded the Rajarajeshvara or Brihadeshvara at Tanjavur (Tanjore) (**24.5**). Eye level here is somewhere down in the sub-base: the tower is 60 metres high. It has been estimated that the tower alone contains 40 times as much stone as an average Chola temple, and that together the Brihadeshvara and Gangaikondacholishvara, erected by Rajaraja's son Rajendra Chola (**2.4**), represent more than half the total building material used during their combined reigns.[23] The Lingaraja temple at Bhuvaneshvara (*c* 1060), almost as high as the Tanjavur temple, became the first imperial temple in Orissa, followed by the Jagannatha, Puri (1135), and the Surya temple, Konarak (1250). In central India, the 11th-century Paramara king Bhoja, a renowned polymath, patron of the arts and

2.4 Shiva garlands the saint Chandesha in a niche at the Brihadeshvara temple, Gangaikondacholapuram (city of the Chola who conquered the Ganges), Tamil Nadu. Images of patrons are rare in the early medieval period, but here the saint is sometimes identified with Rajendra I (1012–44). In erecting this huge imperial temple, Rajendra was following the example of his father, builder of the Brihadeshvara at Tanjavur.

CENTRES OF POWER **31**

paragon of kingly attributes, began (but never completed) a gigantic temple at Bhojpur (MP), linked to a colossal dam and irrigation project.

Resources to undertake such projects became available after about AD 1000 as the period witnessed improvements in irrigation and agriculture, developments in navigation and trade (with the Arabs, whose trade was diverted eastwards by the Crusades, and with South-east Asia), and a greater supply of metal coin.[24] At the same time, given the very extent of the regional empires, the power of feudatory chiefs was increasing relative to the centre. This period has been called the 'heyday of political feudalism',[25] and the Chola empire is Burton Stein's 'segmentary state' *par excellence*. In this context, the giant imperial temples of the second wave seem to have been counterbalancing measures against fragmentation, creating 'a new and *centralised ritual structure*, focused on the new state temple and its royal cult'.[26] Rajaraja's temple at Tanjavur, 'far from representing the self-glorification of a despotic ruler, was in fact a method adopted by an ambitious ruler to enhance his very uncertain power'.[27] In Orissa, rather than creating a new cult centre, the Ganga rulers and their successors patronised and associated themselves with the local, originally tribal cult of Jagannatha, becoming his regents on earth. This achieved a centralised ritual structure along with appeal to popular Bhakti sentiments, catering to a calendar of festivals and creating an enduring node in the burgeoning pilgrimage network. Later Chola kings turned to a similar strategy in their patronage of the cult of Shiva Nataraja at Chidambaram.

Gigantic temples, however, were the exception. In the 10th and 11th centuries various dynasties developed royal cult centres where individual shrines were more modest in scale: examples are the temple complex built by the Chandellas at Khajuraho, and the patronage of the cult of Ekalinga at Eklingji by the Guhilas of Mewar. The Later Chalukyas of Kalyani, the great rivals of the Cholas, seem to have had no imperial cult centre. They built nothing as big as the works of their supposed ancestors at Pattadakal, but erected smaller temples of greater complexity over a much wider area. A series of 11th-century inscriptions at Sudi (Karnataka) gives a glimpse of the administration and life of this provincial capital.[28] For at least 40 years in the first half of the century, Akkadevi, sister of Chalukya Vikramaditya V, administered the districts designated the Kisukad 70, the Torugare 60 and the Masavadi 140. She founded a temple at Sudi, the Akkeshvara, which must be the one now known as the Mallikarjuna. A Kannada inscription dated 981 of the Shaka era (AD 1059–60) attests that

Akkadevi's successor, Nagadeva, a general and Steward of the Royal Household, had founded the Nageshvara temple and a Naga (snake spirit) tank (*naga-gonda*, ie *naga-kunda* in Sanskrit):

> Nagadeva, the Emperor's agreeable High Minister, foremost among councillors, radiant with brilliant glory, raised in the excellent town of Sundi for Nageshvara a surpassing dwelling pre-eminent in the whole world, so that everyone praised it, saying that it is loftier than the Himalaya, more spacious than the great Silver Mountain [Kailasa]. A refuge for sages, in a manner that was not that of a common man, he constructed on each side of the temple white plastered buildings such as might be called a nest of gods, and a quarter for public women. In fair Sundi, while the world praised him and his fame shone brightly, that crest-jewel of royal ministers gladly caused to be dug a pond which may be said to exceed in greatness the Milk-Ocean.[29]

Now known as the Jodu Kalashada, the temple survives (**25.3**); so does the tank (a step well, strictly speaking), encased in an aedicular retaining wall just like an inside-out temple (**2.5**). The temple is about 10 metres high and the tank about 9 metres square. Nagadeva, the inscription continues, assigned the village of Sivunur to Someshvara, a Brahmin votary of Nageshvara. He piously assembled an estate, defined by the Great River, and certain trees and stones, such as the Great Hog's stone, carefully apportioning the income accruing from it to the various needs of the temple. Oblations were provided for, and food for the ascetics, and repair of broken masonry – an income was assigned to a stone-cutter named Candoja. There must have been an attached *matha* or monastery, as the youths studying there are mentioned, and there was income for their teachers, as well as the 'professors lecturing to the ascetics' and the Brahmin officiants. There was generous provision for the public women – including the one 'acting for the god's enjoyment' (who earned more than anyone), the four fan–bearing ones, the four who graced the four pillars of the temple, to the right and the left, and the four dancers – as opposed to the 400 famously assigned to the Brihadeshvara by Rajaraja Chola. Then there was their steward (he earned the same as a dancer), the drummer and the flute-player.

Sudi has changed since Nagadeva's day. I remember arriving by bus, with rucksack, and looking for the temples among lanes of flat-roofed mud houses. The retired schoolmaster lined up the curious villagers in

34 The Temple Architecture of India

2.5 The tank built through the munificence of General Nagadeva at Sudi (Karnataka), 'wider than the Milk Ocean'. Photo © Gerard Foekema

front of me, politely soliciting my 'impression of these simple rustic folk'. I see that, since then, the Archaeological Survey of India has put up a metal fence around the tank.

Notes

1. RS Sharma, *Early Medieval Indian Society: A Study in Feudalisation* (London: Sangam Books, 2001), pp 268–9.
2. *The Rig Veda*, trans Wendy Doniger O'Flaherty (London: Penguin Books, 1981), p 31.
3. AL Basham, *The Wonder That Was India* (London: Fontana, 1971), p 67 (1st edn, 1954).
4. Julia Shaw and John Sutcliffe, 'Water Management, Patronage and Religious Change: New evidence from the Sanchi dam complex and counterparts in Gujarat and Sri Lanka', *South Asian Studies* 19, 2003, pp 73–104.
5. Most importantly, Vishnu and his avatars, Shiva and his family (Parvati, Ganesha, Skanda or Kartikeya), the great Goddess (especially as Durga); see also Chapter 4.
6. Hermann Kulke in H Kulke and Dietmar Rothermund, *A History of India* (Abingdon: Routledge, 2004), pp 89–91 (1st edn, 1986).
7. Ibid, p 114.
8. Ronald Inden, *Imagining India* (Oxford: Basil Blackwell, 1990), p 57.
9. Burton Stein, *Peasant State and Society in Medieval South India* (Delhi: Oxford University Press, 1980).
10. David Schulman, *The King and the Clown in South Indian Myth and Poetry* (Princeton: Princeton University Press, 1985), p 21. This passage is quoted in Julius Lipner, 'Ancient Banyan: an Inquiry into the Meaning of Hinduness', *Religious Studies* 32, 1996, pp 122–3; in this paper Lipner argues that polycentricity is a defining characteristic of Hinduism.
11. Notably the work of BD Chattopadhyaya and H Kulke.
12. Kulke and Rothermund, *A History of India*, pp 147–8.
13. Term coined by BD Chattopadhyaya, see *The Making of Medieval India* (Delhi: Oxford University Press, 1994).
14. Hermann Kulke, 'Royal Temple Policy and the Structure of Medieval Hindu Kingdoms' in A Eschmann, H Kulke and GC Tripathi (eds), *The Cult of Jagganath and the Regional Tradition of Orissa* (Delhi: Manohar, 1978), p 135.
15. Hermann Kulke, 'Fragmentation and Segmentation versus Integration? Reflections on the Concepts of Indian Feudalism and the Segmentary State in Indian History', *Studies in History* 4, no 2 (1982), p 248.
16. BD Chattopadhyaya, 'Historiography, History and Religious Centres: Early Medieval North India, circa A.D. 700–1200' in Vishaka Desai and Darielle Mason (eds), *Gods, Guardians and Lovers* (New York and Ahmedbad: Asia Society Galleries and Mapin Publishing, 1993), pp 33–47 (p 39).
17. See Nicholas Dirks, 'Political Authority and Structural Change in Early South Indian History', *Indian Economic and Social History Review* 13, no 2, pp 125–57.
18. K Ismail, *Karnataka Temples: Their Role in Socio Economic Life* (Delhi: Sundeep Prakashan, 1984), p 49.
19. Michael W Meister, 'Mountain Temples and Temple Mountains: Masrur', *Journal of the Society of Architectural Historians* 65:1, 2006, pp 26–49.
20. Ronald Inden, 'The Temple and the Hindu Chain of Being', *Puruṣārtha* 8, 1985, pp 53–73; see also Chapter 6 in Inden's *Imagining India*, on the imperial formation of the Rashtrakutas.
21. *South Indian Inscriptions* 9, p 147, quoted in Alexander Rea, *Pallava Architecture* (Varanasi: Indological Book House, 1970), reprint of ASI *New Imperial Series* 34, p. 7.
22. Inscription dated AD 778–9, *Indian Antiquary* 11, no 122, p 125, cited in Ismail, *Karnataka Temples*, p 122.
23. Pierre Pichard, *Thanjavur Bṛhadīśvara, An Architectural Study* (Delhi: IGNCA and École Française de l'Extrême Orient, 1995), pp 33–4.
24. Sharma, *Early Medieval Indian Society*, pp 151–3.
25. The phrase is Sharma's.
26. Kulke, 'Royal Temple Policy', p 135. Italics in original.
27. GW Spencer, 'Religious Networks and Royal Influence in Eleventh-Century South India', *Journal of the Economic and Social History of the Orient* 12, 1969, pp 42–56, quoted in Kulke, 'Royal Temple Policy', p 136.
28. 'Inscriptions of Sudi' in *Epigraphia Indica* 15 (1919–20), pp 75–103.
29. Ibid, pp 92–3.

3 TEMPLE, BODY AND MOVEMENT

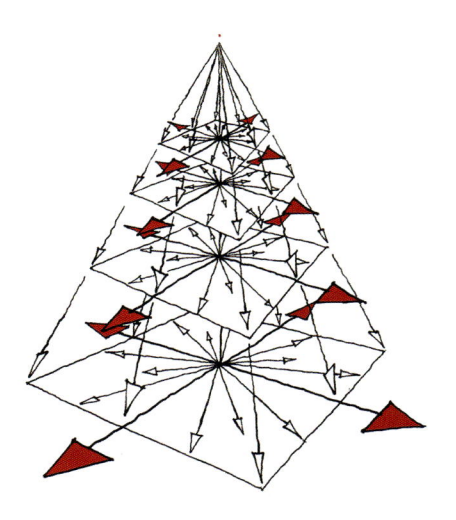

3.2 Main directions of movement expressed in the shrine exteriors.

3.1 Shiva Nataraja (Lord of the Dance) paces out the eternal cycles of creation and destruction in the right-hand lateral shrine of Cave 23, Ellora (Maharashtra), 6th century. To the right are the Saptamatrikas (Seven Mothers).

'The Rich will make temples for Śiva. What shall I, a poor man, do? My legs are the pillars, the body the shrine, the head a cupola of gold.'[1] When Basavanna, the 11th-century religious and social reformer, wrote this verse, the sentiment was radical, but the assimilation between temple and human body, and more specifically the enshrined god's body, was a familiar one. Dozens of Sanskrit architectural terms relate architectural elements to parts of the body in a loose metaphorical way (*griva* = neck, *skandha* = shoulder, *jangha* = shank, most suggestively *garbha* = womb ...), while medieval texts from different religious strands enumerate precise (and varied) correspondences between elements of the temple and the body parts – and indeed the soul – of the enshrined deity.[2] Such connections can seem rather forced, but their purpose is often to provide a graded pattern for meditation, and they are also evoked in consecration or installation rituals for temples and for images. Analogies can readily be drawn between the ascending lotus flowers

36 THE TEMPLE ARCHITECTURE OF INDIA

('wheels', *charkas*) visualised in yogic practices, mounting the subtle spine towards the spiritual goal, and the stages of ascent up the vertical axis of a temple tower, marked by corresponding levels in the exterior. But it is perhaps in the patterns of movement expressed by Indian temple architecture that the connection with the body can be experienced most palpably.

Discussion of movement in architecture can be about how people move through buildings, about how the eye moves over them, or about visual forces; equally, for some kinds of architecture, it can be about how architectural forms represent movement, or even seem to move. In European architectural history, the latter kind of interpretation stems from the characterisation of the Baroque as a dynamic style by Wölfflin, one of the proponents of empathy theory, according to which 'we judge every object by analogy with our own bodies'.[3] Certain means of expressing movement are common to the Baroque and to Indian temples (bursting of boundaries, splitting, multiple projection of interpenetrating elements...), but in no other architecture are such devices used so explicitly, consistently, concertedly and all-pervasively as in certain kinds of medieval Indian temple. These monuments seem to demand to be experienced empathetically, in terms of the human body. Just as the idea of the aedicule, the little god-house, is very concrete and graspable, so the dynamic structure of the relationships between the aedicules is, once seen, eminently human and most easily explained through bodily gestures.

To read Indian art in terms of movement is nothing new. Heinrich Zimmer wrote of the 'phenomenon of the expanding form' in Indian art.[4] One of his examples is a south Indian sculpture of the Lingodbhava (the origin of the *linga*, the phallic emblem of Shiva), now in the Musée Guimet, Paris (cf 3.10), depicting the myth which relates how Shiva appeared and grew from an orifice opening up in the side of an ever expanding *linga*, while Brahma (in bird form) and Vishnu (in boar form) strove vainly to catch up with its respective, ever receding ends. Of this particular representation, stressing the aspect of dissolution as well as

3.3 Architectural means of expressing movement in Indian temples:

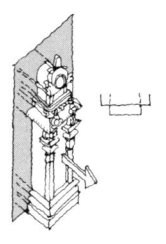

Projection. Projection of an embedded form almost by definition suggests emergence or emanation: pro-jection is 'throwing forward', though (relative to the observer) things can also be thrown sideways, diagonally and backwards.

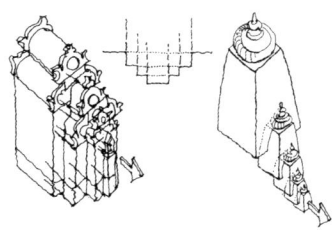

Staggering or multiple projection. Staggering, or progressive stepping out, suggests expansion in stages, a serial emanation. Closely bunched offsets can also create the impression of vibration (*spanda*) as if with inner energy. A staggered sequence of forms, embedded one within another, can be entirely at one level (in which case the elements slide out like an unfolding telescope), or step down as they step out.

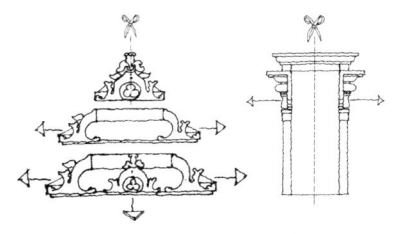

Splitting. Two aligned halves of something familiar as a whole suggest that the whole has split; or even that the halves are still separating, especially if a projected form appears between them, as if emerging from the void.

TEMPLE, BODY AND MOVEMENT **37**

that of growth, Zimmer wrote: 'The solid mass of stone, by a subtle artifice of the craftsman, has been converted into a dynamorphic event. In this respect, this piece of sculpture is more like a motion picture than a painting. The notion that there is nothing static, nothing abiding, but only the flow of a relentless process, with everything originating, growing, decaying, vanishing – this wholly dynamic view of life, of the individual and of the universe, is one of the fundamental conceptions ... of later Hinduism.'[5]

Stella Kramrisch brought together dynamism and temple architecture in her book published in the same year (1946), writing: 'On this vertical axis are threaded the levels of the building, its floors (*bhūmi*) and profiles, their projections and recesses. Expansion proceeds from the central point of the Garbhagriha, in the horizontal, and all the directions of space; this spread with its proliferation and particularisation is gathered up towards the apex; the broad mass with its many forms is reduced to a point, beyond its total form.'[6] Kramrisch's influential interpretation of the Hindu temple as 'monument of manifestation' was related to actual architectural form by herself and others in a rather confusing way. To imagine, as is often implied, that expansion, in an upward-shrinking shape like a Hindu temple, can be upwards at the same time as outwards, is to mistake visual forces, or the trajectory of the eye or mind, for expressed movement. Even within the logic of Kramrisch's metaphysical view, aspiration towards union with the divine must be inwards and upwards to the unity 'beyond form', while manifestation must be downwards and outwards from the one to the many: God is up there, transcendent, and comes down to earth. My purpose in this chapter, however, is not to explore the symbolism of temple dynamics, but to clarify its architectural workings.

The pattern of movement, then, is an animation of the basic axial organisation of the temple. The shrine is invested with a sense of movement that appears to originate at the tip of the finial, or a point just above it, progressing downwards from this point and outwards from the vertical axis, radiating all around, predominantly in the four cardinal directions (**3.2**). This is the pattern in which the aedicular components are made to appear to multiply, to emerge and expand out from the body of the shrine, and out from one another, as interpenetrating elements differentiate themselves and come apart. It is important, once again, to see the full shrine-images, since these are the elements in question: otherwise the heavenly palace will merely vibrate, with agitated huts chattering on its balconies, rather than radiate power through the cumulative force of its constituent mansions. As these forms are

3.3 cont'd

Bursting of boundaries. Where a projecting and enshrined form overlaps the confines of its frame, its emergence is accompanied by a greater sense of expansion.

Progressive multiplication. Proliferation (thus growth of the whole, but not necessarily of the parts) is portrayed where elements are arranged in a sequence of rows, starting with one and then progressively increasing in number.

Expanding repetition. Growth is expressed when, in a series, the elements are similar but get progressively bigger.

conceived as three-dimensional and embedded, the rhythm is not simply a ripple across the surface but an accelerating pulse from within, surging out at the descending stages. Simultaneously with and inseparably from all this downwards and outwards growth and proliferation, the summit recedes as the whole of the shrine swells upwards.

It goes without saying that in a literal sense the architectural elements of a temple are arranged statically in space, their positions and interrelationships fixed in stone. The architecture must, on one level, be viewed and appreciated for the balance and repose of its static composition; but it also has a temporal structure, of which a given spatial arrangement is a momentary glimpse, or rather, a succession of such glimpses. A series of elements, or of configurations of elements, can be sensed not so much as a chain of separate entities, but as the same thing seen several times, at different stages, evolving and proliferating. This dynamism is conceptual in that it is the expression of an idea, but often also illusionistic, almost cinematic (as Zimmer would have it), the forms pouring out in front of our eyes before our minds can reflect on them. More than a thousand years earlier than stroboscopic photographs and the artistic experiments of the Italian Futurist movement, the architects of medieval Indian temples had developed ways of conveying the idea of forms evolving in space, through time. The pattern of centrifugal growth is communicated through clearly identifiable architectural means (**3.3**), not always unambiguously expressive of movement when employed singly, but mutually reinforcing in this expression when working together. These means can be enhanced by direct pictorial or sculptural representation, notably the spewing of arch forms out and down from the jaws of monsters (**3.13**, **3.14**, **3.15**).

Examples

It would be wrong to give the impression that all Indian temple architecture throughout the medieval period has this dynamic character. The Dravida temples of Tamil Nadu and the Nagara ones of Orissa remain relatively static, and are no less magnificent for that, while other traditions show the expression of movement particularly well. A few important examples will serve to illustrate the phenomenon at this stage.

In 7th- to 8th-century Nagara temples of the Valabhi (barrel-roofed) and Latina (single-spire) modes, rhythmic growth is conveyed principally through manipulation of the *gavaksha* or horseshoe arch motif. A typical Valabhi shrine (**3.4**) is crowned by a whole-and-two-halves configuration of *gavakshas*. While this reflects the nave-and-aisles cross section found in early timber structures and in rock-cut *chaitya* halls (**7.7**), it is

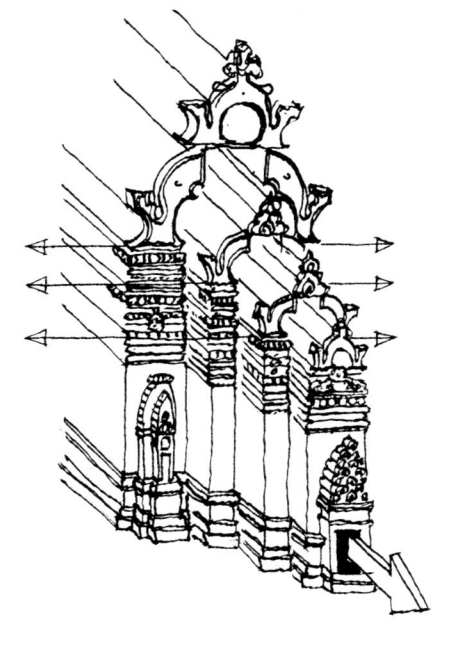

3.4 Dynamics in a shrine of the Valabhi mode of Nagara: the Teli-ka Mandir, Gwalior (MP) (cf 18.5).

TEMPLE, BODY AND MOVEMENT 39

3.6 Dynamics of the central spine in the *shikhara* of the Galaganatha temple: (top) the unfurling of the apex, and (remainder of drawing) a single pair of mouldings with *gavakshas* bursting through them.

3.7 *Gavaksha* cascade of the kind typical of western India in the 9th and 10th centuries. If a pattern is to be accepted as inherent in a design, it must be possible to imagine it clearly and for its visualisation to be communicated. A computer animation – even better than a drawing – can demonstrate that a particular dynamic pattern is conceivable in terms of the forms as they actually are. Easier to do, but jerky, is a Powerpoint presentation, by means of which this drawing can be made to unfold as it bings onto the screen.

3.5 *Shikhara* of the Galaganatha temple, Pattadakal (Karnataka), c late 7th century: a Nagara temple of the Latina mode.

treated in such a way as to imply that the two halves have split from one another and are moving apart. When further forms are projected from inside this pattern, it becomes clear that the splitting is taking place as the elements grow forward from within. The implication of an embedded barrel roof, of which a *gavaksha* is the gable, enhances the directional thrust. Staggered Valabhi shrines are a classic example of sequential emergence expressed through the detelescoping effect, while the ascending expanding repetition of similar forms enhances the sense of simultaneous upward growth.

In the Galaganatha temple, Pattadakal (**3.5**, **3.6**), a Latina shrine of around the late 7th century, the central spine of the tower (*shikhara*) is

3.8 *Mula-prasada* of the Kandariya Mahadeva temple, Khajuraho (MP), 11th century. Photo © Gerard Foekema

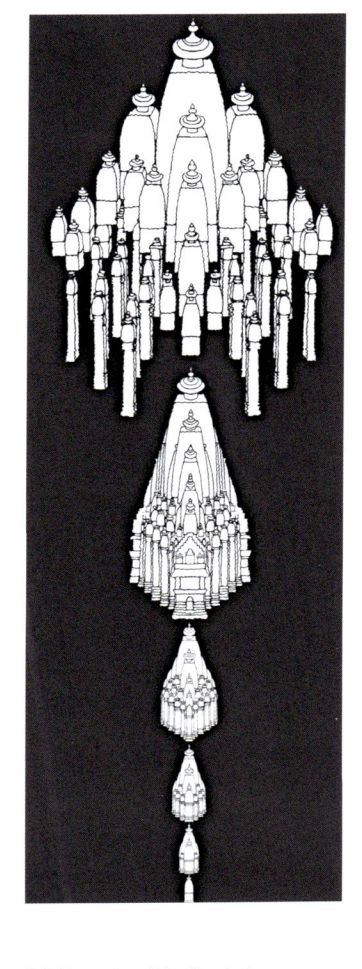

a cascade of horseshoe arches (*gavakshas*). A Valabhi configuration initiates the unfurling, first giving birth to a smaller version of itself. Below, a *gavaksha* window grows through a pair of eave mouldings, splitting, the halves sliding apart, unveiling glimpses of an inner world through tiers of celestial colonnade: another *gavaksha* emerges from within, revealing a heavenly face. This second sequence repeats eight times, descending. In a final crescendo, one appears and splits, another (cusped) appears within it and splits, again below, and finally a Valabhi aedicule stands forward, ready to manifest the deity. Except in this ultimate emergence of a shrine-image, *gavakshas* are not merely parts of larger elements, but have taken the role of abbreviated aedicules, or aedicule-substitutes, as the chief compositional units in the creation of a significant architectural pattern (cf **3.8**).

3.9 Dynamics of the Kandariya Mahadeva, showing how downward and outward emergence is expressed as simultaneous with upward growth of the whole. For anyone seeking the symbolism of divine and cosmic manifestation in these outpouring forms, there are only two ways to imagine the reabsorption that follows creation. If it is a path of return towards the original unity at the summit, then it must be like running the film backwards, hoovering everything up into a black hole in the sky. Otherwise, going with the flow, things fall apart as they appear, swept out to oceanic dissolution.

TEMPLE, BODY AND MOVEMENT

3.10 A split pilaster is especially appropriate for framing the Lingodbhava image, in which Shiva comes forth from an orifice rent in the phallic emblem (*linga*). This example is from the Brihadeshvara temple, Tanjavur. The ensemble calmly projects a sustained sequence of unfolding: emerge–grow–split–move apart–emerge–grow–split–emerge–grow. In some such images there is a 'bursting of boundaries', as Shiva comes out of the hole.

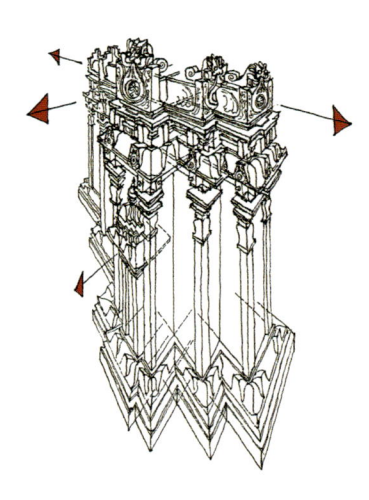

3.11 Dynamics of the double-staggered *shala* aedicule, typical of Karnata Dravida temples from the 11th century onwards. This element is a composite of five interpenetrating *shala* aedicules – representations of two-storey shrines crowned by *shalas* (barrel-roofed pavilions). A central one (end on, and therefore a '*panjara* aedicule') projects forward, another emerges at right angles on either side, each emitting a further one in the same direction. Thus, the sequential and centrifugal swell of the whole is mirrored in the parts.

3.12 Implied unfolding of a double-staggered *shala* aedicule from a '*panjara* aedicule' via a single-staggered *shala* aedicule may be played out in the descending tiers of a *vimana* (eg at the Mallikarjuna temple, Sudi, 11th century).

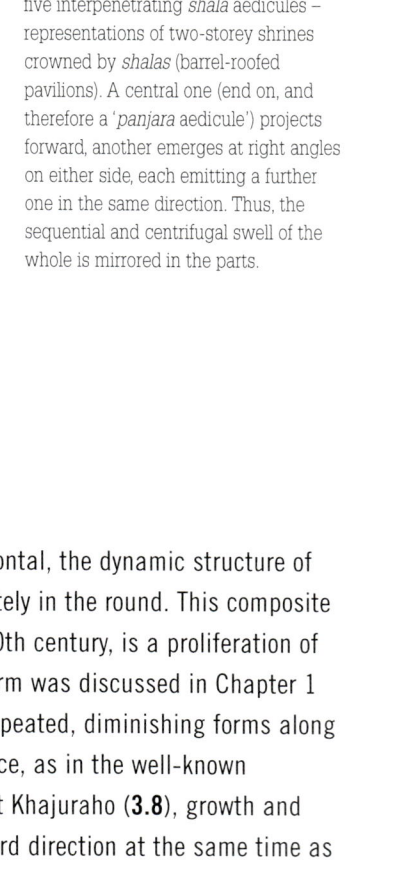

3.13 *Gavaksha* cascade in the late Karnata Dravida tradition: here *gavakshas* alternate with looped archways (*toranas*).

While horseshoe arch patterns are frontal, the dynamic structure of the Shekhari mode of Nagara is completely in the round. This composite type of temple, fully developed by the 10th century, is a proliferation of the unitary Latina, of which a simple form was discussed in Chapter 1 (**1.6**, **1.7**). As soon as the emission of repeated, diminishing forms along the cardinal axes has become a sequence, as in the well-known Kandariya Mahadeva temple (*c* 1030) at Khajuraho (**3.8**), growth and proliferation are expressed in a downward direction at the same time as outwards. Simultaneously, because the repeated forms become larger as the eye moves up ('expanding repetition'), the entire monument appears to swell heavenwards. At the sides of the 'half-*shikharas*' (half-embedded spires) appear 'quarter-*shikharas*' (three-quarters-embedded spires), so that the overall, cruciform pattern of four-emerging-from-one is reflected in embedded clusters: the temple design shown in **1.6** crowns the composition, and also, on each face, emerges twice more from the seething matrix. In other words, the movement pattern of the whole, not purely its shape, is reflected in the parts. Figure **3.9** is an attempt to represent the dynamics of this temple, growing up as it explodes down; the top drawing but one being the shrine as it actually is, and the top one the implied next step, its dissolution.

As already noted, the Dravida temples of the Tamil tradition are relatively static; but they maintain one powerful device to announce emergence at specific points. This is the split pilaster, usually supporting an archway motif (*torana*) and implying that a single pilaster has broken in two, the halves sliding apart like the Nagara half-*gavakshas* we have just observed (**3.10**). Narasimha, Vishnu's man-lion avatar, bursts out of a pillar in a well-known myth, and many gods are represented following suit in temple walls.

The other main branch of Dravida architecture, centred in Karnataka, builds up to extreme dynamism by the 11th century. Here, through a staggered plan progressively stepping forward from corner to centre, each face of a temple grows with an axial bulge culminating in a double-staggered *shala* aedicule (**3.11**), a multiple, interpenetrating version of the simpler form already encountered in Chapter 1 (see **1.5**, lower right). Sometimes the unfolding of this composite element is depicted in the descending stages of the *vimana* (**3.12**). More often, an identical arrangement of aedicules appears at each level, giving radial continuity with expanding repetition downwards (**11.15**). In staggered *shala* aedicules the forward and sideways motion of the *shala* roofs is emphasised by the outpouring of each *gavaksha* gable end from a monster-faced finial, whose snail-like buttress-body rides along on the ridge. This pictorially represented spewing forth is exploited in the Dravida version of a *gavaksha* cascade, where overlapped pairs of *gavakshas* in the *shalas* step down and out along each of the central spines of the temple superstructure, in an overwhelming downward surge (**3.13**, **3.14**, **3.15**).

Notes
1. Basavanna, Poem 820, trans AK Ramanujan, *Speaking of Śiva* (Harmondsworth: Penguin Books, 1973), p 88.
2. See Bruno Dagens, 'Le temple corps du dieu' in *Traités, temples et images du monde indien: études d'histoire et d'archaéologie*, compiled by Marie-Luce Barazier-Billoret and Vincent Lefèvre, Institut Français de Pondichéry and Presses Sorbonne Nouvelle, 2005, pp 125–49.
3. Heinrich Wölfflin, *Renaissance and Baroque*, trans Kathrin Simon (1888; London: Collins, 1964), p 77.
4. Heinrich Zimmer, *Myths and Symbols in Indian Art and Civilization*, ed Joseph Campbell (New York: Pantheon Books, Bollingen Series VI, 1946), p 130.
5. Ibid.
6. S Kramrisch, *The Hindu Temple* (Calcutta: University of Calcutta, 1946), p 167.

3.14 Kashivishveshvara temple, Lakkundi (Karnataka), 11th century. In this Karnata Dravida *vimana*, single-staggered *shalas* issue forth a *gavaksha* cascade culminating in a spectacular central niche, with a Nagara superstructure of the Shekhari mode. The niche bursts its boundaries, usurping the entire central projection of the *shala* aedicule and rising up through the *kapota* cornice. Photo © Gerard Foekema

3.15 South-east *vimana* of the Vira-Narayana temple, Belavadi (Karnataka), 12th century. Here the cascade flows down through double-staggered *shala* aedicules. The *gavakshas* forming the end gables of the *shala* roofs are diagonal ones – folded in half and placed at 45 degrees. Together with the diagonal *makaras* (crocodile monsters) in the *prati* (floor moulding), they add a radial dimension to the centrifugal burst. Photo © Gerard Foekema

4 THE EMANATING UNIVERSE

This chapter is a brief introduction to ideas, practices and movements in Indian religion, focusing on those strands which we now know as Hinduism, leading up to and including our core period of the 5th to 13th centuries. It is intended not so much to be background as to give some sense of the cultural ground against which temple architecture took shape. Chapter 2 threw up analogies between temple designs, with their clusters of aedicules, and the polycentric structures of early medieval states. Analogies, or homologies (structural parallels), are even more evident when Indian temple compositions are compared with certain recurrent religious and philosophical concepts, especially in the light of the sequentially emanating forms discussed in Chapter 3. Architectural patterns of emergence and growth, as if from an all-containing point, will not be illustrated again in the present chapter, but it should become clear that precisely the same kinds of pattern are reflected in the religious ideas surveyed here. Specifically, such patterns underlie a vision of creation which is found repeatedly in many different guises. The manifestation or coming into being of the divine or of the universe is understood as taking place through the sequential emergence, or successive bursting forth, of one form or principle from another. This is not to say that such ideas gave rise to the architectural forms, or that the temple builders deliberately set out to embody these concepts: rather, it would seem, the forms and the ideas both spring from the same way of thinking, the same view of the world.

How should the term 'world' or 'universe' or 'cosmos' be understood in this context? It is the whole of creation, of course, but also the way things are, the order of things (the Greek word *cosmos* means 'order') infused in the whole and reflected in the parts. In Indian traditions the conception of order is perennially a dynamic one: *jagat*, one of the Sanskrit terms for cosmos, comes from the root *gam*, 'to go'. From an early date in India, cosmic order is often seen as integral to the human body, mind and spirit: the human being is a microcosm. The interpretation of Hindu temples, which are also associated with the human body, as symbols of an unfolding universe, is certainly reinforced by the observation that they share an underlying scheme with many accounts of cosmic emanation.

Two typical ways of describing the universe prevail in the religious texts: as a great layered topography of worlds and heavens, and as an unfolding of phenomena from formlessness to form. It is always useful to distinguish between cosmology (the form of the universe) and cosmogony (its birth and process); but it would be wrong to imagine that the first kind of description (of worlds and heavens) is static, since Indian traditions always seem to recognise change and impermanence, with creation followed by dissolution, in endless cycles. If there is a state, it is beyond the process. Sometimes the second kind of description (of an emanatory sequence) does not explicitly mention the universe or its phenomena, explaining everything in terms of a hierarchy of deities. This is because theology and cosmology are seen as virtually the same, whether the gods are understood as real beings or as forces or metaphors, and whether they are seen as many or as aspects of one.

The Vedas and Upanishads

The great collections of Sanskrit hymns to the gods of the Aryans, known as the Vedas ('knowledge'), are for many Hindus the primary revelation from which later sacred texts have issued. The earliest Vedas may have been composed from *c* 1500 BC. Two of the perennial ideas already present in the Vedas are that of the universe originating in an all-containing point of concentration, visualised here as the cosmic egg, and that of the identification of the universe with a cosmic man or being (the Purusha).

During the early centuries of the 1st millennium BC, there developed a range of sacrificial rituals, initially for the wellbeing of the sacrificer, then increasingly for the kingdom and the cosmos. These rituals, intended to accompany the sacrifice of animals or symbolic substitutes, or of various foodstuffs, were focused on altars made of brick, constructed according to rules. The priestly Brahmin (also Brahman, Brahmana) class were the specialists in Vedic sacrificial ritual, as they have remained: this early religion of sacrifice is sometimes referred to as Brahminism.

Around the 8th century BC another of the ubiquitous strands of Indian religiosity, that of ascetic renunciation, began to find expression in a further body of texts known as the Aranyakas ('forest scripture') and Upanishads ('secret scripture'). These emerged from the cultural climate that also gave rise to the great renunciatory religions of Buddhism and Jainism. The Upanishads (the term is often used to include the Aranyakas), with their philosophical and mystical orientation, internalise earlier ritualistic ideas, setting self-realisation through true knowledge as the ultimate goal. The great insight of the Upanishads is the ultimate identity of the inner, true self of the individual (*atman*) with the world soul, the formless Absolute (*brahman*). This *atman/brahman* correspondence is a new, internalised form of the man/universe, microcosm/macrocosm analogy, carrying with it a sense of the miraculous identity of the infinitesimally small with the infinite:

> This self of mine within the heart is smaller than a rice grain or a barleycorn or a mustard-seed or a millet-grain or the kernel of a millet-grain. This self of mine within the heart is greater than the earth, greater than the middle-air, greater than the sky, greater than all these worlds.
> Doing all, desiring all, smelling of all, tasting of all, encompassing all this, unspoken, untroubled, this self of mine within the heart is *brahman*.[1]

Bound up with these notions is the idea of an all-containing unity as the source of creation. The cosmic egg reappears in the Upanishads, splitting open to reveal earth, air, mountains, clouds, rivers and sea.[2] Other passages convey a sense not only of a source but of successive emanation, some enumerating a sequence of cosmic elements or categories rather in the manner of the Samhkya school (see below). In the following example the primal self, in the process of creating the world, gives shape to a man, drawing him out from the waters:

> He heated him up. When he was heated up, a mouth broke out of him, like an egg. From the mouth came speech; from speech, fire. Nostrils broke out. From the nostrils came breath; from breath, air. Eyes broke out. From the eyes came sight; from sight the sun. Ears broke out. From the ears came hearing; from hearing, the directions.[3]

And so continues this serial unfolding, in which cosmos and human being are once again conceived as inseparable.

The Philosophical Schools

Indian philosophy has traditionally been divided into six schools or systems (*darsahas* or 'ways of seeing'). Three of these, Samhkya, Yoga and the Vedanta, are especially significant for our subject.

The Samhkya ('enumeration') philosophy, attributed to the sage Kapila (*c* 7th century BC) has been very influential on a wide variety of later traditions. Emanation or evolution (*parinama*) is at the heart of its vision, which is atheistic (in that god plays no role) and dualistic, seeing existence as springing from the interaction of two fundamentally distinct categories: self or spirit (*purusha*) and primordial matter (*prakriti*). *Purusha* and *prakriti* are the initial two of 25 categories (*tattvas*, 'that-nesses'): from *prakriti* springs the intellect or higher mind (*buddhi*), from which the ego (*ahamkara*), from which the mind (*manas*), along with the five senses and their objects, the five organs of actions, the five subtle elements and the five gross elements.[4] The relevant point in the present context is that, once again, cosmic creation is conceived both in terms of the human body and psyche, and as a process of successive emergence.

Yoga, with its techniques of bodily and mental discipline for the achievement of release (and magic powers along the way), is classed as one of the six systems. Its classical authority is the Yoga Sutra of Patanjali (*c* 100 BC–AD 500), which takes the Samhkya as its philosophical basis, with a similarly integrated conception of body, mind and cosmos. The path to liberation is conceived as inwards and upwards, through graded stages from gross to subtle, against the flow of evolution as visualised by the Samhkya. Many schools of yoga developed, with various religious attitudes. Most envision an esoteric anatomy, a subtle body with centres or 'wheels' (*chakras*), imagined as lotuses mounting in stages up the subtle spine, linked by energy channels (*nadas*), culminating in the blissful thousand-petalled lotus at the crown of the head, or just above it.[5] An analogy with the body of a temple, with its vertical axis marked by stages, is clear; and the Yogic thousand-petalled lotus is often thought of as upside down, like a temple ceiling or the lotus moulding on top of a dome.

The Vedanta ('end of the Veda', meaning the ultimate in Vedic knowledge), rooted in the teachings of the Upanishads, is best known in the version termed advaita, taught by the great Shankara (possibly c ad 788–820). Emphasising knowledge (jnana), and firmly asserting the reality of the transcendent absolute (brahman) over the manifold appearances of existence, this philosophy is monistic (allowing no ultimate distinction between matter and spirit); strictly speaking it is 'non-dual' (*advaita*), holding that even to imagine unity is not to approach the brahman, since the absolute is beyond human conceptualisation, knowable only through direct intuition. Lesser ways, however, including ritual action (*karma*) and devotion to a personal god (Bhakti), are given their place in the system as valid approaches on the long path towards release (*moksha*), and as metaphors through which to approach the ultimate. For this philosophy, even the idea of manifestation is a metaphor, the relationship between the transcendent and the phenomenal world being a mystery, termed *maya*. *Advaita* Vedanta ideas have been given great prominence in modern Hindu thinking and (given their parallels with neo-Platonic idealism) in western understanding of Hinduism.

The Gods, the Epics and the Puranas

By the early centuries AD, the Vedic gods Rudra (god of storms) and Vishnu (solar energy) were becoming fused with various non-Vedic deities to become, respectively, the supreme gods Shiva and Vishnu, whose cults, along with those of the great Goddess, have formed the main theistic traditions of Hinduism to this day. These are the deities whose images have been installed in the sanctums of temples and, with those of their entourages, have animated the temple walls. Other Vedic gods, though retaining their place in Brahminic ritual, lost their earlier significance, finding lesser functions in the later pantheons. Of these, with the emergence of temple building, only Surya, the sun, had a substantial number of temples dedicated to him: Brahma, the creator, has virtually none. Eight of the Vedic gods lived on as the *ashta dikpalas*, guardians of the directions of space, in which role their images appear on the corner projections of many medieval shrines.

Most people find religious meaning not through philosophy but through stories and myths. The Indian epics, the Mahabharata and the Ramayana, first developed in the second half of the 1st millennium BC, and still have universal appeal. Stories from the epics are sometimes depicted in temples, in the form of narrative friezes. Representations of the gods in temple iconography are often allied to descriptions in the Puranas ('stories of old'). These were first compiled in the Gupta period (*c* AD 320–550), and much was added to them during the ensuing centuries. They can be considered 'orthodox' in that they represent the assimilation by the Brahmins of popular mythologies, and the use of these mythologies for propagating theological and ethical doctrines.

Cosmology is a preoccupation of the epics and, especially, of the Puranas. Two kinds of cosmology are typical. One pictures the concentric and layered landscape of the universe, inside the world egg, centred on Mount Meru, with earth and seas, heavens and underworlds, and all kinds of creatures and beings born and reborn in these different realms. In case anything should be thought of as permanent, the Puranas propound a vast and elaborate system of ages and aeons of time, cycles within greater cycles of creation and dissolution rolling on in the eternal play (*lila*) of the Lord. The other kind of cosmology, or, rather, cosmogony (birth of the universe) gives mythological vividness to concepts of emergence and expansion. Several important myths of this kind attained their enduring iconographic patterns in sculpture during the Gupta period, as well as their narrative patterns in words, including the Lingodbhava (**3.10**) and Vishnu Anantashayin (**4.6**, **5.1**).

Tantra

'Tantra' is not a separate cult or movement, but a term used to describe an approach which came to permeate most Indian religious thought and practice, including Jainism and Buddhism, especially the Vajrayana form still practised in Nepal and Tibet. A recent study argues that, rather than Bhakti (devotion), 'Tantra has been the predominant religious paradigm, for over a millennium, of the great majority of the inhabitants of the Indian subcontinent'.[6] The term 'Tantra' derives from the Tantras, a vast corpus of texts which began to appear around the 7th century, many early ones stemming from Kashmir and Nepal. In Tantric traditions, ideas about emanation are more pervasive than ever: even the teachings and liturgies of the Tantras are conceived as having been emitted by the deity and flowing down. Rather as temple designs incorporate earlier designs (see Chapter 6), these texts incorporate earlier orthodox thinking, while considering their own revelation superior.

Tantric practice of rituals and yoga typically involves initiation by a guru. Different strands stress different ends: magical powers (*siddhis*), worldly enjoyments (*bhoga*), or transcendence. *Yantras*, sacred diagrams, often used in conjunction with parallel structures of sound, are especially characteristic. Rather like flat temples, they embody a central deity and a hierarchy of constituent or emanated deities, and symbolise the body, the psyche and the universe (**4.1**). The centre, source and point of equilibrium is called the *bindu* ('drop'): meditation, ritual and the actual construction of a *yantra* can all follow the centrifugal path of emission (towards multiplicity, impurity, the gross) or the centripetal path of reabsorption (towards unity, purity, via the subtle to the supreme). Inwards and upwards are seen as corresponding to the male principle, downwards and outwards to

4.1 The Shri Yantra – diagram of the goddess Shri.

4.2 Circular temple of the 64 Yoginis, Hirapur (Orissa), c 10th century.

the female principle, the two held in balance by the undifferentiated point which is their source and their end.

A defining feature of Tantra is its sexualised imagery and ritual, which ranges from the literal to the symbolic. The literal end of the spectrum follows two main tendencies. The earlier, that of the Kapalikas ('skull men', because they drank from skulls), stemmed from cremation ground asceticism, and involved appeasing the ferocious form of Shiva (Bhairava) or of the Goddess (Kali) with blood sacrifice, and offerings of forbidden substances and acts known as the 'five Ms' (*matsya*, fish; *mamsa*, meat; *mudra*, grain; *mada*, wine; *maithuna*, sex). Magical powers were obtained in return. From around the 9th century there emerged movements referred to as 'Kaula' ('clan') cults, whose adherents conceived of the processes of emission and reabsorption in strikingly physical, liquid terms. For the Kaula initiates, 'clan fluids' and their supernatural powers were obtained from the godhead – again Bhairava or the Goddess – via eight emanated goddesses, who in turn proliferated into 64 semi-divine female emanations called Yoginis. The juices were believed to flow down from the centre through these channels, access to powers being available to male practitioners only through exchange of fluids with human embodiments of the Yoginis. This took place, in a context of ritual, either by drinking sexual or menstrual discharge during mutual oral congress, or through *vajroli mudra*, 'by which the male partner was able, following ejaculation, to draw up into himself the sexual discharge of his female partner'.[7] Not all Yogini worship was Kaula, but some kings and courtiers certainly became involved with Kaula cults (supernatural powers are always useful). Several circular temples in stone dedicated to the 64 Yoginis survive from around the 10th century (**4.2**).

Forms of Tantra in which the sex is not literal but symbolic ranged from practices which demand more or less explicit symbols – the visualisation of *yantras* full of united divine couples, yogic control of semen and ritual substitutes for the 'five Ms' – to far greater degrees of abstraction. Through such abstraction or sublimation, Tantric ideas could be integrated with more orthodox religion, and in this way their influence pervades the theologies of the Goddess, of Shiva and of Vishnu most closely associated with medieval Hindu temples.

4.3 Durga Maishasuramardini (Slayer of the Buffalo Demon), Durga temple, Aihole (Karnataka), *c* 700. Photo © Gerard Foekema

The Goddess

Goddesses habitually appear as the consorts or *shaktis* (energies) of male gods, but for many Hindus the great Goddess (Maha Devi) has been the supreme deity. In the epics and Puranas she is Durga, warrior heroine (**4.3**); all-devouring Kali is her fierce aspect. Her many names derive from her assimilation of countless tribal or village goddesses (just as the goddess Sul at Bath in the west of England came to be identified with the Roman Minerva). Yet many local goddesses survive, independent under trees (**4.4**). Later Shakta cults (the term for cults of the Goddess) are overwhelmingly Tantric. An important tradition is that of the Shri Vidya, in which the goddess Shri or Lakshmi is worshipped in the form of the *shri yantra* or *shri chakra* (**4.1**). This tradition, stemming from Kashmiri Tantra, has long survived in southern India, adopted by the Vedantic, monastic Shankaracharyas and fully absorbed into orthodox Brahminic practice.[8]

4.4 Village goddess, Raghurajpur (Orissa).

a

b

c

d

Shaivism

Shiva ('auspicious') has many names, and many aspects: ferocious and destructive, beneficent, dancing, frenzied, ascetic. He came to represent, for many, the supreme, transcendent and immanent God in the early centuries AD. During that period he also came to be worshipped in the ancient form of the *linga* ('emblem', 'sign', 'phallus'), the generative and expanding form *par excellence*, but equally a form of primal abstraction, an ideal symbol for the transcendent unity of the divine (**4.5a**). Anthropomorphic images of manifest deities are placed at the back of the *garbha-griha* ('womb chamber'): an abstract symbol, the *linga* is the unmanifest; an axis of concentrated power, it sits perfectly at the centre. *Mukha-lingas* ('face *lingas*') with a face at the front had appeared by the 5th century (**4.5b**); after that, three- four- and five-faced *lingas* (**4.5c**). The heads project, half-emerged on the cardinal axes, like the central aedicules in the temple exterior; in a five-faced *linga* the fifth looks up from the top. All these images represent the theological concept of the fivefold Sadashiva coming from the unmanifest (the abstract *linga*) into manifestation.[9]

There are many different Shaiva sects, the oldest known being that of the Pashupatas, its teachings attributed to Shiva via an incarnation, the sage Lakulisha (2nd century AD). The esoteric, proto-Tantric Bhairava cult of the Kapalikas is another early form. Puranic orthodoxy distanced itself from all these Shaiva cults,[10] but Shiva looms large in the Puranas, especially as divine Lord of Mount Kailasa, with wife Parvati and sons Ganesha and Karttikeya. The texts called the Agamas (Shaiva Tantras), emerging and accreting from about the 7th century, were followed by several schools, notably the monist Kashmir Shaiva traditions, and the dualist Shaiva Siddhanta: 'Like the sparkling gem Cintāmaṇi, the Śaiva teachings appear as both one and many. Although they are unitary because of their speaker [Śhiva], they are also multiple because they are divided into many streams.'[11]

The Shaiva Siddhanta ('fully completed') school spread far and wide; it is associated with important medieval temples, and in Tamil Nadu remains firmly rooted today. It represents a respectable face of Tantric Shaivism, an integration of formerly antagonistic Brahminic and Tantric views into a 'composite Tantric-Puranic religion'.[12] The Agamas followed by this school teach a meticulously structured cosmogony, in which transcendent Shiva, remaining whole and unaffected by emanations, activates undifferentiated subtle matter (*maya*), initiating a Samhkya-like sequential and hierarchical emission of the entire universe, correlated with the human mind–body continuum. Everything is subject, after a pause, to reabsorption back

4.5 *Lingas*: (**a**) Plain *linga*, Nand Chand (MP), *c* 9th century. Photo © American Institute of Indian Studies; (**b**) *ekha-mukha-linga* (one-faced), Cave 1, Udayagiri (MP), 5th century; (**c**) *chatur-mukha-linga* (four-faced), Nachna (MP), 9th century – such *lingas* may imply, or explicitly show, a fifth face, looking upwards from the top, thus *pancha-mukha*. Photo © American Institute of Indian Studies; (**d**) *linga* at Kalyanpur (Rajasthan), *c* late 7th century, embodying the process of Shiva's manifestation from formlessness (plain *linga*), via a transitional state (emergent faces), to fully formed (complete anthropomorphic deities). The face of Sadashiva on this side is Sadyojata, and the figure below Shiva is Mahesha (Great Lord). Photo © Frederick M Asher

through the same stages. Each successive stage evolves from a minute fraction of the previous one, and has a proportionately shorter lifespan.[13] The rituals of the Agamas — for purifying the worshipper's body through placement of *mantras*, for arranging concentric layers of water pots for bathing the deity, for constructing a mental image of Shiva's entourage, for invoking Shiva into the *linga* — all follow the same pattern: 'Śavia worship also echoes rhythm. The paired concepts of "emission" (Sṛṣṭi) "reabsorption" (samhāra), with which Saivite cosmology describes the movements of the oscillating universe, are embedded as an organising logic in the patterning of worship.'[14]

Integrated with this whole system is the emanatory hierarchy of deities involved in the emergence of fivefold Sadashiva from formlessness and his progress towards form. In Agamic ritual the priest 'places' the five constituent deities of Sadashiva on his body in the pattern of a five-face (*pancha-mukha*) *linga*, reconstructing the body as a Sadashiva, and thus a stage closer to the supreme.[15] In the Shaiva scheme, Para Shiva is the transcendent unity without form (*nishkala*), Sadashiva is between formlessness and form (*shakala-nishkala*), and Mahesha ('Great Lord') has come fully into form (*shakala*). The unfolding from formless Para Shiva to fully formed Mahesha is embodied in a proliferated development of the *pancha-mukha linga* (**4.5d**),[16] symbolising cosmic manifestation through a sculptural equivalent to the unfurling architecture of a temple exterior.

Vaishnavism

The conception of Vishnu ('all pervading') as supreme deity drew upon three traditions which already existed in the middle of the 1st millennium BC, and which later converged. Two of these were the cults of Vasudeva (identified at an early date with Krishna, a deified king or hero) and of Krishna-Gopala (Krishna the cowherd), and together these strands constituted the basis of the Bhagavata tradition, in which an emphasis on Bhakti, devotion to a personal Lord, was present from an early date. The third strand was the worship of Narayana, who was identified with the cosmic man (*purusha*). Assimilation between these and, indeed, several other traditions must partly account for one Vaishnava concept of emanation, the doctrine of the many *avataras* (avatars, 'descents') or incarnations of Vishnu. Of these the most famous are probably Krishna, Rama, the boar Varaha and the man-lion Narasimha; the Buddha also came to be included in the list.

With its early emphasis on Bhakti, Vaishnavism throughout India was readily influenced by the popular and emotional devotionalism of

THE EMANATING UNIVERSE

the 6th–9th century Tamil poet-saints, the Alvars (though it should be noted that their Shaiva equivalents, the Nayanars, had a similar effect on Shaivism). Vishnu kept the solar associations of his namesake in the Vedas, and represents law, order and ideal kingship. To a great extent he is 'Appolonian' to Shiva's 'Dionysian', light and harmony versus orgiastic fusion.

With this emphasis on human relations, incarnations and attachment to a personal divinity, it might be expected that the cosmos and its evolution would not be prominent in Vaishnavism, but this is far from the case. A recurrent theme is Vishnu as *vishva-rupa* ('universe-form', 'encompassing all the forms of the universe'),[17] a famous instance being Arjuna's vision of *vishva-rupa* Krishna in the Bhagavad Gita, the great 'Song of the Lord' that forms part of the Mahabharata. *Avataras* are one kind of descent, another kind are the *vyuhas*, literally 'emanations'. The tradition known as the Pancharatra ('five nights'), the one associated with the worship of Narayana, has a Samhkya-like scheme of manifestation of the absolute through an

4.6 Vishnu Anantashayin, Mahishasuramardini cave, Mahabalipuram (Tamil Nadu), 7th century. Vishnu sleeps in the cosmic void on the serpent Ananta ('endlessness'). A lotus emerges and grows from his navel; out of the lotus appears Brahma, who begins to create the universe (cf 5.1).

54 THE TEMPLE ARCHITECTURE OF INDIA

emanatory chain of *vyuhas*, already outlined in the Narayania section of the Mahabharata.[18] In this scheme, the absolute is manifest through four primary *vyuhas*, proceeding one from another. These are Vasudeva, then Samkarshana, then Pradyumna, then Aniruddha, from whom descends manifest creation. From about the 7th century ad the Pancharatra school follows texts called the Samhitas (Vaishnava Tantras) and becomes the Vaishnava equivalent of the Shaiva Siddhanta, a respectable Tantric form of Vaishnavism. The *vyuha* system is elaborated by this school, and the *avataras* are seen as emanating through the *vyuhas* rather than directly, as they do in the Puranas.[19]

From as early, perhaps, as the 2nd century BC, ways were being sought to represent Vishnu's emanatory characteristics: deities emerging from the sides of a pillar, a figure with smaller figures springing out at neck-level, the perennial four heads, or a great frothy nimbus of proliferating beings.

Notes
1. Chandogya Upanishad, III 14, 3-4, *The Upaniṣads*, trans Valerie J Roebuck (New Delhi: Penguin Books, 2000), p 164.
2. Ibid, p 169: Chandogya Upanishad, III 19, 1–2.
3. Ibid, p 261: Aitareya Upanishad I.4.
4. Gavin Flood, *An Introduction to Hinduism* (Cambridge: Cambridge University Press, 1996), p 233 (with table).
5. This esoteric anatomy seems to appear from around the 7th century, perhaps as a result of Chinese influence; Geoffrey Samuel (personal communication).
6. David Gordon White, *Kiss of the Yoginī: 'Tantric Sex' in its South Asian Contexts* (Chicago and London: University of Chicago Press, 2003), p 3.
7. Ibid, p 11.
8. Flood, *An Introduction to Hinduism*, pp 187–9.
9. Doris M Srinivasan, 'Śaiva Temple forms: Loci of God's Unfolding Body' in *Investigating Indian Art*, ed M Taldiz and W Labo (Berlin, 1987), pp 335–347 (p 337); also Doris M Srinivasan 'From transcendency to materiality: Para Śiva, Sādaśiva and Maheśa in Indian Art', *Artibus Asiae* 50, 1/2 (1990), pp 108–42.
10. Flood, *An Introduction to Hinduism*, pp 154–5.
11. Kamik Agama 1.1.03, quoted in Richard Davies, *Ritual in an Oscillating Universe: Worshipping Śiva in Medieval India* (Princeton: Princeton University Press, 1991), p 13.
12. Devangana Desai, *The Religious Imagery of Khajuraho* (Mumbai: Franco-Indian Research, 1996), p 11.
13. Ibid, p 152.
14. Davies, *Ritual in an Oscillating Universe*, p 42.
15. Ibid, p 59.
16. Srinivasan, 'Śaiva Temple Forms', p 339.
17. Thomas S Maxwell, *Viśvarūpa* (Delhi: Oxford University Press, 1988).
18. Flood, *An Introduction to Hinduism*, pp 121–2. For an analysis of the *vyuha* concept in iconography, see Doris M Srinivasan, 'Early Vaiṣṇava Imagery: Caturvyūha and Variant Forms', *Archives of Asian Art* 32 (1979), pp 39–54.
19. Desai, *The Religious Imagery of Khajuraho*, p 106.

5   Placing the Gods

Chapter 4 showed how the idea of the cosmos in Indian philosophy and mythology has often been inseparable from a hierarchical structure of gods, often a dynamic one, linked together through sequential emanation. This kind of structure has been embodied in rituals and meditational practices, typically involving the placement of deities onto diagrams, onto arrangements of objects such as pots, or onto the body, conceived as an image of the universe. Housing of divinities in a series goes well beyond the sphere usually thought of as religious: musical notes contain deities, as do the letters of the devanagari alphabet, manifested out from a primal sound.

It should be clear by now that the compositional structure of medieval temples is strikingly homologous with such cosmology, ie they share the same kind of structure. Once it is recognised that shrines are composed of aedicules, their congruence with a hierarchy of gods is obvious, and, in their more dynamic forms, the way in which they mirror a cosmogonic unfolding is irresistible. This parallel is a general one, rather than a precise correspondence between particular deities and architectural elements. However, there are two ways in which deities are explicitly placed in temples: through ritual invocation and through arrangements of iconography – the latter, in fact, is not independent of the former, since divine presence has to be ritually instilled into the images. This chapter will look at these two processes.

Temples and Ritual Placement

In the last few decades, the essence of traditional Indian architecture has for many been associated with a device called the *vastu-purusha-mandala* ('diagram of the spirit of the site'), a pattern to be ritually traced on the site not only of temples, but also of cities and towns, palaces and houses. It consists, with several variants, of a gridded square in which deities of more or less Vedic origin (nothing to do with those in temple walls) are arranged hierarchically in concentric layers. The most commonly reproduced illustration overlays the shape of a legendary cosmic demon, pinned down by the gods, who are assigned to his body parts.[1] A recent study by Sonit Bafna shows that, at an early date, the textual evidence for a connection between the site-demon and grids is tenuous, and that in any case such diagrams are more to do with sites than building forms.[2] More iconoclastically, Bafna argues that linking the site diagram, the *vastu-purusha-mandala*, with Vedic altars and making it the blueprint and, as it were, the genetic coding for the Hindu temple, dates from the monumentally essentialising project of Stella Kramrisch.

Kramrisch herself recognised that the *vastu-purusha-mandala* was not generally a planning grid, though it has been taken as such. An example is the architect Walter Henn's preface to Volwahsen's introductory survey, where the argument is along the lines of 'these ancient Indians were weird, but they used grids, and so do I', as demonstrated by a picture of an open plan *Bürolandschaft* office layout. The architect Charles Correa has made creative use of the *vastu-purusha-mandala* to connote Indianness, as a ground plan if not as a grid, in the Jawahar Kala Kendra, a centre for the arts and crafts in Jaipur. A subtle reconstruction of traditional uses of the diagram – seeing it as a flexible tool, and part of a language shared by client and designer – has been made by Vibhuti Sachdev and Giles Tillotson.[3] However, having seen students design boring square buildings in the name of authenticity, blinded by mystique to the organic plasticity that really is traditional Indian architecture, I would not be upset if the *vastu-purusha-mandala* faded gracefully from the discourse.

Similarly connected with plans are the sacred diagrams or *yantras* found on temple plan drawings in Orissan texts. *Yantras*, as we saw in the previous chapter, have deities placed within them, and they were no doubt ritually inscribed in the plans of temples related to Tantric traditions. Generally, however, there seems to have been little correspondence between the *yantras* and the actual constructional geometry of the temple. The Rajarani temple at Bhuvaneshvara, for example, has been convincingly linked to the Shri Yantra (**4.1**) in terms of its cult affiliation, but superimposition of the *yantra* on the plan shows only a generic connection.[4]

5.1 Vishnu Anantashayin, Vishnu temple, Deogarh (MP), *c* 500. Early temple exteriors usually displayed single images of deities on each face. In this case, the three sides (apart from the west one, with the doorway) have sculptural reliefs of mythic events, equivalent to the reliefs in the cave temples of this period.
Photo © Gerard Foekema

More interesting are the consecration rites which, according to *vastushastra* texts from different regional traditions, call down the cosmos (ie the gods) to inhabit the body of the temple in its full three dimensions. For example, the 11th-century Vastushastra of Vishvakarman (the architect god) prescribes the sequential invocation of deities and features of nature into mouldings and elements.[5] It begins with the tortoise (*kurma*) in the foundation stone, installing the mountains in the pillars and the sky in the great ceiling. The lower series of Shiva's manifestations are allocated to the superstructure: 'Let the five divinities, Brahmā, Viṣṇu, Rudra, Īśvara [Maheśa] and Sadāśiva, live in [each] *uraḥ-srnga* on each *bhadra* offset.'[6] It is tempting to imagine these deities in a vertical sequence of *urah-shringas*, the embedded spire (*shikhara*) forms which emerge along the axes of Shekhari shrines, but the looseness of the fit becomes clear when the higher series – Sadyojata, Vamadeva, Aghora, Tatpurusha and Ishana, who constitute Sadashiva (Vamadeva and Sadyojata are usually the other way round) are placed horizontally in the wall projections. Clearly, there is no logic that binds all the correspondences into a system, and the temple/cosmos analogy is of the same order as the closely enumerated temple/body equations mentioned in Chapter 3. A southern text, the Rauravottar Agama, instructs that once the Sadashiva series have been worshipped in five temporary shrines around the temple, they should be installed in ascending segments of the temple, with Vamadeva in the wall and so on up to Tatpurusha in the roof.[7] This confirms, in case we need reminding, that reabsorption is up, emission down – except that Ishana is not in the finial but in the sanctum. After all, this is not an exact science.

The Iconographic Programme
The placing of iconography generally shows little correspondence with the diagrams and rituals of installation just described, or indeed with many priestly rituals of temple worship.[8] In a temple exterior, pride of place is naturally in the middle of the shrine walls, so the relationship of the deity enshrined in the sanctum to those housed in the cardinal projections is (literally) crucial (**5.1**). The logic of this relationship can be one of family ties (Parvati, Ganesha and Karttikeya in the main niches of a Shiva temple), or perhaps feudal subordination; but the clearest and most influential interpretation, again stemming from Kramrisch, has understood the cardinal deities as the most direct manifestations of the central one, projected forth.

Sometimes this interpretation works, in terms of established hierarchies of gods, and sometimes it does not. It may well be that often the arrangement of gods and demigods is more like a medley of beings visiting a heavenly city.[9] The 'projected manifestations' concept has been criticised as inappropriately monistic and Vedantic (ie seeing the outer multitude as an illusory reflection of one inner reality), but it should become clear that the idea of an emanated universe is by no means uniquely Vedantic; patterns of centrifugal unfurling are open to different philosophical interpretations. In any case, coherent patterns of emanation have certainly been shown to underlie some iconographic programmes, relating most directly not to the Vedanta but to the dualistic, theistic systems. Devangana Desai has demonstrated, for example, that the Laksmana temple (AD 954) and Kandariya Mahadeva temple (*c* 1050) at Khajuraho respectively follow the Pancharatra and Shaiva Siddhanta emanatory theologies/cosmogonies in the placement and graded sizes of images, from the icon in the *garbha-griha*, to the sanctum walls (within the ambulatory), around the temple interior, and out into the exterior.[10]

Deities are sometimes carved in a temple superstructure. This gives extra scope for making downward and outward emanation explicit, and further studies would be needed to find out how often this opportunity was exploited. One case where a downward unfurling has been shown is the 7th-century Parasurameshvara temple, Bhuvaneshvara (**21.3**), where

5.2 Proliferating projections provide places for proliferating pantheons: Temple 1, Khirnivala Group, Kadwaha (MP), 10th century. Gods appear on the main projections, other beings – celestial damsels and musicians, horned lions (*vyalas, shardhulas*) – in recesses. Here damsels also adorn the intermediate projections. Photo © Fiona Buckee

5.3 Vishvanatha temple, Khajuraho (MP), c 1000: south wall, *kapili* recess. The walls provide for images in three registers. Individual deities appear on the projections: to the left is a Latina *kuta-stambha* belonging to the *mula-prasada*, to the right a Phamsana *kuta-stambha* belonging to the *maha-mandapa*. Erotic scenes are shown in the recess between: intercourse in the interstice.

the descending images in the horseshoe arches (*gavakshas*) of the west spine (*lata*) of the tower (*shikhara*) follow an emanatory series of the Shaiva Siddhanta kind.[11] This iconographic sequence parallels the formal unfolding of *gavaksha* chains shown in Chapter 3 (**3.6, 3.7**).

There are, however, no universal recipes for the arrangement of images, partly because the rules were flexible (the texts themselves give alternatives), and partly because, when it came to fitting gods into actual architectural designs, there was no obvious way to do it.[12] Emanation, as we have seen, is conceived as happening downwards and outwards, and temple forms perfectly embody such a pattern: but the alternative idea of anti-clockwise emanation/clockwise reabsorption went better with a circumambulatory viewing sequence. The challenge of placement was compounded by a shrine having a door on one side, usually with a porch or a whole *mandapa*. There were, moreover, symbolic requirements, such as the need for the guardians of the eight directions to face more or less the right way – not easy when your plan is square, and the porch or antechamber covers one whole side. Yet complex iconographic layouts were achieved in spite of these constraints.

While iconographic programmes were certainly made to fit architectural layouts, could architecture also be adapted to fit particular iconographic patterns? Art historians who focus on sculpture tend to see the temple as a glorified picture frame, with the walls as a horizontal frieze. From this perspective, it is natural to interpret the addition of intermediate projections, for example, as a response to a need to accommodate more sculpted deities or their entourages (**5.2**). The proliferation of surfaces is seen as a consequence of the great proliferation of sculpture that took place towards the end of the 1st millennium, a trend which heightened the importance of the overall effect at the expense of the individual figure. It must be recognised that particular iconographic schemes would sometimes have influenced specific architectural layouts; and at times some temple types and sculptural programmes became welded together and helped to fossilise one another, inviting people to prescribe the formula in texts. But iconographic developments cannot explain the subtle and consistent patterns of cumulative unfolding that temple architecture follows (see Chapter 6): it is enough to look at the Dravida architecture in northern Karnataka between the 9th and 12th centuries, where iconography played a negligible role in the temple exterior, to know that this is the case.

A word needs to be said about erotic sculpture. This has a very long history in India. In earlier periods the loving couples in the walls of sacred buildings are simply happy; from around the 9th century they proliferate and, increasingly, copulate. Some readers of Chapter 4 will have been quick to conclude that the erotic sculpture is all Tantric. Some may well have been, in a broad sense, a symbolic substitute for the actual thing. Other well-founded explanations (and many dubious ones) have been suggested, and the reality is surely a combination of these.[13] There is evidence that (following a long tradition) depiction of loving couples was believed to have magical, defensive and propitiatory functions, as well as bringing abundance and fertility. Erotic images would be valued in a courtly milieu, where kings and courtiers were expected to cultivate *kama* (sensual love); *kama*, in fact, is one of life's four goals.[14] Erotic images could be metaphors for the bliss of union with the divine; they could represent the world of the senses which flows out to us, and which spiritual aspiration must transcend. They could be comic. They could make puns: at Khajuraho the well-known images of conjuncture appear at the junction of *mula-prasada* and *mandapa* (**5.4**).[15] They could picture the pleasures of heaven, or simply rejoice in life.

Notes
1. Eg Andreas Volwahsen, *Living Architecture: India* (London: Macdonald, 1970).
2. Sonit Bafna, 'On the Idea of the Mandala as a Governing Device in Indian Architectural Tradition', *Journal of the Society of Architectural Historians* 59:1, March 2000, pp 26–49.
3. Vibhuti Sachdev and Giles Tillotson, *Building Jaipur: The Making of an Indian City* (London: Reaktion Books, 2002).
4. Bettina Bäumer and Rajendra Prasad Das (eds), *Śilparatnakośa – a Glossary of Orissan Temple Architecture* (Delhi: IGNCA, 1994), *passim*.
5. MA Dhaky, 'Prasada as Cosmos', *Adyar Library Bulletin* 35, Pts 3–4 (Madras, 1971), pp 211–26.
6. Dhaky, 'Prāsāda as Cosmos', p 216.
7. Bruno Dagens, 'Le temple corps du dieu' in *Traités, temples et images du monde indien: études d'histoire et d'archaéologie*, compiled by Marie-Luce Barazier-Billoret and Vincent Lefèvre, Institut Français de Pondichéry and Presses Sorbonne Nouvelle, 2005, pp 125–49 (pp 137–8), citing NR Bhatt.
8. Hélène Brunner, 'L'image divine dans la culte āgamique de Śiva. Rapport entre l'image mentale et le support concret du culte', in André Padoux (ed.), in *L'image divine: culte et méditation dans l'hindouisme* (Paris: Editions du CNRS, 1990), pp 9–31.
9. Phyllis Granoff, 'Heaven on Earth: Temples and Temple Cities of Medieval India' in Dick van der Meij (ed), *India and Beyond: Aspects of Literature, Meaning, Ritual and Thought* (London: Routledge & Kegan Paul, 1977), pp 170–93.
10. Devangana Desai, *The Religious Imagery of Khajuraho* (Mumbai: Franco-Indian Research, 1996).
11. Doris M Srinivasan, 'From transcendency to materiality: Para Śiva, Sadāśiva and Maheśa in Indian Art', *Artibus Asiae* 50, 1/2 (1990), pp 108–42 (pp 129–31).
12. For a summary of different logics of placement see Darielle Mason, 'A Sense of Time and Place: Style and Architectural Disposition of Images on the North Indian Temple' in Vishaka Desai and D Mason (eds), *Gods, Guardians and Lovers: Temple Sculpture from North India, AD 700–1200* (New York: Asia Society, 1993), pp 116–37.
13. Devangana Desai, *Erotic Sculpture of India, a Socio-cultural Study* (Delhi: Tata McGraw-Hill, 1975); also Vidya Dehejia, 'Reading Love Imagery on the Indian Temple' in *Love in Asian Art and Culture* (Washington DC: Smithsonian Institution, 1998), pp 97–113.
14. For the householder, together with duty (*dharma*), worldly success (*arhtha*) and release (*moksha*).
15. Michael W Meister, 'Junction and Conjunction: Punning and Temple Architecture', *Artibus Asiae* 41, 2/3, pp 226–34.

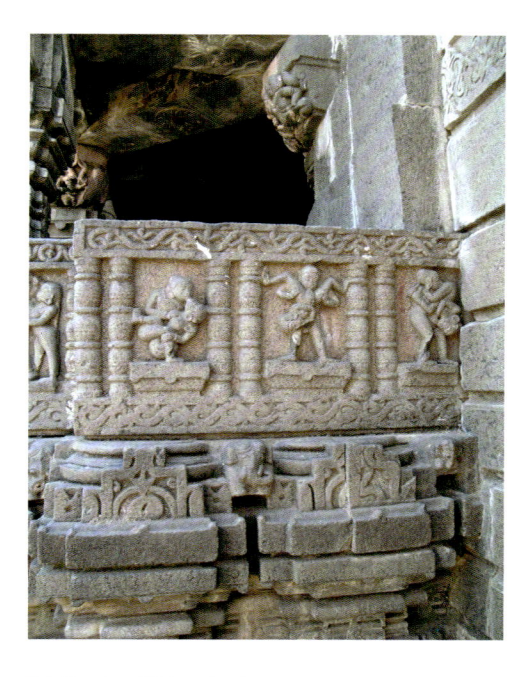

5.4 Devalana (Maharashtra), open *mandapa, c* 12th century: seat back (*kaksasana*). Photo © Gerard Foekema

6 THE ARCHITECT AND UNFOLDING TRADITIONS

The architect is from a renowned land and he is of mixed caste; a man of quality, he must know how to establish buildings and must be well versed in all the sciences; he must be physically perfect, just, compassionate, disinterested, free from envy; without weakness, handsome, and learned in mathematics; he must know the ancient authors, and must be straightforward and master of his senses.[1]

When the canonical texts, the *vastu shastras*, list the qualities expected of the architect (*sthapati*), originality is not one of them. The traditional Indian artist or architect was not the individual genius of post-Romantic myth, even if he was not a selfless channel through which transcendent truths could be given form, as idealists such as Coomaraswamy would have us believe.

An architect's claim to proficiency rested on knowing the *shastras*, or, rather, of *shastra*, the body of knowledge which the texts represent. Traditional practitioners today claim the same authority. The 11th-century *Samarangana Sutradhara*, stressing that neither the theory nor the practice of architecture is useful on its own, without knowledge of the other, declares 'He who begins to work as an architect (sthapati) without knowing the science of architecture (vāstuśāstra) and proud with false knowledge must be put to death by the king as one who ruins the kingdom (rājahiṃsaka); dead before his time his ghost will wander this wide earth...'[2] On a brighter note: 'The prince is obliged to offer land and cows to the tetrad who are led by the architect and who are skilful in measuring. He who does this without reservation shall gain riches in abundance and his kingdom shall extend to the moon and stars so long as the world shall exist.'[3]

The architect's work was team work and, as for the masons of medieval Europe, was not separate from building. It was also bound up with the rituals performed before, during and after construction: these, and other religious aspects of the temple, not least the placement of deities in the iconographic scheme, were presided over by a Brahmin *acharya*. Of the four roles referred to in the previous quotation,[4] the first was that of the *sthapati*, with overall responsibility. Second, the 'drawer of the thread' (*sutra-grahin*), was son or disciple of the *sthapati*, in charge of layout and measurement. Third, the *takshaka* is a cutter (*taksh*) (and carver?) of the stone or other material, and lastly the 'fitter' (*vardhaki*) fits, plasters and paints. These were hereditary vocations in which whole families participated, travelling from site to site, and there is evidence that women could be involved in craft as well as their usual chores. The castes of craftsmen were organised in a system of guilds (*seni*), which, like their European counterparts, carried out functions of welfare as well as regulation, and could become rich and influential bodies.

Inseparable from the masons' work was the work of the *shilpins* (sculptors; the term is sometimes used for craftsmen in general) in their various grades. The range of carving work was great, merging indissolubly with 'architecture', from the central cult icon, through the deities of the exterior and accompanying celestial beings, narrative panels, figurative architectural elements such as brackets and various friezes, to the ornamental enrichment of mouldings. Nor should one forget those who quarried and transported the stone, or those who extracted and cast the iron used for dowels and ties, not to mention the maintainers of oil lamps, the servers of refreshments, and the necessary battalions of labourers.

The design as well as the making of temples was a collective enterprise, to the extent that it is perhaps misleading to speak of 'the architect'. It cannot even be said without qualification that the *sthapati* was responsible for the planning and overall architectural conception of a temple, given the importance of types, of specific architectural compositions and of textual prescriptions of certain types for certain purposes. Wherever types were prescribed, the architect's role in what we know as 'design' would be concentrated on secondary elements and details. While these are essential to the character and quality of a temple, it is not clear to what extent they would have been determined

6.1 Bracket figure at Chenna-Keshava temple, Belur (Karnataka), 1117. The bracket figures at Belur bear inscriptions boasting of the artists' skill. Photo © Gerard Foekema

6.2 Nagara architecture flowing towards fusion: proliferating forms surrender their individuality, like faces swept up in a crowd. Ajitanahta temple, Taranga (Gujarat), 1165. Photo © Gerard Foekema

by the *sthapati*. It is evident just from looking at temples that greater freedom for the individual craftsmen, within the shared medium of the style, was permissible at the lower levels of order, in a manner of which John Ruskin, the great 19th-century English critic, would have approved, despite his strictures against Indian art. It is often in the secondary aedicules or shrine-images, or in even lesser, miniature ones, freer from the requirements of actual construction, that architectural inventiveness is most fertile.

All in all, despite the apparent norms and whatever the distribution of roles, there was ample scope for invention, and admiration for individuals who excelled in it. Some inscriptions from Karnataka are very clear about this. The inscription at Sudi quoted in Chapter 2 relates how the general Nagadeva entrusted the building of his temple to a certain Shamka. He was a 'mine of splendid learning', a 'model for the acquisition of wealth', a 'Vachaspati [poet] of punning phrase'. Virtuosity is prized in architecture as in literature, as the 'finials' of the temple (presumably referring to the ingenious aeducular components) were 'completed in a manner that none could possibly imagine'.[5] Another inscription from Karnataka, of a century or so later, states that, in the village of Kuppatur, was built 'as if by Viśvakarma [the divine architect] himself, out of sublime devotion for the Lord of the Kailāsa mountain [Shiva], the elegant, equipoised and shapely temple of Koṭiśa-Bhava, freely ornamented with Drāviḍa, Bhūmija and Nāgara, and, with bhadra-offsets manipulated in many ways'.[6] The Dravida, Bhumija and Nagara (here meaning Shekhari) are the complex, detailed shrine models found over niches in the walls of later Karnata Dravida temples, including 'exotic' northern modes, and often exhibiting unusual conceptions never realised at full scale. The *bhadra*-offsets (*bhadrōpētadiṁ*, in the original Kannada) seem, again, to be the primary aedicules.

A set of inscriptions of a similar date from further south in Karnataka, on the voluptuous nymph bracket figures of Belur (**6.1**), not only explodes the myth that artists were always anonymous, by giving their names, but also shows that some groups of craftsmen, at least, were able to exhibit the lack of self-effacement expected of kings: 'Hail! Prosperity! to rival titled sculptors like Śiva to Kāma [a glance from Shiva's third eye incinerated him], Cāvaṇa, the son of the artist Dāsōja of Balḷigrāme, made this bracket figure'; 'The bracket figure of the artist Mālliyana, a thunderbolt to the mountain of rival sculptors'; 'Padari Allōya, the sister's son of Vadōja of Nālvattubāḍa a pair of large scissors to the neck of titled sculptors, made this bracket figure...'; and so on.[7] Whether this was workshop banter, or they were really at each other's

64 THE TEMPLE ARCHITECTURE OF INDIA

THE ARCHITECT AND UNFOLDING TRADITIONS **65**

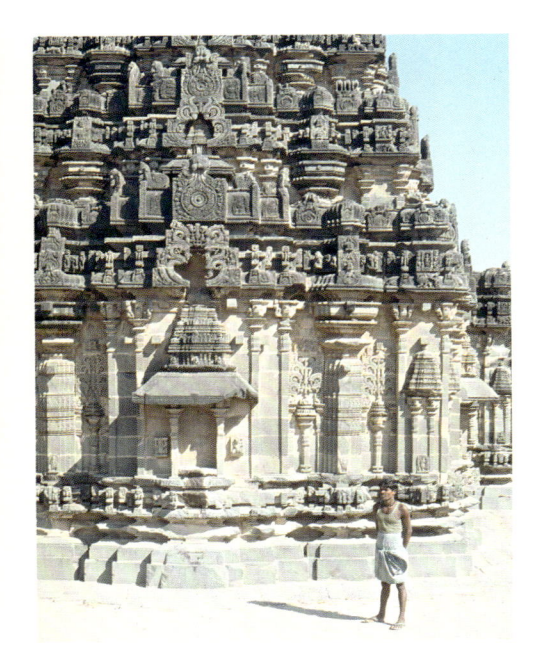

6.3 Dravida architecture flowing towards fusion: the treatment of mouldings reinforces horizontal continuity, so that shapes are crinkled out fleetingly from a teeming matrix, falling back like waves. Mahadeva temple, Ittagi (Karnataka), 1112. Photo © Gerard Foekema

throats, or were actively negotiating meaningful group identity in the social arena, can only be guessed at.

However, norms, conventions and types notwithstanding, inscriptions are not needed to attest to the almost inexhaustible inventiveness of the temple architects and artists through the centuries and to how, when inventiveness was exhausted, it could be renewed. These things can be seen in the temples themselves. Yet, when the development of architectural composition is traced through various strands of Indian temple building – not all, but several important strands – the inescapable fact stands out, that the invention leads in a particular direction. This is not merely from simplicity towards complexity, but towards complexity of a special kind. In the face of dire warnings, from those suspicious of grand historical schemes, against spirits, Kunstwollens and fiendish biological fallacies, an evolutionary pattern emerges. The pattern has two complementary aspects: an overarching tendency towards fusion, and the incorporation of each stage into the next one, creating an effect of unfolding. These will be examined in turn, before I attempt to draw conclusions about where all this leaves the architect and his creativity.

Fusion

The Germanic art historical tradition of the late 19th and early 20th centuries saw a process of fusion between certain European architectural traditions, notably (beginning with Wölfflin) in the contrasting characters of Renaissance and Baroque, and in the change from early to late Gothic. In this understanding, architectural parts or spaces are seen as individually well defined and harmoniously related together in the early or the mature stages, and later as blurred or merged into a powerful whole. The later, fused architecture has been associated with dynamism, often rather vaguely.

A comparable process can be perceived repeatedly in medieval Indian temple architecture. This is not to say that architectural fusion is always the same: fusion can sometimes (as largely with Gothic) imply a reduction in the number of parts, whereas in Indian temples its basis is proliferation, whereby parts get lost like faces in a crowd. Here is the paradox: that the parts dissolve through the very process of their articulation. Differentiation and fusion take place simultaneously. The starting point is always a simple, unitary form – a single aedicule or a single motif such as *gavaksha* arch or a ceiling lotus. Proliferation, through projection, proceeds together with fragmentation and increasing interpenetration, while connections are strengthened through alignments and continuities. Staggering performs multiple functions simultaneously: it brings forward and emphasises the centre, at the expense of the periphery, in the parts as well as the whole; it erodes the definition of edges; and is a prerequisite for interpenetration. The formal language takes hold and obscures the representational origin of forms through abstraction, while elements at first only distantly related in shape and treatment are assimilated to one another.

Some or all of these things happen in different strands of Indian temple architecture,[8] and in every case the effect is one of undermining the independence of the individual part and merging it with the whole. The parts become more difficult to distinguish, and remain centres of attention only fleetingly; as soon as something is seen, the mind is carried off elsewhere. Paradoxically, the whole, increasingly dominant, becomes ever more elusive, graspable only after determined concentration on all its aspects and their relationships.

Apart from the more familiar processes of abstraction and assimilation, the other tendencies towards fusion correspond precisely to various means of conveying movement noted in Chapter 3 (**3.3**), so that dynamism and fusion increase together. This correspondence is no coincidence, but arises from the fact that the same formal properties have two effects: the expression of movement in a single monument and the impression of fusion as the tradition progresses. In addition to the effects of 'staggering' already mentioned, 'progressive multiplication' and 'expanding repetition' are principles of (centrifugal) proliferation, 'splitting' implies fragmentation, and 'bursting of boundaries' creates overlap. Moreover, the more conceptual effects of fusion are difficult to separate from the more illusionistic effects of movement. Is an element jumping into my consciousness or jumping out of the wall? Certainly, the impression of being able to focus only momentarily on a particular part is reinforced by the part seeming to be swept away in a seething swell.

Evolution towards fusion has something of a cyclical character. I confess to having previously exaggerated this, dazzled by the cosmic implications, but the observation is valid in the sense that there is always a limit to the degree of fusion arrived at, a kind of fossilisation. This is not simply because strict norms have set in, although this may also be the case, but because in each situation the architectural game has its limits, at least without the kind of radical transformation – or starting of a new cycle – that occurred when the Shekhari emerged from the Latina. 'Cycles', or the pushing of this characteristic kind of elaboration to its limits, can happen at different times and at different rates, in different parts of temples as well as in different traditions and regions. For example, *gavaksha* patterns quickly dimple out their potential range on the surfaces of Latina shrines which, in their entirety, are developing more slowly. The same example shows that, within a shared vocabulary, the appearance of the same idea in widely separated places does not necessarily imply contact, as the formal system has inherent possibilities. Once these have been exhausted in the development of overall composition, the options short of a new cycle are to develop the parts, to proliferate mindlessly by endless extension (such as adding extra identical rows or tiers), to add some striking new features (such as the banded plinths of the Hoysalas), or to cheat (as in very late Shekhari temples).

In the Indian context it is impossible to resist an analogy between this architectural fusion and the immanent ground, the underlying, all-containing unity beneath the multiplicity of creation, from which all phenomena emerge and to which they return, as waves to the ocean. Such an idea, with different nuances, has been evoked repeatedly in Indian religious and philosophical thinking (see Chapter 5), whether as the World Soul or formless Absolute itself (*brahman*), as primal matter straining towards manifestation (*prakriti*), or as the void (*sunya*) of Mahayana Buddhism. The Yoga Sutras teach techniques of concentration, followed by meditation on relationships, gradually building up to contemplation of an entire field, all aiming towards an increasingly comprehensive vision and, ultimately, to union with the One.[9] Temple architecture cannot literally create a unified field,[10] but progressively it approaches the trance-like effect of a full, vague, fertile continuum, from which forms emerge fleetingly into consciousness, repeated shapes looming out in rhythm like echoing *mantras*, then dying back into pregnant emptiness.

These are the effects of formal evolution towards fusion, but we should be cautious about claiming that they contain deep symbolism, or manifest a specifically Indian way of thinking, let alone a conscious aim. Parallel kinds of development towards fusion (though not necessarily fusion of the same kind) can be found in other cultures; and perhaps the pattern arises from a combination of the common human urge to elaborate, to master each challenge and move on, coupled with the nature of the system or game that has been set up. There is, nevertheless, another aspect to the particular way in which Indian temples so often develop, to which nothing is quite comparable, and which is entirely bound up with their dynamic character.

Unfolding

The same pattern of emergence, expansion and proliferation expressed in a single temple is reflected in the development of forms during the course of various traditions. These forms unfold not just metaphorically, as a tradition developing, say, towards refinement (like Greek Doric temples) or linearity (like some strands of Gothic), but quite literally: new designs are unpacked and pulled out of previous ones. In the process, the sense of emergence and growth within a single composition is enhanced: the evolution is towards an ever greater illusion, in an individual shrine, of evolution. This is surprising, but simple once seen and no more coincidental than the simultaneous effects of dynamism and fusion in a single temple design, since once again it is the same formal characteristics that produce this phenomenon. We are just looking at them from a different point of view. Projection and staggering (**3.3a, b**), progressive multiplication and expanding repetition (**3.3e, f**), and splitting and bursting of boundaries (**3.3c, d**), are not only features to behold, but actions that have been completed. Expanding repetition includes its earlier stages, staggering its earlier steps, literally. The double-staggered *shala* aedicule (**11.13e**), the proliferated and interpenetrating version of the barrel-roofed Dravida pavilion, includes the earlier, single-staggered version (**11.13a**); when it is fronted by two vertically stacked horseshoe arch gables (*gavakshas*) (**11.13f**), the single arch, from which the new one emanates, remains.

Such an unfolding takes place not simply in the details, but at the level of the whole composition. The effect that we can observe in a single, developed temple – of one form putting forth another, which in turn emits another, and so on – is brought about by a cumulative extrapolation and successive incorporation of temple designs: a new design springing from an old one, while preserving the old one within the new. Most typically, the earlier design becomes the superstructure of the later one, which in turn is subject to the same process, the whole composition building up while unfurling downwards and outwards. Another process, while maintaining a given number of storeys, is to fill out an earlier composition by projecting new primary aedicules from the existing ones or from the interstices. At a lower level of order, secondary aedicules are brought out from the primary ones. Because of all this, if one gets to know a particular formal development, closes one's eyes, stands back far enough to see the broad, general lines, and runs it through one's mind's eye like a speeded up film, one will see the same blossoming out as can be experienced by looking solely at one of its later examples. So, figure **3.9**, of the Kandariya Mahadeva, shows not only the

6.4 Evolution: generalised picture of (**a**) the progression of Nagara temples from the Latina through developing types of Shekhari; (**b**) the development of the Karnata Dravida tradition. Such patterns mirror the dynamic unfolding expressed in individual temple designs: in fact, 6.4a shows the same process as 3.9, drawn differently.

6.5 Evolving ceiling designs. At the next stage the individual lobes themselves sprout lobes (cf 15.10, 15.11).

dynamics of the temple, but also (before it all explodes) the general progression of shrine types through the tradition (**6.4a**). Figure **6.4b** shows the evolutionary pattern of the Karnata Dravida tradition.[11]

That a pattern of development can be visualised in this way does not, of course, mean that there is only one route by which the later forms can have emerged, or that temples were necessarily built in the organic sequence. Intermediate stages could be conceived of without actually being built, or come to be built later than their logical moment. Affluent phases would be succeeded by impoverished ones and, although primarily affecting the scale of monuments, this could also influence their degree of complexity. There could be creative phases full of variation with no discernable direction; variation for its own delight is always possible, and outstanding designs are not necessarily those which advance the tradition a step further. At any given time, a range of types would be available, to supply a hierarchy of temple grades. In spite of all this, if a broad perspective is taken — and especially if we look at the emergence of those designs which became established as types — the idealised evolutionary pattern holds true to a remarkable extent. Whatever the actual course taken, the way of development stands out.

Can the designs of the later monuments be predicted by the earlier ones? To claim that they were predestined would be ridiculous. The wisdom of hindsight is dangerous: just because we can trace a set of musical variations back to the original tune does not mean that the later variations were predetermined. Yet, given an architectural language with inherent properties, coupled with a propensity for a particular kind of evolution, certain developments in Indian temple architecture do arrive with an uncanny sense of inevitability. When a staggered *shala* aedicule has spawned a double-staggered version, can the triple-staggered be far behind? We can imagine extrapolations of our own, but it is not easy to beat the temple architects at their game without cheating: starting from the same possibilities, we come up against the same limits.

Continuity and Ingenuity

In the early years of India's great age of temple building in masonry, architects inherited familiar and revered forms from wooden buildings and forged, from their shapes and imagery, expressive architectural languages, each with a range of parts, and ways of combining these into a range of types. These types, in turn, were revered, sometimes prescribed, and to build these types was not a failure of imagination, but a re-creation, like performing music or drama, always bringing out fresh detail and feeling. Often, however, as in a performance, improvisation and even virtuosity were expected, even at the level of the overall composition; but to abandon the architectural language would be meaningless, as it was the very medium of expression. The new designs chosen as new types were those which most directly extended the forms of the earlier types, not through natural selection but through cultural recognition of their power, and partly because the incorporation of lesser types was considered a desirable attribute for a prestigious temple.

Transmitted knowledge of how to make a type would ensure its longevity, since to make a temple requires not only its visualisation and construction, but also the ability to get its relative proportions right. All this has to be mastered before one can change it radically. New types would, in their turn, be revered, and ascribed to divine origin; a band of experts would be at hand to list the types and decree their uses. But texts without pictures, for architects, have as limited power to constrain as they do to inspire: ultimately, constraint was set by the limits of the architectural language itself.

The presence of evolutionary patterns in these traditions was not predestination, or an impersonal will-to-form, but arose because of the way in which the architects extrapolated successively more complex designs from the earlier ones, playing out the potential of the architectural languages they had created. These patterns reflect a way of thought, and so suggestive are the analogies with other cultural domains that it is tempting once again to say that the patterns reflect a whole world view. One certain thing is that, more than fixed forms, a way of designing was passed down.

Notes
1. *Mayamata* 5 14b–18a, trans Bruno Dagens (New Delhi: Sitaram Bharatia Institute of Scientific Research, 1985), p 10.
2. *Samarangana Sutradhara* 44 2–4, quoted in Stella Kramrisch, *The Hindu Temple* (Calcutta: University of Calcutta, 1946), p 8.
3. *Mayamata*, trans Dagens, p 37.
4. Ibid, pp x and 10; also Kramrisch, *The Hindu Temple*, p 10.
5. 'Inscriptions of Sudi' in *Epigraphia Indica* 15 (1919–20), pp 93–4.
6. MA Dhaky, *The Indian Temple Forms in Karṇāṭa Inscriptions and Architecture* (New Delhi: Abhinav Publications, 1977), p 3.
7. Robert J Del Bonta, 'The Madanakais at Belur' in Joanna Williams (ed), *Kalādarśana* (New Delhi: Oxford University Press and IBH, 1981), pp 27–33.
8. For this process in the Karnata Dravida tradition see A Hardy, *Indian Temple Architecture* (New Delhi: IGNCA, 1995).
9. Ernest Wood, *Yoga* (Harmondsworth: Penguin Books, 1959), p 58.
10. Richard Lannoy has interpreted the Ajanta murals in terms of 'unified field awareness' in *The Speaking Tree* (Oxford: Oxford University Press, 1971), pp 31–5.
11. To substantiate this fully, and to be sure that you have not just arranged the monuments in the expected order, the sequence needs to be tied to the securely dated monuments, and every aspect of style has to be taken into account when filling the gaps between them. The general picture is what counts, however, not precise dating and sequence. For a careful analysis, see Hardy, *Indian Temple Architecture*.

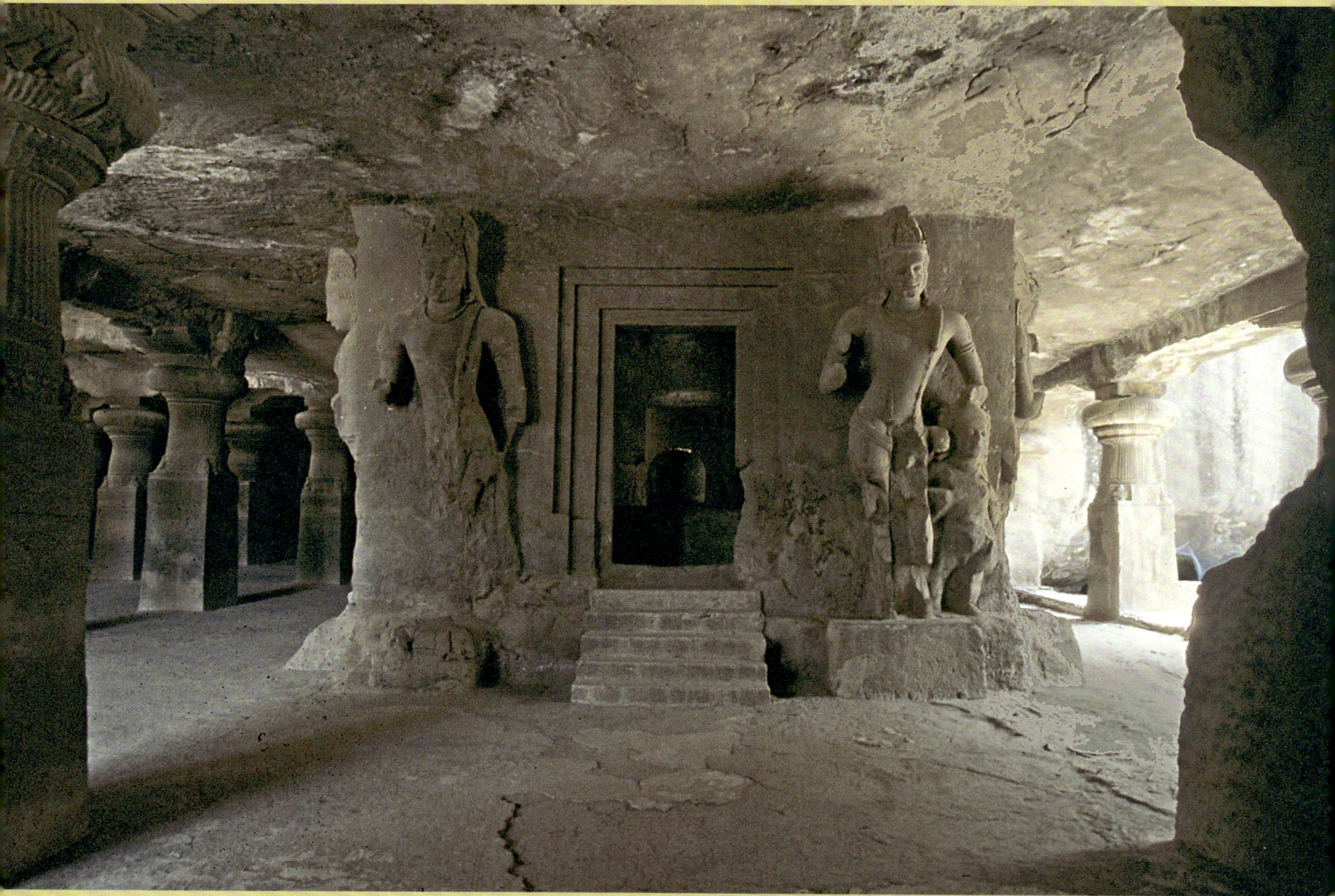

PART 2 PRECURSORS

7   Early Indian Architecture
8   Later Rock-Cut Architecture

Shiva cave, Elephanta (near Mumbai) (**8.8**). Photo © Gerard Foekema

7 Early Indian Architecture

Other than the ruins of the Indus Valley civilisation and various megaliths, the earliest brick or stone architecture surviving in the subcontinent comprises the free-standing columns erected by the Mauryas, most famously by Ashoka (*c* 268–233 BC), and the Buddhist *stupas*, monasteries and *chaitya* halls which grew up from that time onwards along the trade routes of the ancient empires. Ashoka himself almost certainly built *stupas*, made of brick. With its solid dome and cosmic axis, the *stupa*, which has its origins in burial mounds, is the most characteristic sacred monument of Buddhism. One of its multiple associations is the Buddha's achievement of Nirvana on leaving this world. Early *stupas* were raised to encase relics of the Buddha or of a disciple or a saint, and thus radiated miraculous power.[1] The great *stupas* of peninsular India, originally surrounded by thriving monastic complexes, belong to the period between the 2nd century BC and the 3rd century AD (**7.1**).

Thanks to the sublime narrative relief carvings on the gateways and railings of such *stupas*, we learn much about the wooden architecture of that period. Huts, shrines, palaces and city gates are depicted in loving detail, revealing the shapes and components which would later be formalised into the elements, mouldings and motifs of Nagara and Dravida temple architecture. This is not to say that the buildings shown in the reliefs are all 'vernacular' precursors to 'monumental' masonry conceptions. These multi-storey shrines and mansions are monumental wooden structures, combining sophisticated carpentry with refined ornament. Their happy inhabitants, swelling from the balconies and peeping from gables, are clearly well served for shade and ventilation; but the constructional forms are not merely solutions to practical needs. If this were the case, nobody would have gone to the immense trouble of bending beams to make domes and barrel roofs. Structural rationalists needing to find pragmatic origins will have to go further back, to bamboo.

Not only do these wooden buildings provide the vocabulary for later aedicular imagery, but they also contain the beginnings of aedicular thinking: often top storeys, turrets and door and window surrounds are treated like pavilions (**7.4a, d–f, h**). Among the diverse barrel-roofed

7.1 The Great Stupa (Stupa 1), Sanchi (MP), *c* 1st century BC, probably built over an earlier structure, which would have encased a sacred relic. From the top of the dome (*anda*, 'egg') rises a pivotal mast (*yashti*), terminating in a multiple, honorific parasol (*chattravali*), reflecting the Buddha's princely origins. In due course the multiple umbrella would be correlated with cosmic planes and stages of attainment on the path to enlightenment. The mast rises from a railed platform (*harmika*), later transformed into a block crowned by an inverted stepped pyramid (7.8). Railings define a path for ritual circumambulation, with gateways (*toranas*) on the cardinal axes; both the railings and the gateways are massive, stone interpretations of timber detailing. This important *stupa* is raised on a circular platform (*medhi*), reached by a double stairway to the south and providing an upper ambulatory.

EARLY INDIAN ARCHITECTURE 75

7.2 Relief from a *stupa* railing from Bharhut (MP), *c* 2nd century BC, now in the Indian Museum, Kolkata. Photo © American Institute of Indian Studies

7.3 Maya dreams of a white elephant and knows that she will give birth to the Buddha: relief from the Great Stupa, Sanchi, north gateway (*torana*). A city gate is shown lower left (cf 7.4a).

forms are found prototypes for the Dravida *shala* (rectangular and apsidal) and its end view, the *panjara*, along with the Nagara equivalent, the Valabhi shrine. Domed pavilions (square, circular and octagonal) prefigure Dravida and early Nagara domed *kutas* and, before any masonry examples, the idea of a shrine with a *kuta* on top, like a Dravida *alpa vimana* (**11.1–11.5**), was being realised in timber (**7.4b, g**).

Apart from *stupa* gates and railings, the most prominent early translations of timber construction into stone are rock-cut *chaitya* halls. The Lomas Rishi cave in Bihar is a precursor of these (**7.5**). A '*chaitya*' is a sacred place or object (such as a *stupa*), and a '*chaitya* hall' is a building sheltering a *stupa* and providing a space for worship, usually associated with a monastic site. There are archaeological remains of structural *chaitya* halls, but the type is best known from the 'cave' versions in the Western Ghats (Maharashtra), carved out mainly between the 1st century BC and the 2nd century AD, with a second wave in the 5th and 6th centuries AD. They follow various plans, but typically are long, barrel-roofed and apsidal, usually with low aisles (**7.6–7.8**; cf **7.4c**). This form, coincidentally reminiscent of a basilican church, is perfect for encasing a circular *stupa* as the focus, for defining an ambulatory passage around it, and for bathing its dim depths with light from a great gable window in the cliff facade. With their ribcage of hooped beams, and joists shooting out into the sunlight, all carved in stone, the early *chaitya* halls are not far from petrified carpentry.

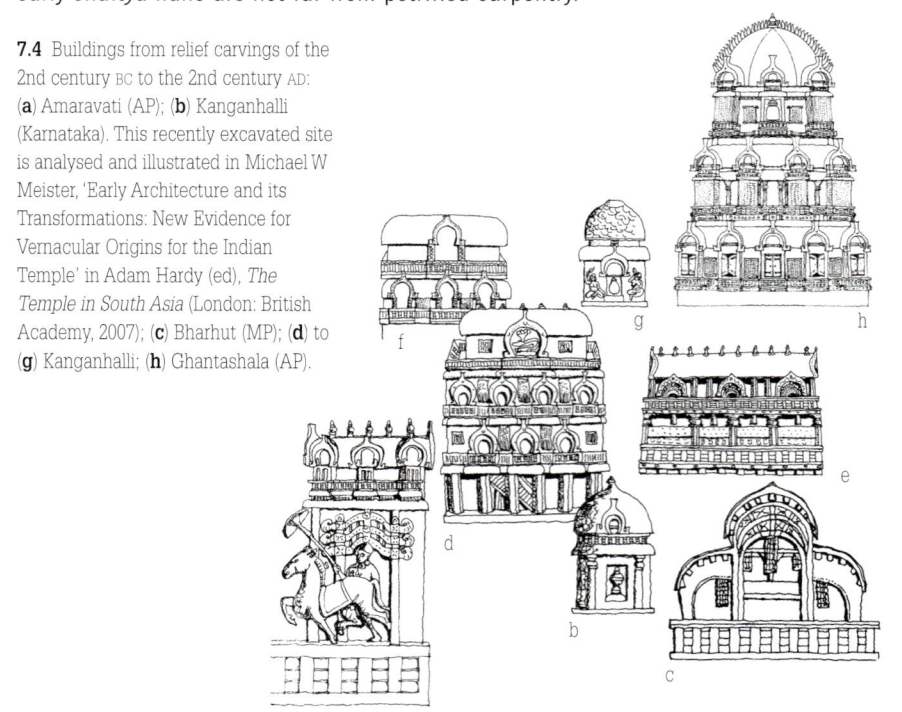

7.4 Buildings from relief carvings of the 2nd century BC to the 2nd century AD: (**a**) Amaravati (AP); (**b**) Kanganhalli (Karnataka). This recently excavated site is analysed and illustrated in Michael W Meister, 'Early Architecture and its Transformations: New Evidence for Vernacular Origins for the Indian Temple' in Adam Hardy (ed), *The Temple in South Asia* (London: British Academy, 2007); (**c**) Bharhut (MP); (**d**) to (**g**) Kanganhalli; (**h**) Ghantashala (AP).

76 THE TEMPLE ARCHITECTURE OF INDIA

7.5 Entrance to the Lomas Rishi cave, Barabar Hills near Gaya (Bihar), *c* 3rd century BC. This leads to a rectangular chamber parallel to the rock face, leading to a circular chamber to the left which probably housed a *stupa*. The facade represents the gable end of a wooden, barrel- or keel-roofed structure.

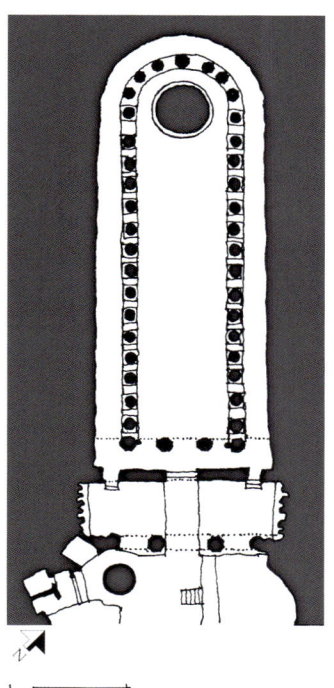

7.6 Buddhist rock-cut hall of worship ('*chaitya* hall') and adjacent monasteries (*viharas*), Bhaja (Maharashtra), *c* early 1st century BC.

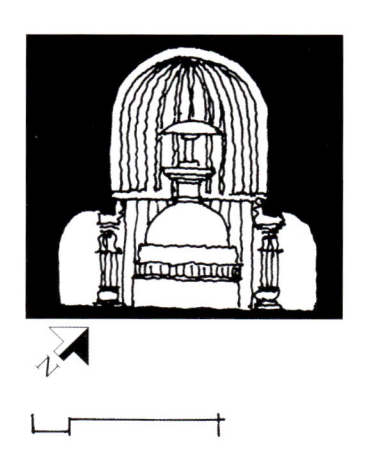

7.7 *Chaitya* hall, Karle (Maharashtra), *c* AD 120, plan and cross section.

EARLY INDIAN ARCHITECTURE   77

However, even here, the extent of the 'copying' can be exaggerated, particularly when it comes to the facades. The horseshoe-gable of the equivalent wooden structure would have stood free, not yoked in the kind of stage-set front drawn by Percy Brown in his conjectural reconstruction of the timber precedent for the *chaitya* hall at Kondane.[2] Along with railings, and sometimes columns and *stupas*, blind horseshoe arch gables – the *chaitya* arches or *gavakshas* to be discussed in Chapter 16 – become motifs arranged on the facade (**7.6**, **7.10**). Sometimes the gables cut straight through the railings, an unlikely state of affairs in a wooden building.

Chaitya halls, typically, are adjacent to *viharas*, monastic courtyards. This is the case both with the structural complexes, known only from remains, and in rock-cut versions (**7.10**, **7.11**). Rock-cut *viharas* also transform timber detailing into stone, but their overall form is not straightforwardly translated, because of their inside-out nature. A square hall, dark and echoing, takes the place of a courtyard open to the blue sky.

7.8 Interior of the *chaitya* hall at Karle. Here the hooped roof beams, usually carved in imitation of timber construction, are actually wooden. Photo © Gerard Foekema

7.10 *Chaitya* hall (Cave 18) at Nasik (Maharashtra), with monastery (*vihara*) Cave 17 to the right, *c* 2nd century AD.

7.9 Solid contentment: loving couple at the entrance to the Karle *chaitya* hall. To the right is a *makara-torana* (archway spewed from the jaws of peacock-tailed crocodiles called *makaras*) with early cushion-type pilaster. Photo © Gerard Foekema

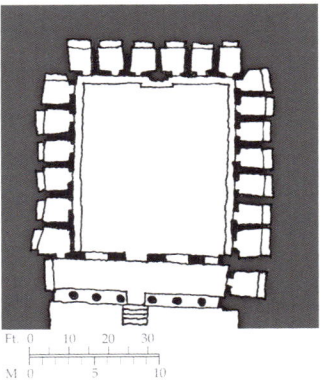

7.11 Plan of Cave 3 (Gautamiputra), Nasik, *c* 2nd century AD; an early rock-cut *vihara*. The doorway to this *vihara* is surrounded by an archway (*torana*, cf 7.1) carved in relief, and the focus of the hall is a *stupa* carved on the rear wall.

EARLY INDIAN ARCHITECTURE 79

Gandhara

Gandhara, or strictly speaking the broader Bactro-Gandharan realm,[3] in present day Pakistan and Afghanistan, experienced constant interchange with the Iranian, Hellenistic and Roman worlds, and to the east with China. Buddhism spread to China via Gandhara. While multicultural fusion is the hallmark of Gandharan art and architecture, they are imbued with the 'pan-Indian' ingredients that we have observed so far.

It may have been the western classical aedicule with triangular pediment that inspired, in Gandhara, the use of more indigenous forms of shrine and entrance in similar ways. Three kinds of aedicular niche are contained in the walls of a *stupa* base at Sirkap dating from about the late 1st century BC (**7.12**). In the Kushana period (1st–3rd centuries AD) the aedicule type based on the gable front of a single barrel-roofed structure (**7.12** middle) gives way to a more complex version, with the ends of side aisles (**7.13c**), representing the same kind of nave-and-aisles wooden structure as the rock-cut *chaitya* halls. Many examples

7.13 Shrine types in Gandhara, *c* 2nd century AD: (**a**) and (**b**) shrines crowned by thatched, domed *kutas*, shown in relief carvings; (**c**) aedicule crowned by a roof like that of *chaitya* hall; (**d**) aedicule crowned by a *kuta* dome (British Museum); (**e**) Court of the Stupa at the monastery of Takht-i-Bahi, surrounded by small shrines of the types depicted in (**b**) and (**c**). These types are precursors of important shrine types for Nagara and Dravida architecture respectively.

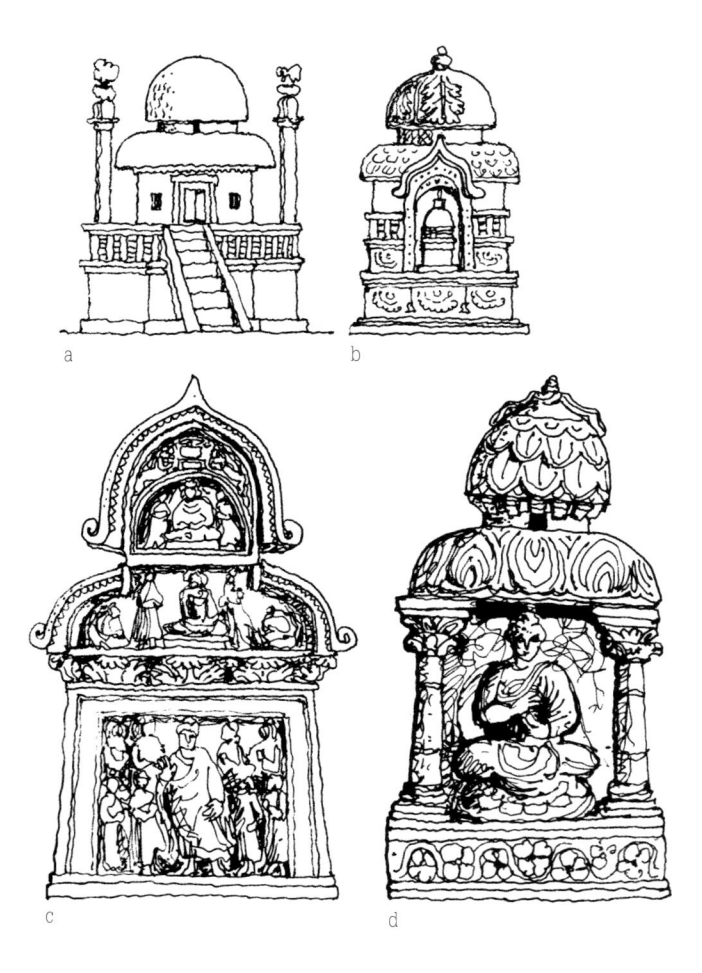

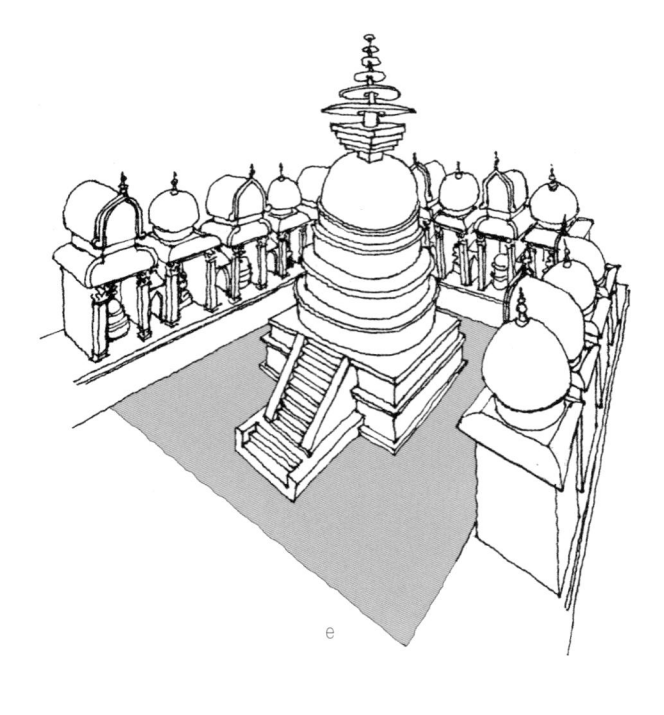

are found in miniature, free-standing shrine reliefs, carved in the characteristic grey schist. The gable generally sits over an 'acanthus leaf' cornice, the full arch often divided from the half-arches for the sake of framing additional sculpted scenes, giving the appearance of two upper storeys. (The sloping sides and the cornice form a trapezoidal doorway that is also used as an aedicule by itself. It looks Egyptian, but the shape doubtless derives from the slanted posts familiar in Indian timber structures.) Another shrine form prominent in Gandhara during the same period is the type with a circular *kuta* on top (**7.13a**, **b**). This is depicted in numerous relief carvings, both as full-size buildings with walls, and as small, open shelters for seated Buddhas, with Corinthian pillars and roofs thatched with leaves (**7.13d**).

In these two Gandharan forms of the Kushana period we have, significantly, two of the basic shrine types — and corresponding aedicules — of subsequent Indian temple architecture: the nave-and-aisles image is equivalent to the Nagara form called the Valabhi (see Chapter 10), and the *kuta*-topped form to the Dravida *alpa vimana* (see Chapter 11). This is not to say that these types spread through influence from Gandhara, but that it seems to have been in Gandhara that these widespread architectural forms were first used in such a markedly aedicular way (**7.14**). Equally interesting is the manner in which these same two timber structural shapes, in the same period, were transformed into masonry shrine types which represented them without literally copying them. This process, in Indian temple architecture generally, normally preceded the adoption of a form as an aedicule. It is apparent in the ruined *stupa* court in the monastery of Takht-i-Bhai (**7.13e**), where these shrine types alternate around the enclosure, sheltering Buddha images (in the *kuta* shrines) and miniature *stupas* (in the 'Valabhi' shrines).[4]

It is no coincidence that it was in Gandhara during this period — along with Mathura, at the other extreme of the Kushana empire — that the sculpted image of the Buddha first developed. Images need to be sheltered, in shrines and in aedicules. The enshrinement of images was a main concern of the later rock-cut architecture dealt with in the next chapter.

7.12 'Shrine of the Double-Headed Eagle', Sirkap, Taxila (Pakistan), *c* late 1st century BC. This 'shrine' is actually the base of a *stupa*. A platform base, later multiplied into tiers, is characteristic of Gandharan *stupas*. Framed by Corinthian pilasters and a bold cornice are three types of aedicule: a classical one (left), a pointed arch one (cf 7.5), and a *torana* (cf 7.1).

7.14 Relief from Gandhara, *c* 2nd century AD, incorporating the aedicules shown in 7.13c and 7.13d. The subject of the relief is possibly the miracle performed by the Buddha at Shrivasti. Photo © The British Library

Notes
1. Michael Willis, *Buddhist Reliquaries from Ancient India* (London: British Museum Press, 2000).
2. As in Percy Brown's drawing of the *chaitya* hall at Kondane: *Indian Architecture (Buddhist and Hindu Periods)*, 3rd edn (Bombay: Taraporevala, 1956), Plate III.
3. Susan L Huntington, *The Art of Indian Asia* (New York: Weatherhill, 1985), p 110.
4. James Harle, *The Art and Architecture of the Indian Subcontinent* (Harmondsworth: Penguin, 1986), fig 52, p 72; and Huntington, *The Art of Indian Asia*, fig 8.7, p 132.

8 LATER ROCK-CUT ARCHITECTURE

A second wave of cave architecture took place between the 5th and early 9th centuries. Early in the 5th century, at Udayagiri near Vidisha (MP) and at Ramgarh in the same region, the Gupta rulers initiated the creation of Brahminical or Hindu cave temples, along with sculpted panels establishing long-lasting formulations for Hindu iconography. During that century at Ajanta (Maharashtra), the site of five earlier caves, a great blossoming of Buddhist rock-cut architecture occurred under the Guptas' allies, the Vakatakas. Buddhist works continued into the 8th century (at Ellora), by which time Buddhism was on the wane through much of India and rock-cut architecture was predominantly Hindu (Shaiva and Vaishnava), and also Jain.

As the age of monumental temple construction gathered pace, rock-cut shrines shared increasingly in the traditions of structural ones. Even the 5th-century caves must reflect contemporary structural temples, now lost, of brick and perhaps of stone as well as of wood, but to a great extent they are still precursors of the masonry traditions. Rock-cut architecture is a storehouse of pillar designs, in which we see enduring types established (see Chapter 14). It also shows, in its increasingly formalised imagery of miniature architecture, the continuing gestation of the aedicular languages of temple architecture.

By the Gupta-Vakataka period, rock-cut monastic courtyards (*viharas*) were more like monastic temples than everyday living quarters, used for worship by the lay community as well as by monks. In the *vihara* plan that is typical at Ajanta, a square of pillars has been introduced into the centre of the hall and a Buddha shrine, often with an antechamber, is placed centrally at the rear (**8.4**). The mandala-like character of the plans is enhanced by lotus-centred patterns painted on the ceilings (**15.1**). This centrality coexists with an axial progression from entrance to shrine, passing through layers defined by steps, thresholds, doorways and lines of pillars. Two of the 6th-century *viharas* at Aurangabad, Maharashtra (Caves 6 and 7), developing from the Ajanta tradition, have Buddha shrines placed in the centre of the hall, allowing circumambulation and creating an inside equivalent to a free-standing shrine in a courtyard. Monastic Caves at nearby Ellora (late 6th to early 8th centuries) show variations on the *vihara* plan, including two- and three-storey versions (Caves 11 and 12, 'Don Thal' and 'Tin Thal').

The extent to which earlier, Theravada ('Hinayana') Buddhism did or did not allow depiction of the Buddha's human form is a matter of scholarly debate, but there is no doubt that the collage of motifs adorning the earlier structures gave way to an architectural framework designed to house the myriad Buddhas and Bodhisattvas of the burgeoning Mahayana pantheon. This is most striking in the two late 5th-century *chaitya* halls at Ajanta (Caves 19 and 26). Inside, a large Buddha emerges from the *stupa* itself, with smaller ones along the 'galleries' of the nave. All over the rock facade, cut through by the sun window, runs a giant relief of a storeyed palace, made regular and rhythmic for the framing of Buddha images.

8.1 Facade of Buddhist hall of worship (*chaitya* hall), Cave 19, Ajanta (Maharashtra), 5th century. Along the top runs a chain of barrel-roofed pavilions, precursors of the '*shalas*' which are an essential element of Dravida temple architecture. Photo © Gerard Foekema

LATER ROCK-CUT ARCHITECTURE **83**

8.3 Interior of Cave 26, Ajanta. Traces of the original painting survive. Photo © Gerard Foekema

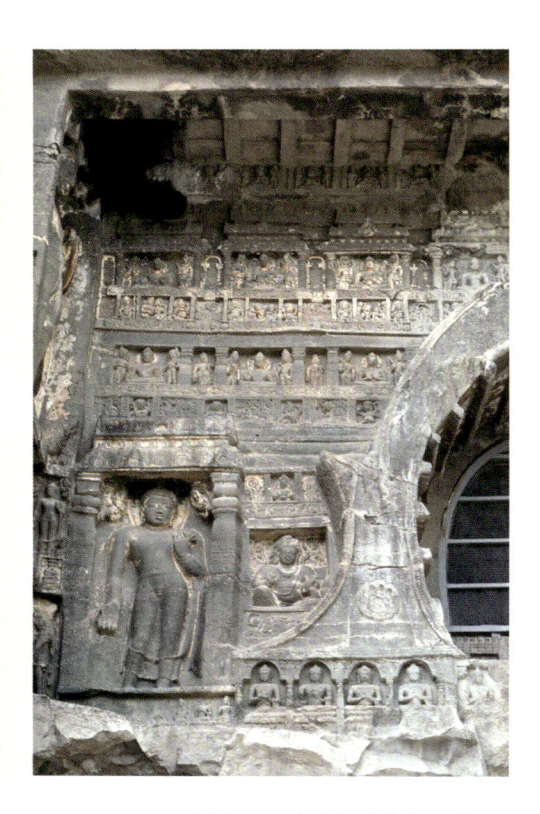

8.2 Facade of *chaitya* hall, Cave 26, Ajanta, 5th century.

This regularisation of miniature architecture is reflected in the presence of chains of pavilions (*haras* in Dravida terminology), like shrines interlinked in a cloister (cf **7.13e**). Such chains, standing on an eave cornice (*kapota* or *kapotali*) begin to appear over doorways and across the top of cave facades. The 'palace' facade of Cave 19, Ajanta, is crowned by a line of Buddha-housing barrel-roofed pavilions, prototypes of Dravida *shalas* (**8.1**; cf **8.5**). Cave 5, Aurangabad, introduces the idea, perennial in structural temples, of a heavenly cloister above the beams. Made up of proto-Phamsana shrines, this runs all around the central bay of the hall. Miniature architecture continues to be a pointer to later forms in the Hindu caves (**8.10**).

Hindu cave temples did not take up the proliferation of small images seen at Ajanta — surprisingly, perhaps, considering the trends soon manifested in structural monuments. Instead, mythological panels (including much of the greatest Indian sculpture) fill whole bays of the interior walls, their power overwhelming in the stillness. Maharashtra again, from the second half of the 6th century onwards, is especially rich in such temples, in the north-west Deccan at Ellora (**8.6**, **8.7**, **8.9**) and neighbouring sites, and in the adjacent coastal region of the Konkan (**8.8**). Stylistically related are the beautiful, late 6th-century Hindu and Jain caves of the Early Chalukyas at Badami and Aihole (Karnataka). At a similar date, traditions of carving cave temples were established in Andhra Pradesh, followed by Tamil Nadu under the Pallavas and Pandyas; these closely related traditions draw on the legacy of Buddhist architecture and narrative carving in Andhra, and

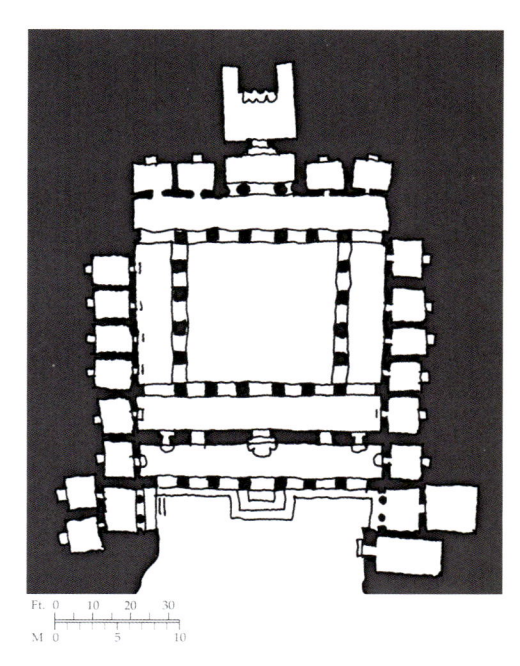

8.4 Plan of the monastery (*vihara*), Cave 1, Ajanta, 5th century.

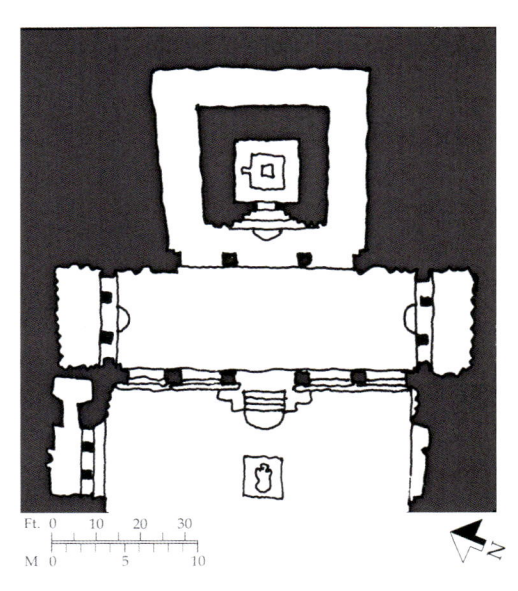

8.6 Cave 21 (Rameshvara), Ellora, 6th century: plan. (Figure 3.1 shows the alcove to the right of the veranda.)

8.5 Facade of Cave 1, Ajanta. The facade is topped by a chain of barrel-roofed *shala* pavilions, with a two-storey domed *kuta* on the return.

LATER ROCK-CUT ARCHITECTURE 85

8.8 Shiva cave, Elephanta (near Mumbai), first half of 6th century. In the vast multi-pillared hall, beams emphasise the east–west orientation, while the longitudinal axis runs towards the free-standing, four-faced sanctum. A transverse axis runs towards the famous Maheshvara image in the south wall.
Photo © Gerard Foekema

8.7 Cave 21, Ellora, interior.
Photo © Gerard Foekema

8.9 Cave 14, Ellora (Ravana-ka-Khai), c late 6th century. Pillars and pilasters are of both the sprouting vase (*ghata-pallava*) type (front) and cushion type (rear).

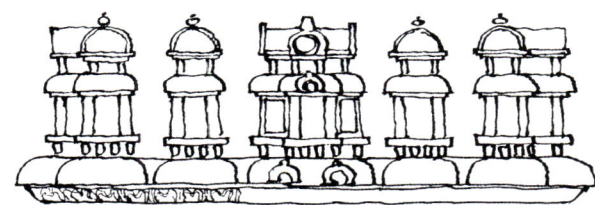

8.10 Cave 3, Badami (Karnataka), AD 578: 'cloister' of pavilions over sanctum doorway. These are *kutas*, with a staggered central *shala*, all of two storeys.

reflect the early stages of Dravida architecture, particularly in the *haras* over their facades. Dravida characteristics also appear during Ellora's second phase of rock-cut architecture, under the Rashtrakutas in the 8th century, as a result of contacts with southern temple-building traditions. In this phase the plans of cave temples often follow those of structural *mandapas*.

Where a cave temple is located beneath a rocky outcrop (as at the Ravana Phadi cave, Aihole), it evokes the idea of a mountain of the gods, like the tower of a structural temple. This is made explicit at the Akkanna-Madanna caves, Vijayawada (AP), where parts of rock-cut proto-Dravida superstructures survive on the hillside above. Monolithic temples realise this concept, completely in the round and carved out of boulders or of mountains. The most spectacular of these is the Kailasa at Ellora (**23.7**), still sometimes quaintly referred to as 'Cave 16'. But these monoliths belong to the realms not of caves but of Dravida and Nagara temple architecture.

LATER ROCK-CUT ARCHITECTURE **87**

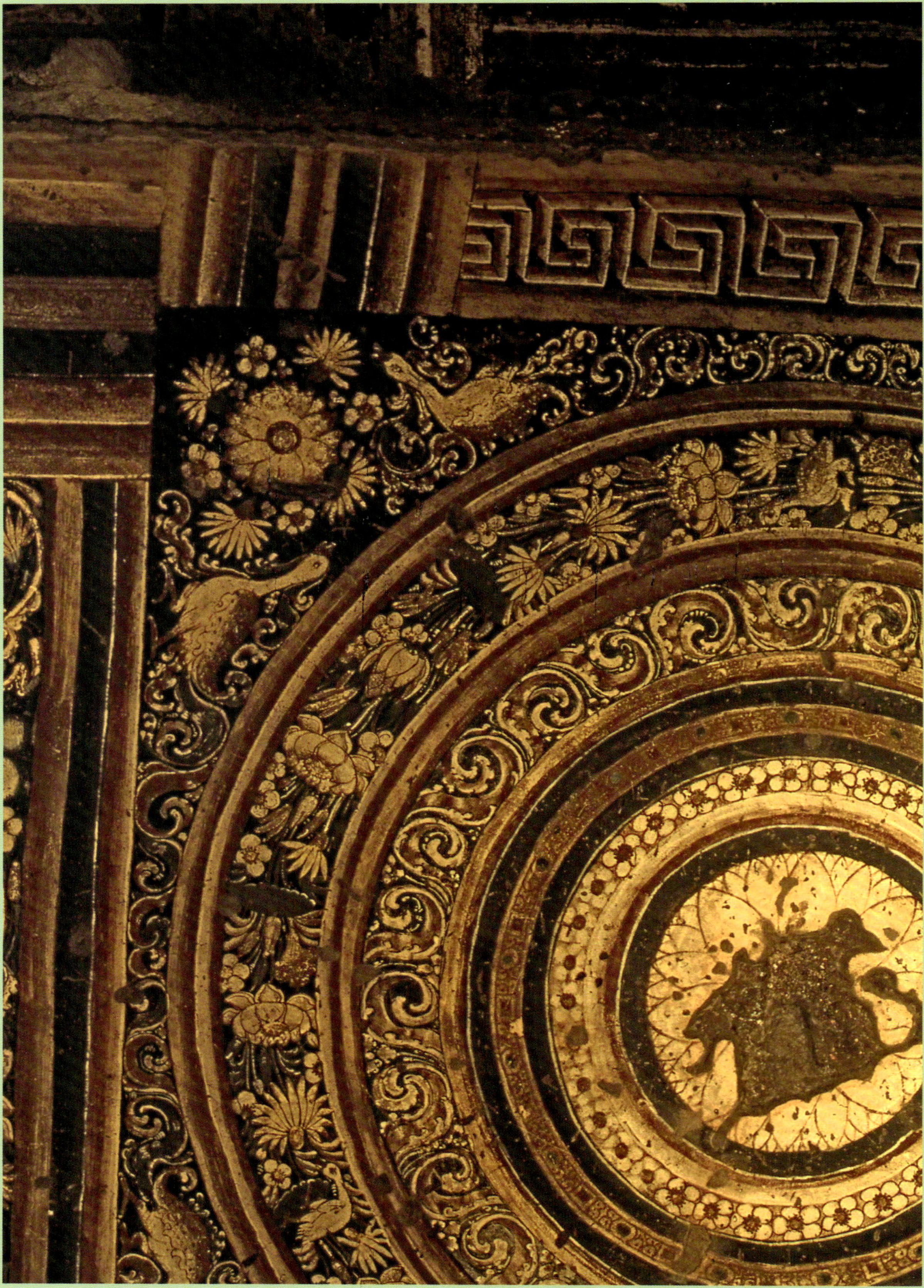

Part 3   TEMPLE DESIGN

9	Plans and Spaces
10	Nagara Shrines
11	Dravida Shrines
12	Geometry
13	Mouldings
14	Pillars
15	Ceilings
16	Gavakshas

Painted lotus ceiling in Cave 2, Ajanta, 5th century (**15.1**).

9   Plans and Spaces

The Shrine

The shrine proper is termed *vimana* ('measured out') in the southern context, the northern equivalent being *prasada* ('palace', literally 'seat' of the deity), or strictly speaking *mula-prasada* (main or 'root' *prasada*). It contains the sanctum, the *garbha-griha* ('womb chamber'), usually square. While some early shrines seem to have been flat roofed, a Nagara or Dravida shrine has a superstructure as an integral part. The interior of the superstructure is rarely accessible, and sometimes filled solid with rubble. However, an upper sanctum at the level of the hall roof is common from an early date in Jain temples (eg the Meguti, Aihole, dated 634–5). A minor temple may consist only of the shrine itself. Normally just one face of a shrine presents the doorway, usually to the east, so that the light of the rising sun will bathe the image of the deity.

Shrines may be rectangular, apsidal, circular or octagonal. However, the sanctum normally remains square, except in rectangular shrines. Most shrines are square or developed from a square; even stellate plans normally retain the four corners of a square quartered by the cardinal axes. Figure **9.1** shows the main kinds of square and square-related plans for a shrine exterior. In general, orthogonal plans evolve towards a greater number of projections and (through staggering) towards more pronounced central emphasis. Different traditions undergo this process at different times. Plans cannot be considered in isolation from the design as a whole: except in the case of the unitary Latina mode of Nagara temple, projections in a plan indicate three-dimensional aedicular components.

Mandapas

All but the humblest shrines have at least a porch (**9.2**). More important ones have a *mandapa*, the audience hall of the god's palace. This in turn may have one, two or three entrance porches. A *mandapa* may be enclosed by thick walls, or open, like an extended porch. Closed *mandapas* generally receive their light through doorways, sometimes supplemented by the bright holes of stone traceries in windows or false porches.

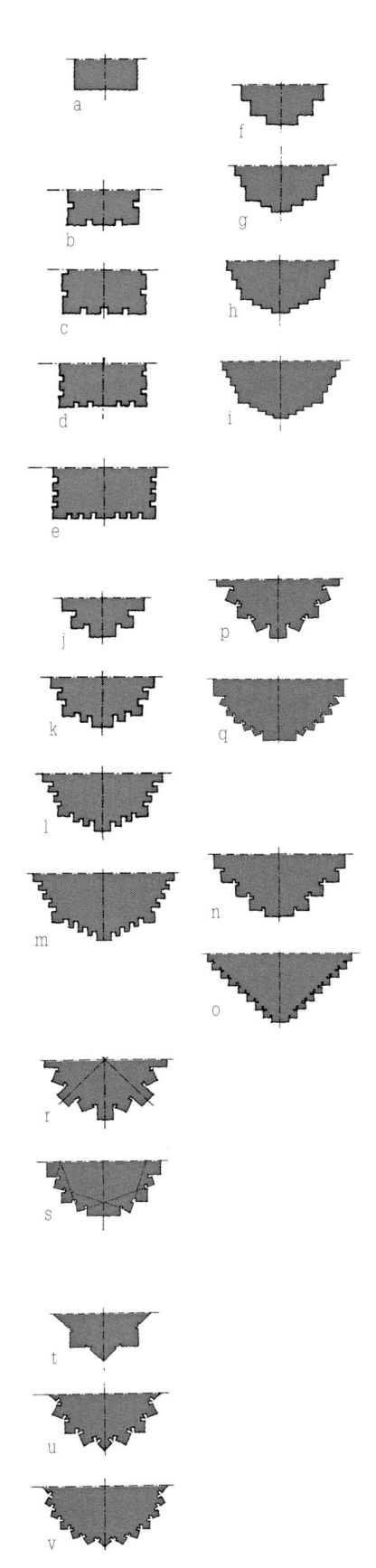

9.1 Typical plan outlines for shrines.

(**a**) Simple square plan – basis of the other types.
(**b–e**) Square plan with simple projections: 3, 4, 5 and 7 projections. Alternatively, the central projection alone may come further out.
(**f–i**) Staggered square plan without recesses: 3, 5, 7 and 9 facets.
(**j–m**) Staggered square plan with recesses: 3, 5, 7 and 9 projections.
(**n, o**) Stepped diamond plan (corner projection the same as others) with 5 and 7 projections (between diagonals).
(**p, q**) Stellate plan with *bhadra* (orthogonal central projection): based on rotated-square star 16 and 32 points.
(**r, s**) Special stellate plans: (**r**) *ashta-bhadra* (with 8 *bhadras*, ie with *bhadras* on the diagonal as well as the orthogonal axes); (**s**) a semi-stellate plan, with the intermediate projection at an angle.
(**t–v**) Uniform stellate plans (no *bhadras*): based on rotated-square star of 8, 16 and 24 points.

Most plans can be classified according to the number of projections between two diagonals: 3, 4, 5, 7 or 9. There are two systems of Sanskrit terminology to describe plans, depending on regional usage in the architectural texts. One counts the number of *rathas* (literally 'chariots' or 'vehicles'): *tri-ratha, chatur-ratha, pancha-ratha, sapta-ratha, nava-ratha*, respectively for 3, 4, 5, 7, 9 projections. The other counts the number of kinds of projections or *angas* ('limbs' or 'members'): *dvi-anga* (2-limbed) for 3 projections, *tri-anga* (3-limbed) for 5-projections, *panch-anga* (5-limbed) for 7 projections, *sapt-anga* (7-limbed) for 9 projections. Notice that stellate and stepped diamond plans have two faces to each projection, and normally have small reentrant projections in the corner between each pair of main projections.

Some of these plans are specific to particular types of shrine, while others lend themselves to a variety of designs. Not shown in these drawings are the additional projections which, in due course, emerge from the main projections to create niches and other secondary aedicules.

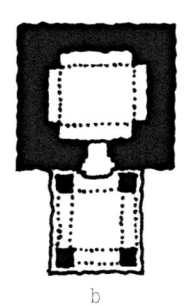

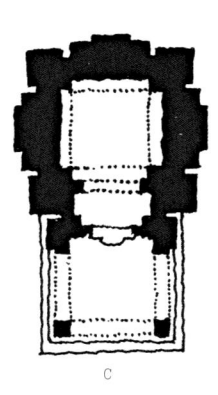

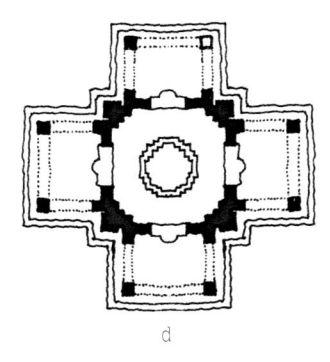

9.2 Basic plan types: (**a**) shrine alone; (**b**) shrine with porch; (**c**) shrine with *antarala* (antechamber) and porch; (**d**) *Sarvatobhadra* shrine (with four entrances).

PLANS AND SPACES 91

9.3 Virupaksha temple, Pattadakal (Karnataka), *c* 742: *mandapa* interior. The structure is of the 'nave-and-aisles' type, shown in 1.4 and 9.4a extended to double aisles. The *mandapa* is square, and the sloping roof-slabs over the aisles are carried round across the front of the *mandapa*, the flat-roofed part of the nave beginning at the central bay. There are lateral porches, and the square central bay, larger than the others, marks a crossing of axes, showing a wish for a 'mandala' plan before this is fully reflected in the roof structure. Roof-slabs have now been removed from one bay. Along the blind clerestory run aerial aedicules.

Whatever sunlight strikes the floor will send its glow to the ceiling, and the divine presence will be sensed in the innermost darkness. It became usual to place an antechamber (*antarala*) in front of the shrine, even if there was no *mandapa*, and to crown the *antarala* with a fronton (*shuka-nasa* – 'parrot's beak') projecting from the main superstructure. In the exterior wall, the antechamber generally corresponds to a recess, termed the *kapili*, separating the shrine from the *mandapa*.

The prototypes of stone *mandapas* were wooden halls of post-and-beam construction, together with the rock-cut halls which themselves reflected the same kind of wooden structure. Spacing of columns was determined by the practicality of quarrying, transporting and lifting beams and slabs, as well as their bearing capacity. Spans are rarely more than about 2.5 metres (8 ft).

Mandapas of the 7th and 8th centuries are characterised by massive roof-slabs. Those of the Early Chalukya temples in Karnataka and Andhra Pradesh are the best preserved from this period. They follow a 'nave and aisles' cross section (**1.4**, **9.3**, **9.4a**), with a central flat-roofed portion flanked in the side aisles by gently sloping slabs. Half-round,

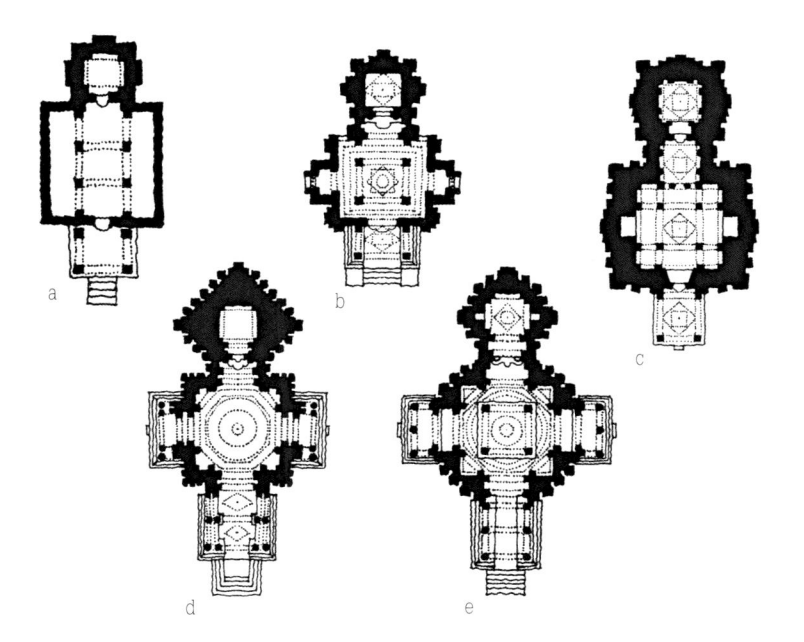

9.4 Plans with a shrine attached to a closed *mandapa* (*gudha-mandapa*), with various ceiling structures (shown dotted): (**a**) shows the early 'nave-and-aisles' type, and as yet no antechamber (*antarala*) to articulate shrine and *mandapa*. The examples shown are: (**a**) Tarappa Basappa, Ahole (Karnataka), 7th century; (**b**) Ambika temple, Jagat (Rajasthan), 10th century; (**c**) Kalleshvara, Kukkanur (Karnataka), 11th century; (**d**) Duladeva, Khajuraho (MP), 12th century; (**e**) Chitradurga, Khajuraho, 11th century.

stone cover pieces are placed over the joints, and the roof is hidden by a parapet. The central bays are covered by single slabs, carved underneath into beautiful figural reliefs which continue the rock-cut tradition of sculptural panels.

From the 8th century onwards, *mandapas* have an increasingly mandala-like character, reflecting that of the shrine itself. A central bay dominates the plan, setting up cross axes. The width of the central bay may correspond to that of the sanctum (*garbha-griha*) antechamber and *antarala*. 'Lantern ceilings' become common, in which triangular slabs are piled up to create receding, nested squares or rectangles (**9.5**; cf **15.3**). Corbelled construction – the method of stepping horizontal courses progressively forward to cover a space, prevented from toppling off by the weight of masonry pressing down at their rear – developed considerably from the 10th century. Previously it had been a pragmatic affair, usually hidden away inside temple superstructures; at this point it is used for creating domed ceilings (**9.6**, **9.9**, **15.9–15.11**). To support these, square bays are reduced to a circle via triangular corner slabs or diagonal beams. In more ambitious schemes, intermediate columns or octagonal central bays are used, allowing for much larger ceilings without increasing the permissible beam span. Throughout northern India, *mandapas* are treated externally as Phamsana or (later) Samvarana shrine forms (see Chapter 10), with pyramidal superstructures (**9.8**). In the lower Deccan, 'nave and aisles' roofs give way to flat roofs covered with mud for waterproofing, still surrounded by a parapet. Here domed ceilings are generally small enough to be covered with a mound of mud.

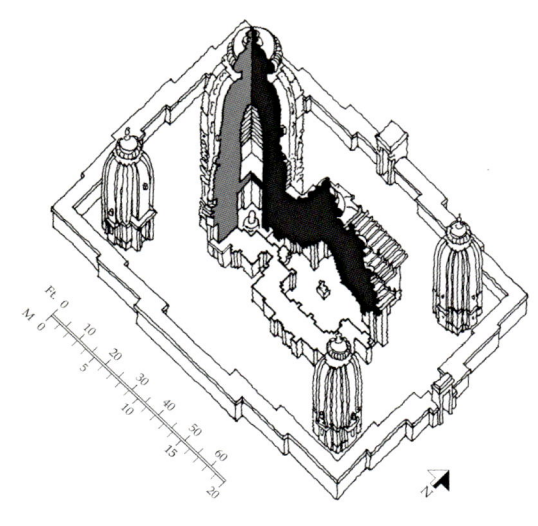

9.7 Brahmeshvara temple, Bhuvaneshvara (Orissa), *c* 1060: axonometric. Orissan *mandapas* rarely have columns: earlier ones are roofed with large slabs, later roofs (like this) being corbelled up from the thick walls.

9.9 (opposite) Jain temple of Vimala Vasahi, Dilwara (Mount Abu) (Rajasthan), 13th century: *mandapa* interior.

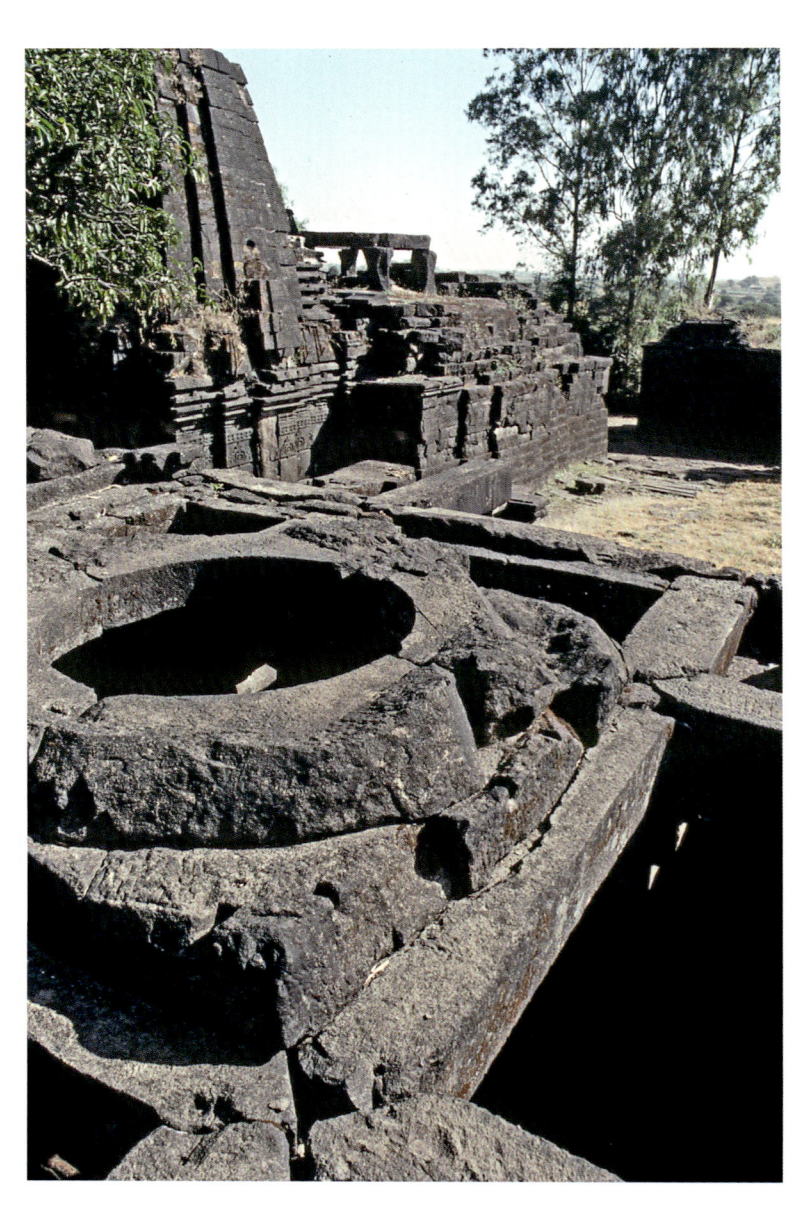

9.6 Ceiling structure of a ruined temple at Anjaneri (Maharashtra), *c* 12th century, showing beams, corner slabs and first course of corbelled dome.

9.5 Porch of small Phamsana temple at Badami (Karnataka), *c* 12th century, with plain 'lantern ceiling'. Beyond are the tank and Bhutanatha temple.

94   THE TEMPLE ARCHITECTURE OF INDIA

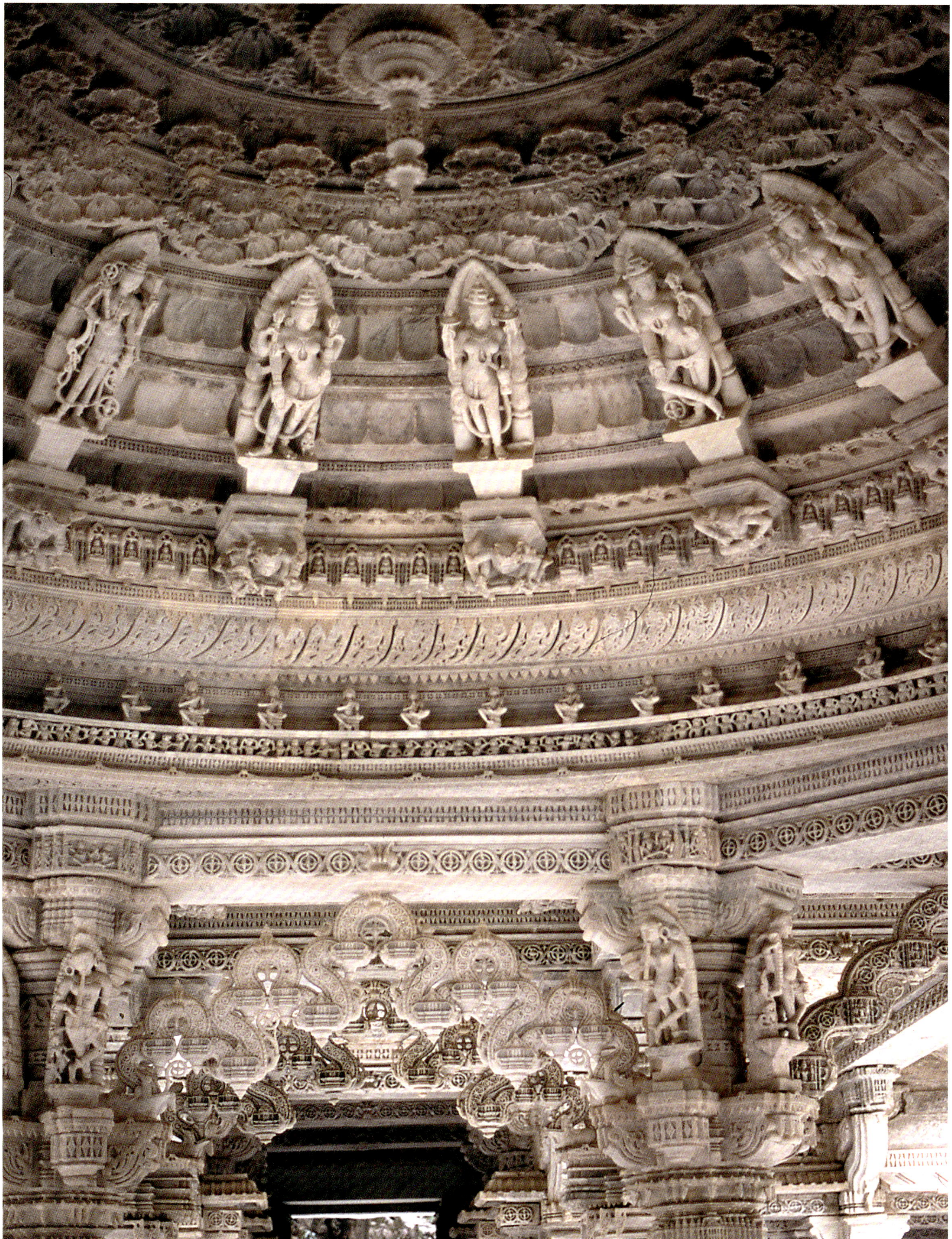

9.10 Plans with a shrine attached to an open *mandapa* (*ranga-mandapa*). Examples shown: (**a**) Yellama Gudi, Badami (Karnataka), 11th century; (**b**) Siddheshvara, Haveri (Karnataka), 11th century; (**c**) Nilakantha Mahadeva, Sunak (Gujarat), *c* 1075; (**d**) Nilakantheshvara Mahadeva, Kekind (Rajasthan); (**e**) Navalakha temple, Sejakpur(Gujarat), 12th century.

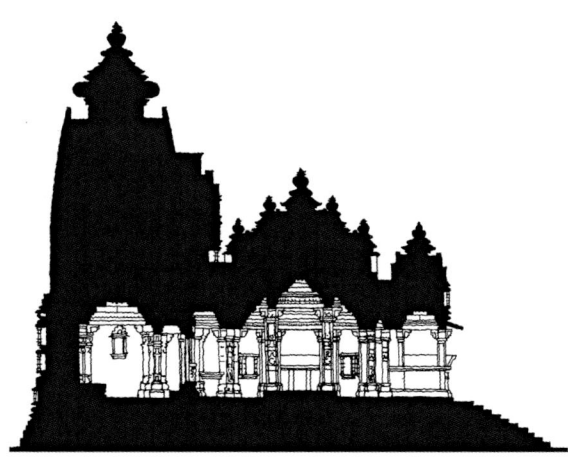

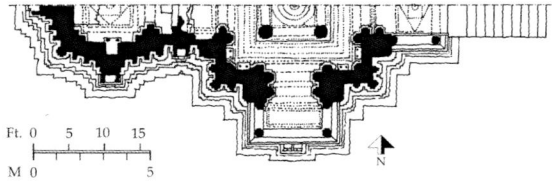

9.8 Vamana temple, Khajuraho, *c* 11th century: half plan and longitudinal section. Adapted from Krishna Deva, *Temples of Khajuraho* (Delhi: ASI, 1990).

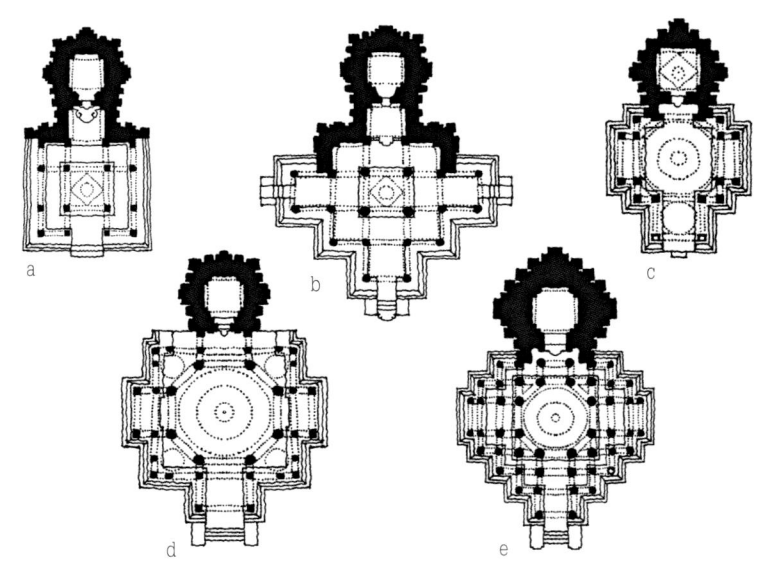

Open *mandapas* of a scale greater than that of a simple porch were known in western India by the end of the 8th century (**9.10**) and were widespread in most regions by the 11th. Their form lends itself to recitations and performances, especially of dance, for which a central platform is often provided. An open *mandapa* can be the only one or (sometimes having been added at a later date) be attached to a closed one, or stand free. Whereas the exterior of a closed hall tends to mirror the treatment of the shrine through an indented plan and aedicular articulation, an open one, requiring beams around its perimeter, must be rectangular, or else push out in bay-size steps. Internally, however, open *mandapas* follow the same range of plans as closed *mandapas*, but can also extend through many more bays, given that they receive more light and need to accommodate more people. The size will be limited by the scale and weight of a pyramidal roof, but there is no such constraint with a flat roof, allowing forests of columns to twirl through the later halls of the lower Deccan (**14.7**). Storeyed open *mandapas* had appeared by the end of the 11th century (eg the Sas-Bahu temple, Gwailor, 1093) and were developed in western India, especially in Jain temples with upper sanctums.

A characteristic cross section is used around the perimeter of open *mandapas* throughout western and central India and the Deccan. The moulded base is surmounted by a seat, facing inwards with its raked back visible from outside (**9.11**, **5.4**, **14.7**), as had been evident in porches and verandas as early as the 6th century (Cave 21, Ellora). The edge pillars stand on the seat, carrying a beam surmounted by a heavy stone canopy (*chhadya*), prevented from tipping off by the weight of the parapet or the superstructure. A bright, horizontal slice cuts through the hall between the seat back and the canopy; seen from outside, the roof seems to hover on a bed of darkness. Sometimes the open slot is filled with a traceried screen (**9.14**). The shaded seats have human scale, invite social gathering and are still popular places for a sleep; except where they are giant-size, made to impress rather than to sit on.

In the far south, before the great temple complexes of later centuries, *mandapas* are unimportant, usually narrower than the *vimana*; here *antaralas* are unusual and *shuka-nasas* unknown. Only from the 11th century do large, rectangular, flat-roofed halls begin to appear, including open ones, entirely open (with no seat) around the edge.

A few generalisations can be made about the character of interior space in Indian temples. As in a cave temple, it is cool, dark and reverberant. It is intimate and enveloping. Progression inwards is from light to darkness, climbing through levels, passing through layers, over thresholds, and through symbol-drenched doorways which, framed by concentric bands, compress several planes of existence into one surge of transition. Space is centralised and hierarchical, yet cellular and polycentric. Structural bays are in this respect a spatial equivalent of the aedicules in a temple exterior, although the structural system never allows the bays to interpenetrate. But there is no question of imagining the shapes of contained spaces as positive volumes, as can easily be done for, say, Byzantine churches. Columns define, of course, but they are made not to delineate but to pulsate with sculptural presence. It is not the bays as spaces that make themselves felt, but their ceilings which blossom and radiate down. Wall surfaces are not shells or limits, or planes even, but the dark ground for pilasters and bulging aedicular niches. Interior elements are their own centres of power, sharing the language and principles of emergent form so manifest in the exterior. Space is not to be located, as stuff, but is the nothing from which things grow.

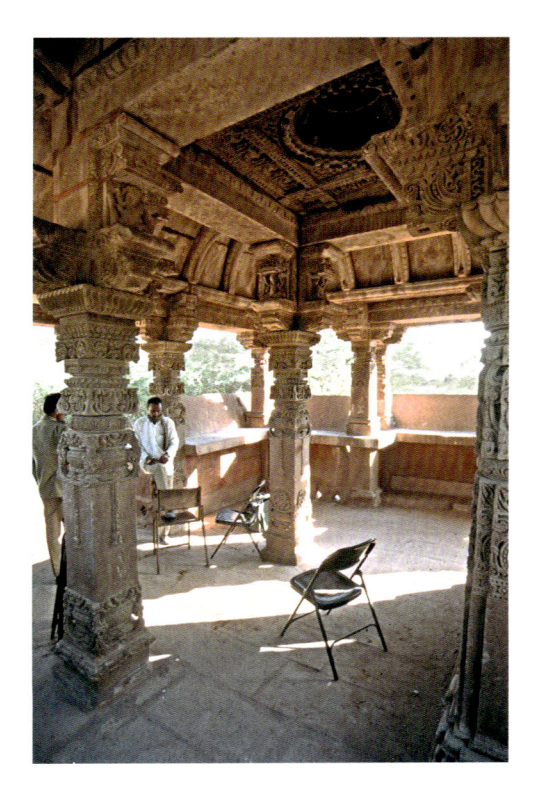

9.11 Harihara Temple 3, Osian (Rajasthan), late 8th century: open *mandapa* interior.
Photo © Gerard Foekema

Sandhara Plans

The act of clockwise circumambulation of the shrine (*pradakshina* – 'going round to the south') was important from the earliest times. Gupta temples of the 5th century already exhibit the two alternative ways of accommodating this rite, which may be used singly or together. First, the temple may be built on a moulded platform (*jagati*), defining an ambulatory path as well as raising the temple to a higher plane, visually and symbolically (**17.2**). The second way, probably originating through enclosing and roofing over the walkway on the podium, is to incorporate an ambulatory passage (*pradakshina-patha*) in the temple interior. Temples with the latter feature are termed *sandhara*, those without *nirandhara*. In early *sandhara* schemes, the superstructure of the shrine rises through a roof of flat or gently sloping slabs, like a temple in a box

(**9.12a**) or a cage (**9.12b**). Only gradually are the shrine and its surrounding ambulatory separated from the hall (**9.12e**), and ultimately fully articulated (**9.12f**). In the Tamil tradition, the passage runs within the thick walls of the *vimana* (**9.24**).

A particular type of *sandhara* plan for major temples had become established in the Nagara traditions of western and central India by the 8th century and continued to be used until at least the 12th (**9.12g**). Here the exterior of the sanctum conveys the idea of an inner temple (**9.13**); the surrounding *pradakshina-patha* is bridged over by slabs or corbelling, lit by traceried windows in false porches, while the exterior of the superstructure flows over the passage without a break. In this tradition, the plan of the main hall (*maha-mandapa*), which also has false porches on the sides, is a square of the same size as the shrine proper (*mula-prasada*). Inside, the structural patterns follow the same variations as for square *mandapas* more generally. The equal internal squares remain a characteristic of this type, even when the exterior of the walls steps outwards.

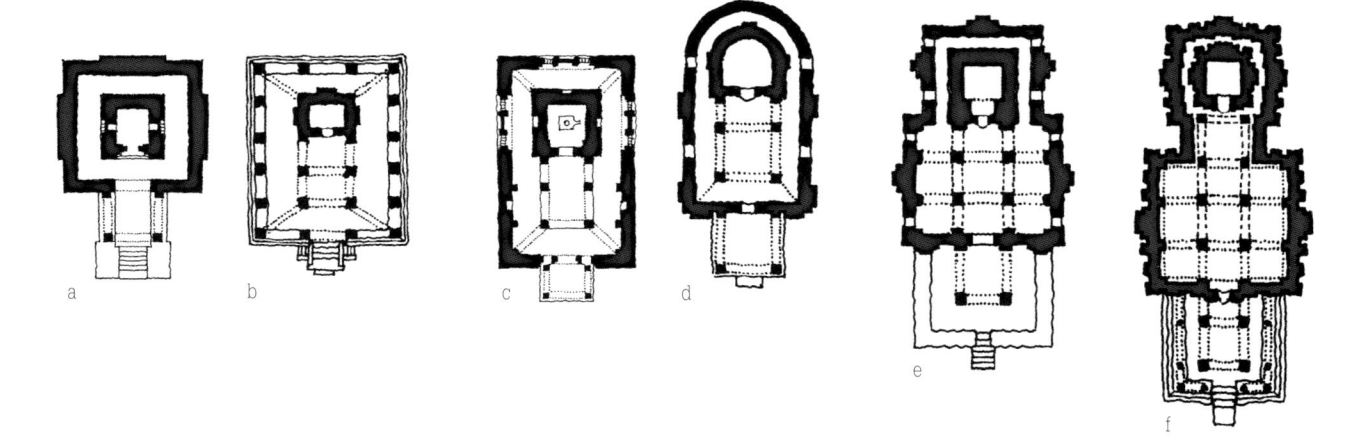

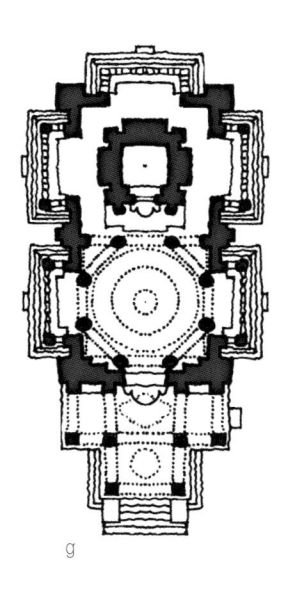

9.12 *Sandhara* plans (with ambulatory or *pradakshina-patha*): (**a**) temple at Nanchna (MP), 5th century; (**b**) Gaudar Gudi, Aihole (Karnataka), 7th century; (**c**) Kumara Brahma temple, Alampur (AP), 7th century; (**d**) temple at Chikka Mahakuta (Karnataka), 7th century; (**e**), Mahakuteshvara, Mahakuta (Karnataka), 7th century; (**f**) Jain temple, Pattadakal (Karnataka), 9th century; (**g**) Mahavira, Ghanerav (Rajasthan), 10th century. Figures (**b–d**) show variants in which the shrine sits within a rectangular hall – open hall (**b**), rectangular closed hall (**c**), apsidal closed hall (**d**). Figures (**e**) and (**f**) show a progressive articulation of the shrine with its ambulatory in relation to the hall. Figure **g** shows a plan type typical in western and central India between the 8th and 12th centuries (see also 9.2a, b).

Multiple Shrines and Ensembles

A temple may have several shrines (southern *vimanas* or northern *prasadas*), adjoining a single mandapa or a series of interlinked *mandapas*. This practice is typical of the Deccan, though occasionally it is seen in western India. The earliest example seems to be the Jambulingeshvara temple, Badami (AD 698–9), where the rectangular hall has a shrine on each of three sides, with an entrance porch on the fourth, facing east. This triple arrangement becomes the most common pattern for multiple plans, the middle shrine inevitably being the most important (**9.14**, **9.15a**). Two shrines, usually a major and a minor one, may be arranged on two sides of a hall, or opposite one another; or (if equal) side-by-side, with two interlinked *mandapas*, an arrangement known to extend to at least five shrines. As many as nine shrines may be interlinked in

9.13 Ambulatory passage (*pradakshina-patha*) of Lakshmana temple, Khajuraho (MP), 954 (cf 9.18a).
Photo © Gerard Foekema

9.14 Keshava temple, Somnathpur (Karnataka), *c* 1268: from east. Three stellate *vimanas* share the *mandapa*, which is closed at the rear, open (with pierced screens) at the front. The temple is raised on a platform (*jagati*) within an enclosure (*prakara*).
Photo © Gerard Foekema

9.15 Examples of temple plans with multiple shrines: (**a**) Temple 1, Balsane (Maharashtra), 11th century; (**b**) Bucheshvara, Koravangala (Karnataka), 12th century; (**c**) Panchalingeshvara, Huli (Karnataka), 11th century; (**d**) Temple 5, Balsane (Maharashtra), 12th century.

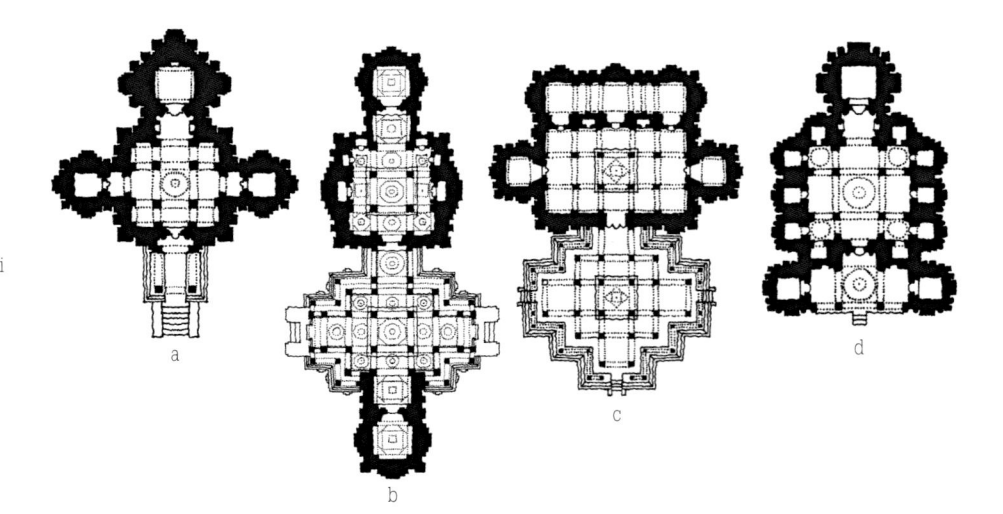

9.16 Rock-cut temple at Masrur (Himachal Pradesh), *c* late 8th century: intended plan according to Meister's analysis. The left half of the plan shows the various superstructures in light grey (cf 2.3).

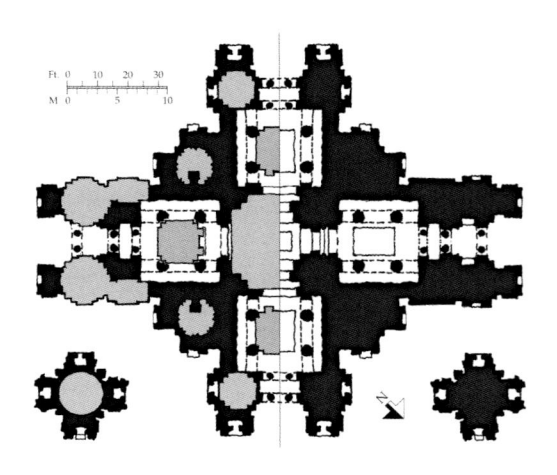

9.18 (**a**) Lakshmana temple, Khajuraho (MP), 954: a *panch-ayatana* temple raised on a *jagati*, the main temple being *sandhara* (cf 19.5); (**b**) Surya temple, Modhera (Gujarat), 1026: *sandhara* temple, open *mandapa* and stepped tank (cf 9.20, 9.21); (**c**) Gondeshvara temple, Sinnar: a *panch-ayatana* temple on a *jagati* (cf 9.17).

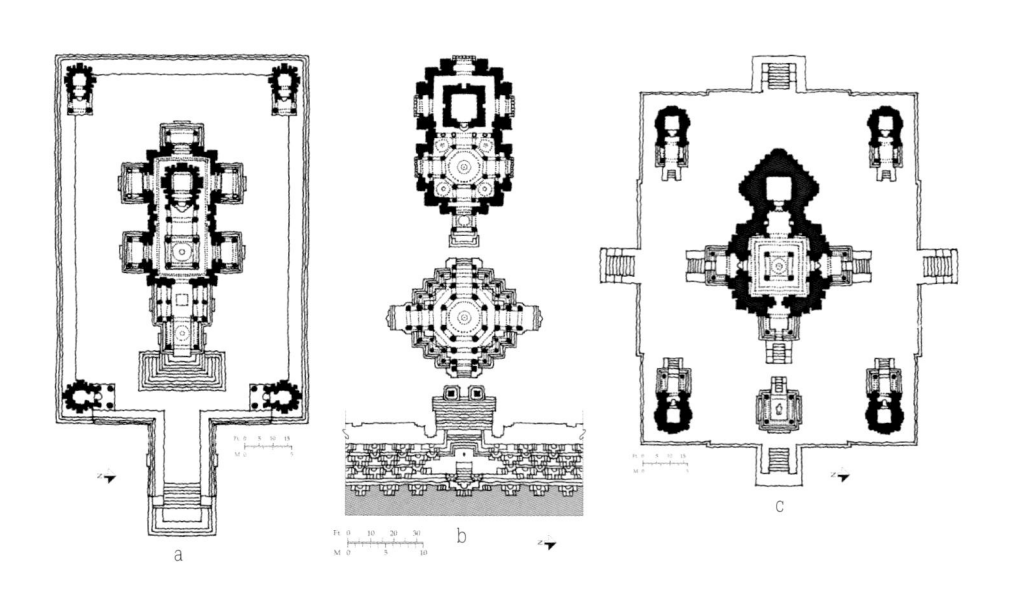

100 THE TEMPLE ARCHITECTURE OF INDIA

9.17 Gondeshvara temple, Sinnar (Maharashtra), 12th century (cf 9.18c). Photo © Gerard Foekema

various ways. Sanctums that are only partly articulated externally and without superstructures can also be grouped around a hall (**9.15c**, **d**).

While these multiple temple plans usually display axial symmetry, they rarely have the completely centralised, 'mandala' plans familiar from the 'temple mountains' of Cambodia, most famously Angkor Wat. However, Michael Meister has recently shown that the extraordinary 8th-century rock-cut cluster at Masrur (Himachal Pradesh) had such a plan (**2.3**, **9.16**).[1] Buddhist *stupas*, on the other hand, having no *mandapa* and not even an entrance, inherently have this kind of plan, and could be developed into elaborate centralised compositions such as the great 8th-century *stupa* court at Paharpur (Bangladesh).

Shrines can, of course, be grouped together without being directly joined. In Tamil Nadu from the 11th century it became common to have a shrine for the goddess consort of the main god alongside his temple. Around established temples, pious donations raised a plethora of subsidiary shrines. These could be planned from the outset in a formal arrangement, by far the most widespread being the 'five-shrine' plan (the *panch-ayatana*), in which the main temple is surrounded by four minor shrines at the corners (**9.17**, **9.18a**, **c**). This concept, predominantly northern, is another one with its origins in the Gupta period. The four corner shrines can sometimes be accompanied by

PLANS AND SPACES 101

9.19 Mukhteshvara temple, Bhuvaneshvara (Orissa), 10th century, with surrounding complex. The temple consists of main shrine (*mula-prasada*) and *mandapa* fronted by an archway (*torana*) and surrounded by a low enclosure wall (*prakara*).

another common free-standing appendage, a small open pavilion or *mandapa* placed on axis in front of the temple. This is often seen outside Shiva temples, where it shelters the bull Nandi, the god's vehicle (*vahana*) (**9.18c**). *Panch-ayatana* groups are usually bound together through being placed on a common podium (**9.18a, c**); alternatively, they can be nestled within an enclosure wall (*prakara*) (**9.7**).

The wall of a temple compound may be moulded to the topography of the site, or make a formal enclosure. This may consist of a wall alone, be lined by a colonnade (**9.14**, **9.24**) or form a necklace of shrines. The latter idea goes back, in India, to the *stupa* courts of early Buddhist monasteries. It appears in south India in the 8th century, as in the Kailasanatha, Kanchipuram (**9.23**), where the enclosure wall is part of a unifying pattern of concentric layers. Cloisters of minor shrines become prominent from the 12th century onwards in the Jain temple enclosures of western India, where the surrounding enclosed sanctums (*cellas*) enshrine 24 *jinas* (**9.22**).

Gateways take the form of the *pratoli* (gatehouse) in northern India, and the *gopura* in the south. *Gopuras* are treated as rectangular, barrel-roofed shrines with a split to let people in and divine power out – a concept indicated by split pilasters framing the openings and vestigial,

9.20 Temple of the sun god Surya at Modhera (Gujarat), 1026: view across tank to open *mandapa* (cf 9.18b). Photo © Gerard Foekema

PLANS AND SPACES 103

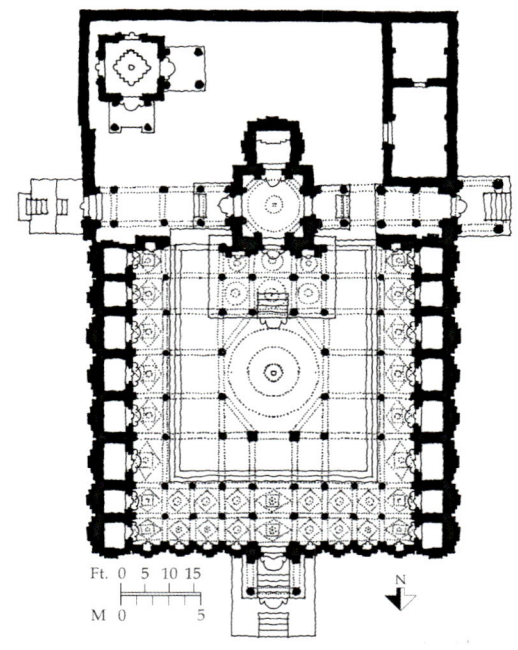

9.22 Jain temple of Shantinatha, Kumbharia (Gujarat), 11th century. *Jinas* (Jain saints) are enshrined in the surrounding cloister. The 'courtyard' between the inner temple and the cloister has a flat roof, with flat ceilings carved in low relief with busy scenes.

9.21 Surya temple, Modhera: looking up in a corner of the closed *mandapa* (cf 9.18b).

9.23 Kailasa temple, Kanchipuram (Tamil Nadu), early 8th century (before the addition of a link between the main shrine and the *mandapa*). To enter the eastern gateway is to pass through the first of five concentric layers of interlinked shrine forms, proceeding inwards and upwards towards the small shrine at the summit of the palace-mountain of Shiva. The second layer, facing in, is the main enclosure wall (*prakara*), not merely a protective container, but integral to the whole design; the further layers are the tiers of the main *vimana*, facing out (cf 11.8, 23.2, 23.3).

104 THE TEMPLE ARCHITECTURE OF INDIA

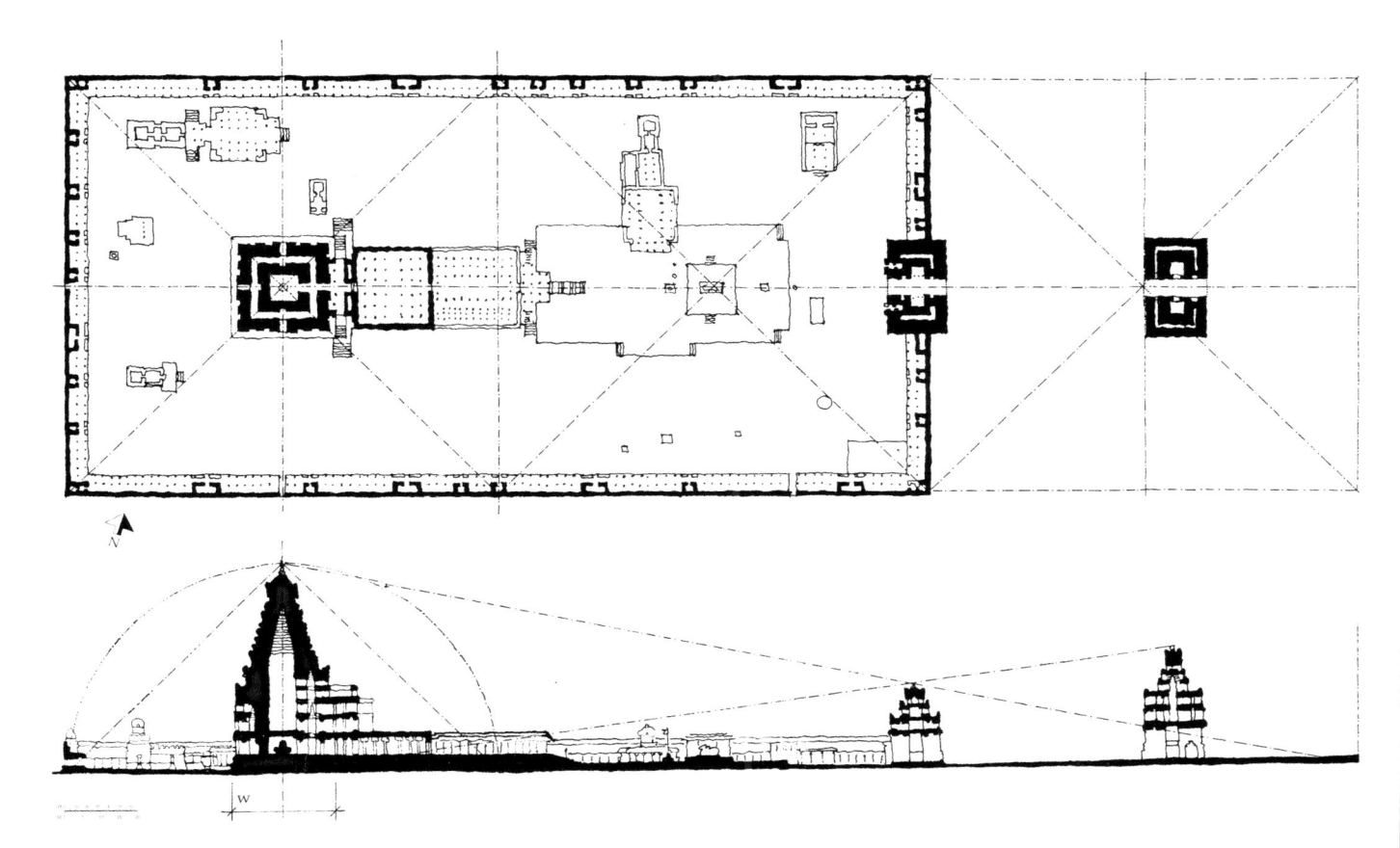

half-sanctums flanking the passage. The Kailasanatha already has a small *gopura*, while the Brihadeshvara, Tanjavur (**9.24**), has the earliest of the monumental, axial *gopura*-sequences typical of the later southern temple complexes, where the gateways belong to concentric enclosures and become larger towards the periphery. Another kind of opening and point of transition is the free-standing archway or *torana* (**9.19**, **9.20**).

Tanks – for irrigation, drinking water, ablutions, laundry, swimming, ritual, festivals and fish (not always all of these together) – are an ubiquitous feature of important temple groups, when these are not built by rivers. As sacred as they are useful, more elaborate tanks are lined with miniature temples. Usually tanks are informally related to the surrounding monuments, but occasionally they are linked by an axis. The Surya temple, Modhera, is organised along a great axial sequence of stepped tank, *torana*, free-standing open *mandapa*, closed *mandapa* and *mula-prasada* (**9.18b**, **9.20**).

9.24 Brihadeshvara temple, Tanjavur (Tamil Nadu), early 11th century (following analysis by Pichard).[2] The height of the *vimana*, about 60 metres, is half the width of the enclosure, and twice the width of the sub-base (W). As in later south Indian temple complexes, the monumental gateways (*gopuras*) increase in size centrifugally. That this signifies expansion, rather than merely reflecting the increasing wealth and pretensions of patrons as they built successive shells, is shown by the fact that the two *gopuras* at Tanjavur, both part of the original scheme, are geometrically related to the whole in a pattern of outward growth.

Notes
1 Michael W Meister, 'Mountain Temples and Temple Mountains: Masrur', *Journal of the Society of Architectural Historians* 65:1, 2006, pp 26–49.
2 Pierre Pichard, *Tanjavur Bṛhadīśvara, An Architectural Study* (Delhi: IGNCA and École Française de l'Extrème Orient, 1995).

10 NAGARA SHRINES

Five Nagara Modes

A traveller through northern India in the 8th century, with an eye for architecture, would have been able to distinguish three general types of monumental shrine: the piled eaves of the Phamsana, the wagon-backed Valabhi and the curved peak of the Latina. Three centuries later the picture was different. Prolific temple building was reaching far wider regions than before; but, except in the east, the Latina form was rising only over the humbler shrines, the Valabhi not at all and the Phamsana mainly as the way to treat *mandapas* and porches. Any important new temples that an 11th-century voyager encountered would have belonged to the clustered Shekhari mode or the ribbed Bhumija.

There are, then, five modes or general types of Nagara temple architecture, although they developed at different times, and once established they went on changing. The names used here for the five modes have been distilled by modern scholarship from the convoluted and shifting typologies of diverse regional textual traditions. These five modes are not enumerated by any text, in the manner of the orders of western classicism. Yet, surveying the whole landscape as we now can, these five species stand out, and that the temple designers understood them as overarching types is borne out by their consistent use of these forms as aedicules.

The five modes, while all ultimately grounded in the imagery of ancient timber forms, have different kinds of origin. The Valabhi begins as a masonry rendering of the barrel-roofed structure, simple or with aisles, familiar through *chaitya* halls. A formalisation of multi-eave towers, wedded to a piling up of slabs, leads to the Phamsana. Both Valabhi and Phamsana have a bearing on the origin of the Latina. This is a more complicated process, and lies at the core of an understanding of the Nagara language in general, not least because the two later modes spring from the Latina, which burgeons out of itself into the Shekhari, and bursts apart into the Bhumija like a ripe seed pod.

While Shekhari and Bhumija are by definition composite or multi-aedicular, the three earlier modes are unitary, in that their basic form

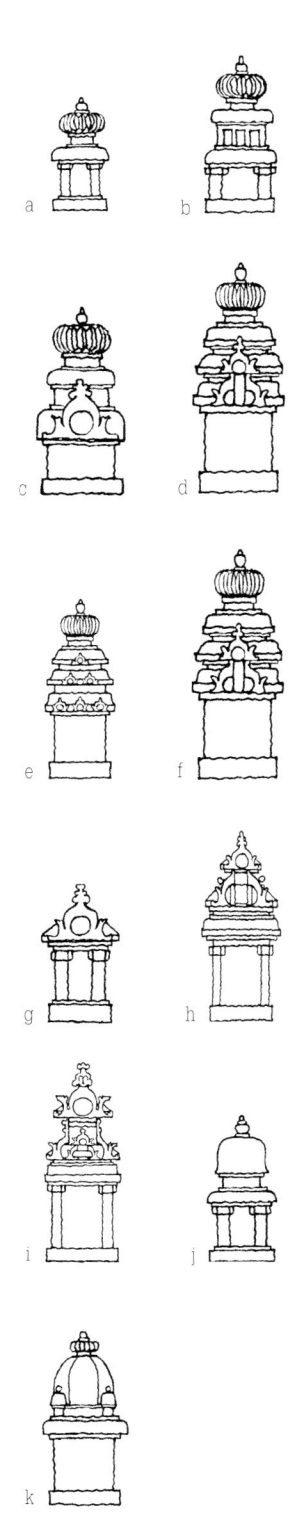

10.1 Early Nagara aedicules:
(**a–d**) amalaka aedicules;
(**e, f**) Phamsana aedicules;
(**g–i**) Valabhi aedicules;
(**j, k**) domed kuta aedicules.

The early Nagara range of aedicules originates in types of full-size shrine, of which the aedicules are images. Two of them have already been met with in Gandhara (17.13c, d): the domed *kuta* aedicule and the Valabhi aedicule. The domed *kuta* aedicule plays a part only in early Nagara traditions, but was to have a lasting presence in Dravida architecture. The Valabhi aedicule is of much greater significance for the Nagara language, as is the Phamsana aedicule. A fourth type, which can be called the '*amalaka* aedicule', after its crowning ribbed cushion, will be shown to be a direct ancestor of the Latina. No full-size '*amalaka* shrines' survive, although a small free-standing example of the simplest version, from as late as the 7th century, forms an island shrine at Mahakuta (1.2). It has been suggested that the form reflects not so much a shrine as an altar; but possibly this interpretation springs from an over-zealous desire to show continuity between Vedic sacrificial ritual and later temple-worship.

Some of the aedicules shown here represent buildings of more than one storey, and it should be borne in mind that, on the piling-up principle, each of the forms shown here can be raised over a further storey (a plain wall or articulated by pilasters) to become the superstructure of a taller shrine form (compare (**k**) with 10.6). In the case of the *amalaka* aedicule, the simple form, presumably via the simple addition of a storey as in (**b**), becomes the crowning element of more elaborate types. (**c**) shows a basic elaboration that creates a type frequently used for corner-pavilions (*karna-kutas*) in 6th-century pre-Latina towers, and long surviving thereafter. The elaboration is simply the addition of a *gavaksha*-dormer to the lower eave. This is often enlarged until it meets the corner (thus touching the corresponding ones on any visible adjacent faces), in which case the effect is of a simple *amalaka* aedicule (**a**) over a simple Valabhi aedicule (**g**). Where a further eave is added, the result is another common and persistent form of corner-pavilion (**d**) which, in effect, has become Phamsana (**d = f**).

This fluidity between categories is the bequest of the imagery of ancient timber forms underlying the Nagara architectural language. An inherent overlap between the Phamsana and the Valabhi arises from the fact that the 'horseshoe arch' or *gavaksha* form refers back both to the end gable of a thatched barrel roof and to the gable of a dormer window projecting out of an overhanging eave or canopy. Thus *gavaksha*-dormers, logically adorning the eave mouldings of a Phamsana shrine or aedicule, come to be placed over half-*gavakshas* derived from the gables or cross sections of side-aisles, and this configuration leads on to splitting, proliferating Valabhi patterns bursting though the Phamsana layers. Conversely, since the new Valabhi patterns have been gestating in a Phamsana matrix, an inconspicuous but unmistakable Phamsana background of curved or triangular eaves is nearly always given to Valabhi aedicules.

10.2 Door jamb of the Gupta period temple of Dash-Avatara, Deogarh (MP), c AD 500, depicting a Valabhi shrine (above) and an 'amalaka shrine' (below). Each ribbed amalaka is topped by a pot-finial (stupi, kalasha, or amrita kalasha, 'vase of divine nectar'). The crowning amalaka of full-size Nagara shrines normally supports this kind of finial, although many have gone missing.

represents a single structure, though frequently elaborated through the addition of shrine-images at lesser scales or levels of order. Fully formed Latina temples of the 7th and 8th centuries are far from simple, however, enveloping deep and complex patterning within their clear outlines. The picture is enriched by 6th-century survivals in the ancient region of Dakshina Koshala and in eastern India at Bodhgaya of completely multi-aedicular designs, which could be said to constitute further Nagara modes, though not as widespread as the others.

Birth of the Latina

Three conceivable routes to the formation of the Latina in all its complexity are suggested by three characteristic kinds of development in Indian temple architecture – the opposite processes of articulation and fusion, and that of piling up. The Latina could have resulted from articulation of the Phamsana, by adding corner pavilions, by bulging out towards the centre, by making recesses, and so on.[1] These things certainly happened to Phamsana designs once the Latina already existed, but that this was not how the Latina came about seems clear from the relatively humble status of the Phamsana, and the peripheral nature of the areas where it was prominent at an early date. A more plausible possibility would be that the Latina arose through compressing and merging together the distinct aedicules, running full height through each tier, seen in the 'early aedicular Nagara' temples discussed below. For a long time I held this view, although it is clear that these temples themselves could not have been the direct forbears of the 'mainstream' Latina appearing in central India early in the 7th century, because they are not quite early enough and in terms of detail are further from this mainstream Latina than are Gupta remains such as the temple at Deogarh (**10.2** and **17.1–17.3**). What does seem to have happened is that the genesis of the Latina took place in the Gupta milieu, beginning with a simple type of shrine with ribbed crown (amalaka), and then developed through the 'piling up' process, by which one shrine form becomes the superstructure of another form. Meanwhile, it was adorned with pavilions at the corners and in the centre. This is the simplest explanation, and best accords with the details of early Latina temples and surviving earlier fragments.

This process is illustrated in **10.3a–c**. Figure **10.3a** is a two-tier amalaka shrine; **10.3b** is a development in which this becomes the superstructure, while the new lower storey supports amalaka aedicules at the corners and displays a central Valabhi aedicule (cf **17.4b**). On the left, **10.3b** shows the corner pavilions as separate from the central

108 THE TEMPLE ARCHITECTURE OF INDIA

Valabhi aedicule. The right-hand side of the drawing shows a development that took place at a certain stage: the eave-canopy links across from the corners to form a false parapet treated as a section of cloister, hiding the feet, as it were, of the pilasters conceived as supporting the superstructure. It will prove to be significant that the *amalaka*, together with its neck, is at the level of the horizontal band formed by what remains of the pilasters.

Figure **10.3c** shows how the shrine in **10.3b** could, in its turn, become the top of a more complex form. For argument's sake I have drawn the pavilions of the first tier as more elaborate than those of the second, the central Valabhi aedicule as proliferated, and the corner *amalaka* aedicules with an additional eave, and thus effectively Phamsana (as **10.1d** and **10.1f**). The three eaves of the first-tier pavilions and the two of the second are carried across as false parapets, against which are placed minor Valabhi aedicules. It will be noticed that the corner *amalakas* still correspond to the band of pilasters, which now has the character of a colonnade. All that remains to transform this into an early Latina tower is to give it a curved profile and merge the central Valabhis into a continuous spine of eave mouldings with a pattern of horseshoe arches (*gavakshas*) running all the way down it.

This is what we see in a fully formed Latina temple, such as the Galaganatha, Pattadakal (**10.4**, **3.5**). Figure **10.4** shows the foot of the tower, with its corner pavilion, a minor Valabhi aedicule (termed '*bala-panjara*') in the recess, and the base of the spine with its climactically unfolding Valabhi configuration. Miniature pillars between pairs of half-*gavakshas*, originally just two pillars reminiscent of the *chaitya* hall cross section, have multiplied to resemble colonnaded storeys revealed within. In the recess, a similar 'colonnade' rises over the eave mouldings that are carried across behind the *bala-panjara* from the corner pavilions, and this colonnade corresponds to the corner *amalaka*, which by this stage has just a recess for a neck (cf **10.3b**, **10.3c**). Conceptually, this colonnade supports the eave sheltering the first storey

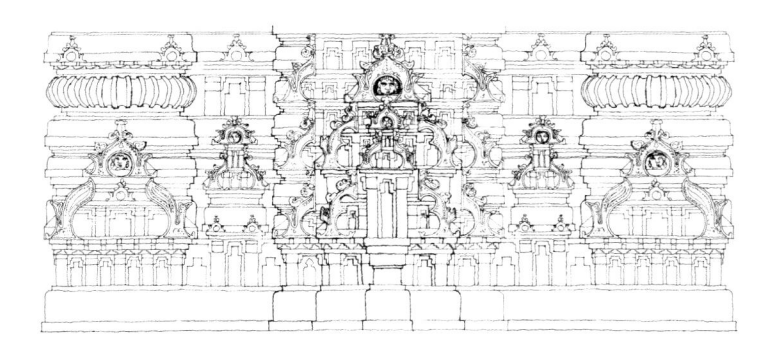

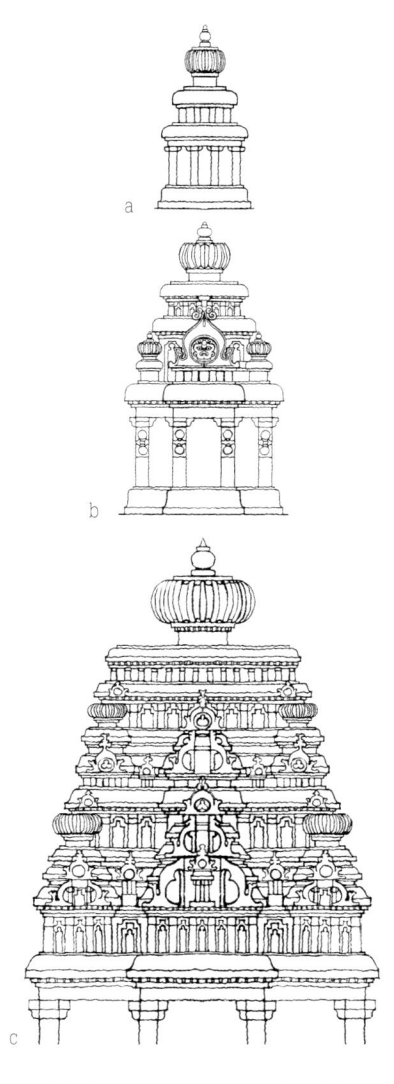

10.3 Hypothetical reconstruction of the piling up of early Nagara shrine forms, leading towards the Latina. A simple '*amalaka* shrine' (**a**) becomes the superstructure of a more complex type (**b**), cf lower shrine in 10.2: a developed form of this, in its turn, is placed above a further tier (**c**). The fusion of the central aedicules into a spine, and the introduction of a curved outline, will result in a Latina spire (*shikhara*).

10.4 Galaganatha temple, Pattadakal (Karnataka), *c* late 7th century: lowest portion of the *shikhara* (cf 3.5).

NAGARA SHRINES

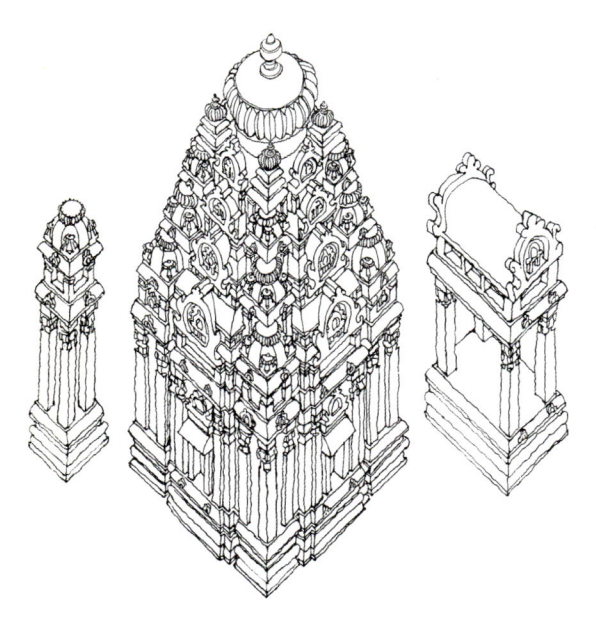

10.5 Rajivalochana temple, Rajim (Chhatisgarh), *c* 600: main shrine with octagonal-domed *kuta* aedicule (left) and simple Valabhi aedicule (right).

10.6 Rajivalochana temple complex, subsidiary shrine, composed of domed *kuta* aedicules. Photo © Gerard Foekema

of the subsequent tier, the feet of the pillars hidden behind a moulded parapet. All this would soon be forgotten, and the levels (*bhumis*) of Latina spires (*shikharas*) would come to be counted from the tops of the corner *amalakas*.

While imaginary structures made of wood are represented in these masonry temples, it is enough to look at the flexible proportions of their imagined storeys to realise that the stone or brick forms were never literal models of timber, and that it is not helpful to try to reconstruct hypothetical timber prototypes for a mature architecture that has evolved consistently within its masonry tradition. As for the curved outline, it is time to abandon the old wives' tale that the Latina form comes from bamboo canes tied together at the top. Admittedly, the curvature of the Latina *shikhara* may well have been inspired by the precedent of curved, tapered, thatched buildings, perhaps even storeyed ones, but curvature was secondary to the piling up of shrine forms, and bent bamboo can tell us little about the Nagara language. To understand the curvature it is enough to consider its advantages: a heightened sense of diminution in the ascending stages, the need for less height to arrive at a given size for the upper platform (normally the same size as the sanctum) and its sheer grace and flow.

Early Aedicular Nagara Traditions (See also Chapter 17)

While the Latina remained unitary until it sprouted into the later composite forms, regions to the south and east of the former Gupta heartland had already by the 7th century digested the 'Gupta' ingredients and articulated them into multi-storeyed, brick temple towers in which each tier, through its entire height, was composed of interlinked shrine-images. This happened in Magadha (now Bihar) at Bodhgaya, and spectacularly in Dakshina Koshala (now Chhatisgarh; see Chapter 17).

An early example from the latter region is the main shrine of the Rajivalochana temple, Rajim, *c* 600 (**10.5**). It is composed of four tiers of linked, full-height aedicules. Those at the corners are octagonal domed *kuta* aedicules (with corner pavilions), replaced by Phamsana aedicules in the top tier. In the centre are Valabhi aedicules, made to stand out against a multi-storeyed background projection through the use of contrasting pilaster types. The drawing illustrates how the aedicules are conceived as three-dimensional, embedded wooden shrines. One of the shrines in the same complex is shown in figure **10.6**, and even the greatest sceptic cannot fail to see that it is conceived entirely in terms of interlinked aedicules of the domed *kuta* type.

Phamsana

Whereas the Valabhi and domed *kuta* forms arise, like the western classical pediment, from basic ways of roofing a single cell, the tiered-roofed Phamsana (the term means 'wedge shaped') is a formalisation in masonry of the more complicated, multi-storeyed, timber *harmyas* (mansions) and palaces that we have already seen well on their way to idealisation, in earlier, Buddhist reliefs and cave facades. At the same time, it is easy to see how the basic procedure of piling up stone roof-slabs would lead, in a tradition disposed to project architectural imagery into its raw material, to the slab edges being treated like roofs. Equally, we have seen how multiple tiers develop through the piling up of shrine forms, and how tempting it is to add an eave moulding or two. Coming effortlessly from all these directions, the Phamsana form seems almost inevitable, springing up in many different places. There is nothing intrinsically Nagara about it, but it informs the Nagara language, and becomes a Nagara mode when adopted by Nagara masons who make it with Nagara details – including the crowning *amalaka*.

Certain regions favoured Nagara versions of Phamsana between the 6th and 8th centuries, including Karnataka under the Early Chalukyas, at Aihole, and the Himalayan foothills, at Jageshvara. Phamsana shrines in both these regions are versions of the type shown in **10.7a**, those at Aihole with schematic colonnades carved in the horizontal recesses to emphasise the idea that these are storeys. In these regions, as more generally, the Phamsana seems to have been a cheap alternative to the Latina; whereas in 7th-century Saurashtra (western Gujarat) the Phamsana was the predominant kind of temple (**17.7**). Here, as well as the multi-eave variety, another type was nurtured, with broad, flat, sloping tiers of 'pent roof', probably in this case reflecting vernacular structures in timber. The earliest example is the temple at Gop dating from about the late 6th century (**10.7b**). Monumental temples of the 8th to 10th centuries in Kashmir follow this general idea (**10.7c**). These are only touched on in this book because they are not Nagara, but follow their own tradition rooted in the earlier art of Gandhara, as can be seen in their gable-crowned, curiously Gothic-looking trefoil 'Valabhis' and transformed Corinthian column type.

While Phamsana shrines continued to be built, from around the 9th century the main use of the different versions of the form was for *mandapas*. Since the later forms manifest the same phenomenon of proliferation that is seen in the Shekhari and the Bhumija, they will be dealt with after those modes.

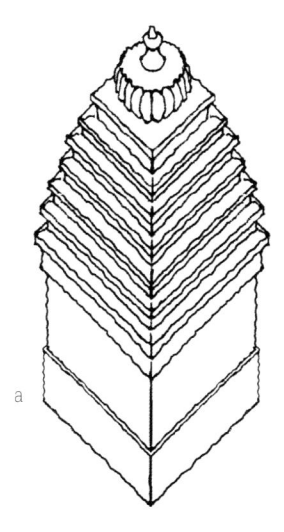

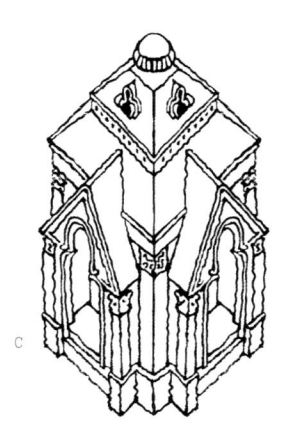

10.7 Phamsana forms: (**a**) early multi-eave type; (**b**) early pent roofed type in Saurashtra; (**c**) Kashmiri type.

10.8 Types of Valabhi shrine: (**a**) simple form; (**b**) simple version with superstructure like an aisled *chaitya* hall; (**c**) central Indian type with *bhumis* like those of Latina temples; (**d**) Orissan fully aedicular type (Vaital Deul, Bhuvaneshvara).

Valabhi (See also Chapters 18 and 21)

Valabhi shrines are rectangular, entered through one of the long sides, and were normally dedicated to goddesses. The term 'Valabhi' is probably derived from *vala*,[2] a curved rafter, like the ones combined in a *valabh* or chassis of the kind that would have supported the tunnel or barrel roof, single or with side-aisles, covering the sort of timber-framed structure represented in masonry by this mode. The *gavaksha*, the horseshoe-arch '*chaitya* window' gable, dominates the Valabhi form, and the evolution of the mode in central and western India, and especially of its representations in wall niches and other aedicules, is tied to spectacular transformations of the *gavaksha* motif (see Chapter 16). Tunnel-roofed timber structures are best known to us through the rock-cut derivatives of their apsidal form, the *chaitya* halls, but no surviving full-size Valabhi shrine is simply a free-standing equivalent of a square-ended *chaitya* hall, since even the simplest versions have an eave-cornice capping the wall, indicating that the superstructure is conceived as a second storey or upper pavilion. The tips of eaves carved more or less conspicuously behind the end *gavakshas* (sometimes sloping back from the gable, so that the roof becomes a rectangular dome), indicative of the close relationship between Valabhi and Phamsana noted in relation to their respective aedicules, further distance the Valabhi form from the *chaitya* hall prototype. In any case, the interior is always a simple rectangular sanctum, never a vaulted space with barrel-vault and aisles, the important idea being the exterior image.

An association between the Valabhi form and a gateway stems from the use in India of barrel-roofed structures for that purpose since ancient times. While gateways opened through the long side of a rectangular structure, the Valabhi gable end also makes a suitable opening, as in a *chaitya* hall facade, and it lends itself especially well to the expression of outpouring divinity, a characteristic that seems to have inspired the particular developments that the mode underwent along with the *gavaksha*. Sideways-on Valabhi aedicules are not uncommon in eastern India, however, where symbolic gateways of this form can be seen fronting Buddhist *stupas*. These *stupa*-fronting Valabhi pavilions are usually the single-roofed type of Valabhi (**10.8a**). The type with 'side aisles' (**10.8b**) is elaborated by projecting a smaller version of itself from the gable end, and sometimes a further, smaller one, and so on in a diminishing sequence. One or more similar projections can also appear on the rear wall. In 8th-century central India, Valabhi temples were made by the same workshops that built Latina shrines, using precisely the same Nagara kit of parts, with levels (*bhumis*) defined by corner

112 THE TEMPLE ARCHITECTURE OF INDIA

kutas, and so on. The basic type with 'side aisles' becomes a top tier or 'upper temple' raised on one or more *bhumis* (**10.8c**).

During the 8th century, the Valabhi concept was extrapolated into complex networks of *gavakshas*, extending downwards through a proliferation of overlapping motifs rather than through the addition of *bhumis*, and more readily applicable to niche 'pediments' (*udgamas*) and to eave-dormers than to full-size Valabhi gables (see Chapter 16).[3] The gable form that appears in response to such patterns has a stepped outline, and sequences of such gables are created, projecting one from another, as in the earlier, detelescoping Valabhi temples, though much transformed (**10.21**).

Valabhi aedicules of intermediate scales, between the scale of a niche and that of an actual temple, are used in modes other than the Valabhi. It has already been seen how the form is deployed as a primary component, indeed the central one, of 'early aedicular Nagara' temples, and later versions of the Valabhi play a comparable role in Shekhari shrines (**10.14h, i**; cf **10.15**). Extra-large central Valabhi aedicules projecting from Latina shrines, and rising right up into the superstructure, are common in Orissa (**21.3**, **21.4**). The same concept is found in many Bhumija temples (**20.6**). Not least, the Valabhi is the form of the antefix or *shukha-nasa* ('parrot's beak') of all the Nagara modes (**10.12**). In these various guises the form continued to play its part and to evolve long after the 9th century, when it ceased to be used for whole temples, at least in central and western India.

In eastern India the Valabhi persisted for longer, and took on a variety of forms, to the extent that it might be more appropriate to refer to Valabhi modes rather than mode. In the Pala domains (Bengal, Bihar, Jharkhand), although virtually nothing survives at full scale,[4] some depictions carved on lintels and door jambs, juxtaposing Valabhi shrines with Latina and Phamsana ones, are clearly realistic representations of actual buildings (**10.9**). In Orissa, where the term for the Valabhi is 'Khakara', three distinct kinds appear. The first (**21.5**) derives, in the 7th to 8th centuries, directly from the central Indian version; the second (Vaital Deul, Bhuvaneshvara, **10.8d** and **21.6**) is fully aedicular and strongly influenced by the tradition of Dakshina Koshala; the third, arising in the 10th century, is of Dravida rather than Nagara inspiration (**21.9**, **21.10**).

Latina (See also Chapter 18)

The term 'Latina' is from '*lata*', meaning 'creeper' and refers to the central spine of the tower, (*shikhara*), so called because of the plant-like patterns of horseshoe arches (*gavakshas*) climbing up it – or

10.9 Archway (*torana*) of the Pala period, *c* 10th century, now in the Ranchi museum (Jharkhand), supporting miniature shrines of the Latina (ends and middle), Phamsana (next to ends) and Valabhi (next to middle) modes. This *torana* was probably over the main image in a shrine (probably Buddhist, in view of the *stupa*-like finials).

10.10 Bateshara Mahadeva temple, Bateshara (MP), *c* late 8th century. This is a temple with an internal ambulatory (thus termed '*sandhara*'), so the shrine walls are below the ambulatory roof. The superstructure has five levels (*bhumis*) and a recess with minor Valabhi aedicules termed '*bala-panjaras*'. The offset next to the spine or *lata* (the *pratilata*) has been treated, like the corners, as a vertical chain of pavilions: this treatment is termed 'double *venukosha*', double 'sheathing of a reed'. A *gavaksha* to cap the central projection has gone missing, and the crowning *amalaka* and its cylindrical neck have been put back the wrong way round (cf 18.2b).
Photo © Gerard Foekema

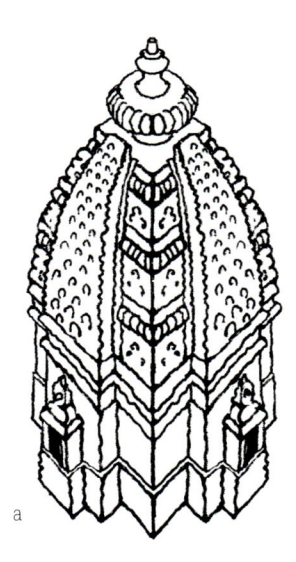

blossoming down it. The mode emerged in the Gupta heartland, was complete with curvature by the early 7th century, and during that century spread across the entire breadth of northern India, as far south as the Chalukya territories in the lower Deccan and as far north as the Salt Range in the upper Indus Valley.[5] For three centuries it reigned supreme, the peak — literally — of Nagara temple architecture; indeed, during that period, it was the Latina form that was meant by the term 'Nagara'. But by the 10th century the Latina had become a dry husk, and the Shekhari had sprung up. From that time the Latina was relegated to increasingly humbler roles; except in the east, where the Orissan masons remained loyal to their version of the mode, known there as the 'Rekha Deul', and still supreme in the mighty towers of Puri and Konarak (12th and 13th centuries).

The basic options for a Latina temple concern the number of segments, or (where there are recesses) projections, in the wall and — usually corresponding — in the *shikhara*, and the number of *bhumis* (levels) in the *shikhara*, marked by the corner pavilions (**10.11a**, **10.11b**). Not counting minor offsets to the central projection (*bhadra*), the number of segments or projections is normally three or five, the number of *bhumis* normally ranging between three and ten, but later with as many as twenty. This number is constrained by local norms at any given moment, but in general terms it increases over time, the height of the *bhumis* being correspondingly compressed. At a secondary level of architectural order comes the disposition and design of niches or wall-shrines, a matter that may be primary in liturgical terms, of course, as it concerns the presence of gods. Much of the life, texture and expression of the Latina mode takes place in the realms that it has taken over from the Valabhi form, through the *gavaksha* patterns chosen for each *shikhara* segment and for each wall-shrine.

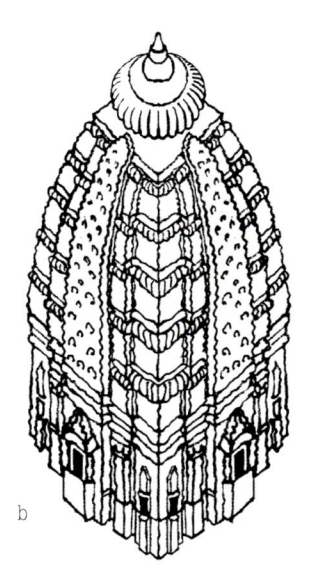

10.11 Latina shrines: (**a**) with three segments and three levels (*bhumis*); (**b**) Latina shrine with five full projections and five *bhumis*.

10.12 The rock-cut Dharmanatha temple, Dhamnar (MP), *c* 850. The main shrine is Latina, with five projections, the intermediate one treated as a pilaster, and six levels. Its fronton (*shukha-nasa*) is as usual Valabhi, and the hall (*mandapa*) a form of Phamsana that is tending towards the composite (cf 10.20a). While the main shrine is Latina, the surrounding subsidiary shrines are already composite or multi-aedicular, the corner ones 'proto-Shekhari' (as 10.13a) and the oblong axial ones composite Phamsana (cf 10.20b).
Photo © Gerard Foekema

114　THE TEMPLE ARCHITECTURE OF INDIA

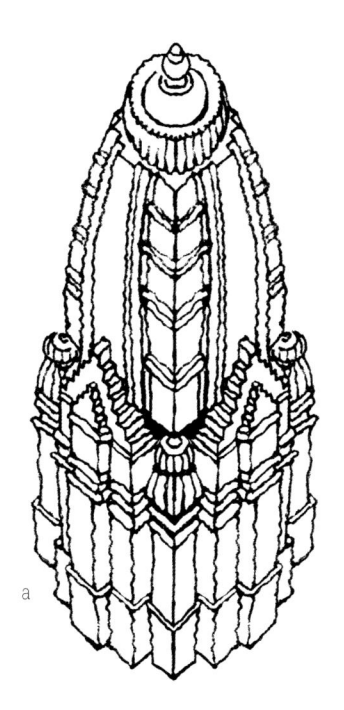

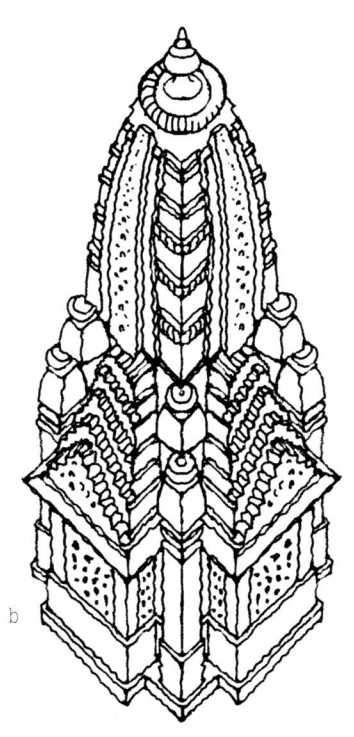

Several details linger as a legacy of the pre-Latina tradition: the broad recess with its minor Valabhi aedicule (*bala-panjara*) and its miniature colonnade supporting an eave-cornice moulding (**10.4**, **18.2a**, **18.2b**), and the option of adding a wide offset next to the *lata* and treating it as a vertical chain of *kutas* like those at the corners (**10.10**, **18.2b**). By the 9th century these features have virtually died out, just at the moment when full projections, with recesses in between, have become commonplace in the wall (**10.17**). In the 9th century, intermediate projections are commonly treated as thick pilasters. From the 10th century, all projections may be given pillar mouldings, following the new composite modes.

Shekhari (See also Chapter 19)

In the 10th century the multi-spired Shekhari mode became the standard one for western and central India. 'Shekhari' is related to '*shikhara*' (spire);[6] another term is Anekandaka ('multi-limbed', literally 'multi-egged'), which can be used to cover the general category of later composite shrine forms, reserving Shekhari for those with *urah-shringas* or 'chest sproutings' in the form of half-*shikharas* (half-embedded *shikharas*) emerging along the cardinal axes. Before the emergence of the Shekhari, two related types appeared which are Anekandaka and 'proto-Shekhari'. These introduce the *shikhara*-topped pillar form (*kuta-stambha*) (**10.14a**). In the simpler type of 'proto-Shekhari' (**10.13a**), a Latina *shikhara* rises over four corner *kuta-stambhas*, with Valabhi-crowned *bhadras* (**10.14h**). A second form (10.13b) is a downward extension of this, with an extra tier, still with three projections, and the Valabhi flowing down and apart into a wide porch-like *bhadra*. These proto-Shekhari compositions are 'types', in that they were used numerous times.

The 10th and early 11th centuries were times of great ingenuity in the design of Shekhari temples, and many were unique. The characteristic way to arrive at new designs was to incorporate existing compositions into new ones: by placing them on top, of course, or by projecting them out as a central aedicule-cluster. From this creative period sprung five Shekhari types that would be repeated down the centuries. Each type is defined by a particular three-dimensional arrangement of its primary elements, its aedicular components. Figure **10.16a–e** shows these types as composed mainly of Latina elements, but it should be borne in mind that variations are possible. Most obviously, the form of a given element within each type may vary: for example, a certain *kuta-stambha* may be Phamsana instead of Latina, or the *bhadra* may be crowned by a Valabhi

10.13 Anekandaka (multi-limbed) or 'proto-Shekhari' shrines: the simpler type (**a**) is expanded downwards to form the more complex version (**b**).

NAGARA SHRINES 115

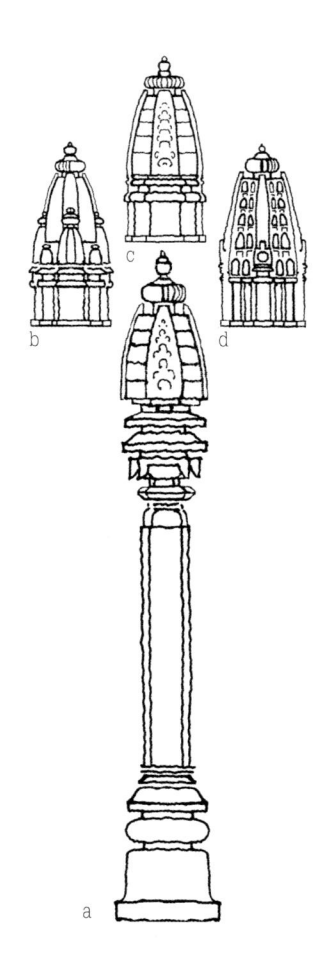

10.14 Aedicular components of later Nagara temples: (**a**) Latina kuta-stambha; (**e**) Phamsana kuta-stambha; (**h**) *bhadra* crowned by a Valabhi pavilion. The aedicules shown along the top, often used to crown kuta-stambhas, are Shekhari (**b**), Latina (**c**), Bhumija (**d**), composite Phamsana (**f**), Dravida-karma (**g**), Valabhi (**i**). Neither a pavilion-topped pillar from (kuta-stambha), nor a cardinal projection (bhadra) crowned by a pavilion, is strictly speaking an aedicule, in the sense of a representation of shrine (unless an elongated one). These are nevertheless 'aedicular components', in that they perform the same function as an aedicule – as primary element of composition.

Already in the 8th century one can sense in the Nagara traditions of central and western India a straining to become composite, in the way that the traditions of Magadha and Dakshina Koshala had earlier articulated temple walls into full aedicularity. Aedicules are, at root, images of known kinds of building, however much they may be stylised and take on their own life. As a general rule, once a new mode or type had appeared, a decent pause would be observed before it would peep out as an aedicule, or to cap an 'aedicular component'. In this way, once the Latina spire had become familiar, its image was used to replace older forms at the ends of door lintels, and then to mark the corners of halls (*mandapas*). Eventually Latina turrets emerged within the curved *shikhara* itself, first at the corners of its base (10.13a) and finally bursting out on the cardinal axes to form the Shekhari. After much proliferation within the whole, Shekhari temples proliferated in their parts and brought forth Shekhari aedicules. Bhumija temples, in a comparable way, developed Bhumija aedicules, and the new derivatives of the Phamsana also became aedicules. All the while, the Valabhi lived on as an aedicule, even when it was no longer built at full scale.

All these shrine forms, then, appear as aedicules, depicted in full or just as a superstructures; and most often, in the later period, they appear at the top of *kuta-stambhas*. A *kuta-stambha* is composed of a body in the form of a pillar (*stambha*), with an aedicule (or just its superstructure) for its head. In the Nagara traditions it was the Latina *kuta-stambha* which emerged first, and inspired the other forms. The idea of a pavilion on a pillar seems archetypal, and there may already have been a long tradition in India of little houses on posts, just as we had on our bollards and lampposts before Modernism abolished imagery. In any case, free-standing *kuta-stambhas* were erected in central India from around the 9th to 11th centuries, in the form of Jain pillars known as '*mana-stambhas*' (for example at Deogarh [UP] and Burhi Chanderi [MP]). The charm of the *kuta-stambhas* seen in temple architecture lies partly in the fact that these are embedded representations of free-standing objects. Their appearance was not sudden, however: their form emerged through the coming together of two separate tendencies – the gradual articulation of shrine walls through projections and recesses (bearing in mind the practice of treating certain projections as pilasters), and a renewed predilection for emphatic pavilions at the corners of a superstructure. The concept of *kuta-stambha* has had a vigorous later history in India, from the towers of victory in the fort at Chittor to the minarets of the Taj Mahal.

aedicule instead of an *urah-shringa*. The latter option, together with a little flexibility as to the number of *urah-shringas* at the lowest levels, means that to count the *urah-shringas* is not a reliable way to define a type. Minor corner pavilions may be added at the base of some of the major elements, and there may be slight variations in the respective springing levels of the latter. The later types are intrinsically wedded to the stepped diamond plan, but can be forced into an expanding square plan to give a similar effect; and the option is always available of cutting corners, so to speak, by making flat walls with no recesses. Because of these possible variations it may not at first sight be clear that a shrine belongs to one of the types. But, in the sense of standard overall relationships of parts, repeated many times, there are indeed five types.[7]

Type 1 (**10.16a** and **1.6**) is the Shekhari idea in pristine form, a Latina *shikhara* rising above four corner *kuta-stambhas*, with a lesser, embedded Latina shrine axially emerging on each face. This is equivalent to the simpler proto-Shekhari, but with a different *bhadra* element. Type 2 (**10.16b**), common from the 10th century onwards, is a downward proliferation of Type 1, which crowns the new form, as if buried to its neck in the lower tier, where the number of projections increases to five. Type 3 (**10.16c**) appears early in the 11th century and, as may be guessed, places Type 2 on top, increasing to five projections in the first tier, a sequence of three *urah-shringas* unfurling on each face and the number of *kuta-stambhas* in each quadrant flowing down from one to three to five. Meanwhile, a radical transformation has taken place in the plan, which is now a stepped diamond, bringing the corners into a line with the adjacent projections. This emphasises the bulging forward of the centre, greatly enhances the diagonal linkages between the *kuta-stambhas* and the main *shikhara* forms, and brings in its train the introduction of reentrant projections, usually treated as quarter-emerged, three-quarters-embedded *kuta-stambhas*. However, the real need for a stepped diamond plan at this stage comes from the fact that, if Type 2 is extended downwards to seven projections on an expanding square plan, it is impossible to avoid an absurdly thin *urah-shringa* in the bottom tier, with a *shikhara* narrower than those of the *kuta-stambhas*.

Types 4 and 5 (**10.16d**, **10.16e**, **10.17**) were established in the 11th and 12th centuries respectively, the Kandariya Mahadeva at Khajuraho (*c* 1030) being an early version of Type 5. Type 4 is a dense, compact, beautifully integrated and enduringly popular model, Type 5 the king of temples. Both types are based on a stepped diamond plan with five principal projections and reentrant projections in between, Type 4 normally with three main springing levels in the *shikhara* and two or

10.15 Shiva Temple 1, Kiradu (Rajasthan), *c* mid-11th century: a Type 4 Shekhari shrine. In this example the reentrant projections do not form *kuta-stambhas*, but are plain supports for the quarter-spire above.
Photo © Gerard Foekema

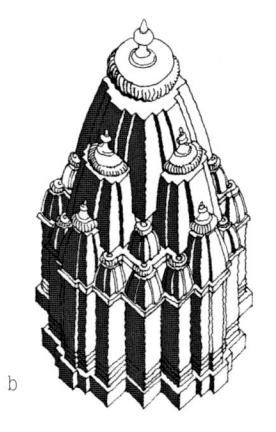

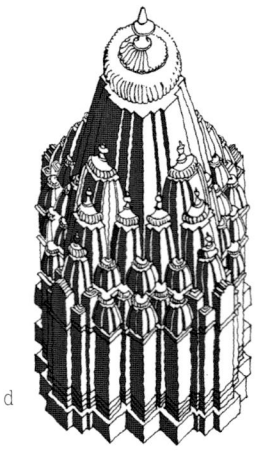

three *urah-shringas* on each face, Type 5 with an additional springing level and the possibility of up to four *urah-shringas*. The inseparability of these two types from their geometry is discussed in Chapter 12. In these types a new level of complexity and interpenetration is achieved through the introduction of quarter-*shringas* (*prati-angas*), or three-quarters-embedded *shikharas*, sitting above the reentrant projections between the *kuta-stambhas*, in the angles between the central *shikhara* form (the *mula-manjari*) and the first (uppermost) *urah-shringa*. The quarter-*shringas* spring at the level of the second *urah-shringa*, and are the same size, together with the first *urah-shringa*, so that, in conjunction with the first *urah-shringa*, they create the figure of an embedded Type 1 shrine emerging from the chest of the *mula-manjari*, and echoing, at a smaller scale, the four-emerging-from-one image formed by the *mula-manjari* and the first *urah-shringas*.

The evolution of these types is a classic example of that sequential unfolding which, as we have observed, follows the same kind of pattern as the centrifugal emergence expressed in a single shrine (Chapter 6). Type 1, a downward growth of the Latina, is expanded downwards to make Type 2, which is expanded downwards to make Type 3. Type 4 is a great bulging forth, splitting open and filling out of Type 2, in the light of Type 3. Type 5 is a downward growth of Type 4, and equally a filling out of Type 3.

Bhumija (See also Chapter 20)

'Bhumija' means 'earth born' or 'country born', most likely referring to its *bhumis* (levels, literally 'grounds').[8] The form emerged in the 11th century, long after the Shekhari, and was neither as widespread nor as durable; nevertheless, for over two centuries it was the preferred type of temple in the important kingdoms of Malwa (or Malava, western MP) and Seunadesha (north-west Maharashtra), extending to other regions in all directions, about a third of surviving examples lying southward in the lower Deccan (Karnataka and adjacent parts of Maharashtra, north-west Andhra Pradesh).

A Bhumija temple is recognised by the radiating, cascading chains of slender *kuta-stambhas* on every angle between its out-thrusting *bhadras*, with the *kuta-stambhas* fully exposed in the first tier and buried to their chests in the serried ranks above. The plan can be orthogonal or (between the *bhadras*) stellate, on the principle of the rotating square, a form to which the Bhumija lends itself perfectly, and sets itself to spin as the eye or the sun, rising or falling, glances around the turning facets. Each *bhadra* is usually treated as a multi-aedicular form of Valabhi, rising as high as the second tier of *kuta-stambhas*, striding

10.16 Shekhari shrine types: (**a**) Type 1; (**b**) Type 2; (**c**) Type 3; (**d**) Type 4.

forth out of the waterfall of the *lata* above, which gushes down from the jaws of a *grasa-mukha* (monster face). Bhumija shrines exist with eight *bhadras* (*ashta-bhadra*), another plan type classified in the texts, and uniform stellate plans (with no *bhadras*) are found among more southerly examples. Stellate Bhumija temples have reentrant projections in the recesses, articulated as pointed tips of embedded *kuta-stambhas*. Reentrants are also present in orthogonal Bhumija temples on stepped diamond plans, and on expanding square plans equivalent to the 'false stepped diamond' plans of some Shekhari designs.

No period of gestation can be traced for the Bhumija, which seems to spring up ready-made: significantly, this is one kind of temple said to have originated with kings rather than gods.[9] This is not to say that these kings, whoever they were, invented it out of nothing: it is not difficult to see how the form arose from the Latina. The idea of the corner *kutas* of a Latina *shikhara* being little Latina *shikharas* had long been made explicit from time to time, and if this idea is applied to that of a *shikhara* with pavilions flanking the *lata* as well as at the corner (**10.10**), and a pilaster is placed below each little *shikhara* to make *kuta-stambhas* (now already familiar in Shekhari temples), then one has an orthogonal Bhumija shrine.

As in the case of the Latina, the basic permutations of the Bhumija lie in the number of projections on plan and the number of *bhumis*. Stellate plans can also be defined by the number of points to the underlying turned-square star, and a certain amount of variety is possible in the choice of star: yet each stellate design with *bhadras* corresponds to a given orthogonal one in terms of the number of visible projections between the 'corners', ie between the points on the diagonals. Thus, in theory there could be plans with three, five, seven, nine or more projections. However, given the norms for height and curvature — based even on a visual judgement of the proportions, regardless of geometrical rules for achieving them — the choice is limited. Five or seven projections are the only real options, since three projections give a single chain of absurdly fat *kuta-stambhas*, while nine make them all pathetically thin. The choice of the number of levels is almost as constrained, since one cannot really compress the *bhumis*: at least, the Bhumija masons were unwilling to change the degree of exposure of their *kuta-stambhas*. With the wrong number of *bhumis* the *shikhara* is too squat or too lanky, so one is more or less limited to five *bhumis* for five projections (**10.18a**, **10.19**) and seven *bhumis* for seven projections (**10.18b**). A few unusual temples break the norms, but these two patterns predominate.

10.16 cont'd (**e**) Type 5.

10.17 Samiddheshvara temple, Chittor (Rajasthan), *c* mid to late 12th century: a Type 5 Shekhari shrine with a Samvarana hall.

NAGARA SHRINES **119**

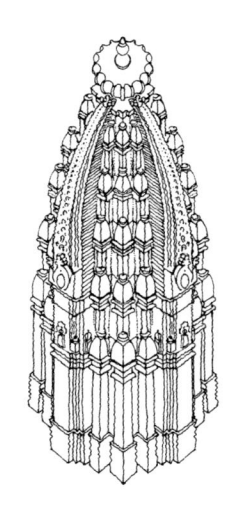

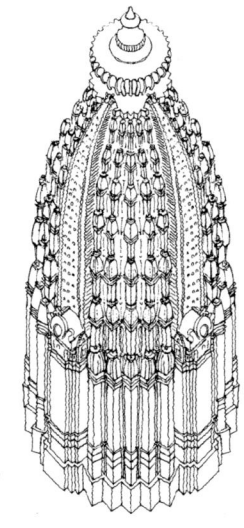

So, while for the Shekhari the inherent possibilities of the form held latent the paths of possible development, for the Bhumija, as soon as it was invented, the range of permutations was laid out from the beginning; and even within the theoretical range, compositions which fitted the desired norms of profile and proportion are barely more than two. This might partly explain why, for all its grace, the Bhumija did not survive as long.

Late Phamsana Forms

The Phamsana mode continued to be used for shrines, but from the 8th century onwards was most prominent as the exterior form for *mandapas*, both for main ones (*maha-mandapas*) and for porches (*mukha-mandapas*), providing a layered foil to the towering verticality of the shrines. As *mandapas* can be either closed or open, the Phamsana roof can either be united with the wall and its projections, or perched on pillars above a stone canopy or awning (*chhadya*).

Several regional varieties emerged. The most spectacular developments happened in western India.[10] These stem from the 'pent roof' kind of Phamsana, seen in the early example at Gop in Saurashtra (**10.7b**), a temple already crowned by a ribbed bell (*ghanta*), as later Nagara *mandapas* almost invariably are. In the second half of the 8th century, the old idea of putting *kutas* at the corners was applied, either Phamsana or Latina ones. This is shown in **10.20a**, which is based on the Mahavira temple, Osian (Rajasthan). By this stage the early *gavaksha*-dormers have become cascades of Valabhi pediments, flooding down to become a Valabhi *bhadra*, often in porch form. The next fundamental step, beginning in the 9th century, was to become truly Anekandaka (multi-limbed) by making the Phamsana roof into an upper pavilion and girdling it with aedicules (**10.20b**, cf **10.13a**). Gradually, in this tradition, the straight roof profiles became double-curved. Such was the prominence of the central Valabhi element, that a Valabhi-dominated Phamsana form took over from the Valabhi as the appropriate kind of shrine to build on a rectangular plan (**10.17, 10.27**).[11]

The ultimate, composite Phamsana-derived form is called Samvarana. Strictly speaking it is no longer Phamsana, in the sense that Shekhari is no longer Latina. The basic principle (**10.22a**) is not difficult. Figure **10.22b** is based on the *mandapa* of the 11th-century Sachiya Mata temple, Osian, which still retains ample bands of sloping roof and alternates bell-topped pavilions with Valabhi dormers in its cruciform unfolding. Its corners, mirroring the whole in microcosm, are treated as a schematically rendered type of Phamsana pavilion which would become

10.18 Bhumija shrines: (**a**) orthogonal with five projections and five levels or *bhumis* (5/5); (**b**) with the equivalent of seven projections between the diagonals, and with seven *bhumis* (7/7), based on a star of 32 points with three hidden in each cardinal projection.

10.19 Bhumija temple at Sakegaon (Maharashtra), *c* 12th century. The shrine is orthogonal 5/5 Bhumija, as 10.18a, but on a stepped diamond plan (corner projection same size as adjacent ones, and in line with them). At the centre of the composition is a composite Valabhi shrine form, reflected at a larger scale by the projecting fronton (*shukha-nasa*) together with the walls of the antechamber over which it rises. The walls of the antechamber (*antarala*) and hall (*mandapa*) have continuous pillar mouldings.
Photo © Gerard Foekema

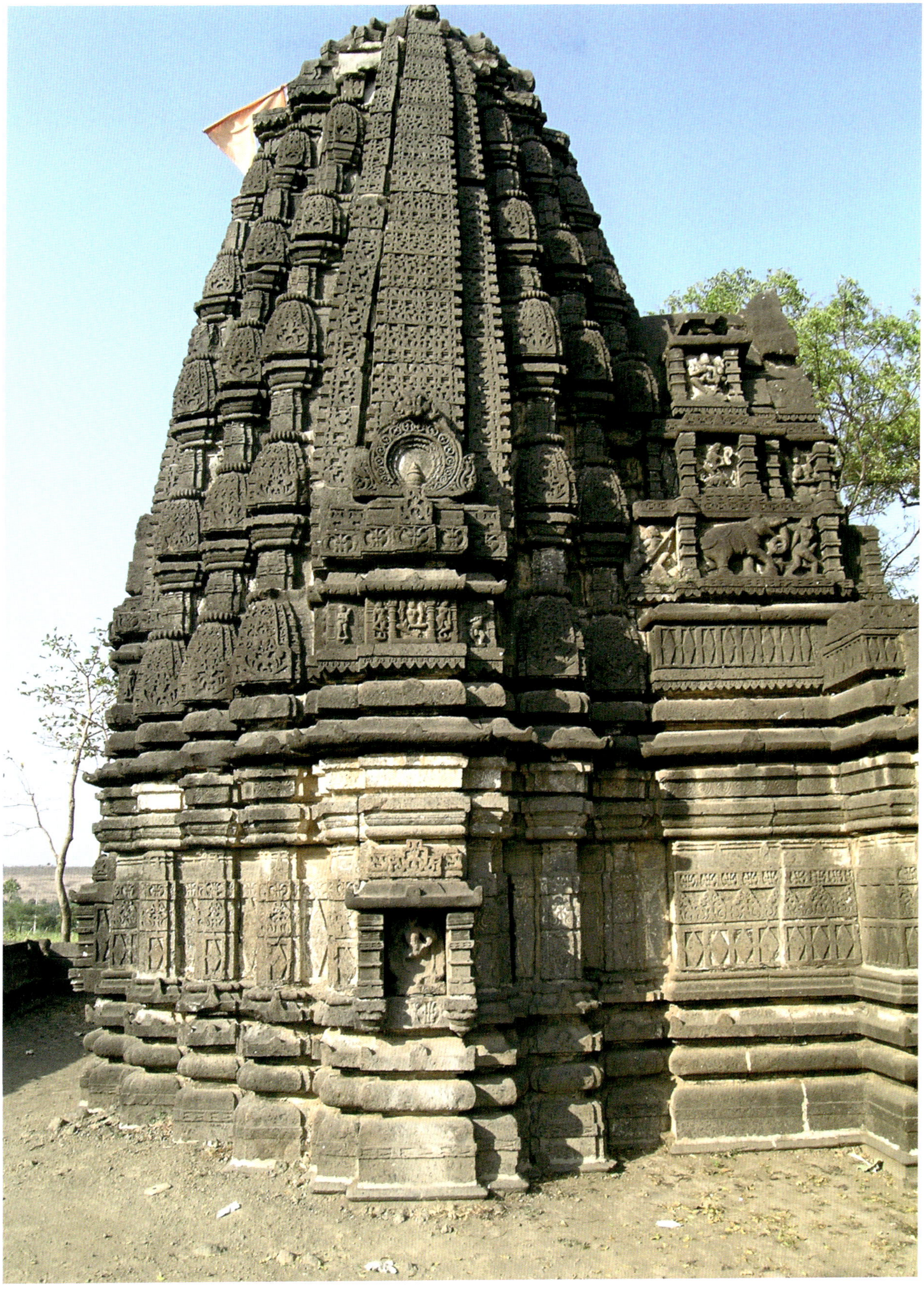

10.20 Later Phamsana forms: (**a**) pent roof with corner pavilions and central Valabhi cascade (the upper two tiers representing a simpler version of this kind of roof); (**b**) upper pent roof surrounded by aedicules and with Valabhi cascade; (**c**) central Indian type (as at Khajuraho), with a projecting Phamsana form reminiscent of the 'half-spires' (*urah-shringas*) that emerge from Shekhari superstructures; (**d**) Orissan Pidha Deul.

10.21 Kameshvara temple, Auwa (Rajasthan), *c* early 9th century. This is a composite Phamsana equivalent of the kind of 'proto-Shekhari' shrine shown in 10.13b. The shrine is rectangular, the shape traditionally reserved for the Valabhi, but it is marked as Phamsana by its summit (restored). Nevertheless, through the magnificent central cascade, it is the Valabhi that sails out triumphant. Photo © Gerard Foekema

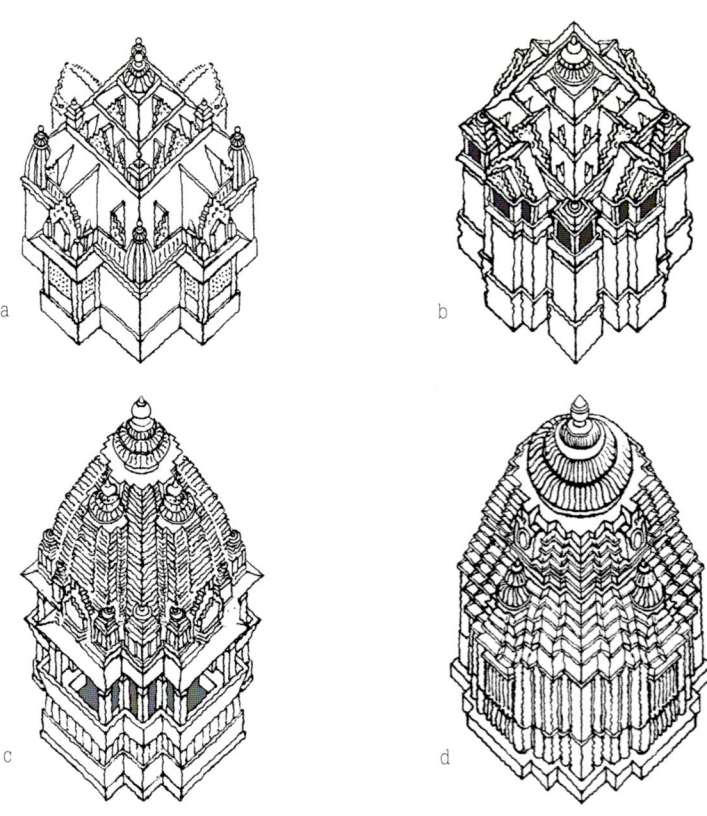

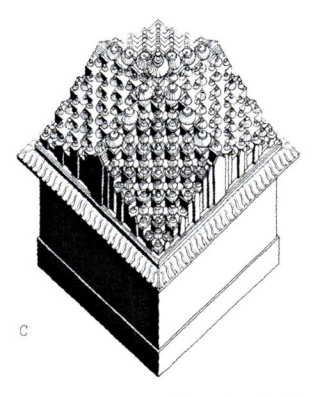

10.22 Samvarana hall (*mandapas*): (**a**) the principle; (**b**) earlier Samvarana, retaining prominent Valabhi gables and sloping roof-slabs; (**c**) typical late Samvarana.

10.23 Samvarana *mandapa* roof at Kasara (Gujarat), 12th century. Photo © Gerard Foekema

the standard component of Samvarana roofs: crowned by a bell, with axial Valabhi projections and small bells at the corners (**10.14f**). By the 12th century the Samvarana principle was being applied more mechanically (**10.22c**). One of the properties of the Samvarana shape is that, along the sides, it steps up vertically towards the middle, giving a surface easily treated as a stepped-up girdle of pavilions, or making a suitable junction with a porch (**10.17**). Clearly, the Samvarana principle can be expanded *ad infinitum*, and the tendency was in that direction.

These western Indian forms spread swiftly into central India, but that region, in parallel, was finding comparable ways to make the Phamsana composite or Shekhari-like, but using the steeper-pitched, multi-eave kind of Phamsana. Thus, at Khajuraho and dating from the 10th century (**10.20c**) there are large, axially projected Phamsanas, equivalent to the *urah-shringas* of the Shekhari, in a girdle of smaller pavilions (crowning *kuta-stambhas* when the *mandapa* is a closed one). A century later, at Khajuraho, the temple architects were experimenting with complex multiple forms, similar to the Samvarana but with reentrant projections.

In Orissa the Phamsana (known there as 'Pidha Deul' or 'Bhadra Deul') supplanted the simpler slab-roofed *mandapa* ('*jagamohana*') in the 10th century (**10.20d**). Strong and powerful, capped by a massive bell, the form can rise in two or even three diminishing tiers of multiple eave mouldings. It remains unitary, though pierced by *bhadra* aedicules extending into the roof. Only occasionally, from the 12th century, does it become composite.

Notes

1. For another analysis of the genesis of the Latina, see Michael W Meister, 'Prāsāda as Palace: Kūṭina Origins of the Nāgara Temple', *Artibus Asiae* 44, 3/4 (1989), pp 254–80, and 'On the Development of a Morphology for a Symbolic Architecture', *Res* 12, 1986, pp 33–50.
2. MA Dhaky, personal communication, 2 March 2006.
3. One full-scale, though small, Valabhi shrine, the Satya Narayana at Osian (Rajasthan), roughly contemporary with the Mata-ka Mandir, is based on a relatively proliferated pattern, with stepped gables to accommodate it.
4. The Sarvamangala temple, Garhbeta (West Bengal) is one example, difficult to date because of restorations: Ajay Khare, *Temple Architecture of Eastern India* (Gurgaon: Shubhi Publications, 2005), p 130.
5. On this outpost of Nagara architecture, see Michael W Meister, 'Temples along the Indus', *Expedition* 38/3 (1996), pp 41–54, and Meister with Abdur Rehman and Farid Khan, 'Discovery of a New Temple on the Indus', *Expedition* 42/1 (2000), pp 37–46.
6. The term has been brought to light by MA Dhaky, on the basis of western Indian architectural texts. In the texts, the multi-spired form is sometimes called Nagaracchanda, or simply Nagara, having wrested that title from the Latina.
7. For a detailed account see Adam Hardy, 'Sekhari Temples', *Artibus Asiae* 62, 1 (2002), pp 81–137.
8. Krishna Deva, 'Bhumija Temples' in Pramod Chandra (ed), *Studies in Indian Temple Architecture* (New Delhi: AIIS, 1975), pp 91–2.
9. Ibid, p 90: reference to *Aparajitaprccha* 112:2–3.
10. See Michael W Meister, 'Phaṁsana in Western India', *Artibus Asiae* 38, 2/3 (1976), pp 167–88.
11. As also the Harihara Temple 3, Osian; see ibid, pp 167–70.

11   Dravida Shrines

At the opening of the previous chapter I launched an 8th-century traveller on an architectural tour of northern India, and made her reincarnation repeat the exercise in the 11th century. It might have been better to send a cloud messenger, who could have sketched some roof plans in passing, but having set the mould I shall dispatch my same explorer southwards in the same centuries. In the 8th-century, lingering in the lower Deccan, and later on the coast of Coromandal, she would espy pyramidal piles crowned by Dravida domes, and at first would find little to distinguish between the temples of those two regions, for they clearly were of common parentage; yet closer inspection would reveal marked differences in character between these siblings. Making the return journey three centuries later, herself untouched by the years, would find the pair estranged, their respective traits and foibles much accentuated. Plodding first the paddy fields of the putatively segmental state of Cholanadu, my slender pilgrim would plainly recognise the old tradition in the new temples hewn from granite; having passed countless graceful, modest shrines, she would gaze in wonder, or possibly take *darshan*, at the highest temple towers ever seen. Wending then northward, she would be greeted on her return to Kuntaladesha, with its wide plateau lands and craggy outcrops, by a scene less grandiose though quite as splendid, but one that at first would seem strange, almost unrecognisable. Yet, after a season's sojourn in that country, its temples would appear familiar, and in their tortuous lineaments she would discern the old accustomed nature, much transformed; and, ere she bade farewell, our wandering *apsara* would come to see what rich and wondrous works of fantasy the masons of that land had teased from stones.

    All this is to say that, from the 7th century, two main traditions of Dravida temple architecture took root in Karnataka and Tamil Nadu (regions which from that time and for centuries after would be rivals for paramount power in southern India), and that, despite a common heritage and early interchanges, the two traditions were distinct from the start and became ever more so. Neither tradition was monolithic:

both comprised various schools and idioms, and the Dravida architecture that spread through the whole of southern India can (until the disruption of the Karnata Dravida schools at the end of the 13th century) be linked to one or other of these traditions, or sometimes to both. Chapter 10 was structured around the different modes of Nagara, but it is not so clear that modes are a useful category for the Dravida – a matter to be discussed at the end of this chapter.

The varieties of Dravida shrine (*vimana*) will therefore be treated in this chapter in a general way, but pointing out the differences between the two main traditions. If these peculiarities seem bewildering, it should be realised that they are not disparate features to be listed, but related aspects of two very different ways of thinking about the same architectural language. In the Tamil temples the architectural elements, while embedded in the whole, remain apart and distinct, bound together by balance and symmetry; in the Karnata tradition – in this way more northern – the parts become increasingly interconnected and interpenetrating, bunched into an ever more powerful axial surge. Both have their own beauty, but a different eye is needed to appreciate each of them. Otherwise, from a Karnata perspective, the temples of Tamil Nadu seem heavy, static and unimaginative and, looking in the opposite direction, Karnata temples seem overdone, muddled and impure.

The Dravida Language and Early Wooden Buildings

Like the Nagara, the Dravida is a language conceived in terms of masonry, depicting an architecture originally made of wood, but formalising it and transforming it into patterns. Dravida temples, even the earliest, are no more copies in stone of timber structures than Nagara temples are: abstraction is there from the start and increases, but the imaginary architecture represented is never entirely lost. Chapter 7 traced the earlier 'pan-Indian' architectural forms that underlie the imagery and system of the Dravida language: huts and *harmyas* (mansions), simple shrines and storeyed towers. Pavilions with two kinds of thatched roof form, the barrel-vaulted and the domical, were

11.1 Varieties of *alpa vimana*, 'minor shrines' consisting of a single aedicule. *Alpa vimanas* are 'one-tier' (*eka-tala*) shrines, but conceptually of two storeys – the real ground floor and an imaginary floor to the upper pavilion that forms the superstructure. This can be either a domed *kuta*, square, circular or octagonal, or else a barrel-roofed *shala*, rectangular or apsidal. Oval forms are also found. *Alpa vimanas* can follow this same range of plan forms in their entirety, but more often the lower parts remain square or rectangular, the change in shape happening in the upper pavilion – or, strictly speaking, only above the 'floor moulding' (*prati*), which provides a platform for sculptures or small pavilions. As in early thatched precedents (7.3, 7.4), domes support a vase-finial (*stupi*, *kalasha*), and the ridges of barrel roofs carry several of them.

DRAVIDA SHRINES **125**

11.2 *Alpa vimana* south of Ravana Phadi cave, Aihole (Karnataka), *c* early 7th century. Mouldings (see Chapter 13), are essential to the imagery. The sanctum walls support a *kapota*, a cornice or entablature representing a thatched eave. This carries a *prati*, the lowest moulding of the upper pavilion, representing a floor with its joists, surmounted by a railing moulding, the *vedika*. A recess or *griva* ('neck') comes below the *shikhara* or roof.
Photo © Gerard Foekema

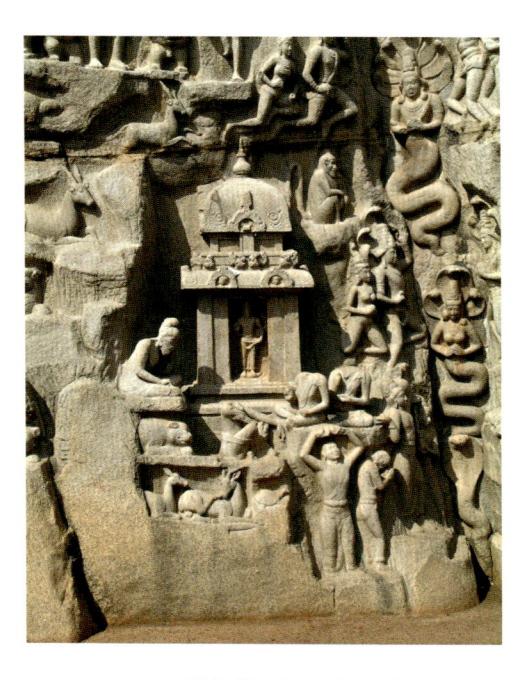

11.3 *Alpa vimana* depicted in the 'Arjuna's Penance' or 'Descent of the Ganges' relief at Mamallapuram (Tamil Nadu), *c* late 7th century. The image shows an architectural vocabulary already transformed to suit stone mouldings (here minus the *vedika*): the proportions of the shrine are close both to its likely timber prototype and to the *kuta* aedicule, the compositional element representing this type of shrine.
Photo © Gerard Foekema

raised aloft on gateways and turrets. One type of shrine had a miniature domed hut as its superstructure, and we have seen how in Gandhara around the 2nd century the image of this type was already used as an aedicule (**7.13d**), and how the same type, originally conceived in wood, was being constructed in masonry and linked with other shrine types into cloister-like courtyards (**7.13e**). Already in the 5th century facades at Ajanta, domes and barrel roofs define miniature pavilions, respectively called *kutas* and *shalas*, linked into ornamental bands called *haras* (**8.1**, **8.5**). *Kutas* and *shalas* are essential parts of Dravida architecture, strung along in *haras* and, more importantly, used singly as the crowning elements of shrines, including the most basic kind known as *alpa vimanas*.

Alpa Vimanas: the Simplest Dravida Shrines

The simplest possible Dravida *vimana* (shrine proper) is a kind of primitive hut with just a base, a wall and a roof. Many village shrines are like this, but the only one known in monumentalised form is Draupadi's *ratha* at Mahabalipuram (**22.5 left**), which demonstrates a theoretical option normally considered too humble for the shelter of a god. In practice, the most basic class of Dravida temple comprises the varieties of *alpa vimana* (minor *vimana*), consisting of a sanctum crowned by a pavilion in one form or another of domed *kuta* or barrel-roofed *shala* (**11.1**). Such shrines, as we have seen, have a long ancestry. A little before the appearance of the first Dravida temples, examples are seen depicted in rock-cut architecture (**8.10**) and in the form of miniature votive shrines. Probably the earliest surviving full-size square *alpa vimana* is a small, sandstone shrine in front of the Ravana Phadi cave at Aihole (*c* early 7th century) (**11.2**); but earlier still are two apsidal, brick *alpa vimanas* at Ter (Maharashtra) and Chezarla (Andhra Pradesh) (see Chapter 17).

126 THE TEMPLE ARCHITECTURE OF INDIA

When *alpa vimanas* are depicted in relief carvings, their proportions are often narrow, like their timber predecessors, and if they have pilasters – representing wooden posts – just two are visible in a side view (**11.3**, **11.4**). In masonry versions, however, where the walls have to enclose a cuboid inner sanctum (*garbha-griha*), the proportions are squatter, and four pilasters are usual, as in the numerous *alpa vimanas* built in Tamil Nadu between the 9th and 11th centuries (**11.5**, **11.6**).

In elaborating the *alpa vimana* form the first impulse (first seen in early 7th-century Karnataka) was the perennial one of piling up, one type becoming the superstructure of another. Just as the *kuta* or *shala* crowns a two-storey *alpa vimana*, so the two-storey types became the superstructures of three-storey ones (**11.7a–b**, **11.8**). *Alpa vimanas* continued to be built after the concept of the multi-aedicular Dravida *vimana* had become established, and indeed they are still built by present-day Tamil temple architects (*sthapatis*). The two-storey *alpa vimana* form also continued to evolve within more complex designs, where it remained at the summit as an 'upper temple' (**11.9**).[1]

Multi-aedicular Vimana Designs

It was during the 7th century that the characteristic stepped form of Dravida shrine emerged, with domed and barrel-roofed pavilions (*kutas* and *shalas*) running along the top of each tier. Sometimes these pavilions would simply form a horizontal garland (**11.7c**), but more often there would be corresponding projections in the wall, framed by pilasters, making the tier into a cloister of two-storey, embedded aedicules (**11.7d**). The *vimana* became a palace wreathed in its many mansions. Figures **11.10** and **11.13** illustrate the range of Dravida aedicules.

In early Dravida temples the aedicules, the representations of shrines that constitute the visual building blocks of an architectural composition, can be widely spaced, standing out against a wall; when they are close together the presence of the intervening recesses barely imposes itself even as background. The 'parapet' above the *kapota* cornice – the band that is formed into pavilions – can be an actual parapet (*anarpita*), as is necessarily the case when an internal ambulatory surrounds the shrine (eg **11.11**). More often, the 'parapet' is simply the top part of a tier (*tala*), and thus can be thought of as false or applied (*arpita*). Whether or not the parapet is detached, each *tala* or tier above the first telescopes out from the one below, as if buried up to its chest. The receding celestial courtyards can be seen as obscured one by another, through an effect of perspective, or they can be seen as embedded one in another.

11.4 *Alpa vimana* over a niche in the Virupaksha temple, Pattadakal (Karnataka), *c* 742. Photo © Gerard Foekema

11.5 *Alpa vimana* at Kilayapatti (Tamil Nadu), *c* 9th century. Photo © Gerard Foekema

11.6 Ganesha shrine in the Sundareshvara temple complex of Nangavaram (Tamil Nadu), early 10th century: an *alpa vimana* with a square sanctum but apsidal above the *prati* moulding.

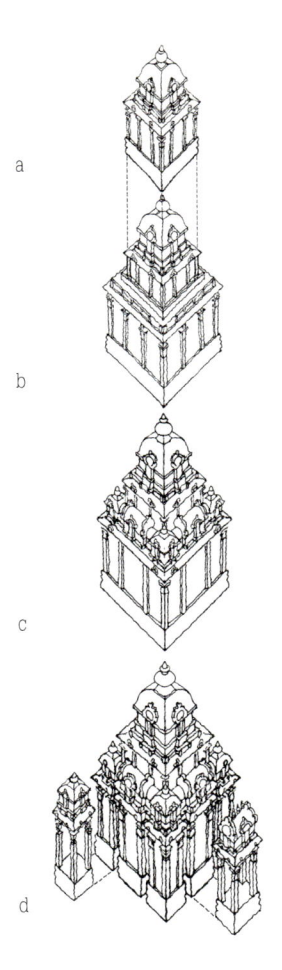

11.7 The two-storey *alpa vimana* form (**a**) becomes the superstructure of a three-storey *alpa vimana* (**b**). The evolution of multi-aedicular Dravida architecture may have followed the steps shown in (**c**) and (**d**): a three-storey *alpa vimana* is given a necklace or *hara* of *kutas* and *shalas* (**c**), then the walls are articulated to form *kuta* aedicules and *shala* aedicules, which portray familiar forms of two-storey *alpa vimanas*.

11.8 Kailasanatha temple, Kanchipuram (Tamil Nadu), early 8th century: enclosure wall and rectangular Mahendravarmeshvara shrine. The shrines lining the wall are three-storey *alpa vimanas*, each fronted by a shallow porch and crowned by a two-storey *kuta*, octagonal in its upper portions. The rectangular shrine (on the longitudinal axis of the compound, but not, as might be expected from later examples, a gateway) is a large, three-storey, *shala*-topped *alpa vimana*. Conspicuous in both are paired '*kapota-panjara* aedicules' (cf 11.10j).

A *vimana* wall can have three, four, five, or (very rarely) seven aedicule-forming projections in the first *tala*. In early Dravida temples, and thereafter in the Tamil tradition, the projections are all in line (**9.1b**); at most, the central projection (*bhadra*) comes further forward. These observations apply principally to square shrines, but different shaped *vimanas* follow the same general principles: a rectangular shrine, for example, will typically have five projections on the long sides, three on the short sides. In the Karnata Dravida tradition, where square shrines are the rule (until the alternative, stellate form is introduced) the walls increasingly become staggered, stepping out towards the centre (**9.1d**), not only in the first *tala* but in the upper ones too. This runs parallel to similar developments in Nagara traditions.

After the plan, the next basic variant is the number of tiers or *talas*, the Dravida equivalent of Nagara *bhumis* (levels). An upper temple in the form of an *alpa vimana* (of whatever shape) counts as the top *tala* (**11.9**). In later Karnata temples, again in contrast to the Tamil tradition, the walls of the top stage receive multi-aedicular articulation just like the other levels (**11.9d**). The convention is to continue to count the crowning dome together with the aedicular tier surrounding it as a single, top *tala*.

Bearing all this in mind, three-projection shrines commonly have two or three *talas*, four-projection shrines three, five-projection shrines three or four. More than four *talas* became usual only in the giant 11th-century temples of the Cholas and the later, towering *gopuras* (gateways). In the Tamil tradition, the number of projections often reduces from level to level:

typically 4–3–1 and 5–4–3–1 (where 1 denotes the unitary upper temple). The temple at Narttamalai, which is *sandhara* (with ambulatory), has 5–4–1 (**11.11**). In Karnataka, an odd number of projections – thus one central projection – was virtually always maintained on every level, and later Karnata Dravida temples invariably have the same number of projections, normally three or five, all the way up (**11.15**). This gives a radial continuity comparable to that of a Latina shrine: variation in the number of projections, and *talas* with four projections, are both incompatible with the staggered plans and central emphasis characteristic of this tradition.

Within these overall patterns of tiers and projections, the next design question is the choice of aedicules. By now it should be clear that *kuta* aedicules are usually placed at the corners, and forms of *shala* aedicule in the centre, where they are appropriate both for their shape and their association with gateways. Intermediate projections, when they first appear, are *panjara* aedicules; in late Karnata Dravida temples their place is taken by *kuta-stambhas*. From the early 8th century onwards, Tamil Dravida temples of any pretension boast two-storey *kutas* and *shalas*, usually placed over projections to form three-storey aedicules (**11.10d–f**). There will at least be a three-storey *shala* aedicule in the *bhadra*, standing head and top shoulders higher than the corners (**11.12**); or all the aedicules of the first *tala* may be three-storey, and even those of the second *tala*. In this tradition, as well as the number of aedicules varying from *tala* to *tala*, corresponding aedicules at the different levels may vary subtly in type, in ways other than the number of storeys – for example, in the shapes of the *kuta* domes (**24.8**).

Karnata Dravida temples, however, never have three-storey aedicules, and never have a marked difference in height between the aedicules within a *tala* – in later ones the roof moulding, including the linking sections between pavilions (roofing the *harantara* recesses), has a common level throughout a given *tala* (**11.15**). Here, reinforcing the radial continuity, corresponding aedicules in different tiers are identical, except in the *bhadra*, where they sometimes follow a pattern of unfolding from the top *tala* downwards (**3.12**). Given the comparative repetitiveness of the aedicules within one Karnata Dravida *vimana*, it may seem paradoxical that the inventiveness and variety of new aedicules in that tradition between the 10th and 12th centuries are unparalleled in any other branch of Indian temple architecture. The invention of new aedicules is based largely on the combination of existing types by embedding them into one another. Two types were intrinsic to the continuing transformation of the Dravida *vimana* by Karnata architects during the 10th and 11th centuries: the staggered

11.9 Variations on the *alpa vimana* form used as the top tier (*tala*) or 'upper temple' of more complex designs: (**a**) with '*kapota-panjara* aedicules' (11.10j) and Nandi bulls on the *prati* platform; (**b**) with central projection and *kutas* on the *prati* platform; (**c**) staggered; (**d**) multi-aedicular. Although the examples shown are square, the range of shapes found in upper temples is the same as for *alpa vimanas* (cf 11.1).

DRAVIDA SHRINES

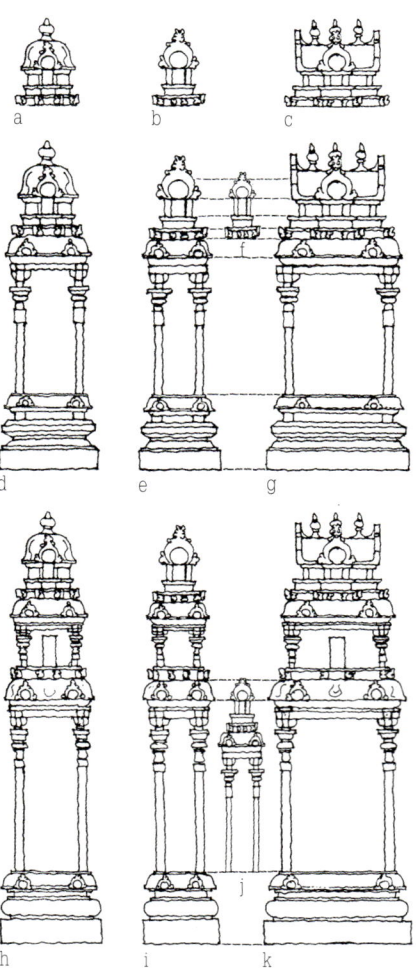

11.10 Dravida aedicules.
Note: the letters in brackets show a simple notation used in this book to describe Dravida aedicules and groups of them.

Crowning pavilions:
(**a**) *kuta*;
(**b**) *panjara*;
(**c**) *shala*. A *panjara* is an end-on *shala*.

The basic two-storey aedicules – images of two-storey alpa vimanas:
(**d**) *kuta* aedicule (K);
(**e**) *panjara* aedicule (P);
(**f**) *shala* aedicule (S);
(**g**) *harantara-panjara* (*harantara* = recess in parapet between pavilions).

Three-storey aedicules – images of three-storey *alpa vimanas* (two-storey aedicules become crowning pavilions):
(**h**) *kuta* aedicule (K̄);
(**i**) *panjara* aedicule (P̄);
(**j**) *kapota-panjara* aedicule, a form between primary and secondary aedicules (niches etc), using a 'horse shoe arch' or *gavaksha*-dormer in the *kapota* eave moulding as its crowning gable.
(**k**) *shala* aedicule (S̄)

11.11 Vijayalaya-Cholishvara temple, Narttamalai (Tamil Nadu), mid-9th century. This is a three-tier (*tri-tala*) shrine, articulated in the first tier as K–P–S'P'S–P–K, where S'P'S is a staggered *shala* aedicule (cf 11.13a), as K–S–S–K in the second tier, while the third takes the form of a circular *alpa vimana*. The circular shape is carried up from the exterior of the sanctum, which is surrounded by an ambulatory. In the foreground is an *alpa vimana* crowned by a circular *kuta*.

11.12 Agastishvara temple, Kilayur (Tamil Nadu), *c* 884. The basic composition is the most widespread and enduring type for a two-tier shrine (*dvi-tala vimana*), with K–S̄–K surmounted by an *alpa vimana* (cf 11.7d). Subtle variations are made on this type: here a three-storey *shala* aedicule dominates the first tier, articulation of two-storey *kuta* aedicules at the corners being deliberately undermined by an absence of recesses. (Compare the *alpa vimana* form above with 11.9a and b.)
Photo © Gerard Foekema

130 THE TEMPLE ARCHITECTURE OF INDIA

DRAVIDA SHRINES 131

11.13 Later Karnata Dravida aedicules
Note: the letters in brackets show a simple notation used in this book to describe Dravida aedicules and groups of them. Composite aedicules are noted according to the aedicules (or parts of aedicules) of which they are constituted (see also 11.10).

(**a**) Staggered *shala* aedicule (S'P'S) (developing the inherent potential of the architectural language by enlarging the *panjara* that had always fronted a *shala*, and projecting the wall below it to create a central *panjara* aedicule);
(**b**) *panjara-stambha* (Ps) (*panjara* on pillar);
(**c**) *kuta-stambha* (Ks) (*kuta* on pillar);
(**d**) staggered *shala* aedicule with *panjara-stambha* at the centre (S'Ps'S');
(**e**) double-staggered *shala* aedicule (S'S'P'S'S) (triple-staggered etc also appear);
(**f**) double-staggered *shala* aedicule (S'S'P'S'S) with special features: diagonal *gavakshas* on *shala* gable ends, double *gavaksha* (*gavaksha* plus *torana*) at centre of *shala*, large niche or wall-shrine usurping the central projection;
(**g**) *kuta* aedicule combined with half-*shala* aedicule (S'K).

Apart from (**a**), also occasionally used in Tamil traditions (cf 11.11), the range of aedicular components shown here, fully established in the 11th century, is particular to Karnata Dravida and related schools. In addition to *kuta* aedicules and *panjara* aedicules (cf 10.10a, b), (**a**), (**b**), (**c**) and (**e**) are the standard range, (**f**) is an elaboration of (**e**), while (**d**) and (**g**) are examples of the huge variety of composite forms that were created.

shala aedicule (**11.13a**), common by the 10th century, and the double-staggered *shala* aedicule (**11.13e**), established by about AD 1000. These central elements, formed through extra offsets in the *bhadra*, advance the progressive stepping forward of the wall surface and reflect within themselves the centrifugal swell pervading the whole.

If we again define a type as a composition repeated several times, the overall patterns of projections and *talas* constitute general types, while more specific types can be identified by particular aedicule forms in particular positions. Specific types have lasted for centuries in Tamil Nadu, notably the type illustrated in **11.7d**; in the heyday of the Karnata Dravida tradition, types would emerge during each phase, only to be transformed in the general evolution (**6.4b**). One needs to remember that at any time a cheap temple may have flat walls, with or without pilasters, thereby abbreviating a type, and that in the Tamil tradition domed *kutas* and barrel-roofed *shalas* sometimes appear purely as a *hara*, a 'parapet' of linked pavilions, without corresponding wall projections (**11.7c**).

One further, obvious difference between the two main branches of Dravida architecture is that, unlike *vimanas* further south, Karnata Dravida shrines from the 8th century onwards have an antefix (*shuka-nasa*) shafting forth divine power from the front of the superstructure, built over the antechamber (*antarala*) to the sanctum (**23.5**, **23.7**, **25.14**). This practice was taken over from Nagara traditions, but the embedded end-on Valabhi shrine forming the Nagara *shuka-nasa* is replaced by its Dravida equivalent, an embedded end-on *shala*-topped *vimana*. Just as the later development of the Valabhi shrine form takes place in *shuka-nasas*, rectangular *vimana* designs, never favoured by the Karnata Dravida tradition, slide forward from its temple towers.

Stellate Vimanas

During the 11th century, Karnata Dravida *vimanas* with stellate plans emerged as an alternative to orthogonal ones. They are contemporary with Bhumija temples further north based on similar plans and, like stellate Bhumija temples, have acute-angled reentrant projections between the main projections, treated as the tips of deeply embedded aedicules. Many render stellate the typical late Karnata Dravida shrine type with five-projections and four tiers (*talas*): either by placing just the intermediate projections at an angle, to create a 'semi-stellate' plan (**9.1g** lower; **25.16**), or by basing every projection but the central one (*bhadra*) on a rotated square star with 16 points (**9.1e**). In both cases the *bhadra* is treated as the now usual stepped cascade of staggered *shala* aedicules. Other stellate *vimanas* omit the *bhadra* to expose a uniform star. The most common stellate type among the 12th- to 13th-century temples of the Hoysalas in southern Karnataka is based on a star of 16 points, with four *talas*, normally composed entirely of *kuta* aedicules (**9.1h**, **9.14**, **11.16**). The Doddabasappa, Dambal (northern Karnataka), had already taken the possibilities of a uniform stellate *vimana* to the limit, with 24 points and seven *talas* (**25.7**).

11.15 Saunshi (Karnataka), shrine model, originally the superstructure of a niche, *c* 12th century. The composition shown here is the established 'top of the range' type in northern Karnataka from the late 11th century. It has four identical tiers (*talas*), each K–Ks– S'S'P'S'S–Ks–K. In the first tier the secondary aedicules (niches) follow the Dravida version of Phamsana (cf 11.17) and in the recesses are Nagara (Latina) *kuta-stambhas*.
Photo © Gerard Foekema

11.14 Amriteshvara temple, Annigeri (Karnataka), late 11th century: three primary aedicules. Left to right: Dravida *kuta-stambha*, *kuta* aedicule, *panjara-stambha*. Miniature *gavaksha* cascades adorn the upper portions of the two *stambha* elements (cf 3.13). The *kuta* aedicule is at the corner of the shrine, the *panjara-stambha* projecting from the recess (termed the *kapili*) between the shrine and the hall, corresponding to the antechamber (*antarala*) inside. A secondary *kuta* aedicule projects from the primary one – not just 'a false niche crowned by a *kuta*', as some would have it. In the recesses generally are small Dravida *kuta-stambhas* below archway motifs (*toranas*). The shrine at Annigeri has the same composition as the miniature one shown in 11.15, and may have been the first of this type.
Photo © Gerard Foekema

Are There Dravida Modes, and What About the Vesara?

In Chapter 10, discussion of Nagara temples centred around 'modes' – general categories of shrine which at first related to earlier structural roof types, and which came (in the case of the Shekhari, the Bhumija and the Samvarana) to imply particular ways of arranging aedicules. Roof types based on timber and thatch construction forms – domed, tunnel-roofed, apsidal – also underlie the earlier Dravida shrine forms. Simple plan shapes, either confined to the crown or extended down through the whole shrine, figure prominently in the classificatory schemes of canonical texts from Tamil Nadu. Notably, they say that square shrines are Nagara, octagonal shrines are Dravida and circular, elliptical or apsidal shrines are Vesara.[2] At one time this caused confusion among scholars, since the terms are being used in a completely different sense from the one indicated in northern texts. Be that as it may, the attachment of such labels does lend weight to the idea of differently shaped south Indian shrines being equivalent to the north Indian modes, and the analogy is reinforced by the fact that in the Dravida language, as in the Nagara, the basic range of shrines is reflected in the basic range of aedicules. However, when it comes to ways of putting aedicules together, it is fruitless to force comparison with Nagara modes. For Dravida temples, beyond unitary shrines consisting of a single tier, the system is always a matter of arranging the aedicules, cloister-like, around the stages of a stepped pyramid, whatever the plan shape of the crowning element or of the shrine as a whole – even if it is stellate.

In this context we need to consider the term 'Vesara' in its more widespread sense. North Indian texts repeatedly use the tripartite classification of Nagara, Dravida and Vesara. Nagara and Dravida, broadly speaking, respectively mean northern and southern temple architecture, while the term 'Vesara', related to the word for a mule, seems to imply some kind of hybrid between the two. It is now generally agreed that 'Vesara' probably refers to the temples typical from the 11th century in Karnataka and elsewhere in the Deccan. This region is geographically between north and south and at certain periods its craftsmen built Nagara as well as Dravida temples. Its typical 11th- to 13th-century temples, while basically Dravida, do have Nagara-like aspects. Their entire architectural vocabulary is Dravida, however, and the characteristics they share with Nagara temples – staggered plans, radial segments including a central spine, a barely stepped profile – do not appear suddenly, as if taken over ready-made, but emerge gradually through tendencies already apparent in Karnataka by the 8th century,

11.16 Chenna-Keshava temple, Aralguppe (Karnataka), *c* early 13th century. This is a uniform stellate shrine based on a 16-point star, with four *talas*, made up entirely of *kuta* aedicules. The aedicular composition is only superficially disguised by features typical of temples built in southern Karnataka under the Hoysalas: the banded plinth and the two-tier wall shaded by a canopy (*chhadya*). Photo © Gerard Foekema

and which distinguish the region's Dravida tradition from that of Tamil Nadu. Although ingenious mixtures of Nagara and Dravida were indeed popular in Karnataka (see Chapter 25), the supposedly Vesara temples are not this kind of deliberate hybrid, but rather are reminiscent of Nagara temples because they have evolved in a similar way, through a similar way of thinking. In the process of transformation, however, there is no decisive stage like the moment when Latina becomes Shekhari: it is impossible to say when temples have ceased to be Dravida and become Vesara. While the later temples look very different from the earlier ones, they are not a new mode, especially as their most basic organising principle remains that of a tiered pyramid. It therefore seems best to abandon the term 'Vesara' in favour of 'late Karnata Dravida', reflecting the continuity of the tradition.

On the question of whether there are Dravida modes, one other kind of temple needs to be mentioned: the Dravida version of Phamsana, common throughout the lower Deccan as a more modest alternative to the usual Dravida. Having already accorded northern Phamsana the status of a Nagara mode, the southern one perhaps deserves similar treatment, although it does not play a comparable role as a primary aedicule form in other kinds of temple. The 7th- to 8th-century Phamsana shrines of the Early Chalukyas were Nagara in their detailing. Phamsana temples reappear in the Deccan from the 11th century, this time built by masons of the Karnata Dravida tradition (**11.17**).

11.17 Lakshmidevi temple, Dodda Gaddavalli (Karnataka), 1117. The shrines here are the Karnata Dravida version of Phamsana, widespread in Karnataka and Andhra Pradesh. They have typical Karnata Dravida bases and walls, roofed by a shallow pyramid of eave mouldings and crowned by a Karnata Dravida dome. The fronton (*shuka-nasa*) of the one shown centre left is entirely Karnata Dravida.
Photo © Gerard Foekema

Notes
1 Stella Kramrisch calls the crowning *kuta* the 'High Temple' (*The Hindu Temple* [Calcutta: University of Calcutta, 1946], p 194), so I am using 'upper temple' to denote the crowning *alpa vimana* to avoid confusion.
2 Ibid.

DRAVIDA SHRINES 135

12   Geometry

While one of the signs of a civilised mind is to be awestruck at the mystery of geometry, one of the quickest routes to mystification is to look for geometry in architecture. It is easy to imagine that a diagram in a plan is more significant than the building itself. Even if one's discoveries are really there in the building, one cannot know for certain whether the building was designed in terms of a geometrical figure, a grid, a system of measurement, a modular system, a set of proportions, or some or all of these things together, since the mystery is such that they all may contain one another. Indian temple architecture gives great scope for delusion in these respects, and all claims to reveal its geometrical principles, even if asserted by the *shastras* themselves, should be treated with scepticism, this chapter included.

That said, far more than most kinds of architecture, Indian temples wear their geometry on their faces, so that sometimes a particular geometry clicks, and it is clear that the shape could not have been made any other way. Architectural imagery did not originate in geometry, but geometrical ideas could lead to new ways of putting it together. Architecture was not simply adapted to fit geometry: the aedicular language had its own formal requirements, and a geometrical pattern was not useful if these had to be distorted beyond recognition. Sometimes a desire to realise a particular formal idea led to new geometrical patterns. Perhaps even new geometrical discoveries were made in the service of architecture: certainly, mathematicians recognise that early Indian geometry owes its sophistication to its practical use in setting out Vedic altars with chords and pegs,[1] as documented in the Sulba Sutras, the 4th- to 3rd-century BC manuals on that subject. If geometry could inspire and be inspired by architectural designs, it could also help to fossilise them: mystery becomes mystique, and a way to do something becomes an instruction.

Most inspiring and mysterious about geometry was the way it starts from a point and unfolds towards infinity, one figure giving birth to another. Relationships between geometry and the emergent forms of Indian temples must be considered not merely in terms of static shapes, but of processes. In the act of orienting and then setting out a temple, geometry unfolded before people's eyes, showing them that a universe of emanation is how things really are.

Orientation, the Extended Gnomon Diagram and the Circle-and-Square Sequence

Apart from any cosmic symbolism in its architectural forms, and aside from astrological calculations for determining the appropriate time for its foundation, the process of establishing the orientation of a temple bound it to the earth, the sun and their relationship at that moment of origination. The method of orientation, known as the 'Indian circle method', was based on the use of an instrument, not unique to India, known as the gnomon or *shanku-yantra* (*yantra* = 'instrument'), an 'ancient device for determining the east–west direction as well as for knowing time'.[2] This method seems to have been a deep inspiration for the geometry of temple plans and its development: at least, the process involved is a perfect starting point for constructing this geometry on the ground. Indian astronomical and architectural texts give detailed instructions for making various kinds of gnomon, but essentially the instrument is a vertical pole, about the size of a cricket stump. It is erected on a level surface, and a small circle drawn around it using a chord. In the morning the shadow of the gnomon will shrink as the sun rises until its tip touches the circumference of the circle; in the afternoon, as the shadow lengthens its tip will again touch the circumference. The line between the two points runs from east to west. Complicated methods were developed for making corrections to take account of variations in the declination of the sun at different latitudes. However, at many sites there are slight differences in the orientation of the shrines, presumably because of uncorrected orientation procedures, suggesting that the place, the time of foundation and the process itself counted more than strict orientation.

If, as can be imagined, it was important to generate a temple plan from the original circle, rather than moving over to the east–west line and drawing a new circle, then a parallel line had to be drawn through the centre of the original circle. Complex methods were apparently devised to do this,[3] although it could easily be done by striking arcs with the chord. Striking arcs will also set up the north–south axis. The next step was to draw four circles of the same size as the original one, centred on the points where the axes cross the circumference, resulting in a figure which may be called the 'extended gnomon diagram' (**12.1a**).[4]

This simple shape is pregnant with further shapes. First, it gives a square fitting perfectly around the first circle. Second, it leads on to the beautiful sequence of nested circles and squares (**12.1b**). If a second circle is drawn around this first square, and the same process repeated as with the first circle, a second square is generated, a third circle, a third square and so on *ad infinitum*. The sides of the third square will measure twice those of the first, its area therefore being four times that of the first square, and so on. Also inherent in this geometry are diagonal squares (**12.1c**), giving the sequence of nested octagons and 8-pointed stars known to the medieval European masons as *ad quadratum*. Furthermore, the 'extended gnomon diagram' contains a hexagon with an inscribed 6-pointed star (hexagram) made of equilateral triangles, and a dodecagon with an inscribed 12-pointed star, which can be made of equilateral triangles or of squares (**12.1d**). All of this has implications for the plans of shrines, both orthogonal and stellate.[5]

Orthogonal Plans

Orthogonal grids are most evident among early Nagara temples of central and western India. Studies by Michael Meister have shown that such temples of the 6th and 7th centuries typically follow a grid of 8 x 8 squares, with the sanctum twice the basic width of the walls (**12.2**).[6] Relevant dimensions must usually be taken at the *khura* ('hoof') of the moulded base. A central projection (*bhadra*) often corresponds in width to the sanctum and a further projection (*subhadra*) to half of this (the 'Brahma-sthana' of the *vastu-purusha-mandala*). An alternative system appeared in the 8th century, using the same grid but with its outer limits in line with the *bhadras* instead of the corners, allowing the walls to be thinner (**12.2c**).

Whether or not these grids have anything to do with the *vastu-purusha-mandala*, their presence is clear. This does not mean that the grid was a primary consideration, or that it was used to generate the plan. After all, the 'extended gnomon diagram' and its further extension into nested squares will give the same result. It is sufficient to expand out from the first square (suitable, perhaps, for the *subhadra* of a small

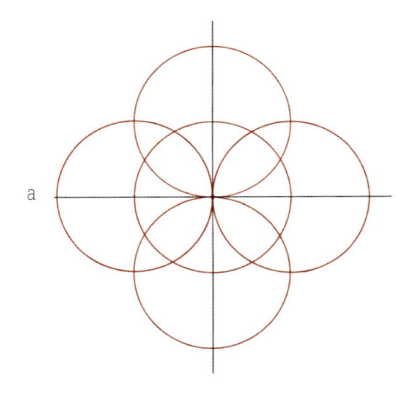

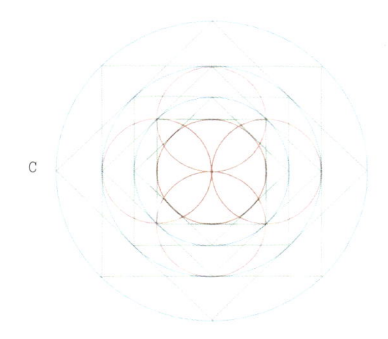

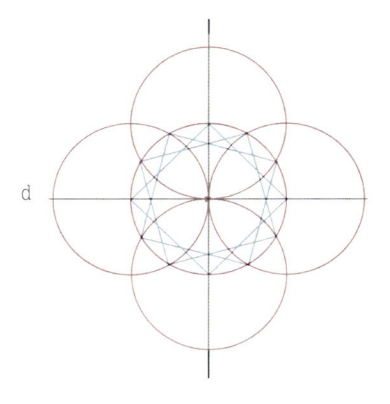

12.1 The extended gnomon diagram: (**a**) basic diagram; (**b**) generating nested squares and circles; (**c**) showing diagonal squares; (**d**) showing the inherent 12-point star.

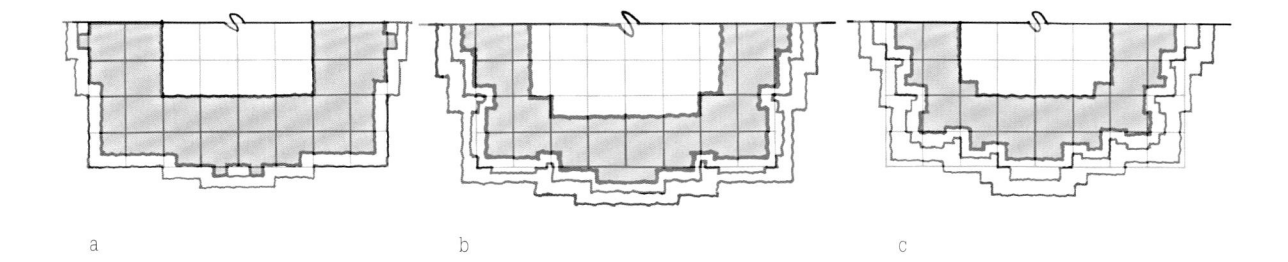

12.2 Plans following an 8 x 8 grid: (**a**) Mahadeva temple, Amrol (MP); (**b**) Surya temple, Umri (MP); (**c**) Surya temple, Madkheda (MP). After Michael Meister.

shrine, or for a *linga* base) to a suitable sanctum size, and then carry on to the second square beyond that, and one can make walls half the width of the sanctum, all perfectly rectilinear and without having to take a single measurement. Grids are less cosmic than this, and much less practical. However, before discounting grids, at least in south India, it should be pointed out that careful measurements of the large Chola temples have revealed planning grids not so easily explained in terms of turning out circles with ropes: 30 x 30 squares for the *vimana* at Tanjavur, and 11 x 11 at Gangaikondacholapuram.[7]

Moreover, in the three-dimensional forms of the more complex Shekhari shrines, grids are not merely present, but intrinsic to the nature of particular types. Figure **12.3** shows the roof plans of the five principal types introduced in Chapter 10. Roof plans are far more important than ground plans for understanding these forms, since the plan changes from level to level. It was by working out the roof plans that I was able to draw the axonometrics (**10.16**). These are the first published roof plans and 3-d drawings of Shekhari shrines done without fudging[8] – any others should be viewed with extreme caution! For the simpler kinds, Types 1 and 2, the grids shown are simply probable ones, but there can easily be variations without changing the basic forms. With Types 3, 4 and 5, however, with their stepped diamond plans, a particular diagonal grid is immutably fixed by lines joining the serrated corners (the *kuta-stambhas*) and linking these to the main *shikhara* forms, ie the central tower (*mula-manjari*) and the first of the emergent *shikharas* (the first *urah-shringas*). This diagonal continuity is enhanced in Types 3 and 4, where reentrant projections (one-quarter exposed *kuta-stambhas*) lead up to quarter *shringas*. A corresponding orthogonal grid underlies the overlapping squares which position the aedicular components.

In Type 3, the first and second *urah-shringas* are defined purely by the orthogonal grid. In Types 4 and 5 a miraculous geometrical figure governs the *urah-shringas*, allowing the intricate three-dimensional composition to snap together with perfection. This is the 8-pointed star obtained when each pair of adjacent corners of a square is linked to the middle of the opposite side.[9] Its operation can be seen in the superstructures of Types 4 and 5, where the second *urah-shringas* (second out from the centre) and the corresponding quarter-*shringas*, which occupy the reentrant positions at the same level, clearly push out beyond the grid lines – their swelling accommodated by the shrinking (within their controlling squares) of the adjacent *kuta-stambhas*. The extent of this transgression of the gridlines is not arbitrary, but governed by the magic lines.

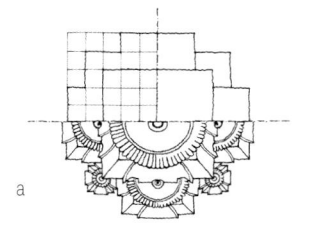

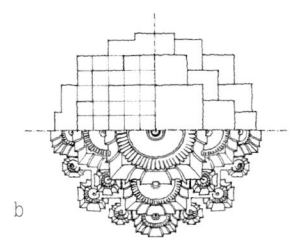

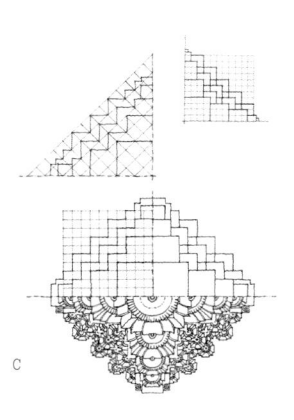

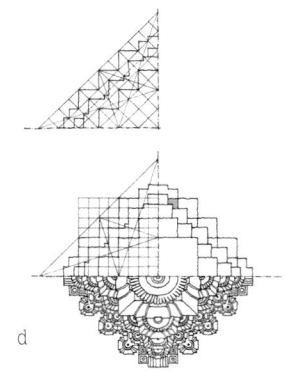

The quasi-organic blossoming out of Shekhari temple designs followed its formal logic of proliferating parts (**6.4**), rather than a quest to fit the forms into a set of preconceived diagrams. Yet this evolution took place through the interplay of compositional ideas and geometrical possibilities, new geometries springing from a desire for new shapes as much as the other way round. Thus, when the architects had progressed from Type 1 via an extra tier to Type 2, and then wished to add another tier with seven projections and a third *urah-shringa*, they would have found that the formal norms have already imposed a limit: if they continued to use an expanding square plan, there would be room only for an absurdly narrow third *urah-shringa*, narrower than the *shikharas* of the *kuta-stambhas*. Fortunately, the solution was to hand in a stepped diamond plan. Not only would this provide a suitable grid and advance the forward bulge of the *bhadra*, but it would also allow plenty of room for a proper third *urah-shringa*. In the transition from Type 4 to Type 5, it was clearly a need to keep the 'magic lines' intact that dictated both the denser orthogonal grid and the compression of the *kuta-stambha* zone, which resulted in protruding reentrants. As for the magic lines themselves, it would be interesting to know whether this geometrical figure was already known. If so, it would have been useful for setting up the grids that it inherently contains, and it might have been brought into service in Shekhari towers because it so neatly solved a formal problem which they posed. Or perhaps it was by working out Shekhari forms that the temple architects discovered the diagram, in which case they must have felt even greater awe than I did when I teased it out of their creations.

Stellate Plans

It is not difficult to see that stellate temple geometry is not a complete departure from orthogonal temple geometry. Both are latent in the extended gnomon diagram and the expanding sequence of circles and squares. It is with stellate plans that architectural designs seem most

12.3 Roof plans of the five standard types of Shekhari temple: (**a**) Type 1; (**b**) Type 2; (**c**) Type 3 (alternative geometry top right); (**d**) Type 4.

directly to have been generated by a range of geometrical possibilities, but even here the geometry can only be useful if it can meaningfully position a collection of aedicules. Stellate temple plans can be grouped into two categories, corresponding to two phases. The first includes the greatly varied stellate and semi-stellate plans of 7th- to 8th-century Dakshina Koshala and a few stellate Latina shrines up to the 10th century, the second comprising the more regular set of permutations applied to stellate Bhumija and stellate Karnata Dravida temples (**9.1f**, **g**, **h**).

Figure **12.5** gives examples of the first category. One repeated underlying pattern among Dakshina Koshala temples fixes the corners on the third square out from the inner sanctum (ie to give a basic wall thickness half the latter's width), and flanks the central projections (*bhadras*) with diagonal or rotated projections relating to a diagonal square constructed by repetition of the first circle along its cardinal axes as in **17.11b**.[10]

In the later stellate shrines, both Bhumija and Karnata Dravida, the basic principle is that of rotated squares (**12.6**). Since points are generally expected to fall on the cardinal axes (even if 'hidden' by the *bhadra*) and the diagonals, the normal range of options consists of stars with 8, 16, 24 and 32 points.[11] An 8-pointed star is inherent in the extended gnomon diagram, so it is a matter of bisecting angles to arrive at 16 and 32, joining appropriate points on the outer circle to make the rotated squares. As we have seen, the extended gnomon diagram also contains 6- and 12-pointed figures, so the same procedure will allow construction of a 24-point star. If preferred, rather than simply bisecting angles, the universe can be churned out through giddy rites of walking in many circles.

As in the case of stepped diamond shrines, scholarship has not appreciated the importance of the reentrant projections between the main ones, in terms of both aedicular composition and geometry. Their points are normally 45° or 60°. An octagon (therefore also the extended gnomon diagram) contains the 'extended star octagon' with points of 45°, as shown inscribed in **12.6a**. Stars with 16, 24 and 32 points can therefore be given reentrant projections with 45° points by joining appropriate groups of 8 inner angles. Stars with 16-points can be given 60° reentrants by joining every 5th inner angle (**12.6b**), 32-point stars by joining every 11th, in both cases carrying on round and round until one gets back to the starting point and the figure closes. A 24-point star, if the appropriate inner angles are joined, contains 8 equilateral triangles, giving 60° points to the reentrants (**12.6c**).

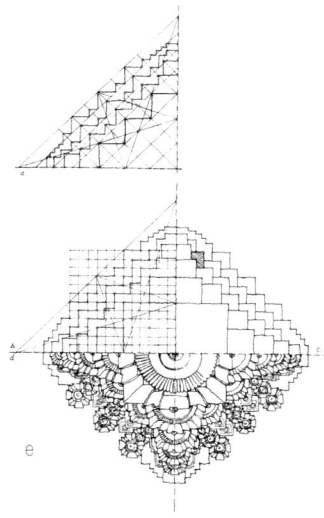

12.3 cont'd: (**e**) Type 5.

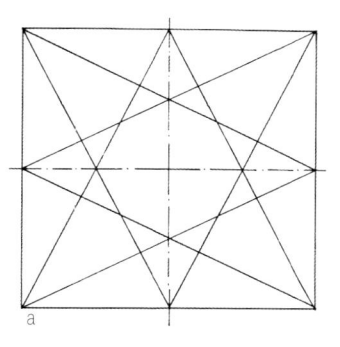

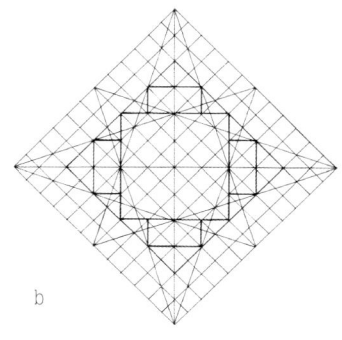

12.4 'Magic lines' governing the half-spires (*urah-shringas*) in Shekhari Types 4 and 5: (**a**) basic diagram; (**b**) showing how it corresponds to the grid of Type 4, and gives first (uppermost) *urah-shringas* which are half the size of the central spire (*mula-manjari*).

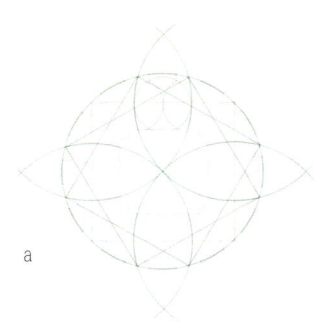

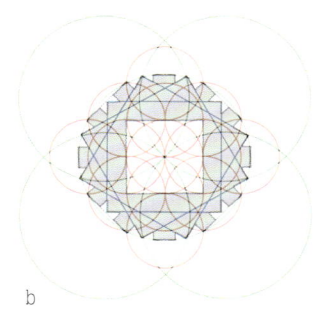

12.5 Stellate plans of c late 8th century: (**a**) Shiva temple, Indor (MP), c 750–75; (**b**) Brick temple, Nimiyakheda (UP). Cf 18.3 and 18.16.

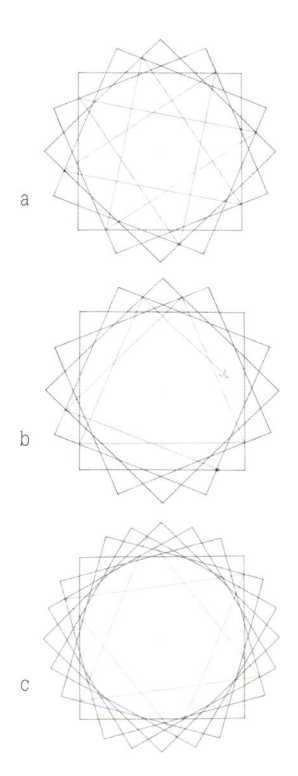

12.6 Stellate geometry: (**a**) 16-point star with 45° reentrant projections; (**b**) 16-point star with 60° reentrant projections; (**c**) 24-point star with 60° reentrant projections.

That the geometry emanating from the extended gnomon diagram can generate and bind together an entire temple plan is shown in figure **12.7**.

Elevations

In building up vertically from a plan, again the visual, representational logic of aedicular forms cannot be transgressed. The familiar images cannot become too fat or too thin; but within these limits there is enormous variety. Texts prescribe relative proportions between the main horizontal divisions of temple elevations, and between their subdivisions, but in the monuments themselves variation is the norm.

There is evidence of the use of modules, and that the module used in an elevation was not necessarily tied to the grid inherent in the plan,[12] and that different modules might even be used for different parts of the building.[13] When I drew the elevations for this book (by eye, from photographs), it often seemed that the pilaster width was a module. This is clearly the case in brick temples where pilasters are one brick wide (eg **17.10**). The grids used to make *gavaksha* patterns and their underlying eave mouldings (see **16.11–16.14**) are intrinsically modular, and instantly readable in an elevation once the system is understood. However, these grids do not necessarily point to an overall system, as they are usually of varying sizes within a single elevation.

The geometry of temple superstructures is more complicated because of the question of diminution and, for Nagara *shikharas*, of curvature. To draw them in elevation is relatively easy. A regularly diminishing, multi-tier Dravida superstructure can be drawn by tracing lines from the horizontal divisions at its base to a point somewhere above the finial: if the resulting fan of lines is crossed by an oblique line, the intersections will mark horizontal divisions in a regularly diminishing series. The curve of a Latina *shikhara* can be drawn with a compass. It follows an arc of a circle, normally beginning one *bhumi* above the *shikhara* base, sweeping up to the shoulder (*skandha*), which is normally the size of the sanctum. The radius of the curve varies greatly, but it is supposedly a multiple of the width of the *shikhara* at its base.[14] In Shekhari superstructures the radii followed by the various species of spire are not all the same, in proportion to the widths, but increase in the larger, higher ones, enhancing the sense of upward swelling. The diminution of the *bhumis* in a Nagara *shikhara* can be drawn in a way similar to the one described for Dravida towers, but with intersecting arcs rather than a fan of straight lines. But one cannot draw lines and circles in the sky. So, if they did not use scale drawings, the builders must have calculated the shrinking of each stage by some kind of arithmetical or geometrical progression.[15]

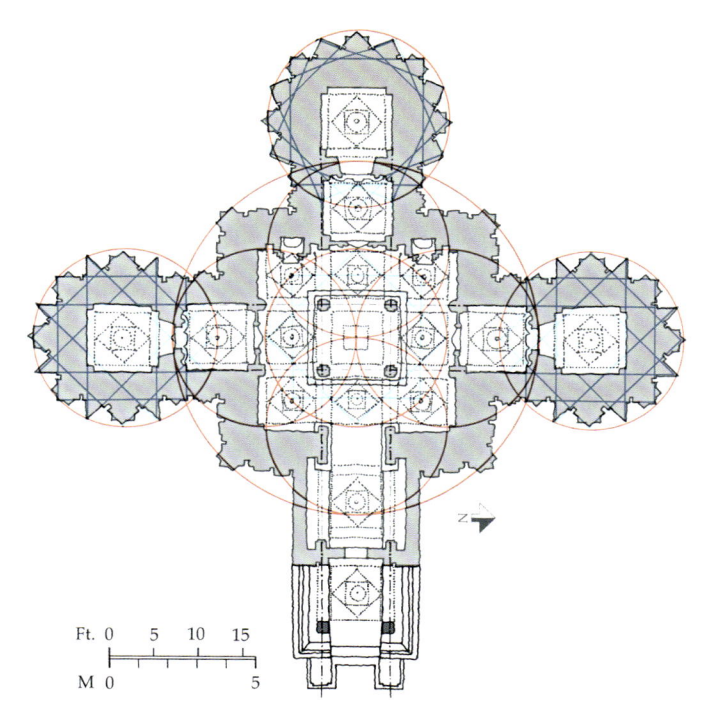

12.7 Geometry of the Lakshmi-Narasimha temple, Bhadravati (Karnataka), 13th century.

Notes

1. Melvin Bragg's *In Our Time* on Indian Mathematics, BBC Radio 4, 14 November 2006.
2. Yujio Ohashi, 'Astronomical Instruments in Classical Siddhantas', *Indian Journal of History of Science* 29(2), 1994, pp 155–313 (p 168).
3. Ibid. pp 182–5; for another method, see Adrian Snodgrass, *The Symbolism of the Stupa* (Delhi: Motilal Banarassidass, 1992), p 15.
4. This geometry was 'prescribed in the texts of the fourth and third centuries BC for locating the square of the brick altar', Michael W Meister, 'Measurement and Proportion in Hindu Temple Architecture', *Interdisciplinary Science Reviews* 10(3), 1985, pp 248–58 (p 255); (and cf note 1).
5. For evidence that various star polygons could determine aspects of non-stellate temples, see Philip E Harding, 'South Asian Geometry and the Durga Temple, Aihole', *South Asian Studies* 20, 2003, pp 25–36.
6. Michael W Meister, 'Mandala and Practice in Nagara Architecture in North India', *Journal of the American Oriental Society* 99, pp 204–19, and reference in note 4.
7. Pierre Pichard, *Tanjavur Bṛhadīśvara, An Architectural Study* (Delhi: IGNCA and École Française de l'Extrème Orient, 1995).
8. See Adam Hardy, 'Sekhari Temples', *Artibus Asiae* 62, 1, (2002), pp 81–137.
9. For properties of this 'extremely well-known' figure see Tons Brunés, *The Secrets of Ancient Geometry* (Copenhagen: Rhodos International Science Publishers, 1967), pp 90–7.
10. Cf analyses by Michael W Meister, 'Measurement and Proportion', p 255 and 'Analysis of temple forms: Indor', *Artibus Asiae* 43 (1982), pp 302–20.
11. Meister points out examples of Bhumija temples with, he argues, stars of 20 and 28 points: see 'Reading monuments and seeing texts' in Anna Dallapoccola (ed), *The Shastric Tradition* (Stuttgart: Franz Steiner, 1989), pp 167–73 (pp 171–2).
12. Pierre Pichard in *Tanjavur Bṛhadīśvara* shows a modular elevation for the Brihadeshvara, Gangaikondacholapuram, in which the module is the pilaster width. The elevation is 73 modules wide, although the plan is based on a grid of 11 x 11 squares.
13. An Orissan text prescribes a vertical module (*mulasutra*) 11/4 times that of the ground plan. See Alice Boner, 'Extracts from the Silpasarini' in P Chandra (ed), *Studies in Indian Temple Architecture* (New Delhi: AIIS, 1975), pp 57–79 (p 68).
14. See Michael W Meister, 'On the development of a morphology for a symbolic architecture', *Res* 12, 1986, pp 33–50 (pp 39–40). Ananya Gandotra argues that these radii follow a circle-square sequence related to the plan in *A Geometrical Analysis of North Indian Style Temple Architecture*, PhD thesis, Cardiff University, 2007.
15. The texts enumerate many kinds of '*rekha*', but it is not clear whether this refers to curvature or diminution. I have not met anybody who could make sense of the drawings and explanations of the *rekha* in Kramrisch's *The Hindu Temple*, pp 205–14. See also Patrick A George, 'Counting Curvature: The numerical roots of North Indian temple architecture and Frank Gehry's "digital curvatures"', *Res* 34, 1998, pp 128–41.

13 MOULDINGS

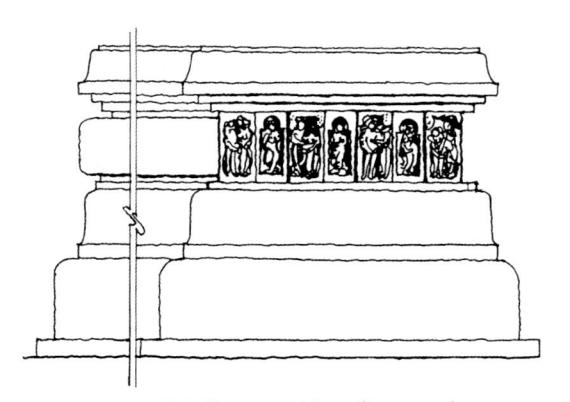

13.1 Nagara mouldings: Gupta temple, Deogarh (MP), *c* 500; mouldings of the platform (*jagati*). To the left, over a plain base course (*bhitta*), rise the three mouldings which would remain the standard ones for a Nagara base (*vedibandha*). First is the *kumbha* ('pot' or 'vase'), a foot moulding. Second comes the *kalasha* (also 'pot' or 'vase'), a cushion moulding. At the top is the *kapotali* ('abode of doves'), an eave moulding. Projections (right) are given an alternative treatment, where the place of the *kalasha* is taken by a recess or *gala*, an inhabitable gallery sheltered by the *kapotali* eave. The base thus represents a miniature storey.

The characteristic, in fact, of Hindu architecture in general is that it is entirely devoid of 'style'; it is a medley or fantastic riot of details crammed together merely for the sake of covering the walls with detail, without any consideration of balance or proportion of parts, or beauty of outline; and as to mouldings, there are no such things in the true sense of the word.[1]

Indian temple mouldings[2] are not the same as western classical ones. While their profiles are often similar, as there are not a hundred ways to shape a stone (so one finds curved mouldings and rounded ones, the Indian equivalents of the cyma and the torus), in Indian temple architecture mouldings exist not as edgings or modulations to other elements, but as elements within larger elements. In this respect they are more akin to the architrave, frieze and cornice in a classical pediment than to mouldings within these. Like Hindu deities or notes on a scale, they are significant entities and come in sequences.

Mouldings run horizontally, closely linked to the process of piling up courses of masonry. Normally each moulding corresponds to one course; confusion arises if its constituent members or 'sub-mouldings' are read as separate mouldings. In a multi-aedicular temple composition, one made up of multiple representations of shrines, it is out of the bed of mouldings that these architectural images are articulated. The only vertical equivalents of the mouldings are the bands bordering doorways and windows: the bands (*shakas*) around doors follow carefully chosen sequences, but, unlike mouldings, are defined more by their ornamental treatment than by their basic shape.

Leaving aside the regular eave strata of a Nagara superstructure, moulding sequences appear principally in the bands of masonry supporting and crowning a temple wall. The moulded base is called *vedibandha* in Nagara architecture, *adisthana* in Dravida: in the former, floor level is normally at the foot of this element, in the latter it sits above it. Sub-bases or pedestals are introduced, and made increasingly elaborate. A sub-base is termed *pitha* for Nagara temples, *upapitha* for

144 THE TEMPLE ARCHITECTURE OF INDIA

13.2 Nagara mouldings: the Latina shrine of the Rameshvara Mahadeva temple, Amrol (MP), c 725–50; central projection (*bhadra*) with lower part of spine (*lata*) in superstructure. The *vedibandha* has the now standard triplet of mouldings, with the *kalasha* more vase-like than the rounded 'torus' at Deogarh (13.1). The cornice zone (*varandika*) is an elaborate one, beginning (as always) with a *kapotali* eave moulding, terminating the 'storey' of the wall. Next is a *chippika* (minor cyma moulding) ornamented with lotus petals, equivalent to the Dravida *vedika* (cf 13.5), but not so obviously representing a railing. The next moulding is a plain *pattika* (fillet). Above is a *tula-pitha*, representing the ends of floor joists, capped by another *kapotali*. This *kapotali*, while terminating the *varandika*, is also logically part of the superstructure (*shikhara*), equivalent to the *kapotalis* commencing each of the subsequent tiers (*bhumis*) (cf 18.2b). At the head of the wall is a decorative band of swags, called a *kinkinika-mala*, named after the little bells (*kinkinika*).

13.3 Nagara mouldings: the main, Bhumija shrine of the Gondeshvara temple, Sinnar (Maharashtra), 12th century; corner projection in first *bhumi*, forming a *kuta-stambha*. By this date, a temple is usually raised on an elaborate sub-base or pedestal (*pitha*), stepping out without recesses. Here this forms a miniature storey in itself. The first three mouldings are compressed equivalents to the *kumbha–kalasha–kapotali* sequence, carrying a double-curved rail moulding (*vedika*) and a colonnaded recess with elephants, sheltered by a *kapotali* roof. The base proper (*vedibandha*) is the normal sequence, but by now the *khura* ('hoof') of the *kumbha* has become differentiated (in this case it is a separate course), giving a composite *khura-kumbha*. Above the *vedibandha*, the projection in the wall (*jangha*, 'thigh') constitutes a pillar (*stambha*) of the cushion type (14.4), on its own moulded base, again equivalent to the *kumbha–kalasha–kapotali* sequence, in miniature. The *varandika* is a single *kapotali* divided from the *jangha* below by a *chhadya* canopy which, like the sub-base, forms a continuous horizontal band, without recesses.

13.4 Nagara mouldings: Navalakha temple, Sejakpur (Gujarat), 12th century open hall; Porches and open halls are often surrounded by a seat (*sopana*) with a raked back (*kash-asana*). This usually sits over a wide frieze of miniature *kuta-stambhas*. Here the *kuta-stambhas* are crowned by the bell-topped pavilions seen in Samvarana (composite Phamsana) roofs; the frieze has Valabhi aedicules at the pillar positions, and is set over a course treated as a miniature colonnade with its own base and eave.

The parts below this are generally, for open halls, a continuation either of the moulded base (*vedibandha* or *adisthana*) or of the sub-base (*pitha* or *upapitha*) of the temple as a whole. Here it is the *pitha* which holds the entire temple aloft, supporting the *vedibandha* in the solid parts of the wall (cf 19.9). The *pitha* mouldings are typical for western India at this date. The lower ones are compressed versions of the *kumbha–kalasha–kapotali* sequence, with a recess (*antara-patta*) below the eave.[3] They support a frieze of monster faces (*kirti-mukha* or *grasa-mukha*, the frieze thus a '*grasa-patti*'), surmounted by a band of elephants (*gaja-pitha*) and of men (*nara-pitha*), each roofed by its own miniature *kapotali*. Even more elaborate temples would interpose a band of horses (*ashva-pitha*) between these. The *pitha* sits over stepped courses or *bhittas*, sometimes ornamented and varying in number.

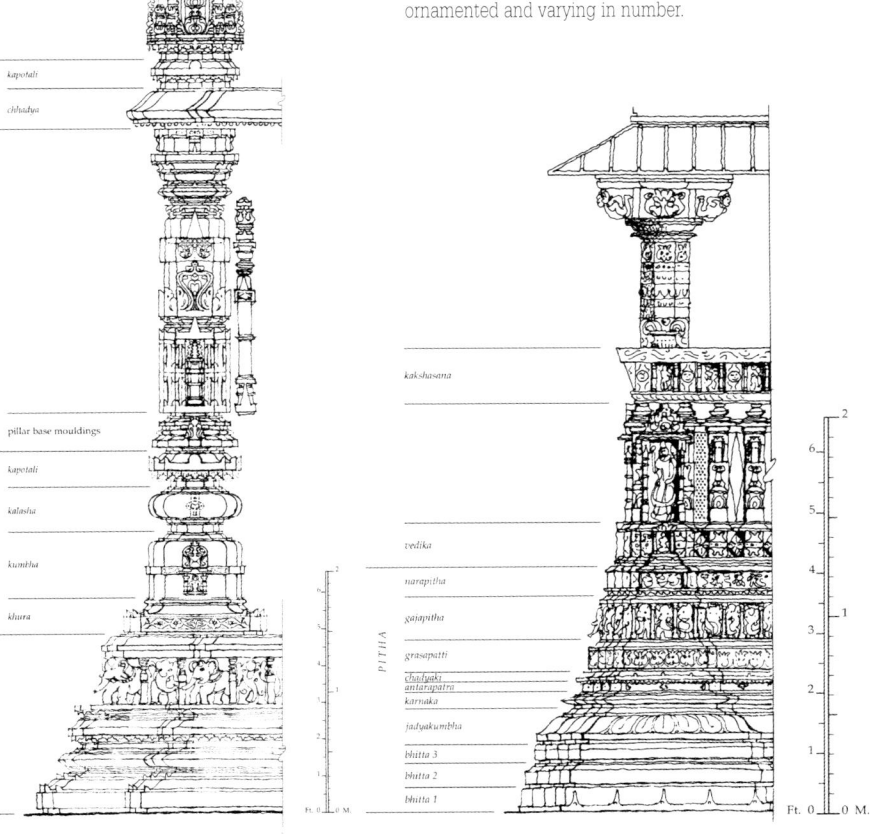

MOULDINGS 145

the populated colonnade that it had once been (Cave 3, Badami; Meguti temple, Aihole). The Dravida *kapota* ('dove') eave moulding is distinguished in contemporary academic usage, following southern texts, from the Nagara *kapotali*, on the basis that the typical Dravida version is a rounded, single curve, whereas in Nagara temples it is a double-curved 'cyma'. To confuse matters, however, Dravida *kapotas* often have a slight outwards sweep at the base, and in Karnataka this becomes usual in the 8th century, thereafter transformed into a distinct 'S' curve. Above the *adisthana* are two optional mouldings at the foot of the wall. First is the floor moulding (usually corresponding to the actual floor level inside), the *prati* or *prati-kantha* ('plank-recess'). This is a complex moulding, far more so than the Nagara *tula-pitha*. Floor planks are represented by a projecting fillet, with the 'joist ends' often treated as creatures, typically, as here, busts of *vyalas* (horned lions) and heads of *makaras* (peacock-tailed crocodiles). Where there are *vyalas*, the moulding is called a *vyala-mala* (garland of *vyalas*). Above sits the *vedika* or rail moulding.

The wall (*pada*, 'leg', literally 'foot') is crowned by a *kapota* eave, which supports the upper pavilion of the aedicule. Tamil Dravida and early Karnata Dravida temples have a decorated sub-moulding under the *kapota*, usually a separate course, treated as a garland of dwarves (*bhuta-mala*) or, as here, of geese (*hamsa-mala*). The upper pavilion, in this case a *panjara*, has a floor (*prati*), a railing (*vedika*), an inhabitable balcony space (*griva*, 'neck') and a roof (*shikhara*). Thus, the sequence *kapota-prati-vedika* appears twice here, above and below the wall. A miniature *kuta* aedicule sits in the gable of the *panjara*.

13.5 Dravida mouldings: Mallikarjuna temple, Pattadakal (Karnataka), *c* 742; intermediate projection of first tier (*tala*), forming a *panjara* aedicule (containing a secondary *panjara* aedicule). Whereas, in the Tamil tradition, a variety of moulding sequences is used for the base (*adisthana*) (13.7), in the Karnata tradition the sequence illustrated here had been established as the norm by the early 8th century. The *adisthana* proper is the Dravida equivalent of the Nagara *vedibandha* sequence. The *jagati* is the foot moulding, equivalent to the Nagara *kumbha* or *khura-kumbha*. Equivalent to the *kalasha* is the cushion moulding, the *kumuda* (one of the words for 'lotus'). This comes in various forms: here it is three-faceted (*tri-patta*). Above this is a recess *gala* which, though still a separate course of masonry, is no longer

13.6 Dravida mouldings: Trikuteshvara temple, Gadag (Karnataka), second half of 11th century; corner projection of first *tala*, forming a *kuta* aedicule (containing a secondary *kuta* aedicule). Although the moulding shapes have been transformed, their sequence is the same as in 13.5, except that the recesses (*gala* and *griva*) have narrowed and ceased to be separate courses, belonging now to the lower *kapota* and the *shikhara* respectively. One or more plain plinth courses (*upana*) are optional. The drawing shows a vase-finial (*stupi* or *kalasha*). As is often the case, these elements have been lost from the actual temple.

146 THE TEMPLE ARCHITECTURE OF INDIA

Dravida ones. At the top of each Dravida tier (*tala*), the eave cornice (*kapota*) supports the mouldings composing the *hara* of pavilions. In Nagara shrines the wall is divided from the superstructure by the mouldings of the cornice zone (*varandika*).

The terminology for mouldings, brought to light by recent scholarship,[4] differed from one region to another. Here I am following the Sanskrit terms now generally accepted for Nagara and Dravida temples respectively. It will be noticed that the mouldings of the two architectural languages are closely related, Dravida moulding types having Nagara equivalents and vice versa. Regardless of names, mouldings are of just a few general kinds. The classes of moulding springing directly from an imagery of wooden buildings are: roof and eave mouldings; recesses treated as habitable spaces such as verandas or colonnades; railing mouldings (*vedika*, 'railing', can also mean and imply 'altar'); floor mouldings. Further categories are cushion mouldings and foot mouldings, both 'bearing elements'; and lastly there are projecting bands or fillets. These representational and expressive characteristics of mouldings govern their relative positions.

As for style, in the sense of the character imparted by the way of making things peculiar to a particular group of people, this is most palpable in the mouldings. Through their shapes and details, regional and local idioms speak. Now, blessed by travel, photography and a notion of history, we can witness the gradual metamorphosis of moulding shapes in the various traditions, across centuries. Not all the variations and transformations were unconscious: it was often on the mouldings of temples that their makers would lavish invention, wit and sensibility. Gods are in the details.

Notes
1. H Heathcote Statham, *Architecture for General Readers* (London: Chapman & Hall, 1909), p 293.
2. 'There is no corresponding term for the word "moulding" in the Sanskrit texts. In Gujarat, the craftsmen use the term "Ghatadum" for it; which is derived from the Sanskrit word "ghata" meaning "form" or "shape".' Personal email communication to author from MA Dhaky, April 2006.
3. The terms used here are from MA Dhaky, 'The Genesis and Development of Maru-Gurjara Temple Architecture' in Pramod Chandra (ed), *Studies in Indian Temple Architecture* (New Delhi: AIIS, 1975).
4. Especially by MA Dhaky, and embodied in the *Encyclopaedia of Indian Temple Architecture*.
5. I am avoiding the typology for *adisthanas* ('*padmabandha*', '*kapotabandha*' etc) given in EITA vol 1, 1999), which I have never understood, as it defines some types by small details and does not make the basic sequences clear, even if it is true to ancient texts.

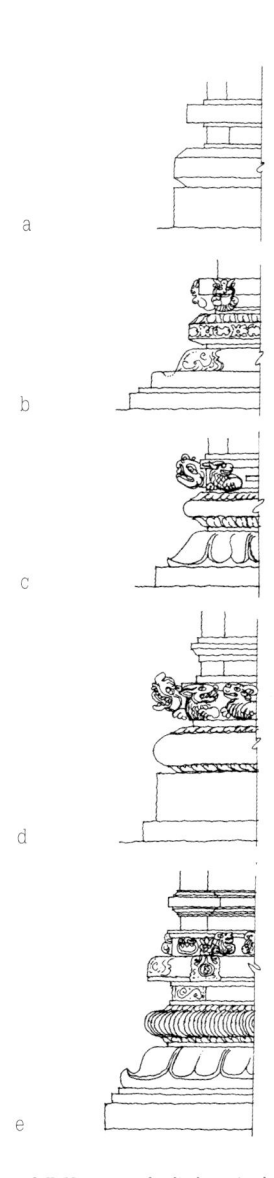

13.7 Varieties of *adisthana* in the Tamil Dravida tradition: (**a**) Bhumishvara temple, Viralur *c* mid-9th century; (**b**) Shore Temple, Mahabalipuram, early 7th century; (**c**) Trutondishvara temple, Tirunamalur, AD 935; (**d**) Koranganatha temple, Srinivasanallur *c* 927; (**e**) Kampahareshvara temple, Tribhuvanam (1178–1218). All begin with a *jagati*, plain or crowned by a *padma* (lotus), surmounted by a cushion moulding (*kumuda*), variously treated. The floor moulding (*prati*), strictly speaking not part of the *adisthana* proper, is often treated as a band of horned lions (*vyalamala*), but the role may be taken by a simple fillet (*pattika*) as in (**a**). A rail moulding (*vedika*) is optional (**d** and **e**). Example (**e**) has a *gala* and *kapota* between the *kumuda* and *prati*. It thus has the same full sequence as 13.5.[5]

14   Pillars

It should by now be more than clear that the defining elements of Nagara and Dravida architecture are not columns, nor even columns plus entablatures, but aedicules or 'little buildings'. Nor do the two languages of temple architecture respectively demand a particular column or pillar type; while the Dravida does have one predominant, stable type, used universally in the slender pilasters of southern temple walls, this form is also found in Nagara temples. If it were as easy to categorise Indian columns as ancient Greek ones, it would have been done. Although it is relatively straightforward to identify types within a given style and period, surveying the whole scene prompts the realisation that, while enduring types are apparent (and a basic typology will be attempted here), they are constantly evolving, and endlessly subject to variation, permutation and cross-fertilisation, with boundaries as fluid as those of kingdoms.

Indian pillars are composed of identifiable parts arranged in vertical sequences, like the mouldings of temple walls, with which these elements are always in dialogue. It is by these piled up parts – the kinds of part used and the order in which they are arranged – that pillar types are best defined. A particular type of part is not, on the whole, confined to a particular pillar type, and the identities of the pillar parts are not entirely fixed. Together with the motifs and patterns which ornament them, these elements constitute families of forms interrelated by shape, image and association, promiscuously mutating one into another, chiselled out in rounds of Chinese whispers. But the relative order in which the parts are placed is not as flexible, and the controlling logic is overwhelmingly anthropomorphic. Vitruvius made explicit the well-known analogy between classical columns and the human form; Indian treatises, which repeatedly relate whole temples to bodies, may not make this connection for pillars, except in the term *jangha* ('thigh') for the shaft. Yet it demands no exceptional empathy to feel that often Indian pillars have not only heads ('capital' is from the Latin *capitellum*, 'little head'), but necks, shoulders, chests, waists, hips, legs and feet.

While there do exist pillars consisting of nothing but shaft, particularly in the earliest Buddhist architecture, generally the shaft or trunk takes up a relatively small proportion of the total height, and is often itself subdivided, adding to the impression of a piled up sequence. This effect is compounded by additional parts below and above the pillar itself. Often a pillar has a base of up to three mouldings from the established range. At the top of a pillar there will more often than not be brackets. Stone brackets provide a good bearing for beams and reduce their spans; but it is surely to their importance in wooden structures, where they also have a bracing function, that brackets owe their prominence in the masonry traditions. Brackets, together with beams, appear above pilasters, notably in the walls of Dravida temples, where the whole assemblage of pilasters, brackets and beams depicts timber construction. Brackets also crown the stacks of moulded parts forming the thick pilasters or pillar images which are the bodies of *kutastambhas* (eg **13.3**, **25.4**).

The Indian texts classify pillars largely in terms of their cross section: *ruchaka* means square and, in the southern terminology, *Rudrakanta* is circular, *Vishnukanta* octagonal, and *Brahmakanta* tetragonal.[1] This is theologically evocative but architecturally unhelpful. If this is the best typology that the *shastras* could come up with, no wonder the design of pillars was so free. Changes in cross section are a way of bringing variety to a given type. Cross sections range from square, circular and polygonal (faceted), through scalloped (fluted), lobed, staggered and stellate. The cross section is commonly varied within a single pillar, and if this is all that the texts mean by '*mishraka*' ('mixed'), then they are blind to the other kinds of mixture, in all their fecundity. As well as variation among the basic components, modulations in cross section are typical of intermediate waists and neckings, and – from the earliest times – of shafts, which often rise from a square base, through an octagon, then 16 facets, to a circle. This transition preserves the stages of progressive reduction from the original block.

Bearing in mind that pillar types evolve and interact, five main types are identified below. Apart from these, two other categories should be mentioned: the Corinthianesque form of Gandhara, bequeathed to the Kashmiri tradition, and the perennial class of 'architectural pillars', in which the shaft is treated as a multi-storeyed, aedicular building.

A The Bell Type

Along with plain, faceted shafts, with or without brackets, the most ancient pillar type, prevalent and originating in Mauryan times (3rd century BC) and still prominent in the Gupta period (5th century AD), can be defined by its bell or tassel-like capital, usually ornamented with petal-like grooves or leaves (**14.1**, **14.2**). Such pillars often support heraldic animals, single or addorsed. This is the type of pillar referred to as Persepolitan or Indo-Persepolitan because it seems to betray early links with Achaemenid Persia.[2] The free-standing pillars erected all over India by the Maurya emperor Ashoka were of this kind, one of which carried the famous, polished stone capital at Sarnath, now the emblem of the Republic of India. Drawing on the imperial associations, the iron pillar ascribed to Chadragupta II (c 376–415), now at Meroli (Delhi), also follows the type.

Above the bell capital is some form of bearing block or abacus, sometimes an inverted, stepped pile resembling the platform for the parasol on a *stupa*, often with a ribbed cushion (*amalaka*) encased in its box-like base. Sometimes the sequence of elements is crowned by a flat wedge shape, usually serving as the brackets (*potika*). Often this has volutes (**14.1b**), and is particularly Achaemenid-looking when adorned with a honeysuckle motif. It is with this pillar type that pots first appeared at the base, similar in profile to the bell capital, but inverted. Symbolic explanations fill such pots with cosmic waters, rationalistic explanations endow them with origins in clay pots used to protect wooden pillars from termites, though they could hardly have withstood the weight.

B Blocks and Roundels

The origins of pillars with roundels (**14.3**), containing lotuses or scenes in low relief, can be traced to similarly treated *stupa* railings. Roundels are carved on the faces of square blocks, the surface on either side treated as leafy ears or tongues, hanging down or growing up. A pattern that is widespread from the 5th century onwards has mirrored roundels (coincidentally, the roundels may be termed *darpanas*, 'mirrors') on each face of a pillar, usually one in a block which forms the capital, the other

14.1 Bell pillars: (**a**) Rock-cut monastery (*vihara*) at Nasik, c 2nd century; (**b**) from a relief from Mathura, c 2nd century; (**c**) Temple 1, Sanchi, 5th century.

14.2 Vaisali (Bihar), Mauryan bell pillar, 3rd century BC. Photo © Gerard Foekema

at the top of the shaft or base block, with a necking in between (**14.3b**). Half-roundels, or some other fraction, are also common, either filling the entire width of a block or as an excrescence protruding up or down from the edge of a block (eg **9.3**).

Block-and-roundel pillars are a familiar type in northern and southern traditions at least until the 8th century. Meanwhile, roundels become a standard part of the repertory of parts for other types, especially at the chest, either filling the block or as an upward excrescence. In the Deccan, roundels metamorphose into *gavakshas* and into ogival 'moonstone' or 'pipal leaf' motifs (**14.6**, second from left; cf **14.4d**, **14.11** rear and **20.5**).

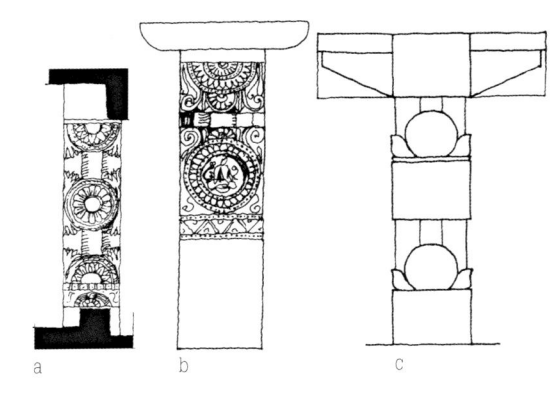

14.3 Pillars and pilasters with roundels: (**a**) Cave 3, Nasik, *c* 2nd century AD, similar to an early *stupa* railing; (**b**) Cave 6, Aurangabad, 6th century; (**c**) Sangameshvara, Pattadakal, early 8th century.

14.4 Right: Cushion pillars: (**a**) Cave 4, Bagh, early 6th century; (**b**) Vaikuntha Perumal, Kanchipuram, late 8th century; (**c**) Siddharameshvara, Niralgi (Karnataka), 12th century; (**d**) Temple 1, Balsane (Maharashtra), 12th century.

14.5 Below: Cushion pilasters: (**a**) typical Dravida pilaster, with names of parts; (**b**) from Cave 19, Ajanta, 5th century (cf 2.1); (**c**) Koranganatha, Srinivasanallur (Tamil Nadu), *c* 927; (**d**) Siddheshvara, Haveri (Karnataka), late 11th century.

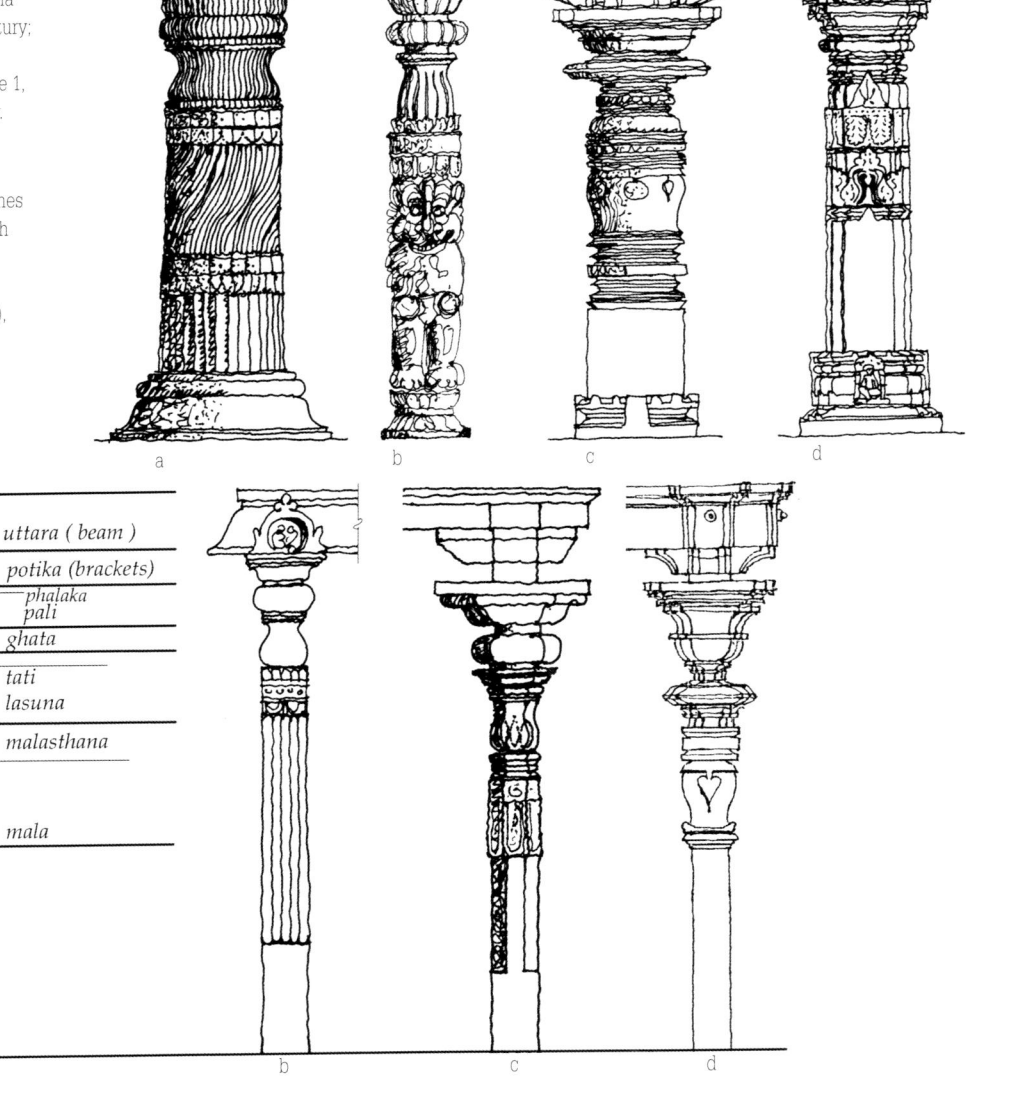

uttara (beam)
potika (brackets)
phalaka
pali
ghata
tati
lasuna
malasthana
mala

14.6 Cushion pillars in the upper veranda of the Jain Cave 32 (Indrasabha), Ellora, *c* late 8th century, with goddess Ambika.

14.7 Cushion pillars with 'bell' hips in the open hall (*range-mandapa*) of the Kalleshvara, Bagali (Karnataka). The type lends itself to variations in cross section. Photo © Gerard Foekema.

C Cushion Pillars

It is difficult to find an appropriate name for this most coherent of types (**14.4**), the pillar equivalent to the ubiquitous Dravida pilaster (**14.5**). It has been termed the 'Dravidian order',[3] but it is by no means confined to Dravida temples or to the south. 'Deccani order' is perhaps more appropriate,[4] as pilasters at Karle are already of this form (**7.9**), and further developments are conspicuous in the 5th- and 6th-century rock-cut traditions of Maharashtra. Its one constant feature is the cushion capital (*ghata*, 'pot'), assimilated to the *amalaka*, the ribbed crowning member, when (in early examples) it is grooved, and later to the range of shapes seen in *kumudas*, the cushion mouldings in the base of Dravida shrines. To have the *ghata* as the only crowning member (as in early *stupa* reliefs, eg at Amaravati) remains an option for some centuries, carrying brackets, and even the beam, directly. In the form which becomes the

152 THE TEMPLE ARCHITECTURE OF INDIA

14.8 *Ghata-pallava* pillars: (**a**) pilaster at Gupta temple, Deogarh, *c* 500; (**b**) Cave 3, Aurangabad, 6th century; (**c**) components in typical sequence; (**d**) Maladevi, Gyaraspur (MP), 9th century; (**e**) Surya temple, Modhera (Gujarat), 1026, dwarf pillar with minor sequence (omitting *ghata-pallava*).

established one, however, the *ghata* is surmounted by a bearing plate (*phalaka*) over a dish or lotus moulding (*pali* or *padma*), normally carrying brackets (*potika*). *Phalaka-padma* are analogous to the abacus-echinus of a Doric capital, although they are not so much the head as something carried on the head – to cushion the load on the cushion capital.

In standard forms of this type, the *ghata* sits over a member termed the *lasuna*, acting as a neck and shoulder, which in turn sits over a chest block, typically a belt (the *mala-sthana*) with dangling pearl-swags (*mala*, 'garland'). A division between blocks of stone is often found at the neck, socketed into the *ghata*, which usually belongs to a block of its own. In the rock-cut traditions of Maharashtra the *lasuna* is like a vase or a tulip, an idea reasserted in Tamil Nadu from around the 9th century. In Karnataka at about the same time the lower part of the chest block is transformed into a similar shape, but the other way up, like a bell (still often hung with pearls, recalling the *mala*). The waist

14.9 *Ghata-pallava* pillar from the gateway known as the 'Hindola Torana' at the Vishnu temple, Gyaraspur (MP), 10th century.

PILLARS 153

thereby moves to the top of the bell, the result being round-hipped and feminine (female hips, too, are hung with pearls). The pearls and other trinkets on their smooth hips are one proof that circular, polished pillars of this kind cannot have been turned on a lathe, as sometimes thought. The chest block without a bell remains an alternative in Karnataka (**9.5**). This is the norm for Bhumija temples (**14.4d**), for which the cushion type is the standard one, and for the various temple types built under the Kakatiyas in Andhra Pradesh (**25.18**).

D Ghata-pallava Pillars

More northerly and more Nagara, the broad class of pillars which have been termed (in their early manifestations) 'Indo-Gangetic'[5] are most easily defined by their brimming vase capital, the *purna-ghata* ('brimming vase') or *ghata-pallava* ('sprouting vase') (**14.8**). The *ghata-pallava* frequently appears at the foot of such pillars as well as the head; it can be one of two or three capitals – since pillars (like gods) can have several heads – or it can be the chest. This kind of pillar represents not only a different type from the cushion category, but a different approach, its sequence of parts being more fluid and extendable. Although shafts, waists and neckings may be polygonal, the type does not lend itself to varied cross sections in the same way as the cushion type because the *ghata-pallava* and other elements demand square blocks, but the type does eventually undergo staggering (**14.9**).

Early examples from the Gupta period are relatively straightforward. The *ghata-pallava* may simply crown a faceted shaft (as often at Ajanta, where the capital may constitute the only difference between this and the cushion type). Alternatively, as at Deogarh (**14.8a**), it resembles the cushion type in the number of elements (but for the addition of a *ghata-pallava* base) and the logic of their arrangement. Here the chest block has a half-roundel, from which hangs a pearl swag *mala*. Similar arrangements remain typical until the 9th century, when a great proliferation of parts takes place. A palette of elements, a kind of resumé of the long-established repertory of pillar parts, is piled up according to the desired degree of complexity. The human form and the previous histories of the respective elements dictate (not too strictly) their relative order. There may be a roundel-chest, or the *ghata-pallava* may become the chest. Between the *ghata-pallava* (whether chest or head) and the crowning brackets may appear one or more of the following, in the following order (upwards): (a) horizontal block with *kirti-mukha* (face of glory), traditionally a chest motif, spewing pearl swags, now also found here; (b) horizontal block with volutes, easily mistaken for

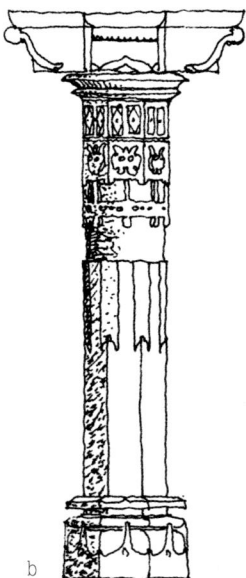

14.10 *Bharana* pillars: (**a**) Surya temple, Modhera (Gujarat), 1026; (**b**) from Somanatha Patan (Gujarat), *c* 12th century.

a *ghata-pallava* but closer to brackets, which are often treated in this way; (c) the *ghata* and *phalaka* typical of cushion pillars, singly or together. These sequences may be carved with unparalleled lushness, as at Osian (**9.11**), or lightly incised and stencil-like, as at Khajuraho (**19.5**).

E Bharana Pillars (14.10)

During the 10th century in most of central and western India, in those Nagara traditions for which the Shekhari was becoming the standard mode of shrine, a new kind of pillar took over from the *ghata-pallava* type as the usual form. This was not entirely new, but took as its sole capital the familiar cushion *ghata*, with a *phalaka* over it, with its usual dish. The result was thus, in effect, a version of the cushion type, but since it was probably not considered as such, it deserves its own category. Typically, the *phalaka* was given foliant ears, reminiscent of the *ghata-pallava*. Cushion and dish are generally ribbed, and the capital-abacus assemblage termed *bharana*, or *bharani* when the ribs are tighter. The cushion tends to atrophy, and sometimes only the abacus and dish remain.

The advantages of the new form are that, unlike the *ghata-pallava* type, the cross section can easily be varied between pillars or within a single one; moreover, it lends itself to a range of treatments, from plain and economical to rich and exuberant. A moulded base is usually present, surmounted by a base block which, as in many cushion pillars of the same period, may display sculpted images under *toranas*. Waist, chest and neck are rarely articulated, but are merged into a long trunk which can be enriched with a varied array of ornamental bands. Loftier *mandapas* with billowing *toranas* under beams led to the development of 'double pillars', with a lower pillar terminating at brackets, then extended upwards with the top part of a further pillar (**9.9**, **9.21**). The *bharana* type, with its simple trunk, was well suited to such upper pillars, and is used as such even where the lower one is of the *ghata-pallava* type.

Notes
1. Terms used in the *Encyclopaedia of Indian Temple Architecture*.
2. Jose Pereira, *Elements of Indian Architecture* (Delhi: Motilal Banarasidass, 1987).
3. G Jouveau-Dubreuil, *Dravidian Architecture* (Varanasi: Bharat-Bharati, 1972 reprint; 1st pub, 1917), p 10.
4. Pereira uses this term for the early ones, *Elements of Indian Architecture*.
5. Ibid.

14.11 Open hall interior at the Vaishnava temple, Anwa (Maharashtra), 12th century. This is a Bhumija temple, and pillars around the perimeter of the *mandapa* are the cushion type favoured by this tradition (cf 14.4d). Those in the foreground are related, but are influenced by the *bharana* pillars of Gujarat, with their ornamental rings. Above the moulded bases are base blocks faced by archways (*toranas*) supported on small pavilion-topped pillars (*kuta-stambhas*) – a common feature in both cushion pillars and *bharana* pillars by this date.
Photo © Gerard Foekema

15 Ceilings

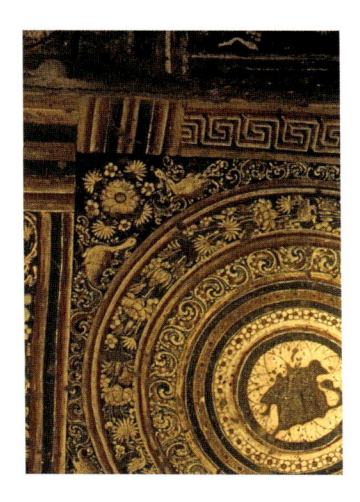

15.1 Painted lotus ceiling in Cave 2, Ajanta, 5th century.

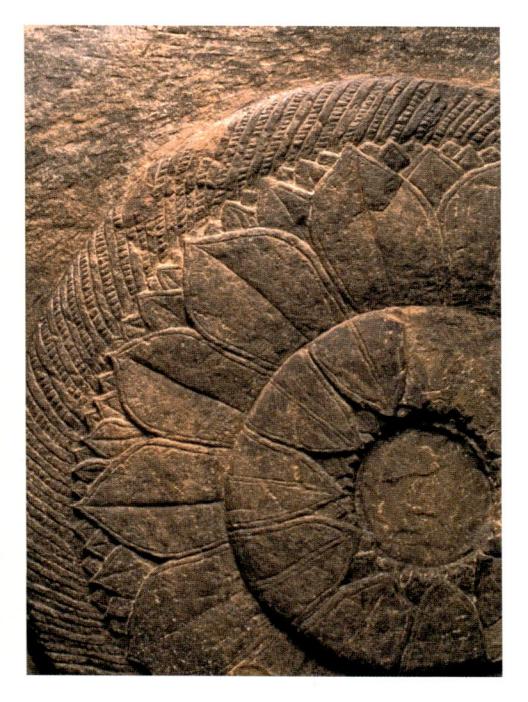

15.2 Carved lotus ceiling at Cave 7, Udayagiri, 5th century.

Before the modern age ceilings had middles and reminded people of the sky ('ceiling', from the French *ciel*). Indian temple ceilings also follow another archetype, the lotus, most multiple of symbols, present in many parts of the temple from top to toe, but especially in ceilings. The lotus blooms up from watery depths, but ceilings blossom downwards, raining beneficence. Even the soffits of beams have lotuses, manifesting polycentric divinity as if through a sprinkler system. All this is no surprise to those of us who have lights hanging from ceiling roses, and roses on watering can spouts. Temple ceilings have petals at their borders, flowerets at their nodes; their pendants push out stamens, and much of their terminology is floral.[1]

If, as we have seen, temples burgeon and flower in their exteriors through formal components that are far more architectural than botanical, then it is to be expected that their ceilings should unfurl, since they depict organisms which do so literally. But before we conclude that they seem organic because they portray natural forms, it must be pointed out that floral motifs in developed 'lotus ceilings' are outweighed by an architectural vocabulary of which the units are not flowers or petals but images of domes. The prototypes, as usual, are in wooden construction and the kind of hooped, radiating beams seen in the apse of a *chaitya* hall (Buddhist hall of worship; see **7.8**), or still, for example, in the palaces of Kerala, with shaped rafters dowelled together by knobbed pegs. A single, ribbed dome image comes often to take the place of a lotus, and the seeming petals of later *padma-shilas* (the central blossom of a corbelled ceiling) are the lobes formed by centrifugally emanating miniature domes. A proliferated ceiling is like a superstructure in negative, the underneath of the jelly mould, and the dome-images are the aedicules, the mansions in the dome of heaven. Temples are made of images of buildings, their ceilings of images of ceilings. It was suggested in Chapter 9 that structural bays are an inside equivalent of aedicules, and that structural necessity prevents them from coalescing. Within each bay, however, dome-image aedicules are free to merge and multiply. They unfurl through expanding repetition

156 THE TEMPLE ARCHITECTURE OF INDIA

and/or progressive multiplication and, when overlapped, through projection, all seen from below. The stages of growth, marked in a tower by its levels (*bhumis* or *talas*), are here traced out by layered planes.

The Indian builders did not struggle with thrust and counterthrust to heave up vast, ribbed cages or mounds of buttressed cupolas. Guardians of architecture as the constructive art might not approve, although these masons cut stone with consummate skill and achieved spectacular feats of corbelling. Relatively free from the constraints of function (in the engineering sense), they followed the demands of form, piling up patterns that Bramante or Sinan could never dream of in their dome clusters,[2] closer to the variegated vaults of late Gothic niche canopies or the stucco stalactites of the Alhambra. Before all these, they hewed and hoisted blocks, chipped into their depths, and built their domes in air for the miniature multitudes who throng celestial courts above the beams.

The first ceilings are flat slabs, and the main exceptions to the lotus pattern are those with figural reliefs, hieratic or narrative. Flat ceilings, painted (**15.1**) or carved (**15.2**), already display lotuses in early cave architecture, and continue to do so. A flat slab may be divided by bands, to make a kind of miniature *mandapa* plan, with a lotus in every square and bud-like bosses where the bands cross. Needless to say, ceilings are like mandalas.

'Lantern ceilings', with their receding/emanating planes of nested squares, are the earliest departure from the flat soffit. These are well suited to construction in piled up slabs, though their origin is in timber, with beams cutting the corners and panels filling the spaces. The early 8th-century example from Charrahi (Himachal Pradesh) shown in **15.3** is a wooden one, decorated just as a contemporary stone one would have been. A happy coincidence of practicality and geometry ensured the perennial popularity of lantern ceilings: they follow the principle of the circle-square sequence or *ad quadratum* (**12.1b**), and can therefore be perfectly integrated with any temple plan based on this geometry.

But recession can also be achieved within a single slab, if it is thick enough, or several blocks can be abutted to provide sufficient depth for

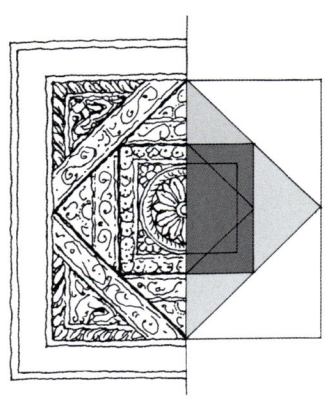

15.3 Lantern ceiling. The example shown is from the early 8th century, from Charrahi (Himachal Pradesh), and is made of wood (cf 9.5).

15.4 Ceiling in the Mahavira temple, Osian, *c* late 8th century. Carved ceilings were cut into stone slabs before they were made by corbelling. Here the ribs take the form of *nagas* (snake spirits), who slide down to peer benignly from the rim with clasped hands. Photo © American Institute of Indian Studies

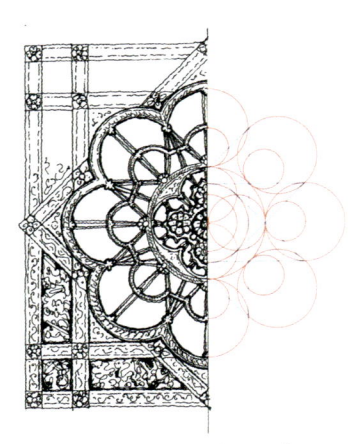

15.5 Ceiling of the Ambika temple, Jagat (Rajasthan), *c* 961 (cf 19.4). Several ceilings of this design are found in western India from this period.

15.6 Ceiling from the Vira-Narayana temple, Belavadi (Karnataka), 12th century. The framework still recalls a shaped timber prototype.
Photo © Gerard Foekema

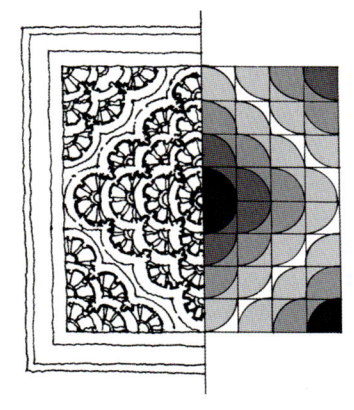

15.7 Lobed ceiling on orthogonal grid.

15.8 Ceiling in the Kandariya Mahadeva, Khajuraho. This is the lobed orthogonal type, with overlapping clusters. Proliferating ceiling patterns are termed *nabhi-chchanda*, *nabhi* meaning 'navel', from the Sanskrit root *nabh*, 'to expand'.

sculpting into (**15.4**, **15.5**, **15.6**). This is what was done before the great developments in corbelling, and it was in western India, in the 8th century, that deep ceilings appeared, where corbelled domes were afterwards perfected, where they flowered most profusely and from where they spread through central India and the Deccan. The first form to be hollowed out as lotus-substitute was the single, circular, ribbed dome-image. From the circle they proceeded, naturally, to the extended gnomon diagram (**12.1a**), one circle emitting four (a concept which could be made to fit rectangular bays as well as square ones, by using ovals rather than circles). Well before this idea was applied to corbelling, they began to multiply the lobes, scooped first around the inner circle, then spreading out like petals. So began an unfolding tradition (**6.5**), closely tied to unfolding geometry (see Chapter 6).

The extended gnomon diagram inherently contains two possibilities of radial expansion: either orthogonally in four directions, or all around. Two paths of development are thus suggested. One, the orthogonal, follows the grid set up by the quartered square which the diagram contains (**15.7**). Shekhari-like half-domes are emitted along the cardinals, quarter domes multiplying diagonally. This type of design, confined to flat slabs, is simple in principle, but creates a profound sense of complexity, especially when clusters are overlapped (**15.8**). The tradition proliferates the patterns, playing with planes, which loom out from the void.

In the other stream of development, the omnidirectional, function follows form, as cusped lobes (called *kolas*, 'boars') come to be carved in concentric rings of corbelled courses (**15.9**, **15.10**, **15.11**); the tradition runs through all the possible sequences of lobe numbers, spreading out from the central circle. Below the central lotus appear plainer concave, ribbed courses (*gajatalus*, 'elephants' palettes'), curved

15.9 Lobed radiating ceiling. The effect is lotus-like, but the unfurling petals are actually half-domes.

15.10 Ceiling in the Luna Vahasi, Dilwara (Rajasthan), *c* 1230s. Photo © American Institute of Indian Studies

versions of the underside of eave mouldings, forming an arena for encircling heavenly maiden bracket figures, and at the base of the dome is a ring of lotus petals (**15.11**, **9.9**).

As usual in the unfolding traditions of Indian temple architecture, parts give birth to parts: here lobes become lobed. But pendants (*lumas*) are the final glory of this tradition of ceiling design, in both its orthogonal and its omnidirectional types, just as they would later be for English Perpendicular vaults. These hanging masses of seemingly weightless stone follow the same patterns as had already been developed, but in negative, the crest of the jelly mould imploding. Bursting in, they become 'thrown out' (*utkshipta*) instead of 'thrown in' (*kshipta*). It becomes a matter of endless ambiguity whether the pendant comes down in a mighty splash from an inverted sea, or spurts up from the fountainhead at the foot of the fountain.

Perhaps these cascading, crystalline domes strike a more universal chord than Hindu temples in their more fleshly embodiments: at least, the sultans of Delhi and of Gujarat, before the one true arch came to reign, eagerly incorporated these products of the infidel, whether plundered or made specially, into their mosques, oblivious that the lacy cusps and pendant lips might be the petticoats of the Goddess; and a thousand ceiling bays breathed unity from their omnipresent centre.

15.11 Main ceiling, Mahavira temple, Kumbhariya (Gujarat), *c* 1062.

Notes

1. See JM Nanavati and MA Dhaky, 'The Ceilings in the Temples of Gujarat', *Bulletin of the Baroda Museum and Picture Gallery* vols 16-28 (whole of one book), 1963; also MA Dhaky and US Moorti, *The Temples in Kumbhariya* (Delhi: AIIS, 2001).
2. Donato Bramante (1444–1514), epitome of High Renaissance architecture in Italy; Mimar Sinan (1489–1588), most celebrated architect of Ottoman Turkey.

16 GAVAKSHAS

The horseshoe arch form, as in the sun window of the Buddhist *chaitya* halls, is most commonly known (particularly in the context of Nagra temples) as the *gavaksha*, 'cow eye' or 'ray-eye'.[1] In its role as an architectural component, the movement that it expresses, and the way in which the motifs and their combinations evolve, the *gavaksha* is a kind of paradigm for Indian temple architecture as a whole: something of the totality can be sensed through this little window. With window imagery and its eye etymology, the ubiquitous *gavaksha* invites symbolic interpretation. For Kramrisch the *gavaksha* motif 'retains as its outline the shape of the arch of vegetation, the shape of Prakrti [primal matter, the female principle]', and as a window embodies the paradoxical, 'retrovert

16.1 Early horseshoe arch gable windows: (**a**) as depicted in *chaitya* hall facades, with open wooden screen; (**b**) as shown in relief carvings, with shading device.

16.2 Early *gavakshas*: (**a**) on a fragment from Mathura, *c* 3rd century AD; (**b**) loose *gavaksha* at Deogarh, *c* AD 500; (**c**) from the Old Temple, Gop (Saurahstra), *c* AD 600; (**d**) from the Lakshmana temple, Sirpur, *c* early 7th century. The examples from Gop and Sirpur contain *chaitya* hall cross sections, the one from Sirpur with a miniature shrine form in an abstracted nave colonnade, comparable to Dravida *gavakshas* of the 7th and 8th centuries (16.10a–c).

function' of radiating divine light out of inner darkness.[2] It seems that, more than through such associations, ideas of divine manifestation are embodied in the unfolding patterns into which the motif is woven.

But, regardless of meaning, the shapes tell their own story, part of which is a matter of styles. There is no better hallmark of style, no better indication of time and place, than the *gavaksha*. In Indian temple architecture, *gavakshas* are the detail closest to calligraphy, manifesting style in the etymological sense of the term – related to the pen or *stylus*. As with calligraphy, their linear flow follows a geometrical framework, and like handwriting they combine cultural norm with personal idiosyncrasy, and carefully learned construction with happy variation and accident.

Shapes

It is because the Nagara and Dravida languages of temple architecture developed from representations of wooden buildings with hooped gables to their roof ends and dormers, that the horseshoe arch form became an inseparable part of both kinds of architecture. Its ornamental function in stone architecture is already apparent in the early *chaitya* halls, where the form is not confined to the actual window. Here the motif still contains details of timber construction, close to those represented in the facade of the Lomas Rishi cave (**7.5**). As explained in Chapter 10, the rock-cut *chaitya* hall cross section lived on as a shape in the Valabhi shrine form, crowned by a whole *gavaksha* placed over two halves. The image of this cross section was also placed inside *gavaksha* arches (**16.3**, **16.10a**), complete with miniature pillars, often abstracted into a trefoil shape. Coincidentally, the trefoil has another, parallel origin, in the shading devices for horseshoe windows, depicted in relief carvings of the early centuries AD (**16.1b**). Reliefs of that period also show the increasing fomalisation of the gable outline, which was not an entirely pragmatic feature even when made of wood. By Gupta times it had grown ears and the Nagara *gavaksha* had been born (**16.2b**).

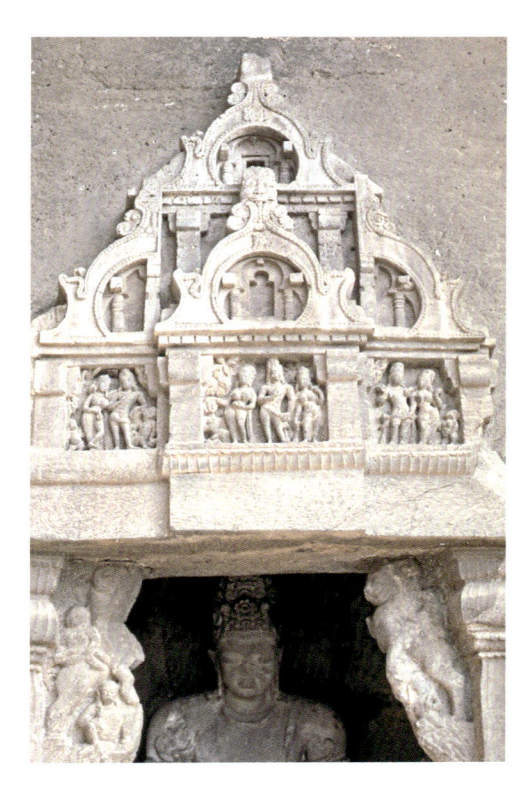

16.3 Niche pediment from the facade of Cave 10 (Vishvakarma), Ellora, a rock-cut *chaitya* hall of *c* 650. Here each *gavaksha* sits on a pair of pilasters, as the crowning element of an aedicule. The pair of half-*gavakshas* imply that a single one has emerged forward and downwards from the upper one, an idea enhanced by the fact that the latter is overlapped by the finials of the former. The projecting front aedicule is seen as emerging last. At its base, each *gavaksha* has a corner of roof, triangular or curved, betraying its origins as a dormer window gable: its parallel origins as the gable-end of a wagon roof is reflected in the schematic *chaitya* hall interior contained within it.

16.4 A 7th-century example of the standard mainstream Nagara *gavaksha* type, from the ruined Temple 2, Nalanda (*c* late 7th century), showing the new standard geometry.

16.5 A mainstream *gavaksha* of the Maha-Gurjara style, from Roda (Gujarat) (late 8th century). Here a second circle defines the outer edge. This example is a linear one: minor *gavakshas* in this style are the negative of this, leaving the surface intact (18.8–18.10).

16.6 The geometry underlying the standard mainstream *gavaksha* remains for centuries, while the *gavaksha* forms themselves are gradually transmuted: top, *c* 7th to 8th centuries; middle *c* 9th to 10th centuries (linear and surface versions); bottom *c* 10th to 13th centuries. While there are clear regional and local variations, making the *gavaksha* a reliable stylistic hallmark, at any one time the same general character is spread over a wide area of central and western India, either because of contact or because the same kinds of transformation occur independently.

Up to the 7th century the general proportions of *gavakshas* varied. Then a norm attained widespread currency from the Gangetic plains to the west coast, at times reaching southward to the Deccan and northward to the Himalayan foothills. The standardisation of this *gavaksha* ('mainstream', at least for central and western India) was due above all to the adoption of one particular grid (**16.4**, **16.5**). To some extent this grid determined the *gavaksha* shape, for example in the flattening of the tops of the ears, level with the top of the inner circle, and their little declivities responding to the vertical gridlines. However, while the grid persists the shape evolves, as shown in **16.6**. Within this norm, regional traditions, even local workshops, had characteristic flourishes and inflections, which also evolved, becoming exaggerated or withering away. Yet the picture is not one of divergence from a common source, but of constant interchange and awareness of the latest fashions. This interchange extends to an alternative, bushy-eared

162 THE TEMPLE ARCHITECTURE OF INDIA

gavaksha form which had become common throughout central and western India by the 10th century. It is found side-by-side with the predominant form, clearly used with deliberate intention, most often fulfilling the lesser function of dormer to an eave moulding in the base or the cornice (**16.7a**).

During the 11th to 13th centuries architects of Bhumija temples, as if for deliberate distinctiveness, chose this as their standard form, in its surface version (**16.7a**) and, especially, its linear one (**16.7b**). They knew the mainstream *gavaksha*, but used it sparingly. For the large *gavaksha* at the foot of a Bhumija superstructure they chose an onion-shaped form of Deccani character (**16.7c**). Eastern India, too, had its own forms of *gavaksha*, more through separation than choice. Nalanda (Bihar), by the 7th century, had its own characteristic types (**21.1**). In that century a temple of the purest 'mainstream' Nagara was built there (**16.4**), but by the 10th century, under the Palas, the region had its own repertoire (**16.8**). In Orissa, the early influx of mainstream Nagara was reflected in a chunky version of the standard *gavaksha*, 7th-century vintage (**16.9a**). A wave of Dravida influence from the Deccan in the 10th century brought a new type (**16.9b**). Renewed contact with central India in the 10th century brought the latest, waspish version of the standard Nagara form (**16.6** bottom; cf **21.14**), but, as the connections were not kept up, this soon became drowsy (**16.9c**).

Dravida *gavakshas* (**16.10**), also termed *nasis* ('little noses'), stem from the same roots as Nagara ones. They appear at a variety of scales, ranging from the gables of barrel-roofed pavilions (*shalas* and *panjaras*) to the dormers projecting from roof elements (*kuta* domes, *harantara* recesses and *kapota* eave mouldings). They give less emphasis to the linear outline than their Nagara counterparts, having foliated ears and generally a monster finial (a *vyala* face or *kirtti-mukha*, face of glory). Their geometrical basis is more varied as they are never combined into patterns.

Unfolding Patterns

In the mainstream Nagara traditions of the 7th century, Valabhi 'pediment' designs became more elaborate, following the typical pattern of an unfurling tradition (Chapter 6). Figure **16.11** shows the 'kit of parts' from which different configurations were made. Proliferation, fragmentation and overlap were already established principles when, early in the 8th century, perhaps in more than one place, the masons discovered a property of the standard grid which ensured its survival for at least seven centuries. It allowed them to overlap and interlock

16.7 *Gavakshas* in Bhumija temples: (**a**) *gavaksha* type selected for Bhumija temples, surface version; (**b**) linear version of the same type; (**c**) onion type used for major *gavakshas*.

16.8 *Gavakshas* of the Pala period (*c* 10th century): (**a**) vase-shaped *gavaksha*; (**b**) relaxed mainstream *gavaksha*; (**c**) form common on Valabhi-fronted *stupas* at Nalanda and Bodhgaya (Bihar).

16.9 Orissan *gavakshas*: (**a**) Orissan version of the 7th-century mainstream *gavaksha*; (**b**) *gavaksha* at the Mukteshvara temple (10th century); (**c**) 11th-century meandering *gavaksha*.

16.10 Dravida *gavakshas*. From Karnataka: (**a**) Upper Shivalaya, Badami, early 7th century (cf 16.1b); (**b**) Virupaksha, Pattadakal, *c* 742; (**c**) Cave 32, Ellora, *c* late 8th century; (**d**) Siddheshvara, Mudhol, 10th century; (**e**) Siddharameshvara, Niralgi, 12th century; (**f**) typical Hoysala diagonal *gavaksha*; (**g**) Rameshvara, Gadag, 12th century. From Tamil Nadu, earlier similar to (**b**): (**h**) Kalugumalai, *c* 800; (**i**) Nelliappar temple, Tirunelveli, 9th century; (**j**) Srangapani temple, Kumbakonam, 10th century.

16.11 Top: 7th-century kit of parts. The *chaitya* hall cross section lives on in the trefoil. Middle: kit of parts invented in the 8th century and then used until at least the 13th, giving notation. Shaded grid squares denote parts which overlap when these components are combined. Bottom: all the later components combined. The grid may be stretched or distorted and was modulated to the curvature and diminution of temple superstructures.

gavakshas and part-*gavakshas* in a rich variety of complicated patterns (**16.12a–d**). These are the *gavaksha* nets (*jalas*), knitted out across northern India, veiling miles of moulded stone. The Bhumija workshops wove their own kind of *jala* (**16.13**), and in Orissa, where they never learnt the secret of the standard system, they took one of their *gavaksha* types and made *jalas* not by overlap but through clever shifts, as if tugging at the weft (**16.14**).

Once, in the 7th century, the new kit of parts became known, the artists proceeded to explore the permutations that they suggested, at first combining them with the earlier shapes, which were then gradually abandoned. After the 8th century, however, no fundamentally new *jala* designs were invented. Further proliferation undermined the individual unit: currency is devalued by inflation. Depth was lost, as *gavakshas* were flattened out, interior vistas forgotten, and coalescence of motifs in a single plane supplanted conceptual overlap. Sequential growth was vestigially implied in the *jalas*, but probably no longer thought about by the craftsmen. By providing a ready-made recipe, the very geometry that had generated the patterns must have contributed to their fossilisation. In any case, the possibilities of the system were exhausted.

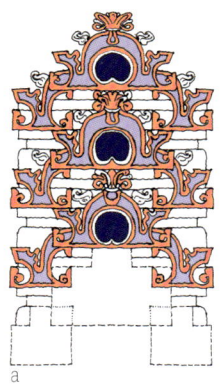

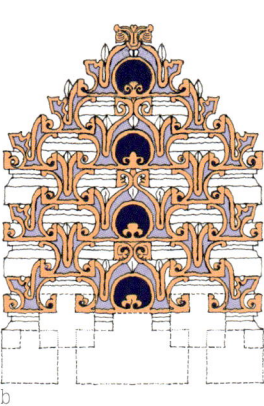

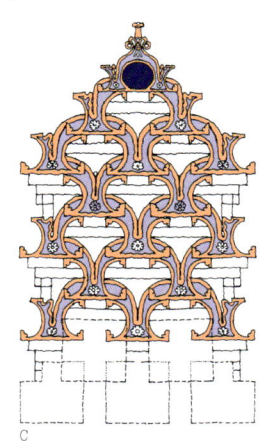

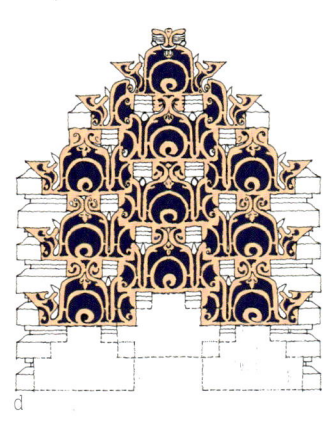

16.12 Varieties of typical *gavaksha* patterns. All of these appeared for about 600 years over a wide area. They are drawn in various styles (stylistic labels following the *Encyclopaedia of Indian Temple Architecture*) to show how composition is independent of the style. These patterns are made from the components shown in 16.11. The grid system allows minor variations to these basic arrangements. For example, 'o' and 'w' motifs are interchangeable, 'o' can be substituted for 'ow' or 'wo'; and 'r' for 'v'.

(**a**) Maha-Maru style,[1] 8th century. This common pattern of 'o' and 'r' motifs provides the starting point (the top) for most other patterns. It is an overlapping version of the whole-over-two-halves configuration.

(**b**) Pattern of 'w', 'v' and 'r' motifs, drawn in Darsanadesha style, *c* 9th century.

(**c**) Pattern of 'ow', 'w' and 'wo' motifs, drawn in Maru-Gurjara style, *c* 12th century. The *gavakshas* are of an extreme kind, with ears that poke half a square beyond the grid.

(**d**) Pattern of 'r' and 'v' motifs, drawn in Karnata Nagara style, *c* 8th century.

16.13 *Gavaksha jala* (net) typical of Bhumija temples, composed of the *gavaksha* type shown in 16.7b.

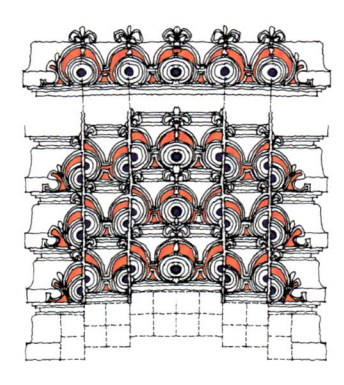

16.14 *Gavaksha jala* appearing in 10th-century Orissan temples, composed of the *gavaksha* type illustrated in 16.9b.

The *gavaksha*, moving along the spectrum from compositional element towards ornament, ceased to be the focus for invention, as the temple architects looked for ways to transform the Latina shrine form into something composite; and new, three-dimensional aedicular components emerged, initiating the grand unfolding of Shekhari temple designs. The rest is history.

Notes
1. The motif is sometimes referred to as a '*chaitya* arch' because of its early prominence as the gable end of a *chaitya* hall. Other Sanskrit terms include *chandra-shala* ('moon house') and, for south Indian temples, *nasi* ('little nose'). The Tamil *kudu* is also used in the latter context.
2. Stella Kramrisch, *The Hindu Temple* (Calcutta: University of Calcutta, 1946), pp 319–20.

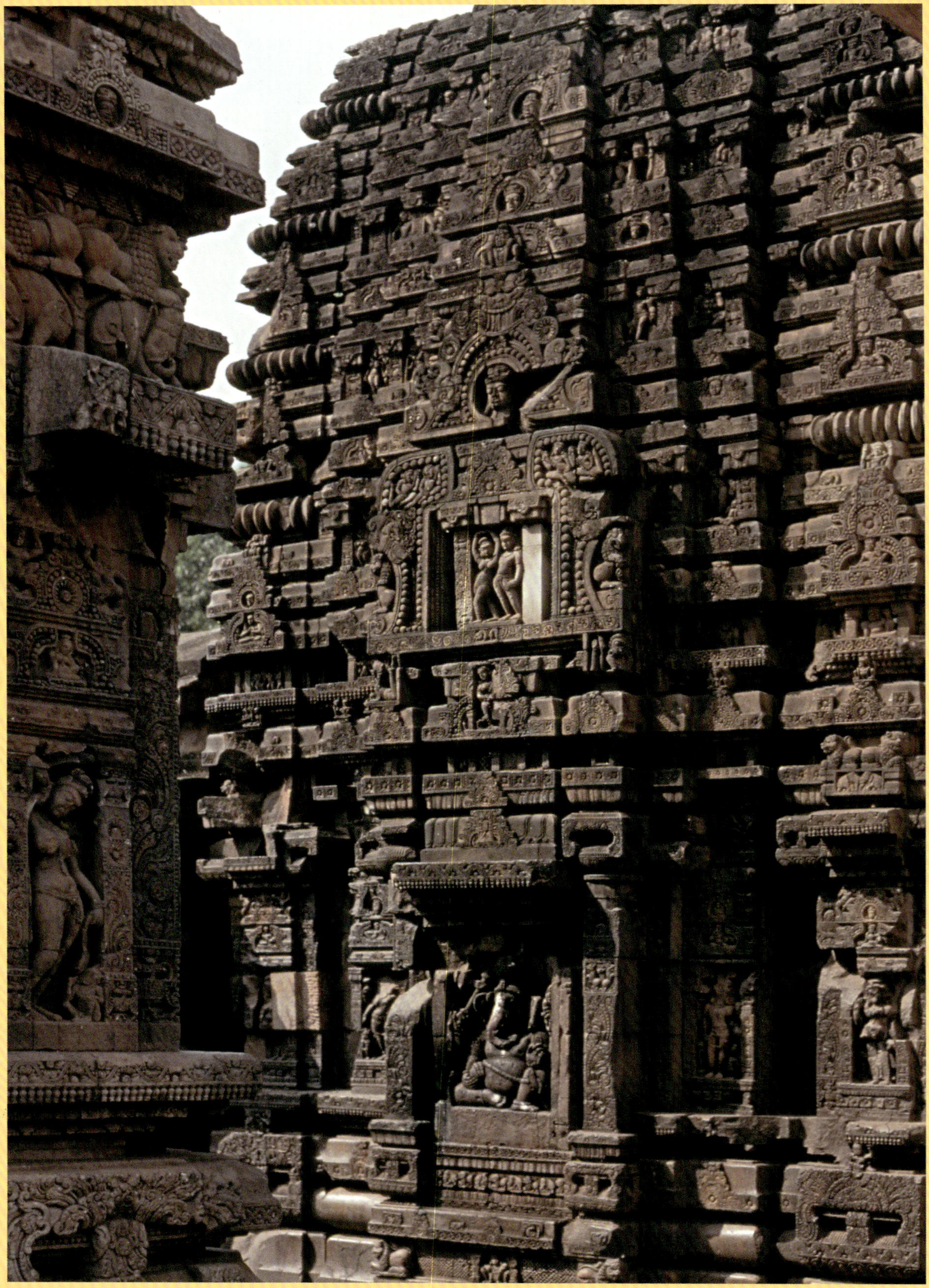

PART 4   **A BRIEF HISTORY OF NAGARA TEMPLES**

17   Early Nagara Temples
18   Latina and Related Valabhi Temples
19   Shekhari Temples
20   Bhumija Temples
21   Temples of Eastern India

Sisireshvara temple, Bhuvaneshvara, *c* 750, with the corner of the Vaital Deul in the foreground (**21.7**).

17 Early Nagara Temples

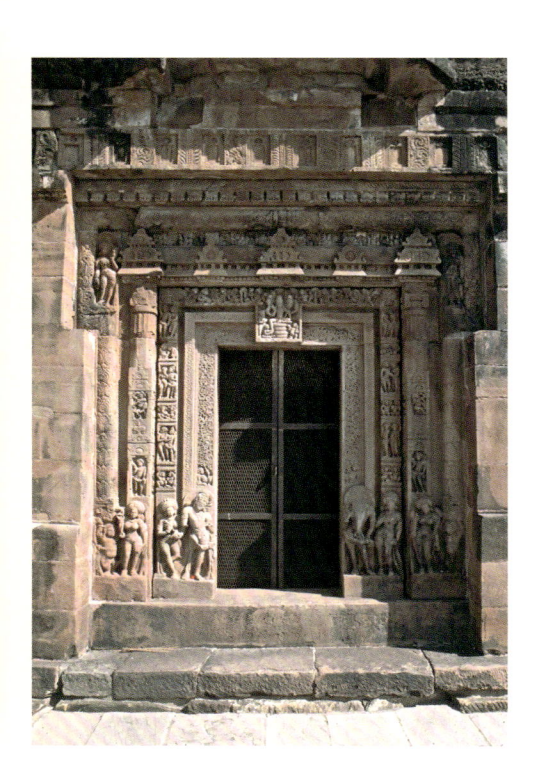

Nagara temple architecture as we now know it falls into three categories during its formative stages. Remains of Gupta structural temples, dating from the 5th century onwards, include the first of these, the kinds of shrine from which the Latina mode, with its curved spire (*shikhara*), eventually emerged, and the second, the shrine form topped by a pile of eave mouldings, known as Phamsana. A third category, apparent by about AD 600, consists of the fully aedicular temples – ie conceived entirely in terms of interlinked shrine images – created by unknown architects for virtually unknown patrons in regions eastwards of ancient Madhyadesha. These constitute a distinct alternative to the 'mainstream' early Nagara which developed into the Latina.

Proto-Latina

Whether or not the small, 5th-century Gupta shrines such as those at Sanchi and Tigawa (MP) were originally flat roofed, or had superstructures (perhaps of brick) which have since been lost, is difficult to know, but there are certainly traces of superstructures from this period. In Chapter 10 it was argued (as illustrated in **10.3**) that the development of the Latina superstructure (*shikhara*) came about through a process of stacking up representations of a type of shrine which I termed the '*amalaka*' shrine, because its defining characteristic is the ribbed crowning member (*amalaka*). Evidence for this process is found in fragments from the Gupta heartland, including '*amalaka* aedicules', architectural components in the form of miniature *amalaka* shrines (**17.4a**; cf **10.1a–d**). Elaborated *amalaka* shrines are depicted on the door jamb of the Gupta temple at Deogarh (**17.1**) and on a small *stupa* at Nalanda (**17.4b**).[1] The Deogarh temple (**17.2**), with its famous sculptural panels (**5.1**), has a ruined superstructure; however, from surviving parts of its lowest courses, a proto-Latina pattern can be deduced (**17.3**).[2]

These general principles seem to have been followed in central India well into the 7th century, when a transition to a continuous (central spine) *lata* and definite curvature brought about the Latina form. A class of small stone temples from that region, with thin, slab walls and

17.1 Doorway to the Gupta temple (Dash-Avatara) at Deogarh (MP), *c* AD 500. Photo © Gerard Foekema closely spaced pillars or pilasters – sometimes termed 'Mandapika shrines' and thought to have been intentionally flat roofed – seem (before they began to receive Latina spires) to have been a developed form of *amalaka* shrine (**17.5**).³

Phamsana

The ruined tower of the large, brick Gupta temple at Bhitargaon (UP), *c* 425–50, follows the general Phamsana principle, with arched hood-mouldings which are loosely Valabhi (ie they represent the arch over two half-arches characteristic of the barrel-roofed Valabhi shrine from). The surviving terracotta images and ornament at Bhitargaon are superb, but the underlying architecture is plain. With more bearing on subsequent traditions is a shrine depicted on a well-published door-lintel from a 6th-century Buddhist temple at Sarnath (UP) (**17.6**), a three-eave Phamsana superstructure rising over an eave-cornice, already with a curved profile and a central projection, through which a large Valabhi element bursts.

The Phamsana was the principal shrine type in Saurashtra during the 7th century, in both its multi-tier (**10.7a**) and its 'pent roof' forms (**10.7b**). Figure **17.7** shows the Mahadeva temple, Bileshvara, which typifies two characteristics of early Phamsana in this region: the progressive multiplication of *gavaksha*-dormers down the face of the superstructure, 1–2–3–4 etc (as opposed to continuous cascades which gradually became the norm), and the addition of corner pavilions illustrating the range of early Nagara aedicules.

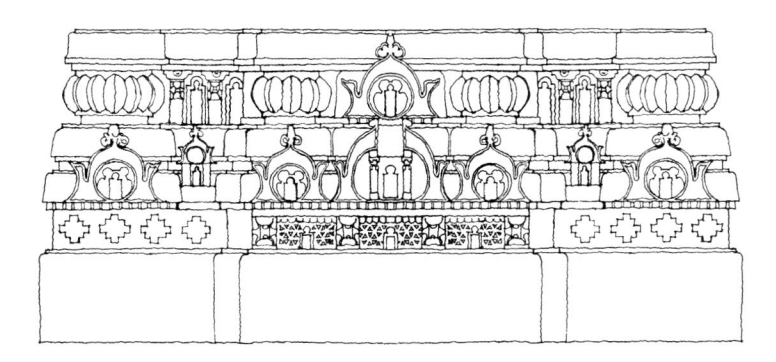

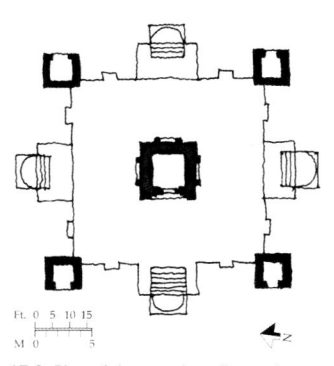

17.2 Plan of the temple at Deogarh, showing presumed corner shrines, now lost. Some form of veranda originally surrounded the sanctum.

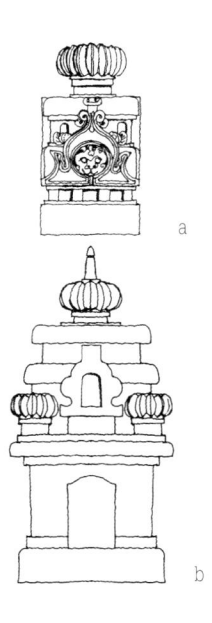

17.4 (**a**) *kuta* from Sarnath, in the form of an '*amalaka* aedicule', *c* 5th century (cf 10.1c); (**b**) an elaborated version projecting from a brick *stupa* at Nalanda, *c* 6th century.

17.3 Conjectural restoration of the base of the superstructure at Deogarh.

EARLY NAGARA TEMPLES **169**

17.5 Doorway in small temple at Chhapara (MP), 7th century. Overdoors, in both Nagara and Dravida traditions, are often treated as a chain of pavilions, making the doorway as a whole into a palatial gatehouse. An overdoor is often, therefore, equivalent to the first stage of a temple tower. The original superstructure of this temple, probably in brick, is likely to have resembled the design shown in 10.3c, minus the lowest stage. Photo © Anne Casile

17.6 Pavilion from overdoor found at Sarnath (UP), 6th century. Here the eave mouldings are double-curved, as would long be usual, although a single rounded curve is an early alternative.

Early Aedicular Nagara

The Magadha tradition has left its traces at Bodhgaya (Bihar), place of the Buddha's enlightenment, principally in the Mahabodi temple, rebuilt c 600–25. Restoration of this brick structure in the 19th century has deadened all detail, but not obscured the original concept.[4] A steep pyramid, with incipient curvature, is treated as seven aedicular tiers: an eighth also has projections, but is subsumed into the restored summit, with its crowning *amalaka* now rendered like a Buddhist *stupa*. The arrangement of aedicules in each tier is shown in figure **17.8**. An ingenious trick is played to imply that each successive tier is behind the one below: in the corner aedicules only the capital of the corner pilaster is visible above the *amalaka* crowning the tier below, while the other pilaster is exposed, as if one leg is hidden and the other one showing.

Far more survives from the inexhaustibly inventive tradition of brick temples of Dakshina (south) Koshala, now Chhatisgarh state. These monuments (of which the details confirm the early dating ascribed to

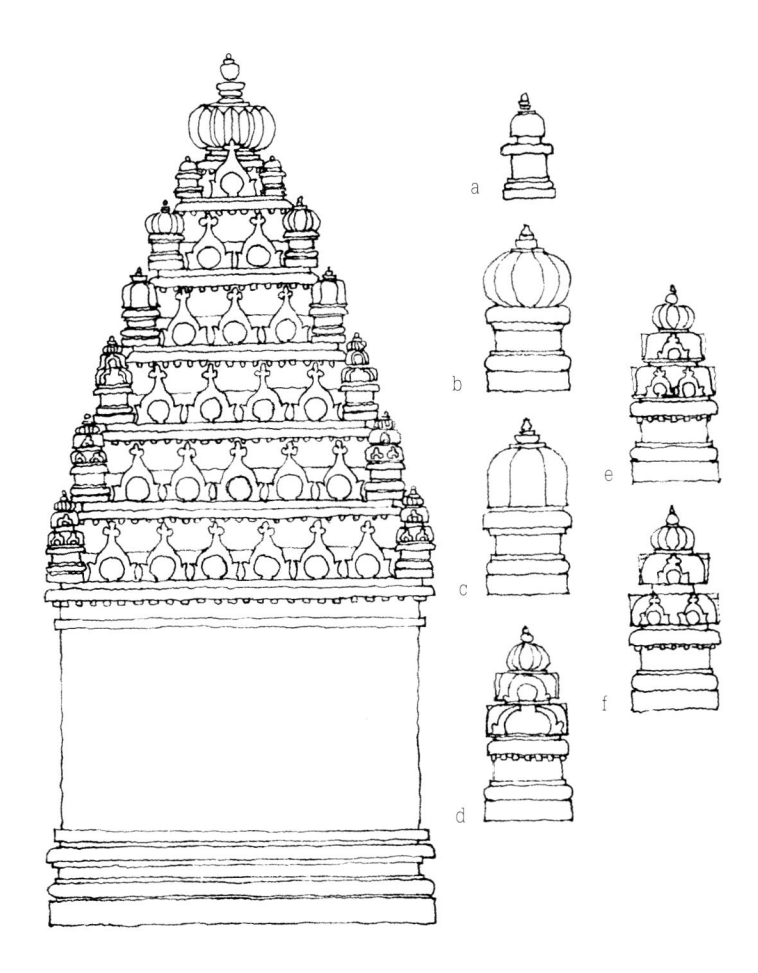

17.7 Mahadeva temple, Bileshvara (Gujarat), early 7th century: Phamsana shrine with aedicules at corners – domed *kuta* (**a**, **c**), *amalaka* aedicule (**b**), Phamsana (**d**, **e**, **f**).

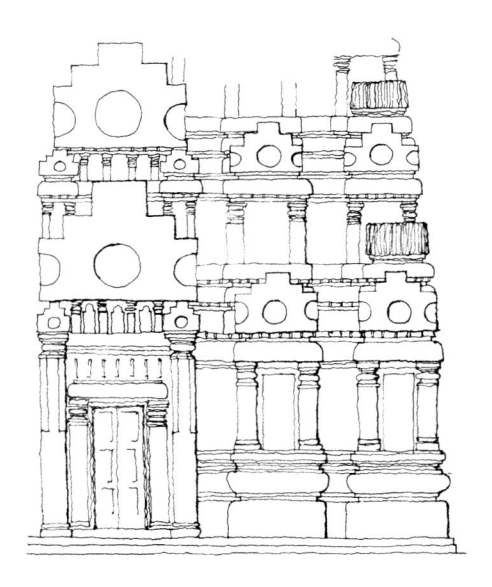

17.8 Mahabodi temple, Bodhgaya (Bihar), *c* AD 600: lower part of superstructure. Each tier, read horizontally, follows the established pattern of Phamsana/*amalaka* aedicule – minor Valabhi – major Valabhi – minor Valabhi – Phamsana/*amalaka* aedicule. The central elements here are composite Valabhi-clusters, the corner aedicules based on the form shown in 10.1c but with three eave mouldings, carried across and projecting in response to the minor Valabhi aedicules, which are also rendered as full-height.

them) do things which other traditions only do much later. With prominent *amalakas*, these temples are predominantly Nagara, although the term is used with hindsight. But the idea of tiers of aedicules with paired pilasters is more like the Dravida, and these works inherit from the storehouse of early Indian architecture various details which were contemporaneously feeding the developing Dravida vocabulary – their particular *gavaksha* form, the octagonal *kuta* domes, cushion pilasters and their use of the rail moulding (*vedika*).

A little later than the examples at Rajim (**10.5**) is the Lakshmana temple, Sirpur (**17.9**, **17.10**). Its sophistication indicates a tradition already well established. Its fully staggered square plan is perhaps the earliest known. The superstructure has a curvature and would have been crowned by an *amalaka*. There seem to have been five tiers, but not in a simple stepped pyramid: as well as stepping out towards the centre, with the staggered plan, the heads of the aedicules step up towards the centre. At first sight the vertical chain of intermediate aedicules appears to consist of two alternating types, but in fact they are made up of two-storey aedicules (domed *kuta* aedicules in the first tier, Valabhi aedicules above) with their heads shifted sideways to allow the profile of the tower to be curved.

EARLY NAGARA TEMPLES **171**

17.9 Lakshmana temple, Sirpur (Chhatisgarh), early 7th century. Photo © Gerard Foekema

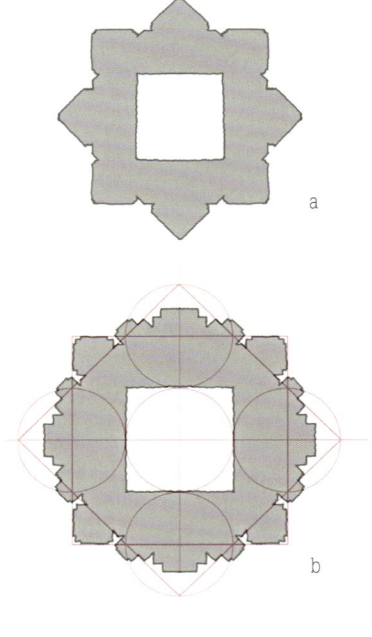

17.11 Stellate plans from Dakshina Koshala, 7th century: (**a**) Shiva temple, Dhobini; (**b**) Siddheshvara, Palari.

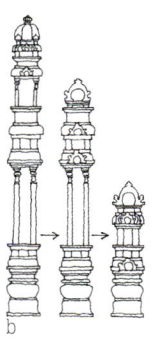

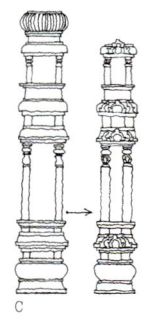

17.10 Part elevation of Lakshmana temple, Sirpur, with explanation of its aedicules: (**a**) three-storey Valabhi aedicule, showing an early example of overlapped *gavakshas*; (**b**) a disaggregated two-storey domed *kuta* aedicule; (**c**) two-storeyed *amalaka* aedicule with staggered corners. Arrows indicate projected secondary and tertiary Valabhi aedicules. The *vedika* moulding gives the aedicules a 'Dravida' character: the Valabhi aedicules are like Dravida *panjara* aedicules. In common with Bodhgaya (17.8), corner *amalakas* are cropped to reveal a pilaster belonging to the aedicule behind.

172 THE TEMPLE ARCHITECTURE OF INDIA

17.12 Shiva temple, Dhobini (Chhatisgarh), 7th century. Photo © Gerard Foekema

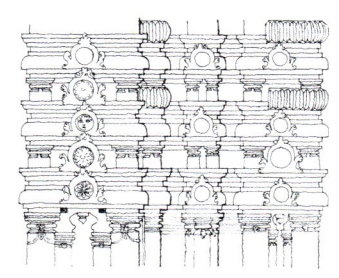

17.13 Siddheshvara temple, Palari (Chhatisgarh), c late 7th century. The shrine is composed of *amalaka* aedicules and Valabhi aedicules. On the *bhadra* (facing), which is a straightforward multi-storeyed band, a Valabhi cascade is created simply by piling up a streak of overlapping Valabhi aedicules on a single projection in the plan. The idea of two lions sitting on a corner and sharing a head goes back to Mauryan column capitals. Photo © Gerard Foekema

17.14 Temple at Ranipur-Jharial, Orissa, c 10th century: lower portions of superstructure. The Dakshina Koshala tradition pursues its own process of fusion.

17.15 Surya temple, Dhank (Gujarat), 7th century: lower portions of superstructure (shown without curvature). The *shikhara* is composed of *amalaka* aedicules fronted by simple Valabhi aedicules (10.1), with an interesting shift in the pattern. Simple Valabhi aedicules form the *lata*.

This tradition invented a great variety of stellate and semi-stellate plans (**17.11**). Force of habit led to some loose interpretations which lose the aedicular plot (**17.12**), but the Siddheshvara, Palari, is dense and meticulously worked out (**17.13**). A couple of later temples of this tradition are found in eastern Orissa. The temple at Ranipur-Jharial (**17.14**), with a *shikhara* profile like the Orissan Latina (or Rekha Deul), shows how the Dakshina Koshala masons happily carried on with a process of fusion using their own ingredients, not taking any ready-made recipe from elsewhere. The tradition shed influence on the Orissan heartland, and had outposts in what is now north-eastern Madhya Pradesh.[5]

Comparable processes to the one observed at Ranipur-Jharial, fusing early Nagara aedicules into something analogous to the Latina, can be observed in far flung places such as Akhodar and Dhank (**17.15**) in Saurashtra, and even at Pagan in Burma.[6]

Notes
1. Illustrated in Michael W Meister, 'On the Development of a Morphology for a Symbolic Architecture', *Res* 12, 1986, pp 33–50, fig 24.
2. The lower courses have recently have completed by the Archaeological Survey of India, based on a surviving portion.
3. Fiona Buckee points out to me that two fat *amalakas* lie next to 'Mandapika Shrine 1' at Mahua (MP).
4. Janice Leoshko (ed), *Bodhgaya: The Site of Enlightenment* (Bombay: Marg Publications, 1987). A pre-restoration photograph is published in this volume.
5. AK Singh, 'The Sūrya temple of Boudha Dauda', *Journal of the Asiatic Society of Bombay* 76, 2002 (for 2001).
6. Email correspondence with Donald Stadtner, who sent me photographs of two temples at Pagan which display this kind of thinking: the temple numbered 966 by Pichard (c 8th–10th century) and the Myebontha (c 1100). See also Pierre Pichard, *Inventory of Monuments at Pagan*, 9 vols (Paris etc: Kiscadale, 1992–) and Donald M Stadtner, *Ancient Pagan: Buddhist Plain of Merit* (Bangkok and London: River Books/Thames and Hudson, 2005).

18 LATINA AND RELATED VALABHI TEMPLES

The Nagara 'Mainstream' of the 7th Century

From the 7th century onwards, central and western India were divided into small kingdoms, many of which were ruled by Rajput clans. Surveying the temple architecture of the period, this region (now MP, Rajasthan and Gujarat) stands out as one broad stylistic zone, with a spectrum of regional styles within it. Stylistic continuity with Madhyadesha ('Middle Land', now UP) is easily overlooked because few traces of its temples remain from this period, but it was in many ways still the centre of things. Its main city, Kanauj (ancient Kanyakubja), from where Harsha had ruled his empire in the 6th century, was the capital of the emperor Yashovarman in the early 8th century, and of the imperial Gurjara-Pratiharas between the late 8th and 10th centuries.

It was during the 7th century that the fully formed Latina form appeared, with its curved spire (*shikhara*) rising to a ribbed *amalaka* and pot finial (*kalasha*). Madhyadesha (as is clear form surviving fragments) was the heartland of a 'mainstream' Nagara architecture which developed directly form the 'proto-Latina' of the Gupta period and its early aftermath. From this tradition the Latina mode inherited the details of a complex architectural language, including the lovingly maintained feature of a recess next to the corner projection of the *shikhara*, containing small Valabhi aedicules called *bala-panjaras* and, above these, strips of schematic colonnade level with the *amalakas* of the corner pavilions (*karna-kutas*) (**10.4**; cf **18.2a, 18.2b**). Beyond this kit of parts, examination of details reveals that most of the significant 7th-century Latina temples were the products of a consistent 'mainstream Nagara' style, of which the early form of 'standard' *gavaksha* is a hallmark (**16.4, 16.6** top). This style covers a wide area, from Nalanda (Bihar) to Alampur (AP) and Pattadakal (Karnataka).

The Galaganatha temple at Pattadakal (*c* late 7th century) has already appeared twice as a representative example of a 7th-century Latina shrine (**3.5, 10.4**). There is no need to describe this Chalukya temple again here, but it should be noted that it is stylistically identical with the group of temples at Alampur, a royal centre of the Chalukyas

250 kilometres to the east. It has the same type of plan as the Alampur temples, with internal ambulatory (**9.12c**), and the *shikhara* design follows a specific type also found at Alampur. (In the core Chalukya area to which Pattadakal belongs, a local school had built a simpler form of Latina temple since around the mid-7th century at Aihole and Mahakuta (**1.2**). Some of these must be the earliest fully Latina temples to survive intact.)

In central India, surviving pre-8th-century Latina temples are very scarce, but the fine, partly ruined Shiva Temple 2 at Mahua (MP) of *c* 675 is an example with 'double *venukosha*' – that is, with pavilions next to the central spine (*lata*) as well as at the corner (**18.1**). This is the earliest Latina example with this feature, but its roots go back to Deogarh (**17.2**). Overlapping *gavakshas* are already seen in the *lata*.

Mention must be made here of Orissa, which received the impact of mainstream Nagara in the 7th century, although this region is discussed in Chapter 21. The Parasurameshvara temple, Bhuvaneshvara (**21.3**,

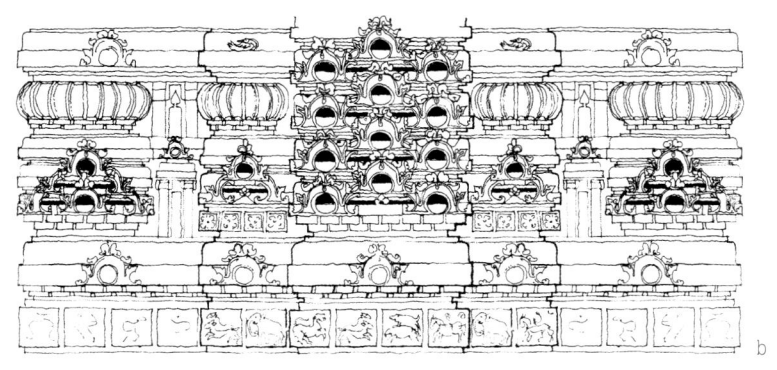

18.1 Shiva Temple 2, Mahua (MP), *c* 675, showing the central projection (*bhadra*).

18.2 Comparison between the lower parts of two Latina superstructures together with their cornice zones (*varandikas*): (**a**) Rameshvara Mahadeva temple, Amrol (MP), *c* early to mid-8th century (cf 13.2); (**b**) Bateshara Mahadeva temple, Bateshara (MP); *c* late 8th century. At Bateshara (cf 10.10) the projection next to spine (*prati-lata*) is articulated as a vertical chain of pavilions, giving a 'double *venukosha*', while at Amrol these have been abbreviated by omitting the crowning *amalakas*. Overlapping *gavaksha* patterns, already present in the *lata* (spine) at Amrol, are more pervasive at Bateshara.

18.3 Shiva temple, Indor (MP), c 750–75 (cf plan, 12.5a). Photo © Gerard Foekema

18.4 Mata-ka-Mandir, Nareshara (MP), c early 8th century: end elevation (upper parts conjecturally restored). A central projection (*bhadra*), rising up into the superstructure, takes the form of a tall Valabhi aedicule that echoes the gable end of the temple itself. In the wall zone, but overlapping the cornice, projects a niche or wall-shrine that is also in the form of a Valabhi aedicule, but one that is already entering the new phase of more complicated, overlapping *gavaksha* patterning.

21.4), follows mainstream details closely, but its style is already typically Orissan. It is usually dated to around 650, but this seems rather early.

8th-century Latina and Valabhi Temples

The 8th-century Nagara architecture of central India is a direct continuation of the 'mainstream'. It flourished notably in Gopakshetra (northern MP), around Gwalior (ancient Gopagiri).[1] Figure **18.2** shows the *shikhara* base of two shrines in that region. Stellate plan geometry, in the same spirit as the stellate plans of Dakshina Koshala, is applied to a Latina temple at Indor (**18.3**, cf **12.5a**).

It is in Gopakshetra, also, that we find two surviving examples of the Nagara language of central India applied to the barrel-roofed Valabhi mode (cf **10.8a–c**). In the Mata-ka-Mandir, Nareshara, a two-storey crowning Valabhi form is raised over one additional level (*bhumi*) (**18.4**). The lower storey of the 'upper temple' is marked, in true early mainstream Nagara fashion, by the band of schematic colonnade in line with the *amalakas* of the corner pavilions belonging to the lower *bhumi*. While the Mata-ka-Mandir is about 6 metres high, the Teli-ka Mandir in the fort at Gwalior (**18.5**), possibly ascribable to Yashovarman of Kanauj,[2] approaches 30 metres, rivalled in that century only by the Kailasa at Ellora. Even the miniature world represented in the colonnaded recess (*antarapatta*) in the base (*vedibandha*) is well above eye level, and the aedicules in the walls above are like full-size Latina and Valabhi shrines. The giant crowning Valabhi is raised on two *bhumis*, mounting with an inward curvature just as they would for a Latina *shikhara*. At the centre of the composition, three further Valabhis, each raised on one *bhumi*, detelescope forward, and yet another, with overlapping *gavakshas*, projects from the wall. As befits the scale, the corner pavilions of the superstructure are themselves composite, with their own small corner pavilions and spines (*latas*). Those of the first *bhumi* are not quite centred on the corner piers which support them, suggesting that, when they began, the builders had not quite come to terms with the scale of their undertaking: if the pavilions had been as wide as the piers, the whole tower would have had to be much higher still.

Central Indian Nagara architecture was carried north to the foothills of the Himalayas, where it ranges from the simple Latina, Valabhi and Phamsana shrines at Jageshvara to the great rock-cut complex at Masrur (**2.3**, **9.16**). The latter, possibly another imperial monument of Yashovarman,[3] assembles a whole range of shrine forms: Valabhi, and Latina shrines which are orthogonal, stellate (like Indor) and round. Southwards meanwhile, in Karnataka, the masons at Pattadakal had

176 THE TEMPLE ARCHITECTURE OF INDIA

imbibed the earlier influx of mainstream Nagara, extracting the inherent possibilities of the language. In their *gavaksha* patterns they ran through a whole cycle of invention in a few decades (**18.6**, **18.7**).

Westwards and north-westwards from central India runs an entire spectrum of styles. Scholars are increasingly abandoning dubious dynastic labels in favour of designations based on ancient geographical divisions. Two such names stand out, referring to two distinctive styles of western India: the lush Maha-Maru and the crisp Maha-Gurjara, originating respectivedly in Gurjaradesha and Marudesha (see Map 1). These are known to art historians through the masterly analysis by MA Dhaky, who identified them and traced their evolution and eventual fusion. In one of the most exciting passages to emerge in this field of scholarship since the 1980s, Dhaky describes this merging of styles: 'It was a tense moment of intense, passionate embrace of the two leading styles of Western India, one virile and handsome, the other ornate and bewitchingly beautiful'[4] (see also Chapter 19). The principal temple sites for the Maha-Maru and Maha-Gurjara in the 8th century are respectively Osian and Roda (**18.8**–**18.12**).

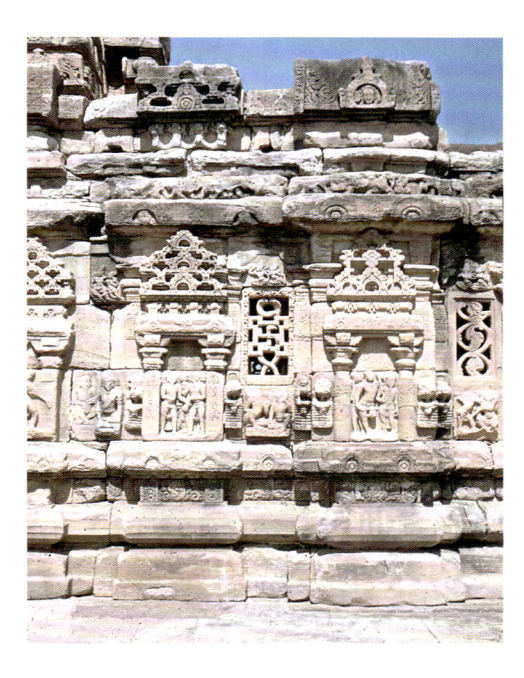

18.6 Papanatha temple, Pattadakal (Karnataka) (720–40): junction of hall and ambulatory passage. This temple shows the inventive mixing of Nagara and Dravida which would reappear in the 11th century. To the right, the wall and parapet project to form a Dravida *shala* aedicule; to the left, the parapet pavilion is a Nagara *kuta* (perhaps originally with a ribbed *amalaka*). The Valabhi wall-shrines explore combinations of the old and new ranges of *gavaksha* components (16.11). Photo © Gerard Foekema

18.5 Teli-ka Mandir, Gwalior, *c* mid-8th century: north view (cf 3.4). As there is no hall, the rectangular sanctum is entered directly via the antechamber (left). This would originally have been crowned by a giant *shuka-nasa*, a lesser version of the shrine ends. Photo © Gerard Foekema

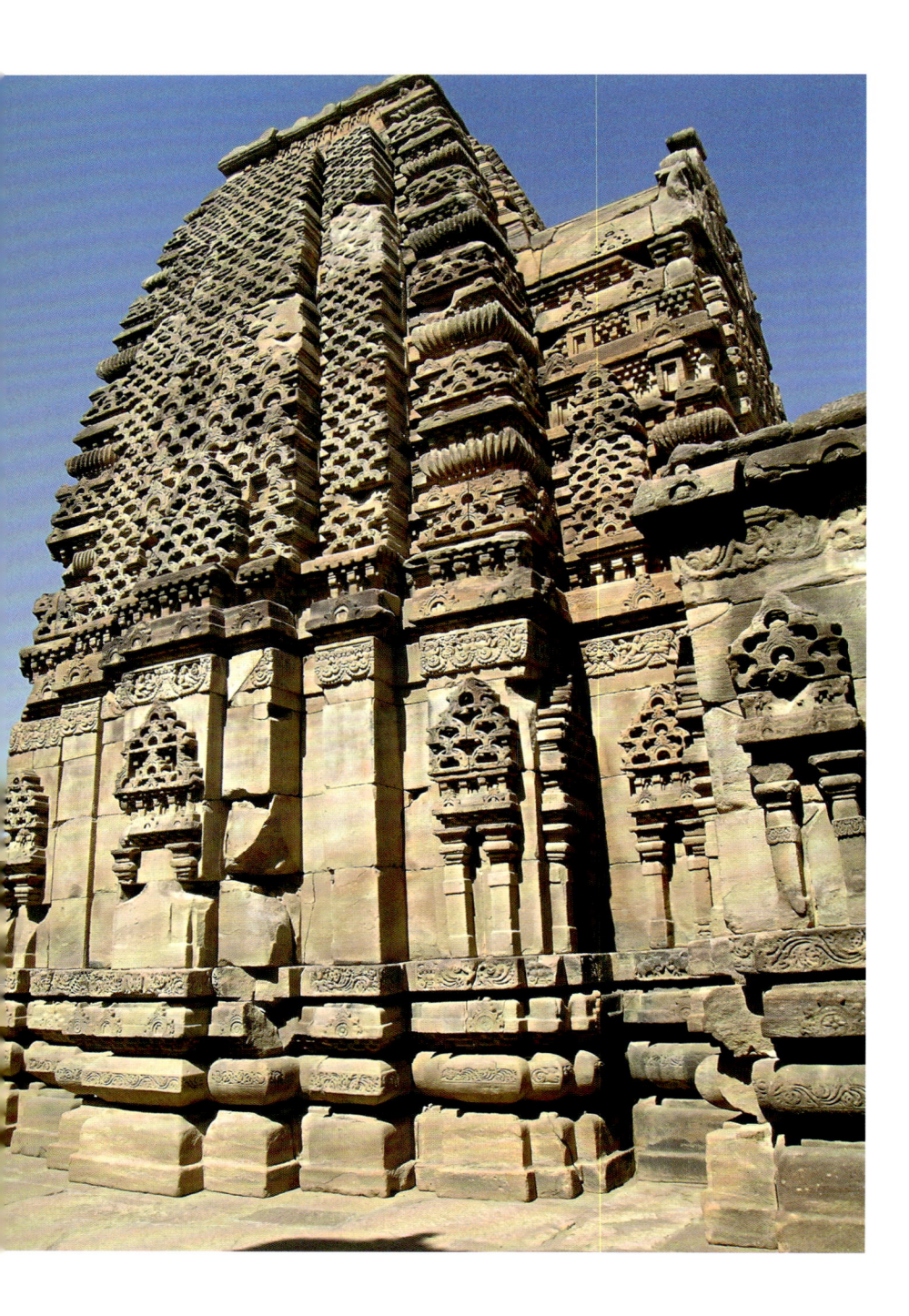

18.7 Kashivishveshvara temple, Pattadakal (Karnataka), post 756. This is a studied exercise in proliferation, advancing to five main projections (the earliest surviving fully staggered wall in a Latina temple) and five tiers (*bhumis*). The beauty of its honeycomb of small, fragmented and overlapping *gavakshas* is that they have not yielded up their depth, still harbouring receding planes of colonnade within their dark eyes. Photo © Gerard Foekema

18.8 The 'virile and handsome' Maha-Gurjara style at Roda (Gujarat), *c* late 8th century: looking from Temple 4 to Temple 3. A pilaster in the intermediate projection (of the cushion type) is rare in this region, but looks forward to a widespread 9th-century feature.

18.9 Temple 4, Roda: lower courses of superstructure. At Roda the distinctive features of pre-Latina Nagara traditions have been abandoned. There is no broad recess, and the offset next to the spine (*prati-lata*) has become, like the spine (*lata*), a band of eave mouldings displaying a *gavaksha* pattern.

178 THE TEMPLE ARCHITECTURE OF INDIA

The 9th century and Later

In the 9th century, staggered plans with recesses became the norm, but wide recesses disappeared in the *shikhara*. There were proportionately more five-projection plans, with six, seven or even nine *bhumis*, and even three-projection shrines might have seven *bhumis*, as at Umri (**18.13**). Despite this creeping inflation, surfaces remained sensuous. With five projections, intermediate projections treated as pilasters became usual (**18.14**, **18.15**, **10.12**). Aedicular niches proliferated, emerging from every available projection and recess, often from the sides of projections as well as the front, and at a smaller scale in the moulded base. Some of these wall-shrines stretched up through the *varandika*; important ones, increasingly salient, were given ribbed awnings (**18.13**, **18.15**), which began to spread across the edges of the projections. Regional traditions retained their character as they evolved, despite cross influences throughout central and western India. One style that seems to have been gloriously separate belonged to the region south of Kanpur on the edge of Madhyadesha (**18.16**).

18.12 Harihara Temple 1, Osian, *c* 725–50. This is a five-shrine (*panch-ayatana*) temple. Its platform (*jagati*) is characteristic of the site, and remains show that it was surrounded by a seat (*sopana*), which would have had the usual racked back (*kaksh-asana*). Photo © Gerard Foekema

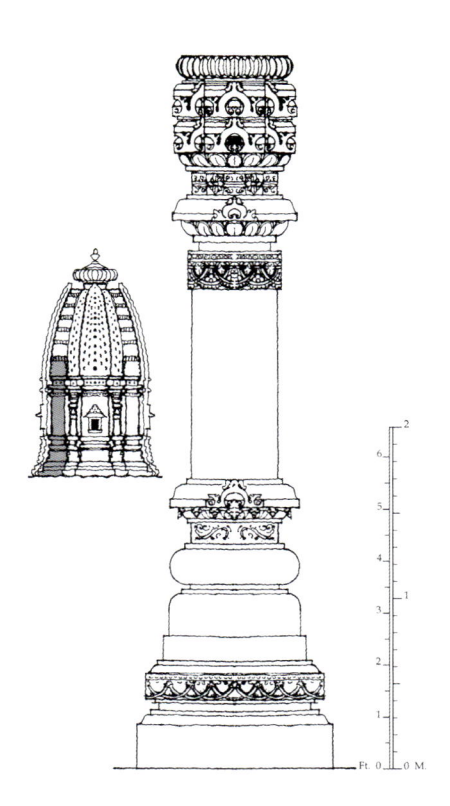

18.10 Temple 3, Roda, corner projection.

18.11 The 'ornate and bewitchingly beautiful' Maha-Maru style: Vishnu Temple 1, Osian (Rajasthan), *c* 775. Early temples at Osian retain the early Nagara features in their towers (recesses with minor Valabhi aedicules called *bala-panjara*, the option, seen here, of additional vertical chains of pavilions, termed 'double *venukosha*'), though these details are becoming less meticulous. Photo © Gerard Foekema

18.13 Surya temple, Umri (MP), *c* 825–50. This three-projection, seven-tier Latina shrine is stylistically typical of 9th-century (Pratihara period) Dasharnadesha (cf 18.1–18.5 for its direct forbears). The central niches enshrine Surya, the sun god, in his chariot; the corner niches, often displaying the guardians of the directions of space (*dikpalas*), here contain their consorts (*dikpalikas*). In the base (*vedibandha*) a floor moulding (*tula-pitha*) alternates with the vase moulding (*kalasha*). Above the eave moulding (*kapotali*) which terminates the base are two Nagara equivalents of the Dravida rail moulding (*vedika*), termed *manchika* and *chippika*. Photo © Gerard Foekema

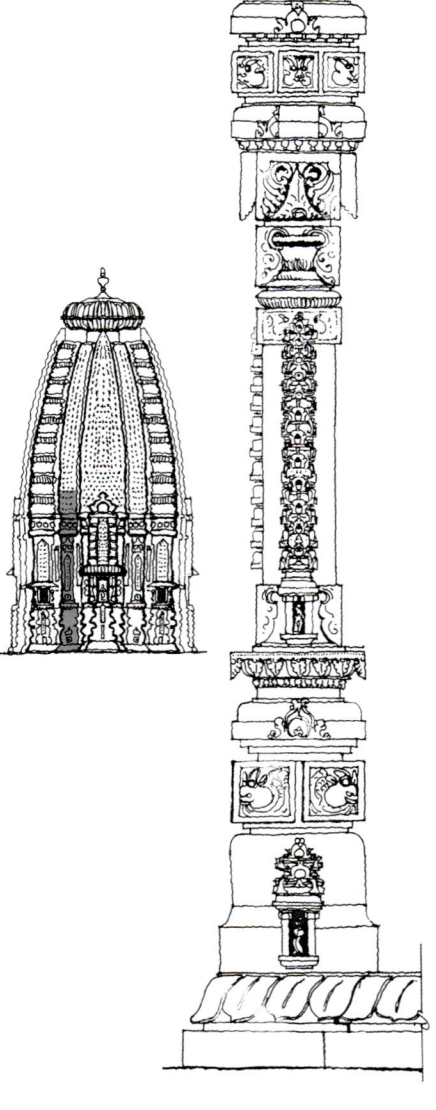

18.14 Surya temple, Madkheda, 825–75: intermediate projections. A grander temple in the same tradition as 18.13.

180 THE TEMPLE ARCHITECTURE OF INDIA

18.16 Brick temple, Nimiyakheda (UP) (cf plan, 12.5b). Photo © Gerard Foekema

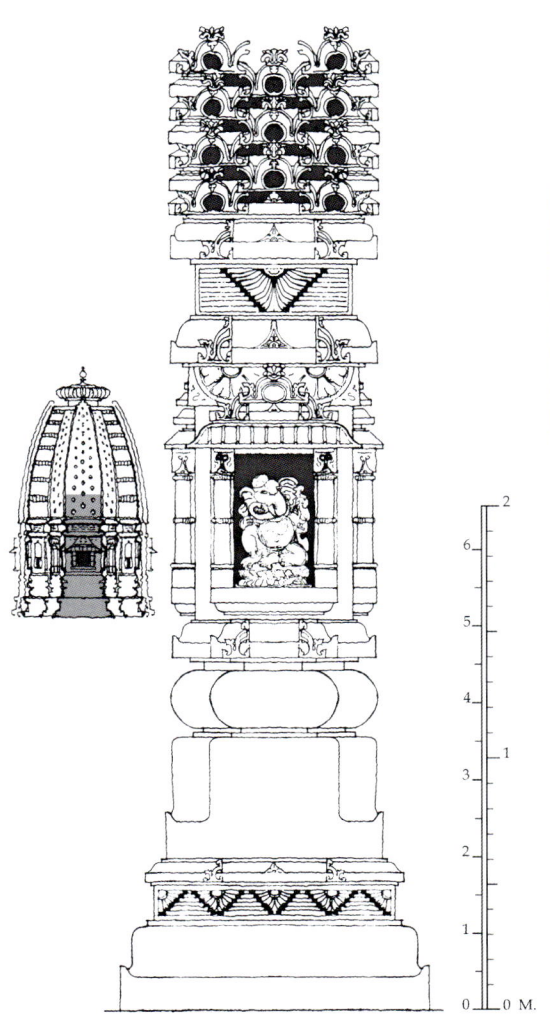

18.15 Shiva temple, Bhavanipur (Rajasthan), c 850–75: the Maha-Maru in the 9th century.

Numbers of *bhumis* continued to increase. In western India by the 10th century all the projections were treated as pillars, from which niches emerged, but in central India, other than in the *bhadra*, the heavenly crew spurned niches, sprinkling themselves in a band around the walls, banishing pediments and pillar mouldings to a zone at the top, if not altogether, and demanding two or three tiers of wall for themselves (**5.2**). The last Latina shrines of pretension have as many as seven projections and 21 *bhumis* (Vamana temple, Khajuraho), but we are now well into the age of the Shekhari.

Notes
1. See Michael D Willis, *Temples of Gopaksetra* (London: British Museum, 1997).
2. *Encyclopaedia of Indian Temple Architecture*, vol 2, pt 2, p 4.
3. Michael W Meister, 'Mountain Temples and Temple Mountains: Masrur', *Journal of the Society of Architectural Historians* 65:1, 2006, pp 26–49.
4. MA Dhaky, 'The Genesis and Development of Maru-Gurjara Temple Architecture' in Pramod Chandra (ed), *Studies in Indian Temple Architecture* (New Delhi: AIIS, 1975), pp 114–65 (p 120).

19   SHEKHARI TEMPLES

The majority of Shekhari temples, the Nagara form with a clustered spine, are found in western India. It was there that their emergence and growth ran parallel to a comparable burgeoning of ceiling designs and Samvarana halls (the composite form of the tiered-roofed Phamsana), and where a rigorous geometry and a lasting typology were developed. Scores of Shekhari temples were built in Gujarat under the Solankis between the 10th and 13th centuries. Jain patronage became increasingly important here and in neighbouring Rajasthan (witnessed in the temple complexes at Kumbhariya and Mount Abu), and played a crucial role in later revivals. In central India, meanwhile, the form was almost as conspicuous, and cannot be ascribed entirely to western Indian influence. By the 11th century the mode had also been imbibed, if not entirely digested, in the Deccan, where Shekhari shrines were built under the Yadavas in Maharashtra and the Later Chalukyas in northern Karnataka. In that century the Shekhari mode also travelled eastwards to the shores of the Bay of Bengal, where it was taken on by the masons of Orissa (see Chapter 21).

The Shekhari, as any other 'mode', took shape in particular 'styles' or regional ways of making things. Many of its early manifestations in western India were created in the Maha-Gurjara (**19.2–19.4**) and the Maha-Maru, the styles of Gurjaradesha and Marudesha introduced in Chapter 18, and in the Saurashtra style (see Map 1). In central India many Shekhari temples exhibit the vertical urgency and the tiered, peopled walls familiar from the famous temples of the Chandellas at Khajuraho in Jejakabhukti (**19.5**), characteristics that belong equally to a spectrum of styles stretching from the realms of the Kalachuris in Dahala to the east, to those of the Kacchapaghatas in Dasharnadesha to the west (**19.1**; cf **5.2**). As for the sequel to Dhaky's love story of the Maha-Gurjara and the Maha-Maru, it relates that when the two styles merged they 'both lost their identity. The result was a beautiful offspring, which was to be honoured, loved and supported by a great empire, that of the Solankis.'[1] The baby was named (by Dhaky) the Maru-Gurjara. It became an enduring and remarkably uniform style over

19.1 Small shrine on roof of monastery at Survaya (MP), 10th century. The basic idea is that of a 'proto-Shekhari' shrine (10.13a), with a central Valabhi porch and *kuta-stambhas* at the corners. This is where the Dasharnadesha/Gopakshetra style has reached by this date.
Photo © Fiona Buckee

182   THE TEMPLE ARCHITECTURE OF INDIA

19.2 Ambika temple, Jagat (Rajasthan), c 961: southern view the Maha-Gurjara style in the 10th century (cf plan 9.4b; mandapa type 10.20b; gavaksha cascade 3.7). Photo © Gerard Foekema

19.4 Interior of the hall at Jagat. The ceiling, which has lost its pendant, is shown in 15.5.

19.3 Ambika temple, Jagat, central projection (*bhadra*): (left) how the central cluster is conceived as a 'proto-Shekhari' shrine (10.13a).

19.5 Lakshmana temple, Khajuraho (MP), dated 954: southern view. In the tradition of central and western Indian *sandhara* temples, ie with an internal ambulatory passage (9.12g, 9.18a), the cardinal projections take the form of an emerging open hall, here expressed frontally with a Valabhi cascade. Photo © Gerard Foekema

SHEKHARI TEMPLES 183

wide regions of western India, and numerous Shekhari temples are its products (**19.8–19.11**, **19.14**, **19.15**).

The Shekhari mode broke out from the chrysalis of the Latina, and took flight. Its gestation had been long. The idea of articulating the walls of Nagara shrines to form full-height aedicular components, other than in the early aedicular Nagara traditions discussed in Chapter 17, had probably already found expression in the 7th century.[2] By the 9th century, Anekandaka ('multi-limbed') forms were well established – the two 'proto-Shekhari' types illustrated in **10.11** (cf **19.1**), and the Anekandaka Phamsana seen at Auwa (**10.21**). The simpler 'proto-Shekhari' was prevalent in what is now western Gujarat, both in Saurashtra (no longer a stronghold of the Phamsana) and in Kachchh (western Gujarat). The extended form (**10.11b**) was well suited to the *sandhara* plan with porch-like projections to admit light to the ambulatory (**9.12g**, **9.18a**, **9.18b**). It is likely to have been the shrine form used at a series of 8th- and 9th-century temples in Rajasthan of this plan type, which have now lost their superstructures, including the sadly ruined Maha-Maru masterpiece at Abaneri (early 9th century), opulent and still bewitching. In any case, the formula appears at the *sandhara* Maladevi, Gyaraspur (Madhya Pradesh) (*c* 850–75).[3] There was, of course, nothing 'proto' about such temples in their own time, and these types continued to be built in the 10th century alongside fully Shekhari ones, as alternative ways of combining the range of aedicular components.

In Chapter 10, I described five principal types of Shekhari shrine (see **10.16**, also **12.3**). At Prachi in Saurahstra there is a precocious Type 2,[4] the Bhim-Deval temple, which on stylistic grounds seems to belong to the 9th century, much earlier than the earliest surviving Type 1 at Nagda (Maha-Gurjara style, *c* 975) (**1.6**). In fact, although Type 1 expresses the Shekhari idea archetypally, and endlessly appears as part of larger compositions, the shrine at Nagda is apparently the only surviving full-scale example of its kind. Establishing types, in any case, was not at the heart of Shekhari temple design in the 10th century, when invention was more a matter of combining existing types into further arrangements. The shrine (*mula-prasada*) of the Ambika temple, Jagat (Rajasthan) (*c* 961) is an exquisite example of the concept of the projected central cluster (**19.2–19.4**). At the centre of the composition appears the simpler form of 'proto-Shekhari'. The concept is made explicit by the smaller scale of the intermediate projections (in the form of *kuta-stambhas*) and their relationship to the chest *shikhara* (*urah-shringa*) – and elsewhere rendered even more explicit when embedded half-*bhadras*

19.6 Lakshmana temple, Khajuraho: Phamsana *kuta-stambha* at the corner of the main hall (*maha-mandapa*).

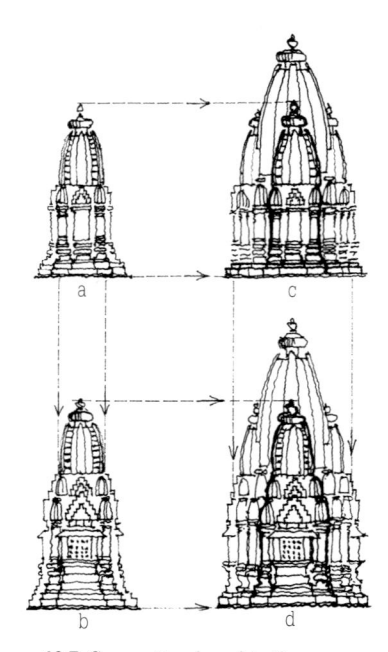

19.7 Compositional combinations: piling up and projecting out.

appear at the sides of the central cluster.[5] The Lakshmana temple, Khajuraho (**19.5**, **19.6**), hosts a galaxy of unfolding configurations, overlapping illusionistically through interpenetration and conceptually through possibilities of alternative readings (**19.7**).

From this melting pot emerged the Shekhari types. Eventually they became fixed, but it should be reiterated that these general types are to do with the three-dimensional relationships between parts, not the identity of the components themselves, which vary. Towards the end of the 10th century, Type 2 became the run-of-the-mill model (**19.8**), but its basic relationships underlie some significant monuments, notably the Vishvanatha at Khajuraho (*c* 999) and the Sun temple at Modhera (**19.15**, **9.18b**). The latter, the first great work of the new-born Maru-Gurjara, instead of rushing ahead into a stepped diamond plan, proliferates by making its components composite.

Downward extension from Type 2 leads, as already explained (Chapter 10), to Type 3 with its stepped diamond plan and reentrant projections. It is first seen at the Someshvara, Kiradu (Rajasthan) (*c* 1020); among several 12th-century examples from Gujarat are the Navalakha, Sejakpur (**19.9**), the Duladeva, Khajuraho, of a similar date, following a slightly different geometry (**12.3c** upper right). Kiradu also has two of the earliest Type 4 shrines, from around the mid-11th century (**10.15**). This dense composition, filling out the reentrants with quarter-*shringas*, was built in large numbers throughout the 12th century (**19.10**, **19.11**).

19.8 Sanderi Mata temple, Sander (Gujarat), *c* 2nd quarter 11th century: Type 2 Shekhari shrine with a Samvarana (composite Phamsana) open hall (*ranga-mandapa*), in the Maru-Gurjara style. The perimeter pillars are of the *bharana* type with a sprouting pot (*ghata-pallava*) chest; the seat back (*kaksh-asana*) is mostly missing. Photo © Gerard Foekema

19.9 Navalakha temple, Sejakpur (Gujarat), early 12th century: Type 3 Shekhari shrine again with a Samvarana hall and in the Maru-Gurjara style (cf 13.4). Photo © Gerard Foekema

19.10 Nilakantha Mahadeva temple, Sunak (Gujarat), *c* 1075 (cf 9.10c): Type 4 Shekhari shrine, once again Maru-Gurjara and with a Samvarana *mandapa*. A sequence of two half-spires (*urah-shringas*) is fundamental to the type, while a third is optional (cf 10.15). The *kuta-stambhas* are crowned by composite spires, which are 'proto-Shekhari' (10.13a). Photo © Gerard Foekema

19.11 Left: Jasmalnatha Mahadeva temple, Asoda (Gujarat), Maru-Gurjara style, 12th century: *kuta-stambha* on sub-base (*pitha*). The Type 4 composition is similar to Sunak (19.10), but the miniature spires on the *kuta-stambhas* are Latina.

19.13 Right: Kandariya Mahadeva, Khajuraho: *kuta-stambha* on sub-base (*pitha*).

19.12 Below: Kandariya Mahadeva temple, Khajuraho, *c* 1030: southern view. The shrine proper (*mula-prasada*) is the earliest Type 5 Shekhari design. The porch-like centrepiece, sliding out from the wall in continuation of the sequence of four half-spires (*urah-shringas*) in the superstructure, and mirrored in the centrepiece of the main hall (*maha-mandapa*), combines the characteristics of the equivalent elements of the neighbouring Vishvanatha and Lakshmana temples – the multiple Phamsana of the former and the frontal Valabhi cascade of the latter.
Photo © Gerard Foekema

19.14 Ajitanatha temple, Taranga (Gujarat), Maru-Gurjara style, 1165: Type 5 Shekhari shrine and Samvarana hall. The *kuta-stambhas* of the shrine are crowned by composite Shekhari towers, rather than unitary Latina ones. Though all Type 2, they increase in complexity as they descend, and those on the corner projection are more elaborate than the adjacent ones. The Samvarana reentrant pavilions are arranged in two steps per tier of *kuta-stambhas* revealing the wall-zones of the latter. Photo © Gerard Foekema

Type 5 appears in the Kandariya Mahadeva, Khajuraho (**19.12**, **3.8**). This giant among temples is not excessively large: about 32 metres high, excluding the platform. Bringing the stepped diamond plan to Khajuraho for the first time, it multiplied the number of wall facets for the play of heavenly multitudes. That many of the crowd disport themselves in cool recesses is because the reentrant projections of the first tier are (as in Type 4) flush with the main projections, not protruding (cf **12.3d**, **12.3e**), as the Kandariya does not follow the later geometry for Type 5. Another difference from the later norm is that, at the cost of forcing a little higher the skirts of the second (from the top) *urah-shringa*, extra quarter-*shringas* are placed in the second tier, the size of the lowest *urah-shringa*, creating a four-emerging-from-one (Type 1) cluster, echoed twice above in an upward-expanding sequence. The later standard Type 5 is seen in two 12th-century examples: the Samiddheshvara, Chittor (**10.17**) and the towering Jain temple of Ajitanatha at Taranga, almost 50 metres high (**19.14**). Type 5 reigned supreme until partially usurped in the later Shekhari revivals. Unexplored extrapolations were then explored, but only through compromises (see Chapter 26).

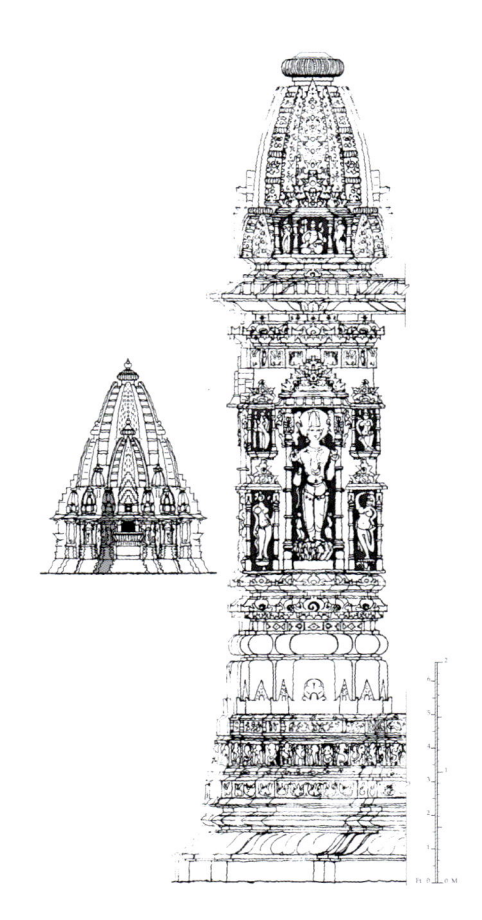

Notes
1 MA Dhaky, 'The Genesis and Development of Maru-Gurjara Temple Architecture' in Pramod Chandra (ed), *Studies in Indian Temple Architecture* (New Delhi: AIIS, 1975), pp 114–65 (p 120).
2 See Michael W Meister on the Shiva temple, Kusuma, and other early *sandhara* temples in *Encyclopaedia of Indian Temple Architecture*, vol 2, pt 1, p 210 and vol 2, pt 2, p 212.
3 Kapilakotta (or Kerakot) in Kachchh (*c* early to mid-10th century).
4 *Encyclopaedia of Indian Temple Architecture*, vol 2, pt 2, plates 750–2. The plates illustrate the temple at Prachi.
5 Elsewhere the idea of an embedded 'proto-Shekhari' shrine is made even more explicit by half-*bhadras* appearing at the sides of the central cluster, as in the Javari temple, Khajuraho.

19.15 Surya temple, Modhera (Gujarat), Maru-Gurjara style, 1026: intermediate projection (*prati-bhadra*) in the form of a 'proto-Shekhari' shrine (10.13a).

20 BHUMIJA TEMPLES

The Paramaras, ambitious rulers of Malava (Malwa, western MP) from the 11th century to the end of the 13th, and no doubt to distinguish themselves from rival dynasties patronising mainly Shekhari temples, chose the Bhumija as their favoured mode, with its vertical chains of *shikhara*-topped pillar forms (*kuta-stambhas*). Of the two dozen temples surviving from their realms, three stand out as imperial monuments. The Udayeshvara at Udayapur (**20.1**) was founded by King Udayaditya in 1059 and consecrated in 1080. On a more gigantic scale are the remnants of the destroyed Bijamandal at Vidisha (*c* late 11th century). Most grandiose of all is the unfinished temple at Bhojpur, ascribed to Bhoja (1000–55), possibly intended as a Phamsana memorial shrine, but of Bhumija 'style' in its detailing. Malava has been seen as the homeland of the Bhumija,[1] but the mode was equally prevalent in Seunadesha (north-western Maharashtra).[2] The Yadava (or Seuna) dynasty were as wedded to Bhumija temples as their Paramara contemporaries. The large Ambaranatha temple at Ambaranath, dated 1060, and the 12th-century Gondeshvara at Sinnar (Srinagara, one-time Yadava capital) are no doubt royal foundations (**9.17**, **13.3**).

A scattering of Bhumija temples radiates out from these regions, some in neighbouring parts of what are now Rajasthan and Gujarat. But outnumbering all of the foregoing are those further south. The Later

20.2 Dattatreya temple, Chattarki (Karnataka), *c* 12th century: hall. The main *kuta-stambhas* have lost their crowning pavilions: the miniature ones below the seat back (*kaksh-asana*) have pavilions of the type called Dravida-karma (10.14g). The foot moulding of the base (*vedibandha*), above the pedestal (*pitha*), is like a Karnata Dravida *jagati*, rather than a *khura-kumbha*. The plan is a staggered square, but each projection has two faces (as in a stepped diamond plan), and there are reentrant projections. Photo © Gerard Foekema

20.1 Udayeshvara temple, Udayapur (MP), founded 1059.
Photo © Gerard Foekema

188 THE TEMPLE ARCHITECTURE OF INDIA

Chalukyas of Kalyana (Kalyani), known for their Karnata Dravida temples, built mainly Bhumija temples in the region of their capital (although nothing survives at Kalyani itself) (**20.2**).[3] Bhumija temples were erected, along with Karnata Dravida and southern-style Phamsana ones, by their feudatories and later successors, the Kakatiyas in Telangana (north-west AP) (**20.3**) and the Hoysalas in southern Karnataka, far to the south. It can be no coincidence that, in 1117, Hoysala Vishnuvardhana, still nominally a feudatory, chose the Bhumija mode for the Chenna-Keshava temple, Belur (**20.4**), and had it built larger than any Chalukya temple. It is not usually realised that this temple, well known to tourists, is a Bhumija one, because it has lost its superstructure — the sad fate of the great majority of surviving Bhumija temples.

In Chapter 10 it was suggested that the sudden appearance of Bhumija temples, with no trace of formative stages, is not difficult to understand, as it can be seen how the form would be invented as a transformation of the Latina. More surprising is the fact that the Bhumija appears largely in hitherto unknown styles, in the sense of the shapes and character of their details — unlike the Shekhari, which takes shape in existing styles. In Seunadesha the novelty arises because virtually no temples are known in Maharashtra from the previous two centuries, but in the eastern fringes of Malava the new Bhumija monuments contrast markedly with established regional styles. Whatever the origins, there were clearly guilds who were Bhumija specialists. When they built Shekhari temples, they did them in their own manner, as at Anjaneri (Maharashtra), Badnavar (MP) and as far north as Bijolia (Rajasthan).

There is a Deccani flavour to these Bhumija styles, naturally more pronounced towards the south, but present throughout, witnessed in the large onion *gavakshas* crowning the central projections (*bhadras*) and the predominantly cushion-type pillars and pilasters. Mouldings share a character that was taking hold in Karnata Dravida traditions, precise and curvaceous (tending towards the dry and mechanical), with knife-edge points and pronounced double flexions, often broken by horizontal fillets (dividing *khura* from *kumbha* [**13.3**] and cleaving the *pali* below the *phalaka* [**14.5d**]) and with bold flourishes at the corners. Beyond details, Bhumija temples share much with Karnata Dravida ones: the piling up of aedicular components in level tiers, the stellate option, a prevalence of multiple shrines around a single hall (**19.15**), rectangular structural bays aligned with the sanctum, and often an aedicular projection in the *kapili* recess (exterior of the antechamber or *antarala*). Just as Bhumija shrines were known in Karnataka, Karnata Dravida shrines appeared in Maharashtra under the Yadavas, executed with

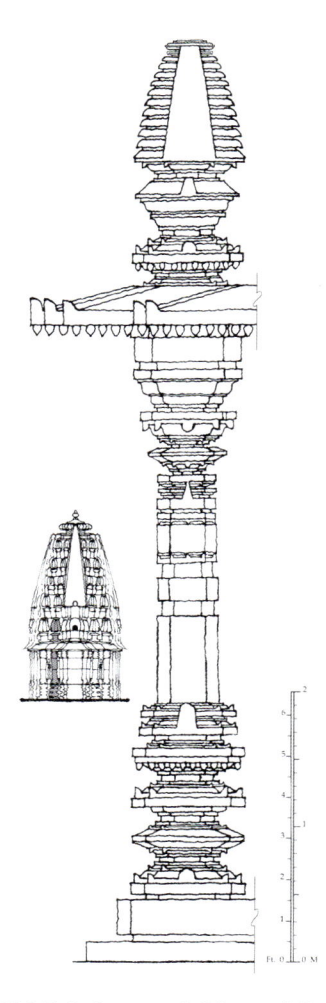

20.3 Erakeshvara temple, Pillamarri (AP), 1208: *kuta-stambha* on sub-base (*pitha*).

20.4 Chenna-Keshava temple, Belur (Karnataka), 1117. The miniature shrines around the platform are varieties of Bhumija, echoing the form of the main shrine before it lost its superstructure. Photo © Gerard Foekema

20.5 'Pipal leaf' or 'moonstone' motif, which became a hallmark of Bhumija temples and of temples in other modes built by the Bhumija masons. The motif evolved from roundels on the waists or chests of pillars: an earlier version is seen in 14.6 (middle left). It was not strictly a *gavaksha*, but was seen as belonging to the same family, to be alternated with varied *gavaksha* forms as a miniature niche pediment.

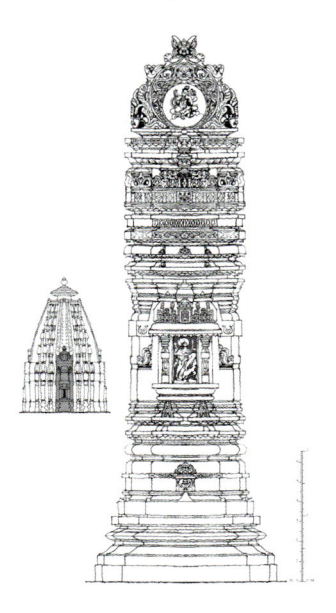

20.6 Mahakaleshvara 2, Un (MP), *c* late 11th century: centre piece in the form of a composite, Valabhi shrine.

20.7 Malavai temple, Alirajpur (MP), 12th century: *shikhara*. This is a 32-point stellate shrine with seven tiers (*bhumis*). The *kuta-stambhas* have Bhumija spires, those at the corner being 8-point stellate. Photo © Gerard Foekema

varying degrees of competence.[4] An exotic *kuta* type is almost ubiquitous among Bhumija temples, with a bell top and flaming tridents billowing from its base (**10.14g**). Doubtless the one referred to in texts as 'Dravida-karma', it must have been thought of as southern: the early ones, of which the main shrine at Amberanath is composed, bristle with strange crocodile-like (*makara*) heads derived from Karnata Dravida 'floor mouldings' (*prati*). All of this might point to the lower Deccan, perhaps the Kalyani region, as the origin of the Bhumija, were it not that the best Bhumija temples of Malava are so much more finely executed than the southern ones which, for one thing, have no curvature.[5]

It is striking that the stylistic details of Bhumija temples are not purely the result of craft habits and norms. Some, at least, were deliberately chosen – not invented out of nothing but fished from the common pool and made into hallmarks. The standard Nagara *gavaksha* was known but used sparingly: the bush-eared, second-class *gavaksha* was adopted, nurtured alongside the onion *gavaksha* and made into net patters (*jalas*) (**16.13**). Another motif, the 'moonstone' (**20.5**), proclaimed Bhumija identity on the waists and chests of pillars and pilasters.

If all this is a story of style, of ornament even, rather than composition, it is because, as explained in Chapter 10, the range of Bhumija types presented itself from the outset, leaving no room for evolution. The Udayeshvara, which has no surviving precedents, is already the deluxe model, based on a 32-point star (equivalent to seven orthogonal projections), with seven *bhumis* (**10.18b**). Occasional attempts to surpass this limit were not really successful: at Nemawar (MP) (*c* early 12th century) they tried the same plan with nine *bhumis*, finding that they had to taper the top abruptly to avoid having to go too high, while at the Undeshvara, Bijolia (similar date), a podium and a tier of headless *kuta-stambhas* were added to mitigate 'the disparity between the heights of the superstructure and the lower structure'.[6]

Within the standard types, however, variations were possible in the usual way – through the choice and design of the aedicular components. Apart from the principal *kuta-stambhas*, the central cluster in the more ambitious examples was a large, composite Valabhi shrine-image, demanding invention (**20.6**). At first sight the main *kuta-stambhas* of a typical Bhumija temple might seem to support simple, curved Latina superstructures, and indeed the lower Deccan used its version of the Latina for this purpose. On closer inspection the characteristic form of a crowning pavilion in Malava and Seunadesha reveals itself to be a schematically rendered form of orthogonal Bhumija, in which the miniature pavilions are not Latina but the bell-crowned Dravida-karma

190 THE TEMPLE ARCHITECTURE OF INDIA

20.8 Galateshvara temple, Sarnel (Gujarat), *c* late 12th century. This is an *ashta-bhadra* ('with eight main projections') shrine based on a 24-point star. It is by a Maru-Gurjara workshop, using their usual detailing entirely. Crowning the main projections (*bhadras*), instead of the typically Bhumija onion *gavakshas*, we find western Indian Valabhi pavilions. Above these they have placed a single exoticism, their own rendition of the moonstone motif (20.5), declaring 'we know how to do Bhumija!'. A comparable interpretation of a Bhumija temple in a foreign style, in this case the Dahala Style of the Kalachuris, is found at Arang (MP).
Photo © Gerard Foekema

20.9 Parvati or Devi temple, Ramgarh (Rajasthan), 12th century. A Latina-Bhumija hybrid is created by alternating segments of spine (*lata*) with *kuta-stambha* chains.
Photo © Gerard Foekema

(**20.1**). These simplified Bhumija shrine-images appear already in the 11th century, before Shekhari temples commonly sported Shekhari towers on their *kuta-stambhas*. Fully articulated Bhumija *kuta-stambhas* are also found, including stellate ones (**20.7**).

Outside this Bhumija heartland, more fundamental alternatives were tried. Uniform stellate (without *bhadras*, ie without main projections **9.1t–v**) and semi-stellate (**9.1s**) Bhumija designs appear over niches in the walls of Karnata Dravida temples: a full-size version of the uniform stellate (16 points, three *bhumis*) at Nandikandi (AP) and of the semi-stellate (five projections, four *bhumis*) at Turuvekere (Karnataka). *Ashta-bhadra* (eight-*bhadra*) plans (**9.1r**) are seen at Sarnel (**20.8**) and Nuggihalli (Karnataka). On the fringes of the heartland are two interesting hybrid (*mishraka*) temples, one crossing the Bhumija with the Latina (**20.9**), another with the Shekhari (**20.10**).[7]

Notes

1. Krishna Deva, 'Bhumija Temples' in Pramod Chandra (ed), *Studies in Indian Temple Architecture* (New Delhi: AIIS, 1975), pp 91–2.
2. Henry Cousens, *Medieval Temples of the Dakhan* (Calcutta: ASI, 1931).
3. Gerard Foekema, *Cālkyan Architecture of Medieval Karnātaka*, 3 vols (Delhi: Munshiram, 2003).
4. The Ayeshvara, Sinnar and *vimanas* at Takahari and Ter.
5. Fragments at Ashapuri (MP) appear to belong to an early (*c* 10th-century) example of the Bhumija 'mode', from before the influx of the Bhumija 'style'.
6. Deva, 'Bhumija Temples', p 106.
7. 'The Surya temple, Ranakpur, Rajasthan, is a spectacular 14th-century Shekhari–Bhumija hybrid'; Deva, 'Bhumija Temples', pp 107–8, plates 46–7.

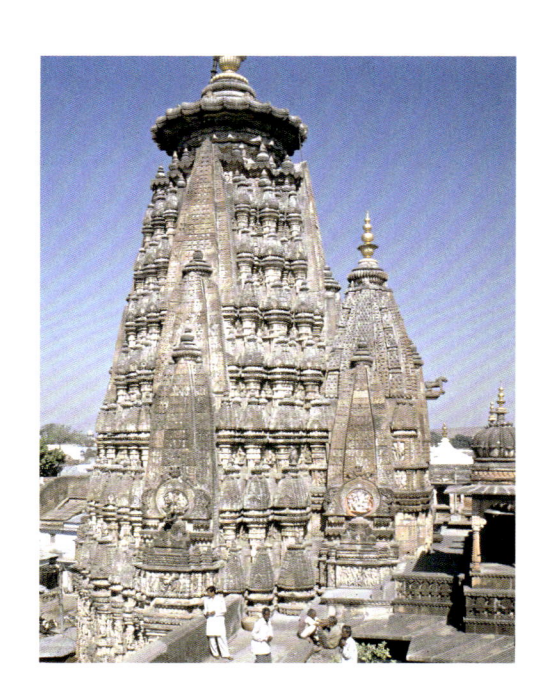

20.10 Surya temple, Jhalarapatan (Rajasthan), *c* 12th century with later additions. This is a Shekhari-Bhumija hybrid, with a Shekhari *shuka-nasa*. The scalloped *amalaka* is common among Bhumija temples.
Photo © Gerard Foekema

21   Temples of Eastern India

The history of medieval temple architecture in eastern India consists of two parallel stories: that of the regions now lying in Bihar, Jarkhand and Bengal (West Bengal and Bangladesh), and that of the coastal region of Orissa. Orissan temples will take up most of this chapter, since many more survive.

In about the 5th century BC, Magadha, around Pataliputra (Patna, Bihar), had formed the backdrop to the lives of the Buddha and of Mahavira, founder of Jainism, both of whom had challenged Brahminical orthodoxy. This fertile region of the lower Gangetic plains had subsequently become the heart of the two most extensive empires of ancient India, those of the Mauryas (late 4th to early 2nd century BC) and the Guptas (*c* AD 320–550). The Mauryas had championed Buddhism, and the Gupta elite, while devotees of the Hindu god Vishnu and establishing 'classical' Brahminical or Hindu cultural patterns, also supported Buddhist institutions. Magadha remained an important centre of power in eastern India after the Guptas and, although its rulers were Hindu, Buddism remained an important force. During the 6th and 7th centuries much building activity took place at the great Buddhist university of Nalanda and at Bodhgaya, where the Buddha attained enlightenment. From the late 8th to early 12th centuries, this region was the home of the Pala dynasty, who extended their empire eastwards across Bengal, and were for a short while the paramount rulers throughout northern India. At a time when Buddhism was declining elsewhere in India, the Palas, who themselves worshipped Shiva, allowed Buddhism to flourish. Buddhist monasteries and *stupas* continued to be built throughout their realms. Nalanda remained a cultural hub during this period, and from here artistic influence followed religious connections to Tibet and South-east Asia. Pala sculpture, much of it in polished black schist, is found in museums all over the world; but of the temple architecture built under the Palas and the Senas, who succeeded them in the 12th century, relatively little remains, as much of it was in brick and much fell victim to conquest. A distinctive tradition can nevertheless be traced.

Ancient states had formed in what we now know as Orissa, including the kingdom of Kalinga, conquered in 261 BC by the Maurya emperor Ashoka, who famously embraced Buddhism, horrified at the carnage caused by his conquest; but for centuries this region remained peripheral, and it was only from around the 7th century AD that a lasting kingdom was formed here. The heartland of Orissa has always been the fertile, rice-growing coastal plains, centred, as still today, on Bhuvaneshvara (Bhubaneshwar) and surrounded by hilly areas inhabited by tribes. Rulers from outside this heartland, descended from tribal chieftains, successively took control, adding their homelands to the expanding kingdom. The Shailodbhavas took over from the south during the 7th century but were ousted by the Bhauma Karas in the 8th century, who were themselves dislodged in the 10th by the Somavamshis who had moved across progressively from Dakshina Koshala. In the early 12th century the Gangas, from what is now northern Andhra Pradesh (by then 'Kalinga' referred to this area), conquered and enlarged the kingdom.

Until around AD 1000, temple building and the settlement of Brahmins went hand in hand with the extension of agriculture and the absorption of indigenous peoples into an expanding Hindu society.[1] To help this process, local tribal cults were assimilated and identified with Hindu deities. By the 11th century the kingdom was well established, but rulers needed more than ever to assert their legitimacy among rivals and feudatories. This situation, in parallel with the rise of Bhakti (devotional worship) and pilgrimage, led to the royal patronage of gigantic 'imperial' temples: the Lingaraja, Bhuvaneshvara (*c* 1060), the Jagannatha, Puri (*c* 1135), and the Surya temple, Konarak (*c* 1250). Since the 12th century, the cult of Jagannatha (a deity of tribal origin assimilated to Vaishnavism) has been an integral part of Orissan culture, Orissan kings being considered his regents.[2]

As Orissa remained comparatively undisturbed by invasions from without, its medieval temples survive in large numbers. In fact, its temple building tradition has trickled on even until today. Given the continuity of this tradition and the unmistakable character of its

21.1 Stupa 3, Nalanda (Bihar), *c* 6th century. A large central structure (now ruined) is raised on a high platform, which has four minor *stupas* at the corners. The south-east corner *stupa* (left), with flight of steps behind, leads to the platform. On the right is a minor *stupa* fronted by a Valabhi aedicule.

21.2 Votive *stupas* of the Pala period, c 10th century, now in the Indian Museum, Kolkata (Calcutta). These have aedicular niches on the cardinal axes and are mainly Phamsana, but the front one on the *stupa* in the foreground is Valabhi, placed sideways (cf 21.1 right). The *stupas*, which have lost their Buddha images and crowning umbrellas, are raised on miniature colonnades, over the three standard Nagara base mouldings. Typically 'Pala' are the relaxed, shrug-shouldered *gavakshas* and the trefoil archways (*toranas*) on bulbous columns, here fronting the Phamsana aedicules and forming a lower storey arcade in the Valabhi aedicule. Such *toranas* are also common in Orissa from this date onwards.

creations, it might be expected to be a classic example of the playing out of some internal logic, resulting in the kind of quasi-organic pattern of unfolding seen elsewhere. That this is not so is partly a matter of conservatism and a propensity to follow given types for a very long time, and partly because the development of Orissan temple architecture, despite its relative isolation, is inextricably connected to a succession of influxes from other parts of India. In other words, this tradition cannot be seen as a continuous progression from spring to ocean, but is better understood in terms of a series of waves flowing in from other seas and merging with the local waters.

Temple Architecture of Bihar, Jarkhand and Bengal

The 6th–7th century brick *stupa* architecture at Nalanda already exhibits features that would become widespread throughout the Pala period. In numerous small votive *stupas* at the site, the circular dome (*anda*) sits on a square, moulded base; aedicular niches project on the cardinal axes, and sometimes also on the diagonals. Often the gateway associations of the Valabhi form are exploited on the front of the *stupa*, where the aedicule is placed sideways-on, as a blind entrance and a niche for the main image (**21.1** left, **21.2**).

The Mahabodi temple at Bodhgaya (*c* early 7th century; see **17.8**) and its subsidiary shrines, as far as can be seen in their restored state, are close in style to contemporary work at Nalanda, but follow an architectural conception different form anything found there. Their architecture represents one of the two strands of 'early aedicular' Nagara discussed in Chapter 17, in which temple exteriors are conceived entirely in terms of interlinked shrine forms. Whereas the other strand, that of Dakshina Koshala, has left traces of a continuing tradition, the Bodhgaya branch is known only from the Mahabodi group. In the mid-7th century, the purest 'mainstream' Nagara architecture, like that of central India, appeared at Nalanda in the now ruined Latina shrine known as Temple 2 (**16.4**). Fragments from the Pala period show that a tradition of Nagara temple architecture still flourished in this part of India, with knowledge of the Latina curved spire, the piled eaves of the Phamsana and the barrel-roofed Valabhi mode (**10.9**). Nagara temples may well have been built by Buddhists as well as Hindus. Not surprisingly, this tradition was stylistically close to that of the Pala *stupas*. In Magadha, 'Pala' details (trefoil archway motifs or *toranas*, the horseshoe arch or *gavaksha* types shown in **16.8**) are found together with central Indian features (*gavaksha* nets, pilasters of the sprouting vase or *ghata-pallava* type [**14.8**] etc);[3] eastwards, in Bengal, the Pala aspects are present without the central Indian ones. This is the case for the brick temples still standing in the south-west of what is now West Bengal.[4] By the 10th century these have something in common with contemporary temple architecture in Orissa, so it makes sense to return to this region after surveying the Orissan tradition.

The Parasurameshvara and Early Orissan Latina

The Orissan style appears as if ready-made and the hypothesis that often comes up in such cases, that stone architecture grew out of an already established wood-carving tradition, seems plausible here, given the lush but shallow relief and the strong presence of the surfaces of the block. Typically, beyond the individual block, each form is bounded within a clear volume, often within a vertical-sided pile, and all these volumes are packed together like children's bricks in a box. As elsewhere, architectural elements are embedded in the body of the temple, but there is a tendency to think frontally, and complex interpenetration is rare. All is broad, rounded, effortless and abundant.

These lasting characteristics of Orissan temple architecture are already conspicuous in the early temples at Bhuvaneshvara. The finest of these is the Parasurameshvara (**21.3**, **21.4**), among the earliest and usually dated to around AD 650. As with several well-known Orissan temples, it is not generally realised that it is of a type, or became so. The source of the Parasurameshvara is clear: it comes directly from the mainstream early Latina that is spread so widely through the centre of India, complete with a broad recess containing minor Valabhi aedicules (*bala-panjaras*). This origin is evident in the mouldings and even in small details, including in the *gavakshas*, which are standard mainstream ones, with the standard geometry. Yet the character is already completely Orissan. Rather than a sense of depth, it is voluptuous surfaces which dominate. Straight-sided *bala-panjaras* fill their allotted space, framing languid couples rather than receding planes. *Gavakshas* look comfortable, wearing big fat pearls, their ears spread out to the limit (**16.9a**).

There are also peculiarities in the overall composition. Projecting from the wall are three aedicules: the wall thus is of three projections, but not in the usual sense whereby the corners form two of the projections. These three aedicules are bold and clear images of Valabhi shrines, the large central one coming further forward and rising up into the tower (*shikhara*). This perennial idea of a large central temple image is almost ubiquitous in Orissa: here it is much bigger than the actual Valabhi shrine of the same style shown in **21.5**. Compared with the norms elsewhere, the

21.3 Parasurameshvara temple, Bhuvaneshvara, *c* 650. One of the earliest surviving Orissan temples, it closely follows the 'mainstream' Latina temples of central India, yet is already completely Orissan in character. Three Valabhi aedicules project boldly from the wall. The design became a 'type', followed by many later temples.
Photo © Gerard Foekema

21.4 Parasurameshvara: wall and lower part of *shikhara*.

21.5 Durga temple, Baideshvara, *c* early 8th century. Like the aedicules in the walls of the Parasurameshvara, this is a Valabhi shrine derived from the widespread Nagara language of central India. Two different kinds of Valabhi (known in Orissa as Khakara) would later appear.

Parasurameshvara shows a striking lack of vertical integration between sanctum wall and superstructure, where the number of projections is not three but five, though both the wall and the tower follow a modular logic (see **21.4**). These peculiarities are faithfully observed in succeeding versions of the type, along with the five levels (*bhumis*), marked by the ribbed *amalakas* at the corners. The only common variation is that minor shrines have three *bhumis* rather than five.

An Influx of Early Aedicular Nagara

The Parasurameshvara type continued to be built right through the 8th and 9th centuries, and is spread from Khiching in the north of Orissa to Mukhalingam (AP) in the south.[5] Three temples in Bhuvaneshvara from around the middle of the 8th century, however, show an entirely different conception. The Sisireshvara temple (**21.7**) and the similar Markandeyesvara are Latina only in their general outline, having a curved superstructure with a central spine: closer inspection reveals that they are fully aedicular in the manner of the tradition of Dakshina Koshala. That the inspiration is from there (long before the Somavamshis linked the two regions politically) is clear both in the aedicular composition and in details such as the vase of plenty in the base, although the character of the lush surfaces is entirely Orissan. The big temple form at the centre is again Valabhi, projecting not from a *lata* spine, but from a multi-storeyed palace with colonnades and overhanging eaves. The corners are full two-storey Phamsana aedicules (**21.8**). Directly from Koshala comes the 'one-leg-showing' trick – the pilaster top is next to the ribbed *amalakas*, implying that each succeeding aedicule is behind the one below.

The third member of this group of temples is the Vaital Deul (**21.6**, **10.8d**). Standing to the south of the smaller Sisireshvara, this is its Valabhi equivalent. It constitutes a second kind of Orissan Valabhi – or Khakara, to use the Orissan term. The Vaital is composed of similar aedicules to the Sisireshvara; two tiers support the crowning Valabhi form. At the centre of the end elevations projects a large Valabhi aedicule, similar to the centrepiece of the Sisireshvara. This is raised on substantial pilasters, topped by sprouting vases and addorsed lions. Each pilaster has its own moulded base, giving rise to a characteristically Orissan slot between the legs, filled up by a further upright projection.

A Southern Wave

Interaction with the architectural traditions of Dakshina Koshala continued, but the particular influx represented by the Vaital Deul and

21.6 Vaital Deul temple, Bhuvaneshvara, *c* 750: end elevation of shrine, southern view. This is the second variety of Orissan Valabhi shrine, inspired by the multi-aedicular temple architecture of Dakshina Koshala.
Photo © Gerard Foekema

21.7 Sisireshvara temple, Bhuvaneshvara, *c* 750, with the corner of the Vaital Deul in the foreground. This is not a Latina temple: it is composed of the same kinds of elements as the Vaital Deul, derived from the tradition of Dakshina Koshala.

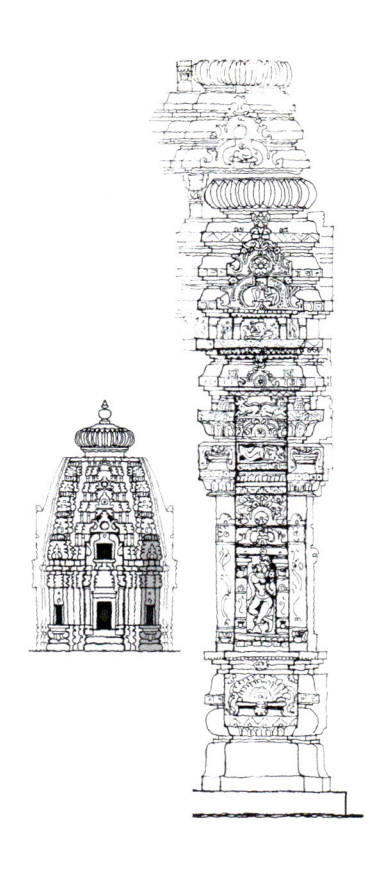

21.8 Sisireshvara temple: corner projection. This is a full two-storey Phamsana aedicule, with sprouting vase (*phata-pallava*) pilasters supporting Phamsana crowning pavilions. It is fronted by a full-height Valabhi *kuta-stambha* containing a secondary Valabhi aedicule within its straight-sided trunk. The base (*vedibandha*) has the usual three mouldings, surmounted by a stepped rail moulding. In the base of the Valabhi *kuta-stambha*, a *ghata-purna* takes the place of the usual *kapotali* and *kalasha* moulding (cf the Dakshina Koshala tradition, where the *kalasha* itself is treated like a *purna-ghata*).

21.9 Varahi temple, Chaurasi, *c* 930: west (long) elevation. This is the third kind of Orissan Valabhi shrine, its multi-aedicular composition inspired by the Dravida traditions of the Deccan. Various details point to this source, especially the floor moulding (*prati*) with crocodilian (*makara*) heads. Photo © Gerard Foekema

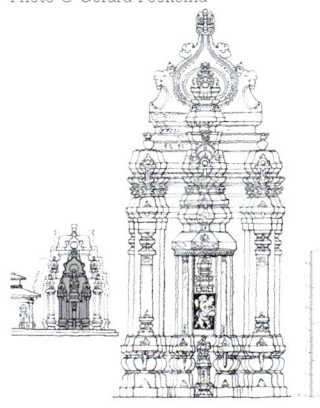

21.10 Varahi temple, Chaurasi, *c* 930: central cluster of the end elevations, in the form of a simpler version of the same kind of shrine.

the Sisireshvara was an interlude, and did not supplant the Parasurameshvara type. Some time in the first half of the 10th century a new wave burst in on the Orissan heartland, this time to become fully and lastingly absorbed. Its vehicle was a third kind of Valabhi or Khakara — at least, it seems to have been classified as such, although it has little in common with the earlier forms beyond its rectangular plan and its use for enshrining goddesses and forming a centrepiece in other kinds of temple design.

The earliest surviving example is the lavish little temple of the goddess Varahi set among the coconut palms at Chaurasi (**21.9**, **21.10**). The style of its carved surfaces is still distinctly Orissan, but luxuriates in a new, bejewelled laciness, which the heavenly maidens, balancing on top of pillars (*stambhas*) wrapped round by snake spirits (*nagas*) in the recesses, seem especially to be enjoying. These *naga*-entwined *stambhas* are shared with later temples of the Dakshina Koshala tradition,[6] as are the particular form of southern 'cushion' pilaster, and the vase-shaped *kalasha* moulding in the base, with its dangling tongues of foliage, traceable back to Sirpur (**17.10**). However, the radically new form of the shrine can only have been created through contact with southern, Dravida temple architecture, as seen in the traditions of Karnataka and Andhra. The crown of the shrine is no Valabhi tunnel-roof, but an elongated dome. In itself this does not make the temple southern, as the vestiges of such a roof had long lurked behind Nagara Valabhi gables; but, together with the chunky lotus-petal

TEMPLES OF EASTERN INDIA **197**

rail moulding (*vedika*) below it, the top of the shrine is the equivalent of an oblong Dravida *kuta* pavilion. This is fronted, on every face, not by northern *gavakshas* but Deccani-looking onion-shaped ones (cf **16.10d, e**), swooping from the jaws of a leonine monster (*vyala*). Looking at the long (west) elevation (**21.9**), we see that the crowning pavilion is raised over two tiers of full-height aedicules, stepping forward progressively in a fully staggered plan.

These aedicules can only be described in Dravida terms. The central element in the first tier (the usual place of a Dravida barrel-roofed *shala* aedicule) is a three-storey rectangular, domed *kuta* aedicule, and in the second tier (omitting the *kuta* dome) the horseshoe gable end of a large *panjara* aedicule. At the corners of the shrine are square *kuta* aedicules, without pilasters but with a full-height projecting *panjara*-on-pilaster (*panjara-stambha*) strip, in the spirit of the Sisireshvara (cf **21.8**). Similar strips are integral to the intermediate elements, which take the form of double-staggered *panjara* aedicules, each crowned by a sequence of three detelescoping *gavakshas*. There is a remarkably Karnata Dravida spirit in this multiple *panjara* and in the central downsurge of *gavakshas* interspersed with secondary aedicules. What marks the Chaurasi aedicules as definitively Dravida is their upper series of mouldings: a double eave moulding (*kapota*), a rail moulding (*vedika*) and in between (in all but the corner aedicules) the unmistakable and entirely Dravida floor moulding (*prati*) with crocodilian (*makara*) heads (cf **13.5, 13.6**).

The Chaurasi type of Khakara is seen a little later in the Gauri temple, Bhuvaneshvara, and as late as the 13th century at Beyalisbati near Konarak, but meanwhile the new wave represented by Chaurasi completely refreshes the Orissan mainstream during the 10th century. Two early flowerings from this assimilation show a new style of Latina shrine, or Rekha Deul, in Orissan terminology: the ruined but exquisite five-shrine (*panch-ayatana*) temple at Ganeshvarpura (**21.11**) and the Mukhteshvara, Bhuvaneshvara (**21.12**), where every surface blooms with sensuous joy.

The layout of the Mukhteshvara, with its archway (*torana*), enclosure wall, surrounding temples and tank, has been illustrated earlier (**9.19**). In certain ways the shrine itself continues the tradition passed down from the Parasurameshvara. This is seen in the superstructure, with its five levels and five segments, its minor offset to the spine and the very late recurrence of miniature Valabhi aedicules (*bala-panjaras*) in the outer recesses. The tradition is also reflected in the big Valabhi (or Khakara) shrine form at the centre of the composition, but now it is the

21.11 An Orissan version of a Dravida *panjara* aedicule, Ganeshvarpura, *c* mid-10th century. The legacy of the 'southern wave' was long-lasting, but the *prati* moulding was gradually lost (cf 21.21).

21.13 Mukhteshvara temple, central cluster, representing the third kind of Orissan Valabhi shrine (cf 21.10). With its large crowning *gavaksha* or *nasi*, flanked by dwarves, this kind of shrine remained a common centrepiece, but soon lost its Dravida character.

new Chaurasi type of 'Dravida Valabhi' that steps out tall and proud (**21.13**). In complete contrast to the Parasurameshvara type, however, is the marked vertical integration between wall and superstructure. This is even more insistent than in other Nagara traditions, and seems to have resulted from the aedicular thinking found at Chaurasi. Each segment is given a distinct treatment, carried from top to toe. Every box of space is filled up, and nothing is allowed to be background, so that if one part could be pushed in, another part would surely have to spring out.

Fresh Nagara Contacts

Dravida influences were not the only ones to refresh the Orissan tradition during the 10th century. Renewed contacts with the Nagara traditions of central India are also evident, not least in the Mukhteshvara. The hall (*mandapa*, or *jagamohana*, the Orissan equivalent), instead of the established rectangular, slab-roofed type, is for the first time square with a tiered roof, and thus Phamsana, or a Pidha Deul, as it is known in Orissa.

Contrary to the subsequent norms, the roof has a rounded profile, is crowned by a simple vase (*kalasha*) rather than a bell shape (*ghanta*) (**10.20d**) and covers a beautiful carved 'lantern' ceiling, rather than plain corbelling. This ceiling in particular suggests that the inspiration for the form of the *mandapa* hall is central Indian rather than from Kalinga (Orissa/Andhra borders), where Phamsana shrines were also well established.

Horseshoe arch motifs (*gavakshas*), as ever, provide conclusive traces of a stylistic connection. Over the porch of the Mukhteshvara and the porch-like projections on the sides of the hall are pediments composed of such elements, following in every detail the contemporary waspish version then sweeping through central and western India (**21.14**; cf **16.6bottom**). It seems as if the Orissan architect on his travels has jotted down the exotic motif in his palm-leaf notebook, or whatever it was he used. He has also seen *gavaksha* nets (*jalas*), as the Mukhteshvara is among the first Orissan temples where these appear,[7] but he has not grasped their system, inventing instead a syncopated pattern made of the onion-like form that had come in with the southern wave (**16.9b**). That these northern contacts were sporadic is clear from the floppy wasp *gavakshas*, fast forgetting what had inspired them, seen in 11th-century temples at Bhuvaneshvara such as the Rajarani and the Brahmeshvara (**16.9c**).

The Rajarani (*c* 1000–30), with its clustered spire or *shikhara*, is another unique temple (**21.15**). Wobbly *gavakshas* notwithstanding, its composite overall form is unmistakably of central Indian inspiration, as

21.12 Mukhteshvara temple, Bhuvaneshvara, *c* 960: *mula-prasada* (Orissan '*rekha deul*'). The centrepiece of the design represents the 'Chaurasi type' of Valabhi shrine (cf 21.9, 10). Every parcel of space is filled, with each segment of the *mula-prasada* given a distinct treatment all the way up. The corner projections are conceived (explicitly in the first *bhumi*) as *kuta-stambhas*; the intermediate ones are bound together by the use of the same *gavaksha* network in both the *shikhara* and the Phamsanaesque aedicule that takes up the entire wall space. Even the main recesses – the rest are mere slots – are treated as vertical chains of positive elements: *naga*-bound pillarets are given small Valabhi aedicules at their base and head, and the same aedicules rise up as *bala-panjaras* in the tower. Each contains a nymph awaiting her lover at an open door – or you can see it as the same girl enjoying a ride up and down in a lift. Photo © Gerard Foekema

21.14 Mukhteshvara temple: pediment projecting from *mandapa* roof, made of careful copies of contemporary central Indian *gavakshas*.

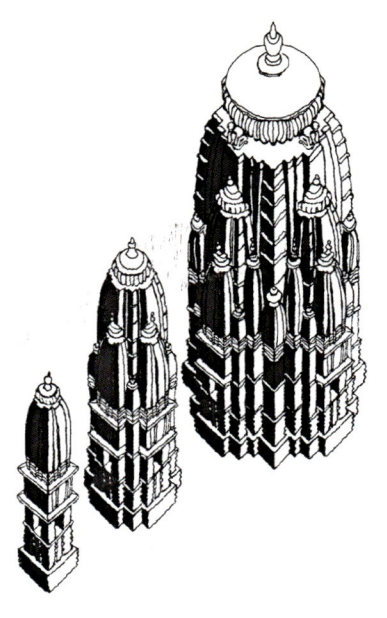

21.16 The central cluster in the design of the Rajarani temple is a Type 1 Shekhari form; in its turn, a Latina aedicule is the centrepiece of a Type 1 Shekhari shrine.

it is a truly Shekhari shrine. Also of central Indian origin are the sub-base (*pitha*), the two-tier wall and the horned lions (*vyalas* or *shardhulas*) lurking in its recesses. All these are common in Orissa from now on. Following the principle of the central cluster, the designer has hit upon the powerful idea, surprisingly not known anywhere else, of embedding a Type 1 Shekhari shrine form (**10.16a**) as the centrepiece (**21.16**). That this is the concept is confirmed by the fact that the intermediate spirelet-topped pillar forms (*kuta-stambhas*) are shorter than the corner ones. One result of the idea is the appearance, at the sides of the centrepiece, of 'quarter-spires' implying embedded half ones at a time when these were only just appearing, for different reasons, in the Shekhari heartlands. The Rajarani is beautifully three-dimensional, but the more-or-less Shekhari works that came in its wake are already reverting to Orissan frontality.[8]

21.15 Rajarani temple, Bhuvaneshvara, *c* 1000–30. This is the one truly, three-dimensionally conceived Shekhari temple in Orissa.

21.17 Brahmeshvara temple, Bhuvaneshvara, *c* 1060: southern view. The temple nestles in an enclosure with its four corner shrines (cf 9.7). Photo © Gerard Foekema.

200 THE TEMPLE ARCHITECTURE OF INDIA

Later Orissan Temples

More than a century of great variety in Orissan temple architecture was followed, from the mid-11th century, by two further centuries of prolific temple building, but now dominated again by standard types. Two basic types were established around 1060 by two temples in Bhuvaneshvara, the Brahmeshvara and the mighty Lingaraja.

Many later temples follow the design of the Brahmeshvara (**21.17**), but without the same richness of surface treatment.[9] In its form we see the afterglow of the Orissan masons' fling with the Shekhari, but they have come home resolutely to frontality. The shrine is Latina, because it has reverted to the single primary unit, but its centrepiece (**21.18**), with a Latina superstructure, still recalls a Shekhari half-spire (*urah-shringa*). Other segments have miniature *shikharas* placed frontally at the base of the tower, thus recalling *kuta-stambhas* but not fully articulated as such. Either side of the spine is a vertical chain of Valabhi aedicules with very tipsy *gavakshas*. These are extremely late echoes of *bala-panjaras* (cf **21.3**, **21.12**), but on a projection rather than in a recess. The curvature of the *shikhara* follows the profile that would from now on be characteristic of Orissan temples: barely curving in as it rises, then sweeping in at the rounded shoulder.

While the scale of the Brahmeshvara is intimate, the Lingaraja (**21.19**) is the first of the Orissan giant temples, towering over the palms and the swelling strata of its surrounding complex. At some 50 metres tall, it rivals the Chola giants of this date. The design takes stock of previous strands, as if trying to incorporate its forbears and surpass them. On each face of the main shrine, the centrepiece, taller than most earlier temples, follows that of the Mukhteshvara (cf **21.13**); though an understanding of the Dravida basis of the Chaurasi-type Valabhi has long been forgotten. Despite the much greater scale, the two-tier wall and its minor aedicules, along with the base mouldings, are essentially like those of the Brahmeshvara. However, in the cornice zone (*varandika*, or Orissan *bada*), multiplied mouldings presage the new striated intensity of the tower.

Until now, Orissan temples had kept conservatively to a maximum of five levels (*bhumis*) in the superstructure;[10] in the Lingaraja this is doubled, while maintaining the now usual five mouldings between each pair of corner *amalakas*. The whole tower is imbued with the post-Mukhteshvara concern for distinctively treated vertical segments. Next to the bold spine is a chain of four Latina-crowned *kuta-stambhas*; an innovation rooted in the earlier Shekhari interlude, but now carried all the way up the *shikhara*, and therefore approaching the concept of the

21.18 Brahmeshvara temple: central projection in the form of a Latina shrine. This is a legacy of the Orissan experiment with the Shekhari mode, as are the miniature Latina *shikharas* at the base of each segment of the tower.

21.19 Lingaraja temple, Bhuvaneshvara, *c* 1060. This vast 'imperial' monument is a model for many later Orissan temples. It introduces a denser texture to the *shikhara* by establishing a new norm of 10 *bhumis* (levels) instead of five. This increase was no doubt seen as appropriate to a superior temple, but the size of the building made it a practical choice, since to maintain five *bhumis* would have required mouldings made of impossibly heavy stones, or else of several courses. Photo © Gerard Foekema

Bhumija mode, of which continuous vertical bands of such forms are the defining characteristic. However, in the Orissan spirit of frontality, and maintaining the integrity of the Latina unit, the *kuta-stambhas* are placed on the segment, rather than constituting it as they do in Shekhari or Bhumija temples. These elements decrease in height by one *bhumi* (as marked by the corner *amalakas*) in each successive stage, creating too rapid a diminution in comparison with the width of the segment. In the corner segment, the increase in the number of levels to 10 would have resulted in very squat corner pavilions. To put this right, an additional projection has been made at the corner itself, forming a vertical tube of little *shikharas*. No corresponding projection has been provided in the wall below: on the contrary, here the corner has been eaten away by offsets, so the corner tube of the superstructure hangs above it.

From this time onwards the Lingaraja becomes the principal model for Orissan temples, with 10 *bhumis* as the norm. While there are variations, some temples follow the type precisely, with the *kuta-stambha* chain (its rate of diminution refined) and the tube of miniature *shikharas* hanging at the corner. Miniature Phamsana cells on the cardinal axes of the main shrine, possibly an afterthought at the Lingaraja, also become a standard feature. The two later 'imperial' temples in Orissa – the Jagannatha temple, Puri, and the sun temple of Konarak[11] – take the Lingaraja as their model and surpass it in scale. Seven-projection plans are also found in this late phase, as at the Megheshvara temple (**21.20**).[12]

The later Orissan temples, standing like giant stacks of assorted biscuits, are no stale leftovers from a more fertile age. Even without the painting that must once have enriched them, they have their own quality of abstraction. Vertically strung and ribbed and slotted, sliced through in varied rhythms, nibbled at every corner, they find, without fragmentation or complex interpenetration, their own way of appearing to loom out of a fertile continuum. Here bareness does not seem to have been a matter of mere economy: nevertheless, when the imperial coffers flowed to wheel forth the mighty chariot-temple of Surya at Konarak (**21.21**), its million mouldings were chipped away with as gentle a sensuality as ever.

Meanwhile in Bengal

Returning to the surviving brick temples of the 'Pala' tradition in West Bengal, it is now possible to appreciate those aspects which, by about the 10th century, they share with contemporary Orissan temples, as well as what is different. The finest and best preserved is the Shiva temple

21.20 *Shikhara* of the Megheshvara temple, Bhuvaneshvara, dated by inscription to between 1170 and 1198. This is a fine example of the abstract and rhythmic qualities of later Orissan monuments. It has seven projections, plus a very thin one next to the *prati-bhadra*. The corner pavilions have circular *amalakas*, now usual, and are fronted by plain, single-*gavaksha* Valabhi projections. This is the closest that the Orissan tradition comes to the Bhumija mode, with four vertical chains of *kuta-stambhas*, though as ever in Orissa these are placed on the front of flat segments.

21.21 Konarak, aedicule from moulded platform (*pitha*), *c* mid-13th century. This type, close to the Dravida *kuta* aedicule, was probably seen as Valabhi (Khakara) in Orissa.

at Bahulara, near Bishnupur (**21.22**), *c* late 11th century. Only the shrine itself still stands, with enough of the original plasterwork (including graceful figures in the swags at the top of the wall) to give a sense of the original delicacy. Before the paintwork was lost, this temple must have been a feast of colour and textured pattern.

The temple at Bahulara belongs to a sophisticated tradition — independent, yet showing much in common with Orissa. Shared with Orissan temples of this date are the two-tier wall divided by three mouldings, the contrasting vertical segments (at least in the superstructure), the circular corner *amalakas*, the vase-like *kalasha* moulding (used here at the foot of the *shikhara* as well as in the base) and above all the curvature of the superstructure.

The geometry of central and western Indian *gavaksha* nets has not reached this far east; as at the Mukhteshvara temple, a special kind of network has been invented, using local arch motifs. These have simply been placed one inside another and joined cheek-to-cheek. The other kind of 'Pala' *gavaksha*, the heart-shaped one (**16.8a**), is used as a contrast: in the photograph, small ones can be seen on the components of the Latina aedicule fronting the central projection,[13] and vestiges at the base of the tower.

Notes

1. This account is based on Hermann Kulke, 'Royal Temple Policy and the Structure of Medieval Hindu Kingdoms' in A Eschmann, H Kulke and GC Tripathi (eds), *The Cult of Jagganath and the Regional Tradition of Orissa* (Delhi: Manohar, 1978), pp 125–37.
2. For a different model of the development of Orissan temple architecture from mine, in which these dynastic events are seen as crucial, and without my emphasis on outside influences, see DR Das, 'Orissan Temple Architecture: from Sub-Regionalism to Regionalism' in *Journal of Ancient Indian History*, date unknown, pp 112–28.
3. Many wonderful sandstone fragments are in the site museum at Itkhore, Jarkhand.
4. See Ajay Khare, *Temple Architecture of Eastern India* (Gurgaon: Shubhi Publications, 2005).
5. The temples in and around Mukhalingam (now in northern AP), ancient Kalinganagara, are stylistically close to those of the Orissan heartland, but show more variation in the number of *bhumis*.
6. Eg the temple at Ranipur-Jharial; see Thomas E Donaldson, *Hindu Temple Art of Orissa*, vol 1 (Leiden: Brill, 1985), figs 515–16.
7. The same *jala* design is seen at Ganeshvarpura; it is subsequently found as far away as Khiching.
8. The Dakra Bhimeshvara and the Ekambareshvara.
9. Including the Siddhesvara, Kedhareshvara and Rameshvara, all at Bhuvaneshvara.
10. A rare exception is the Rajarani, with seven *bhumis* in its *mula-manjari*.
11. At Konarak the shrine proper is ruined, but a 19th-century engraving with part of the tower still standing shows that it followed the Lingaraja type, at least in general terms.
12. The Ananata Vasudeva of *c* 1275 achieves seven projections through a simple refinement to the corner of the Lingaraja type: a corner projection is placed under the previously hanging 'tube', and in the adjacent gap is placed a *kuta-stambha*. As in several works of this period, we thus have the unusual effect of a projection next to the central one (a *pratibhadra*) which is wider than the corner projection (*karna*).
13. This kind of *gavaksha* is most prominent in a Valabhi projection fronting this Latina aedicule, unfortunately worn away in the elevation shown here.

21.22 Shiva temple, Bahulara (West Bengal), *c* late 11th century. The centrepiece, rising up into the superstructure, is an unusual kind of Valabhi shrine image composed of strings of small Latina aedicules, making it a kind of Bhumija Valabhi. Projecting from this, and typical of the tradition already established in 6th-century Nalanda (cf 21.1, 21.2), is a sideways-on Valabhi aedicule; and from this projects a Latina aedicule. Latina forms, with circular *amalakas*, create a necklace around the cornice, and abound in the *shikhara* – at the corners and on three sets of minor offsets to the *lata*.

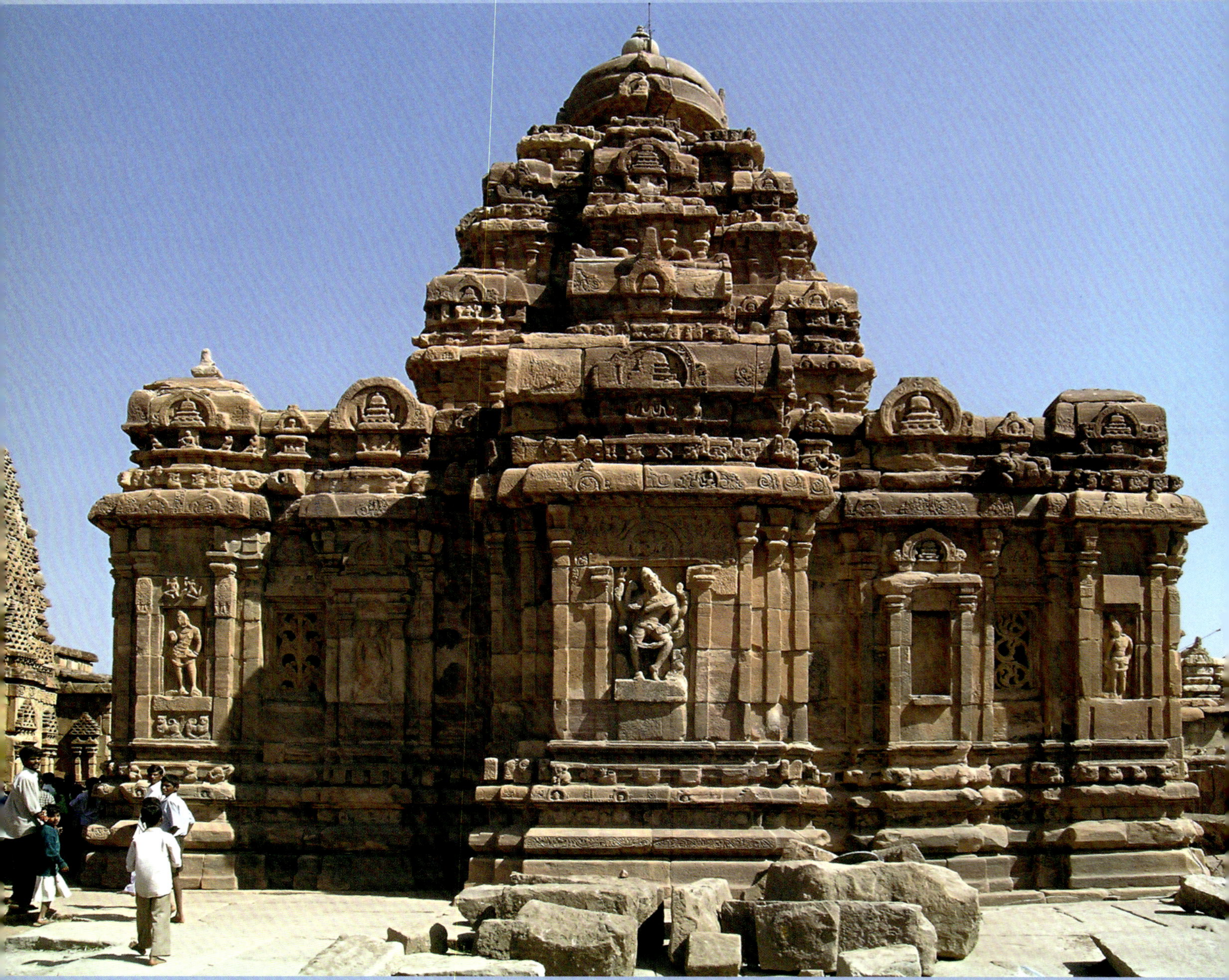

Part 5   A BRIEF HISTORY OF DRAVIDA TEMPLES

22   Early Dravida Temples
23   The Great 8th-Century Dravida Temples
24   Temples of the Cholas and Their Contemporaries
25   The Karnata Dravida Tradition Continued

Mallikarjuna temple, Pattadakal (**23.6**).
Photo © Gerard Foekema

22   Early Dravida Temples

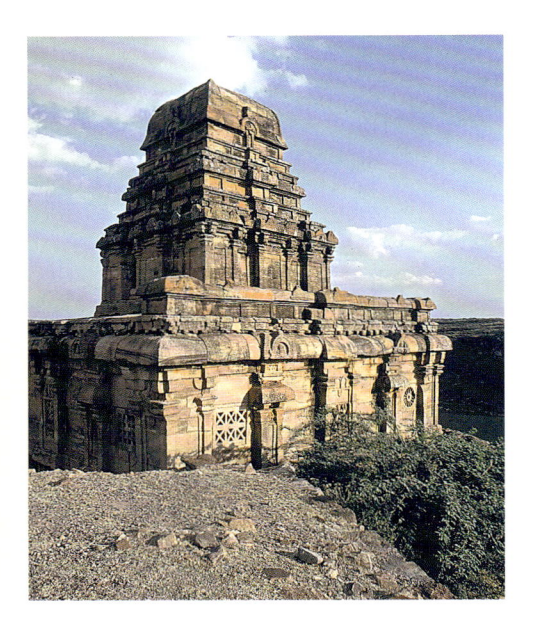

22.1 Upper Shivalaya, Badami (Karnataka), *c* first half of 7th century. The shrine sits within a rectangular envelope, creating a *sandhara* plan, ie with an internal ambulatory (cf 9.12c). Photo © Gerard Foekema

Southern temple architecture grew out of pan-Indian traditions. The precursors of its forms in early architecture made of wood, and in masonry structures faithfully depicting details of timber construction, were dealt with in Chapter 7. Chapter 8 illustrated the development of a more formalised architectural imagery articulating the rock-cut caves of the 5th to 7th centuries, still evoking an architecture of wood and thatch, but in a more stylised and rhythmic fashion, and including elements which would become part of the Dravida vocabulary.

The earliest surviving structures which can be defined as Dravida are probably the brick shrines at Ter (Maharashtra) and Chezarla (Andhra Pradesh). Both are now used for Hindu worship, but are usually thought to have been Buddhist originally, because they are reminiscent of the rock-cut Buddhist halls of worship known as *chaitya* halls. However, whatever their original religious function, their resemblance to *chaitya* halls is relevant in only a general sense, in that they share the same ancient barrel-roof shape (here with corbelled vaults inside). More interesting is the fact that they correspond in every respect to the simplest form of Dravida shrine, with a walled sanctum supporting a single pavilion in the superstructure, and known as an *alpa vimana* ('minor shrine'). More specifically, they are the apsidal type of *alpa vimana* (**11.1**, in foreground), crowned by a round-ended version of a barrel-roofed pavilion (*shala*). The exteriors of these two monuments contain the full range of Dravida mouldings, and the walls of the shrine at Ter, like those of Dravida temples, are punctuated by slender pilasters of the cushion type (**14.5**), complete with brackets (*potika*).

Whether or not these structures are as early as the 3rd century AD, as has been suggested,[1] their mouldings are very like those of the earliest surviving *alpa vimana* of the more usual square form, with a domed upper pavilion (*kuta*). This is a small shrine near the Ravana Phadi cave temple at Aihole (Karnataka) (**11.2**), and probably early 7th century, as the cave itself is of the mid-6th century. Like those at Ter and Chezarla, this shrine is not a literal representation of a wooden building, yet the mouldings do have something of the character of carpentry.

It is in Karnataka, in the heartland of the Early Western Chalukyas – the Chalukyas of Vatapi (now Badami) – that early developments in Dravida temple architecture can best be traced, beginning with the Ravana Phadi *alpa vimana*. The superstructure of the Upper Shivalaya, Badami, has evolved through the principle of cumulative piling up (**22.1**, **22.2**, **11.7**). However, the walls surrounding the hall and ambulatory are already articulated by full-height *kuta* aedicules (K) and *shala* aedicules (S) (representations, respectively, of domed- and barrel-roofed *alpa vimanas*), albeit with wide expanses of wall in between. The same must have been the case with the walls of another temple with an internal ambulatory (thus *sandhara*), the Meguti, Aihole, a Jain temple dated 634; but here the walls have lost their parapet.

A second phase of Early Chalukya temple architecture corresponds roughly to the second half of the 7th century. By this time Nagara temples were being built here, both Latina (**1.2**) and a related variety of the tiered-roofed Phamsana, along with hall temples which were neither Nagara nor Dravida, such as the Lad Khan and Gaudar Gudi at Aihole (**9.12b**). Apsidal shrines also appeared (**9.12d**), notably the Durga temple, Aihole, which, in the gallery of wall-shrines around its exterior ambulatory (**4.3**) shows the Karnata masons deliberately hybridising Nagara and Dravida forms.[2] The Dravida temples of this phase (**1.2** rear, **22.7**) have superstructures consisting of two tiers (*talas*), the first with full aedicules (K–S–K), the second a large *kuta* crowned by an octagonal dome. This is a form which also belongs to the early Nagara range of aedicules (**10.1j**, **k**) and is prominent in the tradition of Dakshina Koshala (**10.5** left, **17.10b**). At Mahakuta, the walls surrounding the halls and ambulatories have corner *kuta* and central *shala* pavilions in the parapets, but only the *shalas* have a corresponding projection below, thus forming a full height, two-storey *shala* aedicule (**22.3**). This projection is staggered, resulting in an early example of a staggered *shala* aedicule. The Malegitti Shivalaya, Badami (**22.4**), arrives at a principle that was resolutely followed by the Karnata Dravida tradition from this time onwards: that of a completely aedicular exterior, with full

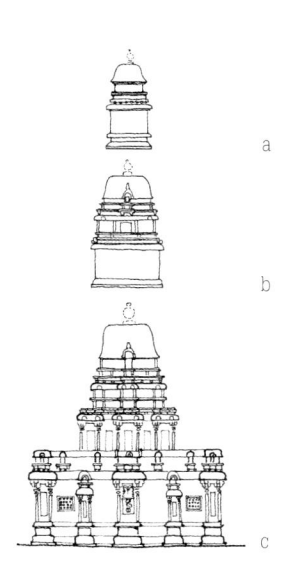

22.2 Piled up *vimana* compositions in Karnataka from the early 7th century: (**a**) *alpa vimana* (mono-aedicular shrine) near Ravana Phadi cave, Aihole (cf 11.2); (**b**) Bananti Gudi, Mahakuta, with (**a**) as superstructure; (**c**) Upper Shivalaya, Badami, with (**b**) as superstructure. The first tier of the superstructure is built as if to support domed *kuta* and barrel-roofed *shala* pavilions, but the tower has been completed simply by piling up mouldings.

22.3 Mahakuteshvara, Mahakuta (Karnataka), *c* last third of 7th century (1.2; plan 9.12e): staggered *shala* aedicule. The lower sequence of mouldings is already the one which would become established in this tradition (13.5), but there is no rail moulding (*vedika*) in the 'parapet'.

EARLY DRAVIDA TEMPLES **207**

22.4 Malegitti Shivalaya, Badami, c early 8th century: fully aedicular articulation. Photo © Gerard Foekema

22.5 The 'five *rathas*', Mahabalipuram (Tamil Nadu), c second half of 7th century. Left to right: Draupadi's *ratha*, Arjuna's *ratha*, Bhima's *ratha*, Dharmarajas' *ratha*, Nakula-Sahadevas' *ratha*. Draupadi's *ratha* is a uni-aedicular primitive hut, a minimalist *kuta*, the Arjuna and Dharmaraja *rathas* are square shrines with octagonal domes, respectively of two and three tiers (*talas*), while the Bhima and Nakula-Sahadeva *rathas* are shala-topped, respectively rectangular and apsidal. The smooth rump of the (*gaja-prishta*) Nakula-Sahadeva is visually punned by the attendant pachyderm. Contrasting with this rotundity, the roofs of the Draupadi and Bhima *rathas* are not the usual, rounded *kuta* and *shala* roofs, but gently curve to a ridge. They look very thatch-like, but there is nothing recently vernacular in their refined innocence.

height shrine-images separated only by narrow recesses. The Bhutanatha temple (**1.3**) follows the same pattern as the Malegitti, while returning to the *alpa vimana* form as the crowning stage of the superstructure.

No trace remains of the earliest masonry temples in Tamil Nadu, no doubt of brick. When Dravida architecture appears here, in the pavilion-chains (*haras*) over the fronts of cave temples and in the monoliths of Mahabalipuram, it is small but perfectly formed. Mahabalipuram (Mamallapuram) was a major port and ritual centre of the Pallava dynasty, who transformed its granite hills and boulders into cave temples, relief carvings (including the great 'Descent of the Ganges' relief [**11.3**], animated on ceremonial occasions by waterworks) and rock-cut shrines known as '*rathas*' (chariots). Best known of these are the 'five *rathas*',[3] carved from a single outcrop (**22.5**, **22.6**, **22.7**).

The *rathas* have often been dated to the mid-7th century, but they could be as late as the early 8th. Though not especially small by Indian temple standards (and their heavenly inhabitants are almost life-size), their dolls' house quality has made them eternally lovable. Such was the care with which they were carved that the hands of embedded gods and guardians stray from their niches, which in a monolith requires forethought. Carved at one time, they illustrate not development but variety of type; which, for the Tamil tradition, principally means bold variety of shape, particularly of plan shape and roof shape (**22.5**). Fully aedicular walls are found here; so are independent bands of *kutas* and *shalas*, as seen necklacing the dome of the Arjuna *ratha* and the rounded wagon roof of the Nakula-Sahadeva (**22.6**). But the Dharmaraja *ratha* has a multi-aedicular top *tala*, later unknown in the Tamil tradition, hitherto unknown but later the norm in the Karnata tradition. The Dharmaraja establishes the predilection among Pallava temples for 'progressive multiplication': the number of *shalas* increases from three to four to five down the faces of its gentle pyramid.

The nearby Ganesha *ratha* (**22.8**), with its trident finials, is a more sprightly version of the Bhima *ratha* with an extra tier (*tala*). Its alert character stems partly from the inspired treatment of the 'parapet' of the second tier. Omission of the linking section (*harantara*) between the *kuta* and *shala* pavilions not only accentuates the two-storey aedicules in that tier, but also reveals, in counterpoint with the latter, the elegant trinity of a two-storey *panjara* aedicule (gable end of a *shala* aedicule) flanked by two *panjaras* (gable end of a *shala*), all standing in the neck of the giant crowning *shala*. On the east side a shallow porch has guardians in sentry boxes and its own pavilion-chain (*hara*) across the top, all framing a typical tripartite Pallava cave facade with lion-based cushion pillars. This porch shows the split pilaster (the earliest surviving) used to brilliant effect, as if a stage curtain has drawn apart to reveal a sacred cave world.

Notes
1 Susan L Huntington, *The Art of Indian Asia* (New York: Weatherhill, 1985), p 180 and fig 9.28.
2 Adam Hardy, 'Hybrid Temples in Karnataka' in *First Under Heaven: The Art of Asia* (London: Hali Publications, 1997), pp 26–43 (pp 31–2).
3 They are known as the 'Pancha Pandava *Rathas*', after the five Pandava brothers of the epic, the Mahabharata, but this association has nothing to do with their original dedications.

22.6 Nakula-Sahadeva *ratha*, with Arjuna's *ratha* (right). Under the gable of the Nakula-Sahadeva, bent pillars and looped arches, distantly abstracted from the *chaitya* hall cross section, surround an emergent octagonal *alpa vimana*. This pattern prefigures, at large scale, a treatment of Dravida horseshoe (*gavakshas*) common in the 8th century (16.10b, c).

22.7 Arjuna's *ratha*: *kuta* aedicule.

22.8 The Ganesha *ratha*, Mahabalipuram east, *c* second half of 7th century.

23 THE GREAT 8TH-CENTURY DRAVIDA TEMPLES

23.1 Iravataneshvara temple, Kanchipuram (Tamil Nadu), *c* early 8th century. Originally protected by limewash and paint, the friable sandstone was covered at a later date in florid stucco work, some of which has been removed. Photo © Gerard Foekema

During the early 8th century the Early Western Chalukyas of Vatapi (Badami) and the Pallavas of Kanchi (Kanchipuram) were consolidating their empires. It was the first time that kings ruling from southern India could justifiably aspire to and compete for the status of universal monarch. As a ritual focus for their realm, each dynasty built an imperial temple mountain dedicated to Shiva. Pallava king Narasimhavarma II Rajasimha (700–*c* 728) erected the Kailasanatha (Lord of Mount Kailasa) at his capital. Following a victory won by their husband over the Pallavas at Kanchi in 742 (see Chapter 2), the two queens of Chalukya king Vikramaditya II built the Virupaksha and Mallikarjuna temples at Pattadakal. Another Shaiva monument in the southern half of India rivals their grandeur: the monolithic Kailasa initiated by Rashtrakuta king Krishna I (766–73) at the established sacred site of Ellora. His father Dantidurga had overthrown the Chalukyas around 754 and subsequently, through much of the 9th century, the Rashtrakutas wielded the main power in India. Mutual awareness of these imperial monuments among their respective architects is evident, rather than a simplistic chain of influence.

A new phase of temple architecture began at Kanchipuram under Rajasimha. As well as the great Kailasanatha, many smaller temples were built, of which the Iravataneshvara is a typical two-tier (*dvi-tala*) example (**23.1**). As often in works of the Pallava period, the wall has been thought of as an entity, without projections, only weakly corresponding with the parapet pavilions that it bears; but the latter are themselves two-storey aedicules – a barrel-roofed *shala* aedicule (S) flanked by two domed *kuta* aedicules (K). The second tier, as would be universal from this time onwards for an 'upper temple' in the Tamil tradition, takes the form of a single-aedicule shrine (*alpa vimana*) – in this case the type crowned by a large domed pavilion (*kuta*). On each face of the crowning *kuta*, sheltering beneath its gable arch, projects a miniature *alpa vimana*, a *kuta* aedicule, forming the apex of a cascade of diminutive shrine-images in a progressively multiplying pattern characteristic of Pallava monuments. At the next level down, in the wall

210   THE TEMPLE ARCHITECTURE OF INDIA

23.2 Kailasanatha, Kanchipuram, *c* first quarter 8th century. To be in the intimate passageways, teeming with gods, between the engirdling shrines of the enclosure and the taller ones around the main shrine (*vimana*), is like being inside the heavenly city, embraced by one of the imaginary spaces of the temple pyramid, where successive celestial courtyards rise towards the abode of Shiva. Photo © Gerard Foekema

THE GREAT 8TH-CENTURY DRAVIDA TEMPLES 211

zone of the 'upper temple', are a pair of elements of the kind that I call '*kapota-panjara* aedicules' (**11.10j**), end-on *shala* aedicules with their gable arches in the eave moulding (*kapota*). This pair has been fully exposed by leaving out the usual link (*harantara*) sections between the three pavilions crowning the first tier (cf **22.8**). A progression from one to two to three aedicules is boldly displayed, without any of them being 'primary' aedicules, standing the full height of a *tala*.

The Kailasanatha is a consummate expression of concentric and mounting cloisteredness (see **9.23** and **11.8**). This whole assemblage is made up of *kuta*- and *shala*-topped shrines, whether actual *alpa vimanas* containing chambers for sculpted deities, or aedicules. *Shalas* crown all those on the cardinal axes, including the eastern entrance (a simple version of a monumental south Indian gateway or *goprura*), and the three-storey Mahendravarmeshvara shrine (**11.8**). The main shrine (*vimana*), the cosmic mountain itself, is 20 metres high, and has four tiers, more than any previous Dravida monument. This is the first temple in Tamil Nadu to have an internal ambulatory, which helps to reinforce the expression of the superstructure as a temple in itself, raised proudly over the sanctum, and to define the first tier as a real cloister. At this level the central (*shala*) and corner (square *kuta*) shrines are fully projected out from the wall, and thus not purely aedicules but three-storey *alpa vimanas*, each containing a sanctum. At parapet level there are intermediate *shala* pavilions, so the pattern is K̄–S̄–S̄–S̄–K̄. The succeeding tiers, diminishing upwards, run K̄–S̄–S̄–K̄ and K–S–K, to the single, large K̄ at the summit. Thus, reading downwards, there is a progressive multiplication, 1–3–4–5, with *kapota-panjara* aedicules providing a two between the one and the three. Uniquely for an upper level, the aedicules of the second *tala* are three-storey, proclaiming the grandeur of the monument and further enhancing the idea of the superstructure as a complete *vimana*. In turn, the top two tiers alone constitute a *vimana* design (one like that of the Iravataneshvara, but with an octagonal dome, and full aedicules in the first tier), and again in turn the crowning element is an *alpa vimana*.

Whereas the Kailasanatha takes the Pallava tradition in the direction of weight and solidity, the Shore temple, Mahabalipuram, another work which may also be attributable to Rajasimha, is slender. The last important Pallava monument of the 8th century is the Vaikuntha Perumal (temple of Vishnu's heaven), Kanchipuram. Here concentric layers are realised completely, in that one can physically go inside them, from the tight passage between the enclosure and the *vimana*, through double ambulatories on two levels and a single one on the third, leaving

23.3 Kailasanatha: the magnificent central shrines in the *vimana* walls are, like the larger Mahendravarmeshvara shrine (11.8), three-storey, single-aedicule shrines (*alpa vimanas*) with barrel-roofed *shalas* for their crowning pavilions; they face smaller versions of the same form on axis in the enclosure wall. Staggering of the walls is rare in the Tamil Dravida tradition. Here the step forward creates a full-height projection in the form of a three-storey *panjara*-aedicule, equivalent to the ends of this shrine. The effect of dynamism here is less insistent than the increased weight and presence of the aedicule imparted by the extra corners.

212 THE TEMPLE ARCHITECTURE OF INDIA

only the 'upper temple' inaccessible. These layers surround three superimposed sanctums, enshrining three forms of Vishnu.

At about the same time as Rajasimha was building the Kailasanatha, Chalukya king Vijayaditya (reigned *c* 696–733) built the Vijayeshvara (now Sangameshvara) at Pattadakal (**23.4**). When built it would have been the largest temple in the Deccan, elaborating the Chalukya three-aisle hall type to five aisles. Virtually everything about it has local precedents (and ramifications), but details favoured by the Pallavas are prominent – *kapota-panjara* aedicules, corner figures supporting roofs, miniature aedicules under the horseshoe arch gables. What makes this the most 'Pallava' of Chalukya temples, however, is the progressive multiplication in its aedicular composition: from one, a *shala* pavilion in the neck of the 'upper temple', to three (K–S–K) in the middle stage, to four (K–S–S–K) around the ambulatory, which centres on a wide recess.

So any 'Pallava influx' had happened before Vikramaditya's wonderment at the Kailasanatha (Chapter 2). But the Virupaksha temple, also at Pattadakal, maintains the 'Pallava' details and, no doubt intended to rival the Kailasanatha, has a four-tier shrine, sits in a walled enclosure and staggers the corners of aedicules (**23.5**; see also **9.3**). Yet this monument reinforces tendencies which are characteristically Karnata Dravida as opposed to Tamil Dravida. With its light pilasters, the effect of the staggering in the Virupaksha is not to add weight but to break down

23.4 Sangameshvara temple, Pattadakal (Karnataka), *c* first quarter 8th century: *shala* aedicule.

23.5 Virupaksha temple, Pattadakal, *c* 742 (cf 9.3). Compared with earlier temples there is a much denser concentration of aedicules, because of their close spacing and the proliferation of secondary aedicules. The Mahendravarmeshvara shrine at Kanchipuram (11.8) was probably the model for the great antefix (*shuka-nasa*) projected over the *antarala*: a southern form for a northern feature.
Photo © Gerard Foekema

THE GREAT 8TH-CENTURY DRAVIDA TEMPLES 213

23.6 Mallikarjuna temple, Pattadakal, west. From now on K–P–S–P–K would be the standard pattern for five projections. The Virupaksha is behind to the right, the Kashivishveshvara (Chapter 18) to the left. Photo © Gerard Foekema

23.7 Kailasa temple, Ellora (Maharashtra), *c* second half 8th century. Lotuses lie face down on the flat roofs, radiating divinity through the ceiling. The external circumambulatory passage is surrounded by subsidiary shrines, which are full-size *vimanas*. Photo © Gerard Foekema

boundaries, move planes forward and make ripples along walls. The *vimana* has five projections in the first tier, around the ambulatory (K–P–S–P–K, where P indicates *panjara* aedicules, ie end-on *shala* aedicules), three in the second and third (K–S–K), and at the summit an *alpa vimana* form with corner *kutas*. Thus, no tier has an even number of projections: the centre is emphasised and 'progressive multiplication' of aedicular components is abolished from the Chalukya realms in favour of 'expanding repetition' (**3.3e**, **f**). Wide recesses are also abandoned in this dense congregation of aedicules.

The Mallikarjuna follows the same general scheme as its senior twin, but takes the evolutionary logic a step further (**23.6**, **13.5**). All the primary *kuta* and *shala* aedicules are staggered at the corners, and in the top tier the *alpa vimana* form is replaced by three projections supporting a circular dome. The arrangement of the mouldings over the eave cornice (*kapota*) indicates that these were intended to be the lower mouldings of *kutas* and *shalas*, carrying the K–S–K scheme all the way up; the dome (for Karnataka a very rare departure from the square) must have been added after a short interruption, probably the Rashtrakuta takeover. This extended radial continuity is complemented by greater central emphasis, the *shala* aedicules sliding forward (especially from

214 THE TEMPLE ARCHITECTURE OF INDIA

the first tier) in a chain of expanding repetition. The dynamic fusion fermenting here would be taken up and swept along in the continuing Karnata Dravida tradition.

At Ellora, Mount Kailasa was carved from the mountainside (**23.7**), held high on the backs of life-size elephants. More than in the actual height of 30 metres, the effect of grandeur lies in the setting of the Kailasa temple, and the sense of scale as you walk in the chasm from which the great monolith rises, elephants' feet above your head, the tower up in the sun.

Maharashtra, most visibly through its cave temple traditions (Chapters 7 and 8), had fed the developing Dravida language; now the architecture of the south returned, and mingled with the local character. Most obviously from Pattadakal is the layout, with its enclosure (the pit), and its sequence of gateway, pavilion for Nandi (Shiva's bull), 16-pillared hall with three porches and antechamber surmounted by a barrel-roofed fronton (*shuka-nasa*). Instead of a nave-and-aisled cross section, the hall ceiling is flat and divided into panels, further emphasising the central bay and cross axes; and rather than having an internal ambulatory passage, the base (*adisthana*) of the temple forms a lofty platform, providing an external ambulatory. Chalukya connections extend to details, though these are chunkier in Deccan trap, the coarse volcanic stone from which the Kailasa was hewn, than in sandstone; and there is inscriptional as well as stylistic evidence that sculptors were brought here from Pattadakal.[1] As at Pattadakal, there are none of the Tamil three-storey aedicules; aedicule corners are not staggered, but, going beyond the Mallikarjuna, the whole *vimana* plan steps forward, although the intermediate offsets in fact form only secondary *panjara* aedicules in wide recesses. Yet there are Tamil resonances too in the Kailasa, direct rather than via Pattadakal, most obviously in the crowning *kuta* with its octagonal dome and Nandi bulls on the platform afforded by the 'floor moulding' (*prati*). Contacts might have been Pandya more than Pallava (cf **23.9**); in any case, these imports from other kingdoms show no meek acceptance of influence, but the will to extract tributes and surpass them all.

Two slightly later Dravida monoliths at Ellora, the Chota ('Little') Kailasa and the Sarvatobhadra (four-faced) shrine at Cave 32 (**23.8**), both Jain foundations, radically manipulate Dravida principles simply by swivelling the *shalas* through 90 degrees.

Note
1 See Doris Clark Chatham, 'Stylistic Sources and Relationships of the Kailā Temple at Ellora', PhD dissertation, University of California, Berkeley, 1977.

23.8 Sarvatobhadra shrine at Cave 32 (Indrasabha), Ellora, *c* late 8th century. A Dravida *gavaksha* cascade (an idea later exploited in the Karnata Dravida tradition) is achieved by presenting the central *shalas* end on.
Photo © Gerard Foekema

23.9 Vetuvankovil, Kalugumalai, *c* 800. This exquisite and robustly voluptuous rock-cut *vimana*, left unfinished, was made under the Pandya dynasty in southern Tamil Nadu. It seems to have affinities with Ellora.
Photo © Gerard Foekema

24 Temples of the Cholas and Their Contemporaries

The Pallavas in Tondainadu and the Pandyas in the extreme south remained the main forces in the Tamil country into the 9th century, when the Chola dynasty rose to power, at first in the rice bowl of the Kaveri delta. In the 11th century they controlled south India (perhaps through a decentralised 'segmentary state', as discussed in Chapter 2), conquered Sri Lanka, forced Bengali princes (it is said) to carry Ganges water to their capital, expanded trade in South-east Asia and exchanged ambassadors with China. But other dynasties ruled and built temples, in regions other than Cholanadu: a tendency to label the productions of the period 'Chola' indiscriminately can perhaps be blamed on the prestige that the modern-day art market has attached to the name.

The architectural principle of progressive multiplication of aedicular elements continued through time as well as temple superstructures under the later Pallavas, extending to five tiers (*talas*) (Tirupatti) and as many as seven projections (Alambakkam). In 'Chola' times, as state society and agriculture spread, temples became more numerous but were generally modest in size and in their degree of elaboration. The simple shrine form composed of a single aedicule, termed '*alpa vimana*', sprang up everywhere in its various shapes (**11.1**, **11.5**, **11.6**). A new character is discernible in the proportions and details of temples, not so much a transformation as an intensification of certain qualities: boldness, clarity, massiveness, roundedness, contrast of smooth and rough... Much of this can be attributed to the new preference for granite, but not all. The details of the sandstone Kailasanatha, after all, had already become more massive than those of the monolithic '*rathas*' ('chariots') at Mahabalipuram; and the new shapes are the same in brick temples.

Beautiful 9th-century two-tier (*dvi-tala*) shrines (*vimanas*) are found at Kilayur (**11.12**) and Kodumbalur, ascribed respectively to the Irrukuvel and Muttaraiyar dynasties. The Muvarkovil at Kodumbalur (**24.1**, **24.2**) was originally an enclosed complex with three main shrines in a line, and the work is pervaded by patterns of three. Two of the shrines survive: the central one, built to increase the religious merit of King Bhuti Vikramakesari, and one of the others, which were for his two

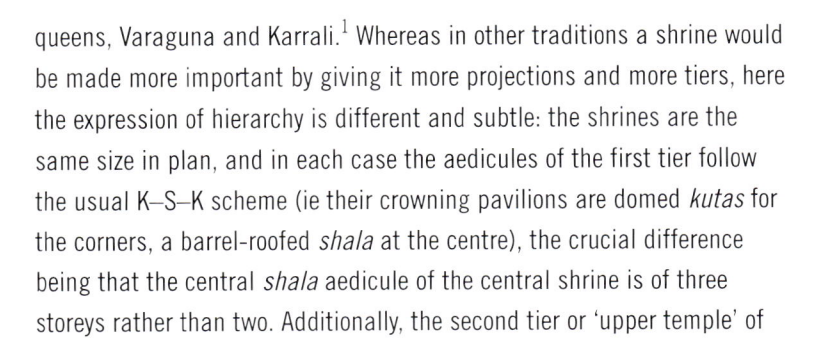

24.2 Muvarkovil, Kodumbalur: three-storey *shala* aedicule in central shrine.

24.1 Muvarkovil, Kodumbalur (Tamil Nadu), *c* mid-to late 9th century: southern shrine. Spilt-pilaster niches open a vertical triad of slots for deities. Three manifestations of Shiva appear here: (top to bottom) Vireshvara, Natesha and Gajasamhara. Photo © Gerard Foekema

queens, Varaguna and Karrali.[1] Whereas in other traditions a shrine would be made more important by giving it more projections and more tiers, here the expression of hierarchy is different and subtle: the shrines are the same size in plan, and in each case the aedicules of the first tier follow the usual K–S–K scheme (ie their crowning pavilions are domed *kutas* for the corners, a barrel-roofed *shala* at the centre), the crucial difference being that the central *shala* aedicule of the central shrine is of three storeys rather than two. Additionally, the second tier or 'upper temple' of this principal shrine is graced with paired '*kapota-panjara* aedicules' (**11.10j**) – *panjara* aedicules (ie shrine-images crowned by end-on *shalas*) with their gables in the eave moulding (*kapota*), in this case with circular bodies. One further distinguishing feature of this central *vimana* was a continuous gallery of deities at parapet level, now lost.

The composition of the individual shrines at Kodumbalur is bold, varied and balanced, each element standing out, with no repetition except through symmetry. Emergence, central emphasis and fusion are brought about, but at a calm pace, and by different means from the more northerly principles of staggering, proliferation and enhanced continuities. The central aedicule, even the two-storey one, is simply higher than the corners, and it is the only one to have a niche in the wall. By not recessing the wall and *kapota* cornice, the *kuta* aedicules at the corners are implied but de-articulated, further undermining them by fusing them into the whole. Moreover, the bulging of the centre and bursting open of its split-pilaster niche are enhanced by a further treatment of the corner which makes the wall elevation even more of a trio dominated by its centre, its three primary aedicules standing like a bronze Vishnu flanked by two poised goddesses. The device is the closeness of the paired pilasters, spaced so that their abacuses (*phalakas*) just touch. The implied *kuta* aedicules are thrust to the sides, clasping their hands together beneath the tight *décolletés* of their paired *gavakshas*.

Symmetrical pairs about the centre of the wall are favoured in this tradition, whether sculpted (eg attendant deities), split pilasters, or aedicular niches. Where there are recesses next to the central projection (*bhadra*), they tend to contain *panjara* aedicules, secondary but prominent, often to form a K–p–S–p–K pattern. At Pullamangai (**24.3**),

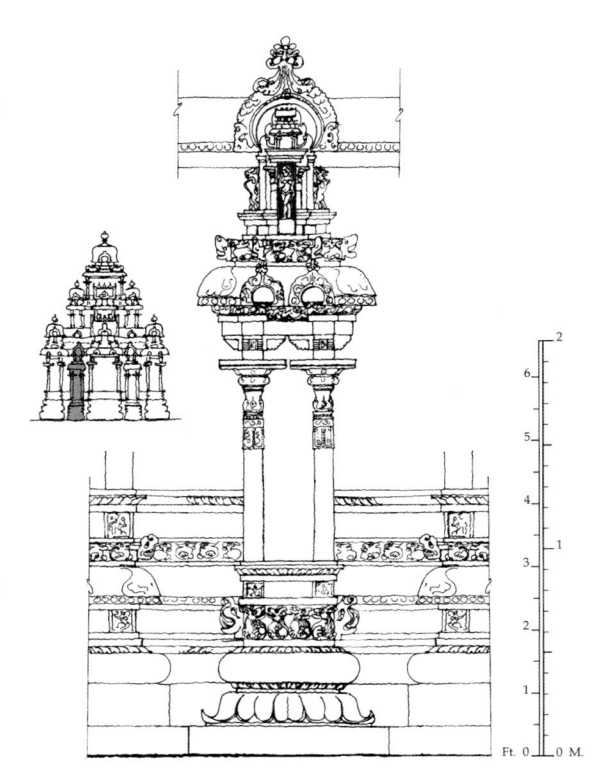

24.3 Brahmapurishvara temple, Pullamangai, *c* 910: *panjara* aedicule in recess.

24.4 Moulded temple base (*adisthana*) at Narttamalai, *c* 9th century. The mouldings are *jagati*, round *kumuda* and *prati*, surmounted by a *vedika*. The *prati* (floor moulding), with its joist-end creatures, can be the most tightly rhythmic of mouldings, but this one is at the free end of the spectrum, strolled along by elephants, horned lions (*vyalas*) and others friends.

218 THE TEMPLE ARCHITECTURE OF INDIA

24.5 Brihadeshvara temple, Tanjavur, founded c 1003: *vimana*. That an earthen ramp was used is doubtless true, but that the dome is a single stone is just a legend shrouded in plaster. Photo © Gerard Foekema

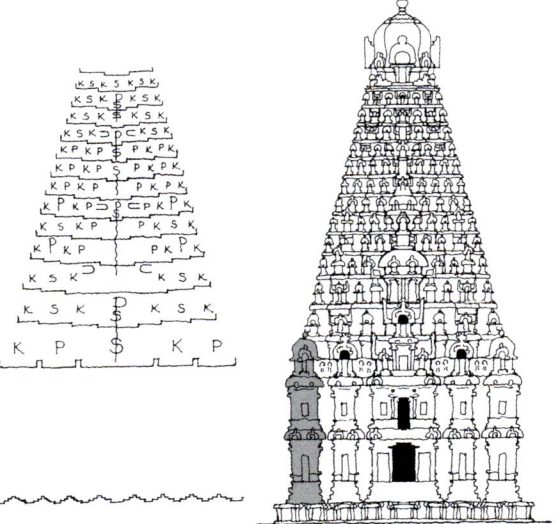

24.6 Brihadeshvara, Tanjavur. Right: elevation with key to aedicule types. The sideways 'U' symbols indicate apsidal *shalas*. Left: three-storey *kuta* aedicule on sub-base or pedestal (*upapitha*). Would it have been easier to keep to radial chains? There is a perceptible change of pitch after the fourth *tala*, presumably because to have continued at the same angle would have led to a much wider dome platform, or a much higher tower.

TEMPLES OF THE CHOLAS AND THEIR CONTEMPORARIES **219**

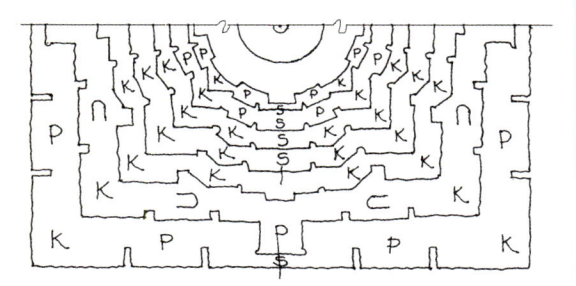

24.7 Brihadeshvara temple, Gangaikondacholapuram, built by Rajendra Chola I (1012–44): half roof plan of shrine (after Pichard) showing aedicule types. The superstructure makes a transition from square to circle.

24.8 Airavateshvara temple, Darasuram, mid-12th century: *vimana*. Photo © Gerard Foekema

24.9 Airavateshvara temple, Darasuram: *panjara* aedicule on sub-base (*upapitha*).

for example, not only are they *kapota-panjara* aedicules (with their heads in the *kapota*), but they have their own moulded base standing out from the main one. They emerge out of the recess, bursting boundaries above and below.

The Pullamangai temple, with its three tiers, is a grand one for its time, but intimate and perfect. All this changed with Rajaraja's supreme achievement, the Brihadeshvara (or Brihadishvara), Tanjavur (Tanjore), filling its 60 metres not with four or five tiers or *talas*, but 14 (**24.5**, **24.6**; plan **9.24**). The formal challenges of such an unprecedented venture, let alone the logistical ones, are evident even in the sub-base (*upapitha*), which has nine staggered projections, intended for a more complex scheme which, visually, could never have been adapted to the

220 THE TEMPLE ARCHITECTURE OF INDIA

required height. On this they built a wall of five massive projections, the central one slightly forward, making the mouldings of the moulded base (*adisthana*) gigantic rather than proliferated. Confusion about the number of tiers arises because the first one is wrongly understood as two. Literally, it contains two storeys, each with an ambulatory passage lit by windows in the *bhadra*; the lower one around the sanctum, which contains a huge Shiva *linga*; the upper one at the foot of the hidden void inside the tower. Conceptually, as the mouldings indicate, the vertical wall represents a single *tala* of three-storey aedicules. Confusion arises because (to fit with the interior) the second 'storey' of the aedicules is as wide and nearly as tall as the first, and the interstices (*harantaras*) are treated like the wall below. These contain the '*kumbha-panjaras*' (*panjara-stambhas* on pots), common in the Tamil Dravida tradition ever since.

In the first tier the scheme is K–P–S–P–K. At the centre of the *shala* is a two-storey *panjara* aedicule, identical to the upper two stages of the intermediate aedicules, forming one of those triplets. Furthermore, this *panjara* aedicule has its *panjara* in the *shala* of the next stage, so there is conceptual as well as spatial overlap: does it belong to the upper *shala*, the lower one, or purely to itself? Comparable clusters, generally without the subtle ambiguity, were to have a long history in the design of monumental gateways (*gopuras*), beginning with those (now caked in later plasterwork) at the Brihadeshvara itself. Other kinds of groupings appear at higher levels of the *vimana* superstructure, the lowest of them piercing through as many as four *talas*. But, despite this inventiveness, the problems of the new profusion of architectural parts were not fully resolved. The effect of the tower is multitudinous but monotonous, and if there are patterns here, they have abandoned the 'Early Chola' virtue of clarity.

Ambitious and more lucid pattern-making was undertaken at the imperial temple of Rajaraja's son Rajendra Chola I (1012–44) at Gangaikondacholapuram, 'Town of the Chola who conquered the Ganges' (**24.7**), and visual clarity along with approachability returned in the large but not gigantic royal temples at Darasuram (**24.8–24.9**) and, now hidden beneath later stucco, Tribhuvanam (built respectively by Rajaraja II, 1146–72, and Kullotunga III, 1178–1218). But, when it comes to 'Late Chola', I would give Tanjavur and the rest, and all the gold heaped at their doors by pious pilgrims, for the little temple at Melai-Kkadambur (**24.10**), which bulges with innocence and delight.

24.10 Melai-Kkadambur Melaikkadambur, Amritaghateshvara, before 1113: shrine wall.

Note
1 *Encyclopaedia of Indian Temple Architecture*, vol 1, Part 1, South India: Lower Drāviḍadēśa, 200 BC–AD 1324 (Delhi: AIIS and Manohar, 1999), p 202.

25 THE KARNATA DRAVIDA TRADITION CONTINUED

During the 9th and 10th centuries, several regional dynasties on the border zones between Chola and Rashtrakuta hegemonies built impressive groups of Dravida temples, notably the Eastern Chalukyas of Vengi, especially at Biccavolu (AP), the Western Gangas of Talkad at Sravana Belagola and Kambadahalli (Karnataka) and the Nolambas of Hemavati at Nandi (Karnataka). Other important sites are in areas that were probably ruled more directly by the Rashtrakutas, such as Bhavanasi Sangam (AP) and Sirval (northern Karnataka). In terms of style all these lie along the spectrum of Dravida architecture that runs between that of the broad Tamil tradition and the continuing Karnata Dravida still centred on the former Chalukya heartland.

This statement needs to be qualified, as the Badami region, no longer the political centre that it had been, produced mainly modest works during this period, but these form a conduit between the monuments of the Early Chalukyas and the 11th-century explosion of temple architecture under the Later Chalukyas of Kalyani. Although this is only apparent with hindsight, Aihole and surrounding sites during the Rashtrakuta period (up to 973) were a crucible in which the transformational tendencies incipient in the mid-8th century lay smouldering until, at the end of the 10th, the winds of the Chalukya revival ignited them, and in all the fireworks which followed, at some indefinable point, temple architecture had undergone such metamorphosis that sages began to waggle their heads and say 'This is not Dravida, it is Vesara'. As explained in Chapter 11, the domed, stepped pyramid of a typical Dravida shrine was, in the Karnata Dravida tradition, progressively transformed to the extent that it could be mistaken for a different form of temple. This later form was probably the one referred to as 'Vesara' in texts and inscriptions, and it was brought about chiefly through increasing central emphasis and staggering, in the whole and in the parts, and through radial continuity, enhanced by making the uppermost tier (*tala*) the same as the other ones, ie composite or multi-aedicular. Essential to the transformation was the staggering, at first in a single step (**11.13a**), of the shrine-image

25.1 Left: Jain temple, Pattadakal, *c* 900: elevation. Right: Navalinga temple, Kukkanur, staggered *shala* aedicule. The wall-shrine is a *kuta* aedicule. In this tradition, pilasters, the ends of the barrel-roofed *shala*, dormer gables (*gavakshas*) in eave mouldings (*kapotas*) and corner blocks in floor mouldings (*pratis*) are now all aligned vertically. Horizontal recesses (*griva*, *gala*) are becoming narrower. The style here is a direct forbear of the Karnata Dravida mainstream style found at Lakkundi (cf 25.2).

222 THE TEMPLE ARCHITECTURE OF INDIA

normally placed at the centre of each *tala*, the barrel-roofed *shala* aedicule. These kinds of feature were not unique to the Badami region: staggered *shala* aedicules were not unusual elsewhere by the 10th century, and this region was relatively slow to adopt multi-aedicular top *talas*. But it was here that centrifugal forces began to transform the whole and the parts together; for example, in the Jain temple, Pattadakal (*c* 900) (**25.1**).

Furthermore, as revealed by an increasing number of temples exhibiting their particular style of chiselwork, it was the guilds of this region who first received the renewed flow of patronage under the Later Chalukyas, and whose tradition developed into a style that can be called the late Karnata Dravida mainstream. Temple building, hand in hand with agriculture and state society, spread mainly southwards from here through the 11th century. Lakkundi (Lokkigundi), some 80 kilometres south of Badami, became the most important political centre and temple site in Karnataka, and the heart of the region then known as Kuntaladesha, where most 'Chalukyan' temples are concentrated. (Surviving temples around Kalyani on the borders of Maharashtra, not mentioned as the capital before the mid-11th century, are mainly Bhumija: see Chapter 20.) A guild previously active south of Badami built dozens of temples in and around Lakkundi, forming the core of the 'mainstream' style (**25.1**, **25.2**). The preferred material was now chloritic schist or 'soapstone', which allowed virtuosic undercutting and polished pillars (**1.10**); but, even more than is the case with granite and Chola temples, the material suits the style but cannot be the whole reason for it, as the style was already developing in sandstone. A gradual transformation of the shapes of mouldings can be seen to have been taking place as early as the Early Chalukya period. Single curves have given way to 'S' curves, profiles becoming sharper and flatter, while recesses have narrowed. The blocked out shapes of elements remain conspicuous, whether or not they have been carved into (**25.3**, **25.4**, **25.6**).

In terms of the overall composition of shrines, the unfolding of the Karnata Dravida (**6.4**), including its metamorphosis into the 'Vesara',

25.2 Kashivishveshvara temple, Lakkundi, before 1087, east shrine dedicated to Surya, from south (cf 3.14); Chlorotic schist or 'soapstone'. The central elements are *panjara* aedicules, the intermediate ones *kuta-stambhas* crowned by a novel kind of Phamsana *kuta*. The fronton (*shuka-nasa*) has a Phamsana roof.
Photo © Gerard Foekema

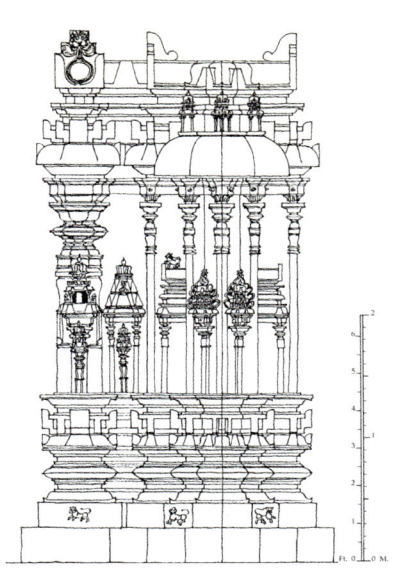

25.3 Jodu-Kalashada temple, Sudi, c 1060: central and intermediate elements. This was the Nageshvara temple mentioned in Chapter 2. In the central cluster an eight-point stellate *kuta* aedicule projects from a *shala* aedicule. The latter has *kuta-stambhas* within the wall and thrusts through a minor *shala* aedicule. It also has a necklace of small *kuta* aedicules. The intermediate projection (*prati-bhadra*) is a *panjara-stambha*, putting forth two lesser orders of *kuta-stambha*. In the recess, a Nagara-inspired wall-shrine shelters a small *kuta-stambha*.

25.5 Mahadeva temple, Ittagi, dedicated 1112: shrine (*vimana*), with later addition replacing the original dome. A general named Mahadeva was the founder, and a foundation inscription calls it 'an Emperor among temples'. The composition consists of four identical tiers of five main projections, double-staggered *shala* aedicules at the centre, Dravida *kuta* aedicules at the corners and Dravida *kuta-stambhas* in between. This is essentially the same as the widespread design shown in 11.5, but in the wall of the central element the forwardmost plane has been usurped by the emerging wall-shrine. A cascade of arch forms (*gavaksha* gables and looped *toranas*) has been created on the spine (cf 3.13). Refinements to the mouldings reinforce vertical and horizontal continuities, enhancing the sense of fusion (cf 6.3). Photo © Gerard Foekema

25.4 Yellama Gudi, Badami, *c* early 11th century: double-staggered *shala* aedicule. A miniature two-tier (*dvi-tala*) superstructure crowns the wall-shrine, which has begun to burst boundaries.

amounted to a great blossoming out and bursting forth of multiplicity, suffusing the whole and reflected in the parts. The staggering of forms, already mentioned, made the whole wall bulge and allowed its central elements to be transformed into clusters of interpenetrating, centrifugally separating shrine-images. If there was a stage in this evolution which marked a wholesale departure from earlier Dravida architecture, it was the arrival of the double-staggered *shala* aedicule, in which five barrel-roofed shrine forms emerge from one another (**3.11**, **3.12**, **11.13e**, **25.4**). This became the standard central aedicule of the 11th century, and by the end of that century was appearing at every level of a five-projection, four-tier (*chatus-tala*) shrine composition which was to become the typical one for the grander temples of this tradition (**11.15**; cf **25.5**).

Even stellate shrines, which appeared among Karnata Dravida monuments around this same time, though certainly linked with the contemporaneous appearance of the stellate Bhumija further north (see Chapter 20), can be visualised in terms of an organic outgrowth. Diagonal *shala* ends and diagonal joist-blocks in the floor moulding (*prati*) (**25.14**, **3.15**, **11.13f**), emerging at the corners of the bulging centre, presage the bursting of the bubble, as everything is pushed out at an angle, and melts into the descending spiral of the uniform stellate plan (**9.1t–v**). The temple at Dambal (**25.7**) is at the edge of final fusion: every aedicule is identical, and it is impossible to increase their number (with more points to the star plan) without changing them beyond recognition.

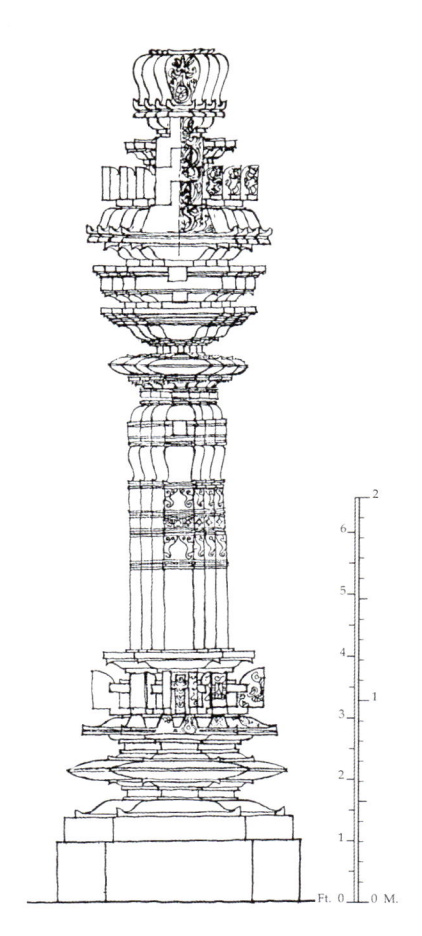

25.6 Mahadeva, Ittagi, *kuta-stambha*.

25.7 Doddabasappa, Dambal, early 12th century. The shrine has seven *talas* and is based on a 24-point star (12.6c), the hall on a 32-point star. All the primary components are elongated *kuta* aedicules. Photo © Gerard Foekema

225

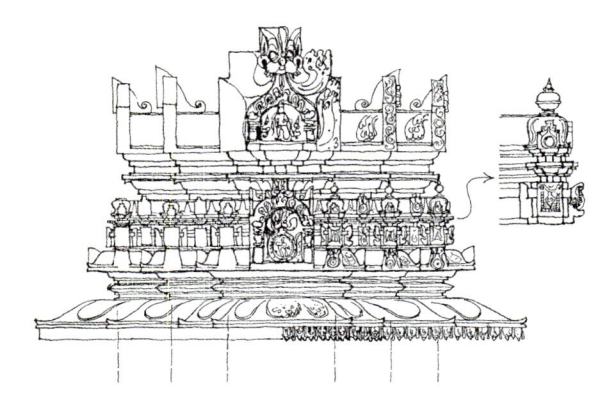

25.8 Katteshvara temple, Hirehadgalli, c late 11th century: double-staggered *shala*. A sophisticated game is played with the mouldings, replacing the *prati* with a chain of miniature *kutas* and *panjaras*.

25.9 Wall-shrine from the Katteshvara temple, Hirehadgalli.
Photo © Gerard Foekema

But maybe, after all, it is the individual acts of creation from which the broader patterns emerged that draw us to the artists of the Karnata Dravida tradition, more than the collective destiny which they unwittingly chiselled out. That their genius concentrated on aedicular architecture more than sculpture (though their rare surviving sculpture is superb) must be partly because, during the 10th century, when northern walls were being covered with deities, here they could only afford to evoke the gods through further images of their shelters. Blind niches proliferated, forming a lesser register of aedicules projecting from the primary ones and in the recesses. At first these secondary elements were *kuta*, *shala* and *panjara* aedicules. With time and new patronage the niches began to be crowned with complex temple superstructures, with correct proportions and in all their detail. So, when one full-size *vimana* was designed, the team of craftsmen might have a dozen or so more to design in miniature. Here the constraints were fewer and thus there was scope for greater inventiveness. Architectural ingenuity, in the 11th century and into the 12th, was applied to the real and miniature shrines at every level of the composition,[1] from the overall form (with experiments in orthogonal and then with stellate and semi-stellate plans), through the inseparable issue of aedicule design (inventing new types through new combinations of the existing range), to the shapes and details of mouldings, which were sometimes deliberately manipulated to create particular and surprising qualities of rhythm and surface (**25.5**, **25.8**).

Epitomising the spirit of invention are experiments in hybridisation applied at all these levels.[2] The hybridisation in question here is not a matter of the characteristics which the 'Vesara', formed of Dravida parts, has in common with the Nagara because of the way it has evolved (see Chapter 11), but of deliberate attempts to invent mixed (*mishraka*) forms. Nagara temples had been unknown in Karnataka after the 8th century, except as glories from the past in and around Aihole and Pattadakal. In the 11th century there was again contact with northern schools. A Nagara tradition developed around Kalyani, and the temple architects of Kuntaladesha began to design Nagara temples among their miniature shrine-images and then to build them full size, even if their interpretations betrayed certain 'southernisms'. They knew the curved spire of the Latina, the clustered superstructure of Shekhari and the Bhumija with its vertical chains of miniature turrets (see Chapter 10).

There were different means of combining Nagara and Dravida. A temple such as the Kashivishveshvara, Lakkundi (**3.14**), in its west *vimana*, centres on a prominent Shekhari niche and displays Nagara forms in its intermediate projections. But it remains essentially Karnata

226 THE TEMPLE ARCHITECTURE OF INDIA

Dravida rather than mixed. A more equal mixture of Nagara and Dravida aedicules is tried in some miniature shrines, while others use the perennial principle of centrally projecting a 'foreign' form at full scale from the chest of the *vimana* – Nagara from Dravida and vice versa. But the subtlest kind of mixture is seen at the Someshvara temple, Lakshmeshvara, where Dravida elements are organised according to Nagara principles, without using a single Nagara detail (**25.11, 25.12**).

The Someshvara, along with its namesake at Gadag (**25.13**), belongs to one of the more active of many schools or workshops which sprung up towards the end of the 11th century in parallel with the Later Chalukya 'mainstream' style, which was gradually engulfed in the new currents. Some of these schools are known from just a single work; some can be ascribed to local rulers. Two important, geographically distant 'non-mainstream' Karnata Dravida offshoots are the schools of Telangana (north-west AP), first patronised by the Chalukyas and later the Kakatiyas, and that of southern Karnataka, under the Hoysalas. The latter, local rulers from the hills, surpassed the scale of Chalukya temples while still nominally feudatories, in the Chenna-Keshava temple, Belur (**20.4**) and the Hoysaleshvara, Halebid (completed *c* 1160) (**1.10**). After the demise of the Chalukyas of Kalyani at the end of the 12th century, the Hoysalas and Kakatiyas vied for control of former Chalukya territories, as did the Yadavas from the north.

About 300 Hoysala temples survive. Their shrines are on the whole less complex than those in northern Karnataka (the type shown in **3.15** is widespread), but they are often more ornate, the soapstone drilled, grooved and undercut, while maintaining the volumes of the blocks. Great galleries of jewelled gods line the walls, often pushing the niche canopies to an upper wall zone, divided from the sculpture frieze by a continuous eave moulding (*kapota*) (**25.14**). Miniature *vimana* designs remain abundant and varied, but often careless about proportions and verging on caricature. Stellate shrines are common, beginning with Belur and Halebid. While the former (**20.4**), is Bhumija and the latter (in both of its twin *vimanas*) Karnata Dravida, both are based on 16-point stars with cardinal projections from which overgrown niches have burst out as three-dimensional attached shrines. Both stand on platforms (*jagatis*). The axial shrines and the *jagati*, along with the two-tier wall and the banded base (*adisthana*), both introduced at Halebid, remain optional special features for Hoysala temples. *Jagati*, banded base, two-tier wall and the now universal overhanging canopy (*chhadya*), all contribute to a sense of horizontality (an impression exaggerated when, as at Halebid, no superstructure survives).

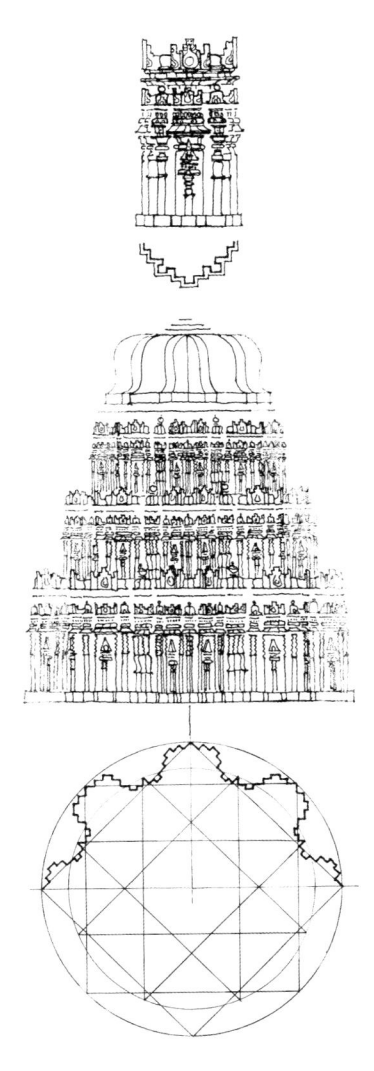

25.10 Analysis of the wall-shrine shown in 25.9. centre: elevation. From top: main aedicule type, elevation, plan geometry. The aedicules are S'K'S'P'S'K'S (notation as in 11.13) and, in the spirit of the full-size pavilions (25.8), have a miniature pavilion-chain (*hara*) at neck level, forming *kuta-stambhas* and *shala-stambhas* in conjunction with the pilasters of the wall below.

25.11 Someshvara temple, Lakshmeshvara, *c* first half 12th century: *vimana*. Photo © Gerard Foekema

25.12 Analysis of the *vimana* of the Someshvara temple, Lakshmeshvara. The design uses Karnata Dravida components, organised on principles inspired by the Shekhari mode of Nagara architecture. The plan is a stepped diamond with reentrants (9.1n), and clusters projecting from the chest of the tower simulate the half-spires (*urah-shringas*) of a Shekhari shrine.

25.13 Someshvara temple, Gadag, 12th century: double-staggered *shala* aedicule. Temples of this local school (cf 25.11; 14.5d) have blockish and shallowly encrusted mouldings, with rectangular arch panels in place of major dormer gables (*gavakshas*). Interwoven with their encrustation are precise and curvaceous details of a character shared with other 'non-mainstream' Karnata Dravida schools and with Bhumija temples (see Chapter 20).

228 THE TEMPLE ARCHITECTURE OF INDIA

25.14 Vira-Narayana temple, Belavadi, north-east shrine, *c* late 12th century. The intermediate projections are in the form of *kuta-stambhas* set at an angle, making the plan semi-stellate (9.1s). Photo © Gerard Foekema

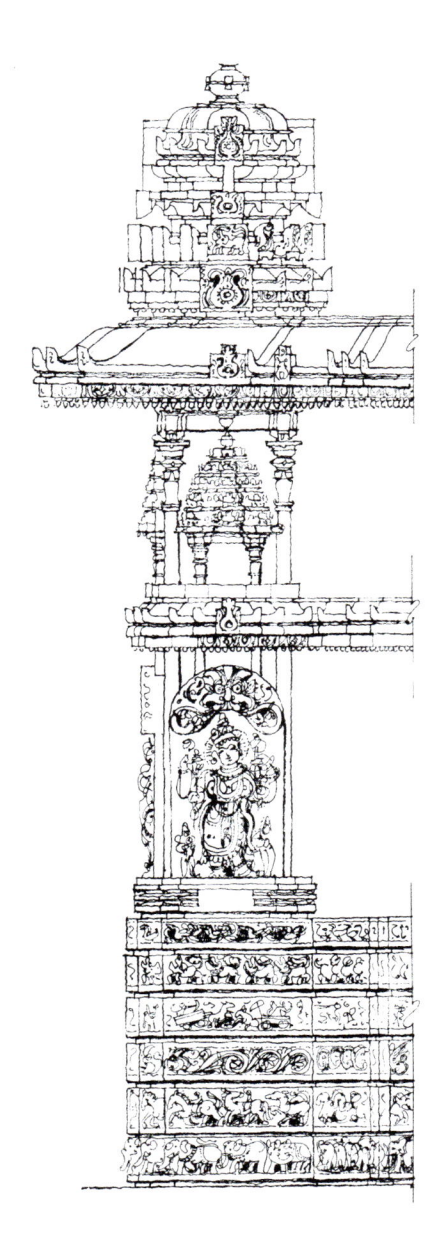

25.15 Keshava temple, Somnathpur, 1268: *kuta* aedicule (cf 9.14). Many Hoysala temples have an alternative form of base (*adisthana*), made of banded courses carved in relief.

THE KARNATA DRAVIDA TRADITION CONTINUED   **229**

25.16 Ishvara temple, Arsikere, 1220: stellate shrine (*vimana*), semi-stellate closed hall (*gudha-mandapa*) and stellate open hall (*ranga-mandapa*). The shrine is *ashta-bhadra* (with eight principal projections or *bhadras*) (9.1r), the eight *bhadras* being *panjara-stambhas* emerging from *shala* aedicules. Intermediate projections are *kuta-stambhas*, alternately square and stellate, enhancing the sense of rotation. Photo © Gerard Foekema

25.17 Rameshvara temple, Ramanathpura, *c* 12th–13th century. The composition and geometry are those of the lateral *vimanas* at Bhadravati (12.7), eight-point stellate *kuta* aedicules alternate with S–Ks–S elements (notation as 11.13). This temple is complex but not ornate. Photo © Gerard Foekema

230 THE TEMPLE ARCHITECTURE OF INDIA

25.18 Bracket figures from Ramappa temple, Palampet (AP), early 13th century. Photo © Gerard Foekema

The most common stellate form among Hoysala temples is the 16-point uniform star, typically composed entirely of *kuta* aedicules (**25.15**), but occasionally the basis of highly inventive forms (**25.16**, **25.17**); semi-stellate forms are also found (**25.14**).

Kakatiya temples are mostly of grey basalt and many had brick superstructures which no longer survive. The Karnata Dravida ones, though plainer than their Hoysala counterparts, share many features with them, including a predilection for *jagati* platforms and *bhadra* shrines. But, rather than emphasising the horizontal, their proportions are extremely slender and vertical. The respective characters of the traditions of Telangana, southern Karnataka and northern Karnataka are epitomised by their bracket figures: elegantly elongated (**25.18**), buxom and bedecked (**6.1**), and just hauntingly beautiful (**25.19**).

Notes
1. MA Dhaky, *The Indian Temple Forms in Karṇāta Inscriptions and Architecture* (New Delhi: Abhinav Publications, 1977); Gerard Foekema, *Architecture Decorated with Architecture: Later Medieval Temples of Karnātaka* (Delhi: Munshiram, 2003); Ajay Sinha, *Imagining Architects: Creativity in the Religious Monuments of India* (Newark: University of Delaware Press, 2000); Adam Hardy, *Indian Temple Architecture – Form and Transformation: The Karṇāta Drāviḍa Tradition, 7th–13th centuries* (New Delhi: IGNCA, 1995).
2. Adam Hardy, 'Hybrid Temples in Karnataka' in *First Under Heaven: The Art of Asia* (London: Hali Publications, 1997), pp 26–43.

25.19 Bracket figure from Mallikarjuna temple, Kuruvatti (Karnataka), *c* early 12th century. Photo © Gerard Foekema

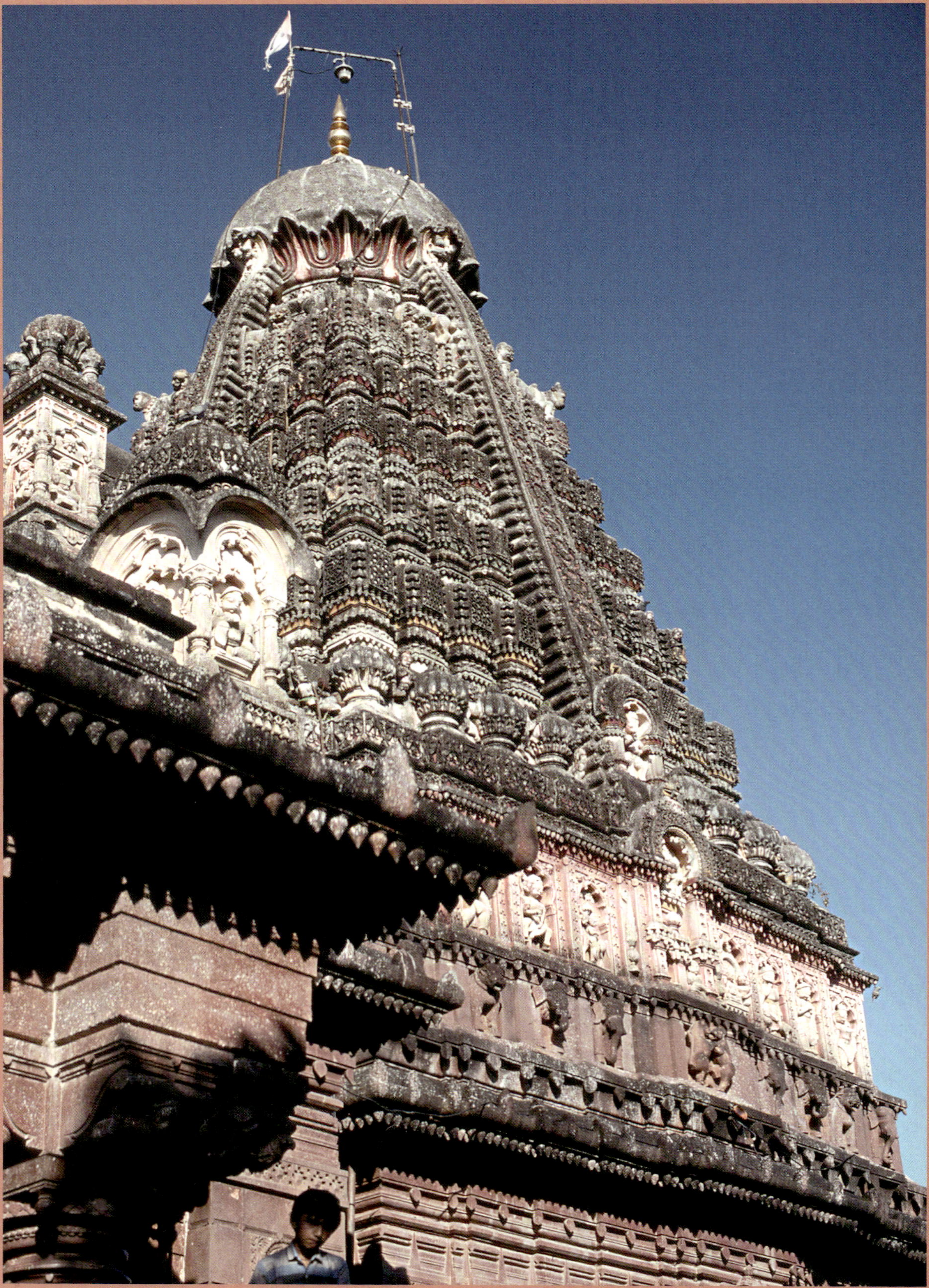

Part 6   LEGACY

26   What Happened Afterwards
27   What Next?

Grishneshvara temple, Ellora (Maharashtra) (**26.12**).

26   WHAT HAPPENED AFTERWARDS

In 1210 the Afghan leader Muhammad of Gaur established a new north Indian empire, the Sultanate of Delhi. Bengal became its offshoot shortly afterwards. A century later, Ala-ud-din waged a campaign in the south, annexing the Deccan. Here the Bahmani sultanate declared independence in 1345 and, following Timur's sack of Delhi in 1398, several independent regional sultanates emerged, including that of Gujarat. During that period, the south came under the domination of the powerful Hindu empire of Vijayanagara (Karnataka), with its new style of 'military feudalism'[1] inspired by developments under the Muslim rulers. Throughout the 15th century, Vijayanagara was in competition with the Bahmani sultanate, and its successor states in the Deccan, and with the regents of Lord Jagannatha in Orissa, who controlled most of the east coast. The Vijayanagara empire was succeeded in the south by smaller states ruled by dynasties of Nayakas (officers), previously subordinates of Vijayanagara. From the beginning of the 16th century, while the mighty Mughals gained control of the whole of the north, the Nayakas continued to flourish in the south, and the Portuguese established their colonies, chief of which was Goa. Mughal power was undermined in the 18th century by the commercial, diplomatic and military exploits of the British and French, and by the Hindu empire of the Marathas of Maharashtra. Then along came the British empire, then Independence.

Under these changing conditions, the building and support of monumental temples took various forms. Royal patronage continued for centuries in the Hindu realms of the south, at a grand scale befitting ritual sovereignty, and also in Orissa. Mercantile Jain patronage was periodically renewed in western India. Revivals of royal support took place under the Marathas in their homeland and their provinces (notably at Benares), and the various Rajput rulers who remained in power under the Mughal and British empires. In colonial times, many temples were funded by merchants and government officials, and during the 20th century it was rich industrialists who were most munificent. Recent years have seen a florescence of middle-class, community temple culture in India and among Hindu and Jain diasporas worldwide,[2] alongside temples of 'pizza effect' (exported and re-imported) Hinduism, such as the Hare Krishna movement.

At the end of Chapter 15, I may have maligned the sultans for ignoring the feminine principle; certainly Sultan Ibrahim Adil Shah, the Muslim ruler of Bijapur in the late 16th century, was devoted to the goddess Saraswati.[3] From our present vantage point, creative hybridity seems both truer to what went on and more attractive than purity. With the arrival of Islam, guilds of masons adapted their traditions to Muslim patronage: the earlier mosques of Bengal, and later of Gujarat, although planned differently from temples and avoiding sculptures of living beings, follow temple mouldings, pillars and corbelled domes. 'Indo-Islamic' architectures developed. Across northern India in the 17th and 18th centuries there appeared an architectural vocabulary shared by Mughal mosques, Rajput palaces, the courtyard houses (*havelis*) of nobles and merchants, Hindu temples and Sikh *gurudwaras*. This vocabulary has its own kinds of aedicule: arch shapes in a rectangular panel – pointed, or cusped in distant homage to the *chaitya* hall cross section, *chhatris* (umbrella-like pavilions) with domes or rectangular vaults, some with the vernacular Bengali (*bangaldar*) curved roof ridge and eaves. The new pavilions were projected as balconies (*jarokhas*), lined up in *haras* against the sky, placed at corners around a dome in the time-honoured manner of *kutas*, or mounted on pillars to make *kuta-stambhas*, as in the minarets of the Taj Mahal. The Hindu rulers in Bengal, loyal to the Mughals, erected brick temples fusing the now established Bengali mosque architecture with the local vernacular forms, while Maratha temples recombined elements from the Deccani Islamic tradition. Meanwhile, the Greek temple image with triangular pediment took its place in the Indian aedicule range for the first time since ancient Gandhara. But all that is beyond the scope of this book, which is about the Nagara and Dravida languages. These, it must be admitted, have from time to time become bearers of Purity, and are pressed into her service even today.

26.1 Vitthala temple, Hampi (Vijayanagara) (Karnataka), 1554: interior of open hall (*ranga-mandapa*) with composite piers.
Photo © Gerard Foekema

26.2 Arunachaleshvara temple, Tiruvannamalai (Tamil Nadu): within the second enclosure wall (*prakara*) looking east. The gateway (*gopura*) in the foreground is *c* 1200, the one beyond dates from the 14th century and the two giant ones from the mid-16th century. (Crispin Branfoot, personal communication.)
Photo © Gerard Foekema

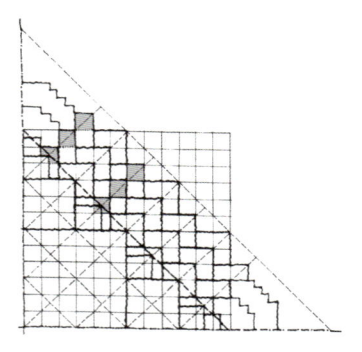

26.3 Late variant of Type 5 Shekhari shrine: roof plan. The geometry has been simplified, placing all the main elements within a diagonal square.

The Dravida Continued

The continuity of the Karnata Dravida tradition was broken with the establishment of the Deccani sultanates, and the rulers of Vijayanagara (present-day Hampi, Karnataka) brought craftsmen from Tamil Nadu to transform the granite boulders of their capital into temple complexes. Occasionally the regional predilection for staggered shapes burst through, but architectural inventiveness was applied not so much to the inherited Dravida vocabulary as to the layout of temple complexes and the planning of the whole city. With a growing need for large open halls for congregational gatherings, a highly sculptural form of composite pier was developed (**26.1**). Such piers reached gigantic proportions in the temple cities of the Nayakas in Tamil Nadu (**26.2**),[4] lining ceremonial corridors for the processional outings of the deity at festival times. In these complexes it was again — apart from the composite piers and the ever-increasing height of the *gopuras* — in the overall planning that innovations were made. The underlying designs of *vimanas*, and of *gopuras* (except for the number of storeys), remained as those of the Chola period. Mouldings and details also stayed close to Chola ones, but became more florid, especially when made in stucco. However, the notion of two- or three-storey aedicules, though sometimes emphatically present even in the 17th century, tended on the whole to give way to parapet pavilions arranged without vertical connections, like pots on a shelf.

And the Nagara Continued

Unlike the Dravida, Nagara temple architecture in northern India received no lavish royal patronage after the 13th century, yet in its various revivals, especially in the Shekhari mode, untried possibilities were attempted in shrine composition, alongside the numerous repetitions of established types. The most coherent extrapolations were, admittedly, relatively early, notably in the 15th-century Jain temple complex at Ranakpur (Rajasthan) (**26.4–26.6**). The Surya temple here, on an *ashta-bhadra* stellate plan (with eight main projections), and with a stellate hall, is a dazzling hybrid, combining Shekhari chains of half-spires with Bhumija full-height bands of radiating pavilion-topped pillar forms (*kuta-stambhas*). Development of the Shekhari mode is seen in the nearby Parsvanatha temple (**26.5, 26.6**), a fine example of a type which reappeared several times up to the 17th century.[5] In common with a new version of Type 5 (**26.3**; cf **12.3e**), half-spires (*urah-shringas*) sit within a diagonal square — a simplification which offsets a new level of complexity attained though the addition of a further, inferior order of quarter-*shringas* emerging from the first order. These lesser quarter-spires (not exactly a

26.4 Adinatha temple, Ranakpur (Rajasthan), 15th century. The multi-shrine enclosure seen at Kumbhariya and Dilwara was, on a more mandala-like plan, raised through two storeys, pierced by full-height spaces which provide diagonal vistas from level to level, enhancing an almost diaphanous character unprecedented in Indian temple architecture.
Photo © Gerard Foekema

quarter on plan) are organically related to the stages below through corresponding cardinal projections in the reentrants.

This line of thinking is taken a stage further in another Jain monument, the late 16th-century Navi Adinatha temple in the Adisvara Tuk on Mount Shatrunjaya (Palitana, Gujarat). Here the reentrants have been brought out into line with, and made identical to, the main *kuta-stambhas*, to make a row of seven in each quadrant (**26.7**). In other words, a Shekhari shrine, for the first time, has nine main projections on each face. A new set of reentrants appears in the crevices, leading up diagonally to the minor quarter-spires. The main temple in the same enclosure, the large Adinatha, foregoes minor quarter-spires in order to display a record number of *urah-shringas* – six on each face (**26.8**). This is achieved only through compromise. The half-spires are packed in by making them shallow – considerably less than half a square – so that the intermediate *kuta-stambhas*, normally leading up to the first half-spires, now lead up to the second. The third half-spire is still within the central diamond: then, within the widening, concentric diamonds, stepping down, it is possible to have three more, but these are all smaller than the turrets of the lowest *kuta-stambhas*.

Another strand of development, also using two orders of quarter-spires, extrapolates from the old idea of the emergent central cluster. One type of shrine begins from the concept of a projected Type 1 cluster (cf **21.16**) and brings out a smaller Type 1 from this (**26.9c**).[6] The large, 18th-century Trimbakesvara temple built by the Marathas at Trimbak (Maharashtra) goes a step further, with a cardinal detelescoping of four diminishing Type 1 images (**26.10**). This is a nine-projection temple, with a sequence of four very shallow half-spires, all within a diagonal

26.5 Parsvanatha temple, Ranakpur, 15th century. An additional order of quarter-spires brings additional complexity to the Shekhari mode. Further proliferation is manifested in the miniature turrets piled up at the corners of the central spire (*mula-manjari*) and of all the lesser spire forms.

WHAT HAPPENED AFTERWARDS 237

26.6 Parsvanatha temple, Ranakpur: roof plan geometry.

26.7 Nava Adinatha temple, Adishvara Tuk, Mount Shatrunjaya (Palitana) (Gujarat), late 16th century: roof plan geometry.

square. The reentrants support three orders of quarter-spires flanking the first, second and third half-spires. But all of the half-spires project by the same amount, and the quarter spires are like bananas; so, in terms of the earlier norms, this degree of development is achieved only by cheating. Contemporary Maratha works in distant Varanasi are also Shekhari, in a more relaxed way, again achieving novelty through ignorance of the earlier constraints, and no less charming for the bizarre shapes and proportions of their constituent parts. A similar approach is seen in **26.11**.

So, although Shekhari designs in general became less varied in the late medieval period, some remarkable developments took place, extending the earlier evolutionary pattern, even if the quality of sculpture and surface declined. Even revived traditions, involving a certain amount of copying, were able to explore the inherent potential of the language once its formal principles were understood, although their ultimate inventions rested on compromise. Other than by engendering increasingly minor orders of quarter-*shringas*, or by successively incorporating (as in **26.9**) *ad infinitum* – both possible, but very fiddly – it is difficult to see how the same kind of evolution could have continued without abandoning the rules. So, quite apart from any socio-historical explanations for the fossilisation of the Shekhari mode, its formal possibilities had largely been exhausted. In other circumstances, perhaps, people might have transformed it into something quite different, starting a whole new cycle.

The Bhumija mode did not attract renewed attention to the same extent as the Shekhari, but in Maharashtra the Marathas, before discovering the Shekhari (no doubt through links with Gujarat), first drew from Deccani sultanate architecture and then began to mould this into a Bhumija pattern, reviving the chosen temple form of their Yadava predecessors (**26.12**).

Until Today

For Hindu reform movements during the colonial period, worshipping 'idols' in temples was seen, at best, as a lower path to spiritual attainment. Yet the monumental traditions were revived through the efforts of merchant classes, especially in the south, while the shrines of the fields and villages went on springing up as they always had. A new phenomenon of the 20th century was patronage by the great industrial houses, most prominently the Birlas, whose temples commissioned in the 1930s were rather Art Deco. In recent years there has been an increasing demand for new temples, especially 'traditional' ones.

Contemporary Indian temples can be divided into three categories: folk/popular; those designed by 'traditional architects'; and those designed by architects qualified in the modern profession.

The wide spectrum that runs from 'folk' (naive good taste, from the perspective of elite architecture) to 'popular' (naive bad taste, from the same perspective) includes much more than forms derived from Nagara or Dravida. But echoes of the classical forms abound, from mud mandirs in Maharashtra to brick boxes in Birmingham with fibreglass *shikharas* on the roof. Within this broad category are the prodigious modern complexes that have appeared in Indian cities over the last couple of decades, such as the Chhattarpur complex, New Delhi. Described by AGK Menon as 'pastiche par excellence',[7] these are undeniably kitsch. But would they not be boring without their embellishments, and would the brick box be better without its plastic spire?

'Authentic' Dravida temples are now designed mainly by *sthapatis* from Tamil Nadu, Nagara ones (Jain as well as Hindu) by the Sompura caste from Gujarat. These traditional architects stress their credentials in terms of ancient professional lineage and knowledge of the *Shastras*. They copy medieval forms, but adapt construction methods and planning

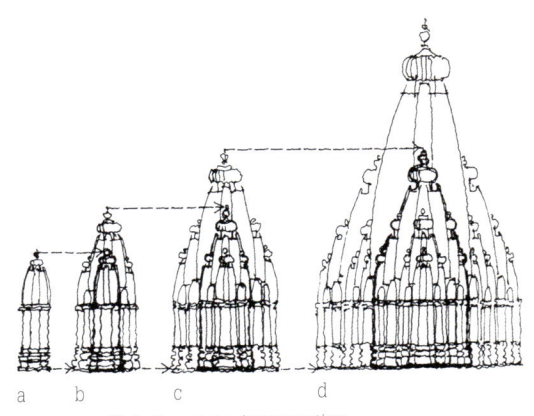

26.9 Successive incorporation.

26.8 Adinatha temple, Adishvara Tuk, Mount Shatrunjaya. The design of the Adinatha is constrained by the fact that the superstructure of 1585 is built over a sanctum of 1155–7. The sanctum walls dictate a stepped diamond plan with three main *kuta-stambhas* and protruding reentrants, as for Type 5. Photo © Dr Julia AB Hegewald

26.10 Trimbakeshvara temple, Trimbak (Maharashtra), 18th century. Photo © Gerard Foekema

26.11 Shiva temple, Dulhinganj (Bihar): a vaguely Shekhari temple, showing that blissful ignorance of classical subtleties can bring its own vigour.

(often, outside India, collaborating with local architectural practices) to new climates and needs, in particular to modes of worship which are more congregational than those of the past. If stone is too expensive, they use cement. Stylistically, their work is closest to the florescence that the respective traditions enjoyed in the 16th and 17th centuries under the Nayakas in Tamil Nadu and with Jain patronage in Gujarat. They also use older models, particularly 'late Chola' in the south and 'Solanki' (Maru-Gurjara) in the north.

In terms of composition, only simple shrine forms have been built recently by traditional temple architects, although a Sompura text of the 1930s, with plans and elevations of superstructures, shows full knowledge of the Shekhari types discussed in Chapter 10.[8] Even more than their 17th-century predecessors, contemporary traditional practitioners are oblivious to the vertical connections which are the basis of a multi-aedicular composition. This is their prerogative, of course, but such decapitated thinking divorces towers from walls. So, for example, when the concept of a south Indian temple enclosure is roofed over for a cold climate, it is given a suspended ceiling throughout, with no view from inside of the towers, which poke up like pimples on the roof of a supermarket (cf **26.13**).[9]

One of my few realised contributions to the Sri Venkateshvara temple of the United Kingdom at Oldbury (West Midlands, UK) is the simple idea of the towers coming up through roof lights, so that you can see them from below and the walls have proper light. Yes, as it is the end of a chapter and not of the book, I may weave myself into the story, having designed several Hindu temples in England. There is not much to tell, as I am not good with committees, some of them had no money anyway, and the final designs cannot be shown as they followed the romantic notion that they would grow organically within a framework for collaborative craft work. And there is little more to say of work by professional architects generally, since temples have not received their attention to nearly the same extent as churches or mosques. Modern architects, Indian ones foremost among them, crippled by the fear of committing pastiche, find Indian temples embarrassing in their complexity and their supposed ornateness, in their spirituality and their sensuality. None of today's categories of temple design can claim to show the way to what could happen next.

Notes

1. Hermann Kulke in H Kulke and Dietmar Rothermund, *A History of India* (Abingdon: Routledge, 2004), pp 162–95.
2. Joanna Punzo Waghorne, *Diaspora of the Gods: Modern Hindu Temples in an Urban Middle-Class World* (New York: Oxford University Press, 2004).
3. Mentioned in the Persian text Sahifat-i Ahl-i Huda, cited in Richard M Eaton, *Sufis of Bijapur, 1300–1700: Social Roles of Sufis in Medieval India* (Princeton: Princeton University Press, 1978), p 101. See also Philip B Wagoner, 'Reviving the Chalukyan Past in the 16th Century Deccan: Archaeological and Literary Perspectives', *South Asian Studies* 24, 2007 (forthcoming).
4. Crispin Branfoot, '"Expanding Form": The Architectural Sculpture of the South Indian Temple *c.* 1500–1700' in *Artibus Asiae* 57, 2 (2002), pp 189–245.
5. Variants are found in several 15th-century temples in Rajasthan, and later in two of the 17th-century memorial *chhatris* at Mandor. Perhaps the earliest example is the Meera temple at Eklingji.
6. Three examples are the 15th-century Lakhema temple, Abhapur (Gujarat), the 18th-century Shiva temple, Vadnagar (Gujarat), and an 18th-century Maratha work, the Narayana temple, Nasik (Maharashtra). See Adam Hardy, 'Sekhari Temples', *Artibus Asiae* 62, 1 (2002), pp 81–137.
7. AGK Menon, 'Contemporary Patterns in Religious Architecture', *Architecture + Design*, Nov–Dec 1997, pp 23–9 (p 27).
8. Narmadashankar Sompura (ed), *Silparatnakar* (Dhuangdhra, Kathiawar: Shilpashastri Shri Narmadashankar Muljibhai Sompura, 1939). The text shows many more types than my basic five, different names being given on the basis of minor variations.
9. Eg the Shiva-Vishu temple near Washington, DC.

26.12 Grishneshvara temple, Ellora (Maharashtra), 18th century. This loosely Bhumija temple has stone mouldings and pillars derived directly from medieval forms, while its plastered pavilions carry lotus-necked onion domes typical of Deccani Islamic architecture, and sport cusped arches, tracery (*jalis*) and curved '*bangaldar*' roofs.

26.13 Hindu temple of Central Florida, Casselberry, USA. This south Indian temple proclaims its ecumenism through four Shekhari-esque spires, which complement the main shrine (*vimana*) and four barrel-roofed gateways (*gopuras*). The towers are cut off by the roof, but are visible from inside through a large central rooflight. Photo © Adrian Smythies

27 WHAT NEXT?

What new cycle of creation could await us? That carved temples are still appearing in the world is a marvel, but I wonder (dare I say this?) whether their realisation would not be improved upon if their designers read this book. The temple architecture of India reveals an inexhaustible variety, along with means of creating it. Among these are the processes of starting from a palette of aedicules, manipulating and combining these to make new ones, putting them together according to various three-dimensional arrangements and, when these are exhausted, inventing new kinds of arrangement. Contemporary 'traditional' temple architects could learn not just from the forms but from the ways of designing still palpable in the works of their forbears, keeping in mind that the most perfect composition will be sterile if there is no life or human feeling in the making of it. That, in the Indian context, handmade work can be used in buildings of the silicon age is something to be cherished, for the benefit of both maker and beholder.

But there is room for temples made in neon lights as well as ones of mud, for temples in the heart and the home and on the outer ring road, for temples in virtual reality as well as real stone. Modern architects, too, can design temples, if they can learn that greater than the danger of pastiche is that of blindness to other ways of architectural thought than those they have been trained in. Indian temple architecture cannot be reduced to axes and grids, and no abstract diagram, even one termed *vastu-purusha-mandala*, can be a stamp of identity. If a Critical Regionalism can be found, it will not be through qualities approved by Modernist sensibilities but which have nothing to do with Hindu temples, such as 'tectonic form' – the expression of construction and of 'the way in which the syntactical form of the structure explicitly resists the action of gravity'.[1] The new temple can follow an architecture of imagery, and of patterns with potential for endless development and transformation, inviting contemplation through a focused mind, yet sensuous, brimming with life, calling out to be experienced in terms of the human body and its movements.

Needless to say, I do not think that the legacy of Indian temple architecture is only for India, and it is certainly not the property of some imaginary pure Hinduness. The world's heritage belongs to all of us, and the principles embodied in the shrines of South Asia may blossom in new, multicultural architectures, in infinitely self-replicating, fractal-like structures, or in monumental paradigms of an expanding cosmos.

The aim of this book, however, has not been to provide recipes for transforming a great architectural tradition into new architecture, but to attempt a prerequisite for that: to see the tradition clearly, in the fruits of its unfurling branches. Before any question of how that tradition might live on, this same aim has been pursued simply for the sake of understanding it and to try to make some sense of it as a whole. Valuable detailed studies of Indian architecture continue to be made, but it is also necessary to survey the broader scene, trying not to get lost in the particular, yet not to let general patterns blot out whatever does not fit them.

In order to understand visual things, to look at forms is not formalism but the only way to begin and the only way to make meaningful connections with other human realms. Architecture, politics and religion cannot be reduced one to another. If the source of culture is a silent voice in the Beyond, then religion, politics, architecture and all the arts are its varied expressions on earth; but if culture is interminably remade in a great identity parade, then maybe politics and religion are different kinds of architecture. In any case, the connections cannot be explained in terms of causes, but, if a clear enough picture is painted, they can be seen.

> The eye is truth: the eye indeed, is truth. So if now two people were to come arguing, one saying, 'I have seen', the other saying 'I have heard', we would believe the one saying 'I have seen'.[2]

Enough of words, then. There are people who are impatient to bypass what they see and jump to meanings, and others so busy trying to be methodologically correct that they have no time to look at all. There will always be those who, in museums, spend longer reading labels than looking at art. But this book will have fulfilled its aim if it has opened a little window into another architectural universe, and begun to sketch out its overall shapes and to fill in its details, watching its unfolding from the alpha of the aedicule to the omega of last *gavaksha*. This might not be the noblest end, but it will have made a good start.

Notes
1 Kenneth Frampton, 'Towards a Critical Regionalism: Six Points for an Architecture of Resistance' in Hal Foster (ed), *Postmodern Culture* (London: Pluto Press, 1985), pp 16–31.
2 Brihadaranyaka Upanishad, V.14, 4, *The Upaniṣads*, trans Valerie J Roebuck (New Delhi: Penguin Books, 2000), p 101.

Glossary

The words in brackets follow the International Alphabet of Sanskrit Transliteration, which conveys pronunciation more accurately than the anglicised versions.

adisthana (adiṣṭhāna): moulded base of a Dravida shrine aedicule: image of a building used as a compositional element
alpa vimana (alpa vimāna): minor vimana (uni-aedicular)
amalaka (āmalaka): 'myrobolan fruit'; ribbed crowning member of a Nagara shrine
antarala (antarāla): antechamber in front of sanctum
aspara (apsara): celestial nymph
bala-panjara (balapañjara): small Valabhi aedicule in recess of a Latina shikhara
bhadra (bhadra): main projection, normally on cardinal axis
bhumi (bhūmi): tier or storey of a Nagara shrine
Bhumija (Bhūmija): Nagara shrine with continuous vertical chains of khuta-stambhas
chhadya (chādya): stone canopy
Dravida (Drāviḍa): belonging to south Indian temple architecture
gavaksha (gavākṣa): 'cow eye'; horseshoe arch
gopura (Tamil gopuram) (gōpura): shala-topped temple gateway
hara (hāra): band of pavilions, usually Dravida
harantara (hāntāra: linking section of a hara, between pavilions
jagati (jagatī): temple platform; lowest base moulding in a Dravida adisthana
kalasha (kalaśa): 'pot', rounded moulding in Nagara vedibandha; vase-finial
kapota (kapōta): rounded Dravida eave moulding
kapotali (kapōtālī): double-curved Nagara eave moulding
'kapota-panjara aedicule': panjara aedicule with its crowning gavaksha in the kapota moulding (see 11.10j)
kuta (kūṭa): 'peak'; crowning pavilion, especially domed Dravida type (see 11.10a)
'kuta aedicule': aedicule crowned by a kuta (see 11.10d)
kuta-stambha (kūṭastambha): pillar or pilaster with kuta on top (see 10.14 and 11.13c)
lata (latā): 'creeper'; central spine of a Nagara (especially Latina) shikhara
Latina (Latina): mode of Nagara shrine with curved shikhara
linga (liṅga), Tamil lingam: phallic emblem of Shiva
mandapa (maṇḍapa): hall; maha-mandapa = main hall; mukha-mandapa = 'face hall', porch
mula-prasada (mulaprāsāda): main shrine, shrine proper, of a Nagara temple
Nagara (Nāgara): belonging to north Indian temple architecture
panjara (pañjara): 'cage'; Dravida pavilion with gavaksha gable roof (end of a shala) (see 11.10b)
'panjara aedicule': aedicule crowned by a panjara (see 11.10e)
'panjara-stambha': pillar or pilaster with panjara on top (see 11.13b)
Phamsana (Phāṁsana): type of shrine crowned by a pyramid of eave mouldings
pitha (pīṭha): pedestal or sub-base of a Nagara temple
prasada (prāsāda): palace; Nagara shrine
prati (pratī): Dravida floor moulding
sandhara (sandhāra): with internal ambulatory (pradakshina-patha)
shala (śālā): Dravida pavilion with barrel roof (11.10c)
'shala aedicule': aedicule crowned by a shala (see 11.10g)
Shekhari (Śekharī): mode of Nagara shrine with clustered shikhara
shikhara: (śikhara): superstructure (tower or spire) of a Nagara temple
shuka-nasa (śukanāsa): antefix or fronton to temple tower
stambha (stambha): pillar
stupa (stūpa): dome-like Buddhist sacred monument (early ones encased relics)
tala (tāla): tier or storey of a Dravida shrine
torana (tōraṇa): gateway, archway; gateway/archway motif
upapitha (upapīṭha): pedestal or sub-base of a Nagara temple
urah-shringa (uraḥsṛṅga): 'chest-sprouting', half-spire or half-shikhara (half-embedded shikhara) in a Shekhari superstructure
Valabhi (Valabhī): mode of Nagara shrine with barrel-roofed superstructure
varandika (varaṇḍikā): band of mouldings between wall and superstructure of a Nagara temple
vedibandha (vēdibandha): moulded base of a Nagara temple
vedika (vēdikā): railing: rail moulding
venukosha (vēnukōśa): 'bamboo sheath': segment of Nagara shikhara (esp. at corners) consisting of piled up kutas
vimana (vimāna): Dravida shrine; main shrine, shrine proper, of a Dravida temple

---

Bibliography

Ali, Daud, *Courtly Culture and Political Life in Early Medieval India* (Cambridge: Cambridge University Press, 2004)
Asher, Frederick M, *The Art of Eastern India, 300–800* (Minneapolis: University of Minnesota Press, 1980)
Basham, AL, *The Wonder That Was India* (London: Fontana, 1971)
Bäumer, Bettina and Rajendra Prasad Das (eds), *Śilparatnakośa– A Glossary of Orissan Temple Architecture* (Delhi: IGNCA, 1994)
Behrend, Kurt A, *The Buddhist Architecture of Gandhara* (Leiden: Brill, 2004)
Berkson, Carmel, *Ellora, Concept and Style* (Delhi: IGNCA, 1992)
—*Elephanta: The Cave of Shiva* (Princeton: Princeton University Press, 1983)
—*The Caves at Aurangabad: Early Buddhist Tantric Art in India* (Ahmedabad: Mapin, 1986)
Blurton, Richard, *Hindu Art* (Cambridge, Mass: Harvard University Press, 1993)
Branfoot, Crispin, *Gods on the Move: Architecture and Ritual in the South Indian Temple* (London: British Academy and Erskine Press, 2007)
Brown, Percy, *Indian Architecture (Buddhist and Hindu Periods)*, 3rd edn (Bombay: Taraporevala, 1956)
Chandra, Pramod (ed), *Studies in Indian Temple Architecture* (New Delhi: AIIS, 1975)
—*On the Study of Indian Art* (Cambridge, Mass: Harvard University Press, 1983)
Chattopadhyaya, BD, *The Making of Early Medieval India* (New Delhi: Oxford University Press, 1994)
Cohen, Andrew, *Temple Architecture and Sculpture of the Nolambas* (Delhi: Manohar, 1998)
Cousens, Henry, *The Chalukyan Architecture of the Kanarese Districts* (Calcutta: ASI, 1926)
—*Medieval Temples of the Dakhan* (Calcutta: ASI, 1931)
Dagens, Bruno (ed), *Mayamata: an Indian Treatise on Housing, Architecture and Iconography* (Delhi: Siataram Bharatia Institute, 1985)
—*Traités, temples et images du monde indien: études d'histoire et d'archaeologie*, compiled by Marie-Luce Barazier-Billoret and Vincent Lefèvre (Institut Français de Pondichéry and Presses Sorbonne Nouvelle, 2005)
Davies, Richard, *Ritual in an Oscillating Universe: Worshipping Śiva in Medieval India* (Princeton: Princeton University Press, 1991)
Deheja, Vidya, *Indian Art* (London: Phaidon, 1997)
—*Early Buddhist Rock Temples: A Chronological Study* (London: Thames and Hudson, 1972)
Desai, Devangana, *The Religious*

Imagery of Khajuraho (Mumbai: Franco-Indian Research, 1996)
Desai, Vishaka and Darielle Mason (eds), *Gods, Guardians and Lovers* (New York and Ahmedabad: Asia Society Galleries and Mapin Publishing, 1993)
Deva, Krishna, *Temples of Khajuraho*, 2 vols (Delhi: ASI, 1990)
Dhaky, MA, *The Indian Temple Forms in Karṇāta Inscriptions and Architecture* (New Delhi: Abhinav Publications, 1977)
Dhaky, MA and US Moorti, *The Temples in Kumbhariya* (Delhi: AIIS, 2001)
Donaldson, Thomas E, *Hindu Temple Art of Orissa*, 3 vols (Leiden: Brill, 1985)
Eck, Diana L, *Darśan: Seeing the Divine Image in India*, 2nd edn (Chambersburg, PA: Anima Books, 1985)
Encyclopaedia of Indian Temple Architecture (EITA) Vol I, Part 1, *South India: Lower Dravidadeśa, 200 BC–AD 1324*, ed Michael W Meister (Delhi: American Institute of Indian Studies and Manohar, 1999)
—Vol I, Part 2, *South India: Upper Dravidadeśa, Early Phase, AD 550–1075*, ed Michael W Meister and MA Dhaky (Delhi: AIIS and Oxford University Press, 1999)
—Vol I, Part 3, *South India: Upper Dravidadeśa, Later Phase AD 973–1326*, ed MA Dhaky (Delhi: AIIS, 1996)
—Vol 1, Part 4, *South India: Dravidadeśa, Later Phase*, ed George Michell (Delhi: AIIS, 2001)
—Vol II, Part 1, *North India: Foundations of North Indian Style, c 250 BC–AD 1100*, ed Michael W Meister, MA Dhaky, Krishna Deva (Delhi: AIIS and Oxford University Press, 1998)
—Vol II, Part 2, *North India: Period of Early Maturity, c AD 700–900*, ed Michael W Meister and MA Dhaky (Delhi: AIIS and Oxford University Press, 1991)
—Vol II, Part 3, *North India: Beginnings of Medieval Idiom c AD 900–1000*, ed MA Dhaky (Delhi: AIIS and IGNCA, 1998)
Fergusson, James, *A History of Indian and Eastern Architecture* (London: John Murray, 1876)
—and James Burgess, *The Cave Temples of India*, (Delhi: Munshiram, 1988; 1st edn, 1880)
Flood, Gavin, *An Introduction to Hinduism* (Cambridge: Cambridge University Press, 1996)
Foekema, Gerard, *Hoysala Temples* (Delhi: Books and Books, 1994)
—*Calkyan Architecture of Medieval Karnataka*, 3 vols (Delhi: Munshiram, 2003)
—*Architecture Decorated with Architecture: Later Medieval Temples of Karnataka, 1000–1300 AD* (Delhi: Munshiram, 2003)
Grover, Satish, *The Architecture of India, Buddhist and Hindu* (Delhi: Vikas Publishing House, 1980)
Guy, John, *Indian Temple Sculpture* (London: V&A Publications, 2007)
Hardy, Adam, *Indian Temple Architecture, Form and Transformation: The Karnataka Dravida Tradition, 7th–13th Centuries* (New Delhi: IGNCA, 1995)
—(ed), *The Temple in South Asia* (London: British Academy, 2007)
Harle, James, *The Art and Architecture of the Indian Subcontinent* (Harmondsworth: Penguin, 1986)
Hegewald, Julia B, *Water Architecture in South Asia: A Study of Types, Developments and Meanings* (Leiden: Brill, 2002)
Huntington, Susan L, *The Art of Indian Asia* (New York: Weatherhill, 1985)
Inden, Ronal, *Imagining India* (Oxford: Basil Blackwell, 1990)
Knox, Robert, *Amaravati: Buddhist Sculpture from the Great Stupa* (London: British Museum, 1992)
Kramrisch, Stella, *The Hindu Temple* (Calcutta: University of Calcutta, 1946)
Kulke, Hermann and Dietmar Rothermund, *A History of India* (Abingdon: Routledge, 2004)
Lannoy, Richard, *The Speaking Tree* (Oxford: Oxford University Press, 1971)
Michell, George, *The Hindu Temple: An Introduction to its Meaning and Form*, (Chicago: University of Chicago Press, 1988; 1st edn, 1977)
—*Hindu Art and Architecture* (London: Thames and Hudson, 2000)
—*The Penguin Guide to the Monuments of India*, Vol 1: *Buddhist, Jain, Hindu* (London: Viking, 1989)
Mitter, Partha, *Indian Art* (Oxford: Oxford University Press, 2001)
Pichard, Pierre, *Thanjavur Bṛhadīsvara, An Architectural Study* (Delhi: IGNCA and École Française de l'Extrème Orient, 1995)
Rea, Alexander, *Chalukyan Architecture: Including Examples from the Bellary District, Madras Presidency* (Madras: ASI, 1896)
—*Pallava Architecture* (Varanasi: Indological Book House, reprint 1970)
Sachdev, Vibhuti and Giles Tillotson, *Building Jaipur: The Making of an Indian City* (London: Reaktion Books, 2002)
Samuel, Geoffrey, *The Origins of the Indic Religions: Yoga and Tantra before the 13th Century* (Cambridge: Cambridge University Press, 2007)
Sinha, Ajay J, *Imagining Architects: Creativity in the Religious Monuments of India* (Newark: University of Delaware Press, 2000)
Snodgrass, Adrian, *The Symbolism of the Stupa* (Delhi: Motilal Banarassidass, 1992)
Sompura, Narmadashankar (ed), *Shilparatnakar* (Dhuangdhra, Kathiawar: Shilpashastri Shri Narmadashankar Muljibhai Sompura, 1939)
Soundara Rajan, KR, *Indian Temple Styles: The Personality of Hindu Architecture* (Delhi: Munshiram, 1972)
— *Cave Temples of the Deccan* (Delhi: ASI, 1981)
Spink, Walter, *Ajanta: History and Development*, 5 vols (Leiden: Brill, 2005 onwards)
Stein, Burton, *Peasant State and Society in Medieval South India* (Delhi: Oxford University Press, 1980)
Tadgell, Christopher, *The History of Architecture in India, From the Dawn of Civilization to the End of the Raj* (London: ADT Press, 1990)
Tillotson, Giles (ed), *Paradigms of Indian Architecture* (London: Curzon Press, 1997)
Viennot, Odette, *Temples de l'Inde centrale et occidentale*, 2 vols (Paris: École Française d'Extrème Orient, 1976)
Volwahsen, Andreas, *Living Architecture: India* (London: Macdonald, 1970).
Waghorne, Joanna Punzo, *Diaspora of the Gods: Modern Hindu Temples in an Urban Middle-Class World* (New York: Oxford University Press, 2004)
White, David Gordon, *Kiss of the Yoginī: 'Tantric Sex' in its South Asian Contexts* (Chicago and London: University of Chicago Press, 2003)
Williams, Joanna (ed), *Kaladarśana: American Studies in the Art of India* (New Delhi: Oxford University Press and India Book House, 1981)
Williams, Joanna G, *The Art of Gupta India: Empire and Province* (Pinceton: Princeton University Press, 1982)
Willis, Michael D, *Temples of Gopaksetra* (London: British Museum, 1997)
—*Buddhist Reliquaries from Ancient India* (London: British Museum, 2000)
Zimmer, Heinrich, *Myths and Symbols in Indian Art and Civilization*, ed Joseph Campbell (New York: Pantheon Books, Bollingen Series VI, 1946)

INDEX

Figures in italics indicate captions.

abacus-echninus 153
Abaneri 184
Achaemenid Persia 150
acharyas (religious teachers) 63
Adinatha temple, Ranakpur (Rajasthan) 237, *237*
Adishvara Tuk, Mount Shatrunjaya (Palitana) (Gujarat): Nava Adinatha temple 237, *238*, *239*
adisthana (moulded base) 144, *145*, *146*, 215, *218*, 221, 227, *229*
advaita (non-duality) 47, 48
aedicules *17*, 44, 52, *122*, 134, 148, 176, 198
   abbreviated (aedicule-substitutes) 41
   aedicular niches 80, 97
   aedicular thinking 74
   aerial 92
   amalaka *107*, 108, 168, *169*, *171*, *172*, *173*
   bala-panjara see *bala-panjara*
   bhadra 123
   Bhumija *116*
   Chaurasi 198
   classical 80, *81*
   components of the *vimana* *14*, *15*
   composite *132*
   corner 170, *171*, 198
   definition 10
   dome-images 156-57
   Dravida 14, *127*, *130*, *132*
   Dravida-karma *116*
   dynamic relationships 17-18
   early aedicular Nagara traditions 110
   embedded *16*
   emerging centrifugally *16*
   framing religious images 12
   increasing abstraction 15
   interpenetrating 22
   kapota-panjara *129*, *130*, 212, 213, 218, 220
   kuta 16, *126*, *128*, *130*, *132*, *146*, 198, *202*, 207, 210, 218, *219*, *222*, *225*, 226, *229*
      16-point uniform star 231
      domed *107*, 110, *110*, 171, *172*, 198
      eight-point stellate *230*
      Latina *114*, 203, *203*
      Nagara 14, *107*, 169, 173
   panjara 42, 129, *130*, *132*, *146*, *172*, 198, *198*, 209, 214, 215, 218, 221, *223*, 226
   Phamsana *107*, 112, *116*, 171, 197, 199
   pointed arch *81*
   preceded by shrines 11
   primary 64, 69, 212, 218
   relationships between 37
   secondary 64, 69, *91*, *130*, 198, 212, *213*
   shala 16, *43*, *128*, *130*, 132, *177*, 198, 207, 210, *213*, 214-15, 217, *217*, 223, *224*, 226
      double-staggered 42, 43, *43*, 69, 70, 132, *132*, *224*, 225, *228*
      single-staggered 42
      staggered *43*, 70, 129, 132, *132*, 207, *207*
   Shekhari *116*
   stellate *kuta* 224
   three-storey 129, *130*, *172*, 215, 217, *217*, *219*
   torana *81*
   two-storey 16, *130*, 171, *172*, 207, 209, 210, 221
   Valabhi 41, *107*, 108, 109, 110, 112, 113, 115, *116*, 117, 171, *171*, *172*, *173*, 174, *176*, *179*, *193*, 195, 198, 201
Afghanistan 23, 80
Agamas (Shaiva Tantras) 52, 53
Agastishvara temple, Kilayur (Tamil Nadu) *130*
Aghora 58
agriculture 223
   agriculturalists 22
   Brahmins' teaching 28
   extension of 27, 193
   improvements in 32
Aihole (Karnataka) 111, 222
   caves 85
   Durga temple *18*, 207
   Durga Maishasuramardini (Slayer of the Buffalo Demon) *51*
   Gaudar Gudi *98*, 207
   Lad Khan 207
   Latina temple 175
   Meguti temple 90, *146*, 207
   Ravana Phadi cave 87, *126*
      alpa vimana 206, *207*
   Tarappa Basappa *93*
Airavateshvara temple, Darasuram (Tamil Nadu)
   panjara aedicule on sub-base (*upapitha*) 220
   vimana 220
Ajanta (Maharashtra)
   blossoming of rock-cut architecture 82

Cave 1
   facade *85*
   monastery 85
Cave 2: painted lotus ceiling *89*, 156
Cave 17 24
Cave 19
   chaitya hall *83*
   cushion pilaster *151*
   'palace' facade *84*
Cave 26 *84*
   chaitya hall *84*
   ghata-pallava pillars 154
   miniature pavilions *126*
   murals 24, 71n10
Ajanta tradition 82
Ajitanatha temple, Taranga (Gujarat) 64, *187*, 187
Akhodar 173
Akkadevi 32, 33
Akkanna-Madanna caves, Vijayawada (AP) 87
Akkeshvara temple (now Mallikarjuna), Sudi 32
Ala-ud-din 234
Alampur (AP)
   Kumara Brahma temple *98*
   temples 174-75
Alexander the Great 23
Alhambra, Spain 157
Alirajpur (MP): Malaval temple 190
alpa vimana 16, 76, 81, *125*, 126-27, *126*, *127*, *128*, *129*, *130*, 135n1, 206, 207, 210, 212, 214, 216
Alvars 54
amalakas 108-11, *108*, *109*, *113*, 150, 152, *168*, *169*, 170, *170*, 171, 174, *175*, 176, 196, 201, 202, *202*, 203, *203*
Amaravati (AP) *76*
   early stupa reliefs 152
Ambaranath
   Ambaranatha temple 188
   main shrine 190
Ambika (goddess) *152*
Ambika temple, Jagat (Rajasthan) *93*, *157*, *183*, 184
ambulatory passage (*pradakshina-patha*) *97*, 98, *98*, *99*, *183*
American Institute of Indian Studies: *Encyclopaedia of Indian Temple Architecture* 21
Amritaghateshvara: Melai-Kkadambur Melaikkadambur 221, *221*
Amriteshvara temple, Annigeri (Karnataka) *133*
Amrol (MP): Rameshvara Mahadeva temple *139*, *175*

Ananata Vasudeva 203n12
Ananta (serpent) 54
anarpita (parapet) 127
Andhra Pradesh (AP) 85, 92, 119, 154, 193, 197
Anekandaka ('multi-limbed') forms 184
Anekandaka Phamsana, Auwa 184
angas (projections) 91
Angkor Wat, Cambodia 101
Aniruddha 55
Anjaneri (Maharashtra) 189
   ruined temple *94*
antarala (antechamber) *91*, 92, 93, *93*, 97, *120*, 132, 189, *213*
antarapatta (colonnaded recess) 176
Anwa (Maharashtra): Vaishnava temple *155*
AP *see* Andhra Pradesh
Arabs 32
Aralguppe (Karnataka): Chenna-Keshava temple *134*
Arang (MP) *191*
Aranyakas 46
Archaeological Survey of India 19, 35, 173n2
architect (*sthapati*)
   alpa vimanas 127
   design of 'authentic' Dravida temples 239
   knowledge of the *shastras* 62, 239
   qualities 62
   role of 63-64
   team work 62
   traditional 239-40
architectural language 21, 36, 70, 71, *107*, *132*, 147, 174
archways *see* toranos
arhtha (worldly success) 61n14
Arjuna 54
   ratha 208, *208*
arpita (false or applied) 127
Arrangabad: Cave 6 *151*
Arsikere: Ishvara temple *230*
Arunachaleshvara temple, Tiruvannamalai (Tamil Nadu) *236*
Aryans 11, 22, 45
ascetic renunciation 46
asceticism 12
Ashoka, Emperor 12, 23, 74, 150, 193
ashta dikpalas (guardians of the directions of space) 48
ashta-bhadra 119, 191, *191*, *230*, 236
ashvamedha (Vedic horse sacrifice) 24
Asoda (Gujarat): Jasmalnatha Mahadeva temple *186*
atman (the individual) 46

Aurangabad (Maharashtra)
    Cave 3 *153*
    Cave 5 84
    Caves 6 and 7: *viharas* 82
Auwa (Rajasthan)
    Anekandaka Phamsana 184
    Kameshvara temple *122*

Bactro-Gandharan realm 80
Badami (Karnataka)
    Bhutanatha temple *14*, 15-16, *15*, 208
    Cave 3 *87*, *146*
    caves 85
    Jambulingeshvara temple 98
    Lower Shivalaya *11*
    Malegitti Shivalaya *11*, 207-8, *208*
    Phamsana temple *94*
    Upper Shivalaya *11*
    Yellama Gudi *11*, *224*
Badnavar (MP) 189
Bafna, Sonit 57
Bagali: Kalleshvara (Karnataka) *152*
Bagh: Cave 4 *151*
Bahulara: Shiva temple 202-3
Baideshvara: Durga temple *196*
bala-panjara (small Valabhi aedicule) 109, *113*, 115, 174, *179*, 195, 198, 201
Balsane (Maharashtra)
    Temple 1 *100*, *151*
    Temple 5 *100*
Bananti Gudi, Mahakuta *207*
Bangladesh 192
Barabar Hills near Gaya (Bihar): Lomas Rishi cave 77, 161
Baroque 37, 66
Basavanna 36
Bateshara (MP): Bateshara Mahadeva temple *113*, *175*
Bath, west of England 51
Bay of Bengal 182
beams 15, 76, 78, 84, *86*, 93, *94*, 96, 149, 152, 156, 157
Belavadi (Karnataka)
    Vira-Narayana temple *9*, *43*
    ceiling *158*
Belur (Karnataka)
    Chenna-Keshava temple 189, *189*, 227
    bracket figure 64, *64*
    stellate shrine 227
Benares 234
Bengal 25, 113, 192, 194-95, 202-3, 234, 235
Beyalisbati, near Konarak 198
Bhadra Deul 123
bhadra (orthogonal central projection) 21, 64, *91*, 114, 115, *116*, 118-19, 120, 128, 129, 132, 133, 138, 140, *145*, *173*, *175*, *176*, 181, *183*, 189, 191, *191*, 218, 221, *230*
Bhadravati (Karnataka): Lakshmi-Narasimha temple *143*
Bhagavad Gita 54
Bhagavata tradition 53
Bhairava (ferocious form of Shiva) 50, 51, 52
Bhaja (Maharashtra): *chaitya* hall *77*
Bhakti (devotion to a personal god) 28, 32, 48, 49, 53, 193
Bharhut (MP) *76*
    stupa railing 76
Bhauma Karas 193
Bhavanasi Sangam (AP) 222
Bhavanipur (Rajasthan): Shiva temple *181*
Bhim-Deval temple, Prachi, Saurashtra 184
Bhima: *ratha* 208, 209
Bhitargaon (UP): Gupta temple 169
bhoga (world enjoyments) 49
Bhoja (Paramara king) 31-32, 188
Bhojpur temple (MP) 32, 188
Bhumija mode 64, 106, 111, 118-20, 134, *155*, 226, 238
Bhumija shrine, Gondeshvara temple, Sinnar (Maharashtra) *145*, 225
Bhumija temples 113, *116*, 133, 143n11, 154, *163*, 188-91, *228*, *241*
Bhumija workshops: *jala* 164
bhumis (levels) 112-13, 114, *114*, *120*, 128, 142, *145*, 157, 176, *178*, 179, 181, 190, *190*, 191, 196, 201, 202, 203n10
Bhutanatha temple, Badami (Karnataka) *14*, 15-16, *15*, *208*
Bhuti Vikramakesari, King 216-17
Bhuvaneshvara (Orissa) 195
    Brahmeshvara temple *94*, 199, *200*, 201
    Gauei temple 198
    Lingaraja temple 31, 201, *201*
    Megheshvara temple 202, *202*
    Mukhteshvara temple *102*, 198, 201
        central cluster *198*
        meandering *gavaksha* 164
        mula-prasada 199
    in Orissa's heartland 193
    Parasurameshvara temple 59-60, 175-76, 195, *195*, *196*
    Rajarani temple 57
    Sisireshvara temple *167*, 196, *197*, *197*
Vaital Deul shrine *112*, 113, *167*, 196, *196*, *197*
Biccavolu (AP) 222
Bihar 113, 192
    see also Bodhgaya
Bijamandal, Vidisha 188
Bijolia (Rajasthan) 189, 190
Bileshvara: Mahadeva temple (Gujarat) 169
    Phamsana shrine *171*
bindu ('drop') 49
Birlas 238
Bodhgaya, Magadha (now Bihar) 108, 110
    Buddha attains enlightenment 192
    Mahabodi temple 170, *171*, 194
    Valabhi-fronted *stupa* 163
Bodhisattvas (saints) 12, 83
bracket figures 64, *64*, 231, *231*
brackets (*potika*) 149, 150, 152-55, 206
Brahma
    the creator 48, 54
    linga myth 37
brahman (transcendent absolute) 46, 47, 48, 68
Brahmapurishvara temple, Pullamangai 218
    panjara aedicule 218
Brahmeshvara temple, Bhuvaneshvara *94*, 199, *200*, 201, *201*
Brahminism 11, 45
Brahmins
    acharyas 62-63
    assimilation of popular mythologies 48
    as priests 11, 22, 23
    religious and agricultural teaching 28
    settlement of 193
    spiritual and intellectual elite 28
Bramante, Donato 157
Brihadeshvara (Brihadishvara) temple, Tanjavur (Tanjore) 31, *31*, 32, 33, *42*, 105, *105*, *219*, 220-21
Brihadeshvara temple, Gangaikondacholapuram (Tamil Nadu) 31, *31*, 143n12, *220*
British empire 234
Brown, Percy 78
Bucheshvara, Koravangala (Karnataka) *100*
Buddha (Siddhartha Gautama) 53, 74, 76
    enlightenment 170, 192
    images enshrined 12
    miracle at Shrivasti *81*
    as Prince Vessantra *24*
    sculpted image developed 81
Buddhas 83
buddhi (intellect) 20, 47
Buddhism
    Ashoka supports 12, 23
    development of 12
    dies out in most of the subcontinent 13
    a great renunciatory religion 46
    Mahayana 12, 68
    spreads to China 80
    tenets of 11-12
    texts 17
    Theravada ('Hinayana') 83
Buddhist architecture 12, 14, 74, 85
Buddhist art 21
Burhi Chanderi (MP) *116*
Bürolandschaft 57
bursting of boundaries 38, *38*, *42*, 67, 69, *224*
Byzantine churches 97

Cambodia: 'temple mountains' 101
Candoja (stone-cutter) 33
canonical texts 21
canopy (*chhadya*) 96, 120, *134*, *145*, 227
cardinal axes 16, *74*, 141
Casselberry, USA: Hindu temple of Central Florida *241*
castes (*jatis*) 11, 22, 27
ceilings 97, 156-59, 182, *183*
    carved *104*, *156*, 157, *157*
    corbelled 156, 158
    designs *70*
    domed 93
    lantern 93, *94*, 157, *157*, 199
    lobed *158*
    lotus 156, *156*, 157, 158, 159
    painted *156*, 157
    proliferated 156, *158*
Central Asia 22
Chadragupta II 150
'chain of being' 26, 30
chaitya hall 39, 76, *77*, 78, *78*, 79, 80, 83, *83*, 109, 112, 156, *160*, *161*, 206
    prototype of the Valabhi form 112, 161, 196
    the trefoil 161, *164*
chakras (wheels) 47
chakravartins (universal rulers) 24
Chalukya dynasty 30, 114, 174, 175, 207, 223, 227
Chalukya heartland 222
Chandella dynasty 32, 182
Chandesha, Saint *31*
Chandragupta II 24
Charrahi (Himachal Pradesh): lantern

INDEX **247**

ceiling 157, *157*
Chattarki (Karnataka): Dattatreya temple *188*
chattravali (multiple umbrella) 74
Chaurasi: Varahi temple 197, *197*
Chenna-Keshava temple, Aralguppe (Karnataka) *134*
Chenna-Keshava temple, Belur (Karnataka) 189, *189*, 227
   bracket figure 64, *64*
chess 24
Chezarla (Andhra Pradesh) 206
   alpa vimanas 126
Chhapara (MP): doorway in small temple *170*
Chhattarpur complex, New Delhi 239
Chidambaram: cult of Shiva Nataraja 32
Chikka Mahakuta (Karnataka): temple *98*
China 80, 216
chippika (minor cyma moulding) *145*, *180*
Chitradurga, Khajuraho *93*
Chittor fort *116*
Chittor (Rajasthan): Samiddheshvara temple *119*, 187
chloritic schist ('soapstone') *223*, 223
Chola dynasty 31, 32, 201, 216, 236
Cholanadu 124
Chota ('Little') Kailasa, Cave 32, Ellora (Maharashtra) 215
'circle of kings' (*rajamandala*) 24
circle-and-square sequence 138, *138*, *157*
Circular temple of the 64 Yoginis, Hirapur (Orissa) *50*
circumambulation, ritual 74, 82, 97
cities
   decline of 26
   expansion of 23
'clan fluids' 51
collective unconscious 17
colonialism 19
colonnades 103, 109, 174, 176, *178*
columns 148
   Corinthian 111
   free-standing 74
   intermediate 93
   Mauryan *173*
   role of 97
consecration rites 58
Coomaraswamy, Ananda 20, 62
corbelling 15, 93, *94*, 98, 157, *157*, *158*
cornices
   'acanthus leaf' 81
   eave 84

kapota 15, *43*, 84, 127, 147, 218
Coromandal 124
Correa, Charles 57
cosmic egg 45, 46, 49
cosmic order 44
cosmogenesis 17
cosmogony 45, 49, 52, 56, 59
cosmology 45, 48-49, 56
   Saivite 53
cosmomoral order 30
cosmos 44, 45, 56, 58
Court of the Stupa, Takht-i-Bahi 80
creation myths 17
cremation ground asceticism 50
cross axes 17
Crusades 32
cupolas, buttressed 157
curvature 142
cycles 67-68
cyma 144, *145*, 146

Dahala Style of the Kalachuris *191*
Dakshina Koshala (now Chhatisgarh) 108, 110, 113, *116*, 141, 170-71, 176, 193, 194, 207
   multi-aedicular temple architecture *196*
   Shiva temple, Dhobini *173*
      stellate plans *172*
   Siddheshvara, Palari *173*, 173
      stellate plans 172
Dambal (northern Karnataka): Doddabasappa 225, *225*
dancers 13, 31, 33
Dantidurga 210
Darasuram (Tamil Nadu)
   Airavateshvara temple 221
   panjara aedicule on sub-base (*upapitha*) *220*
   vimana *220*
Dash-Avatara temple, Deogarth (MP) *108*
Dashamadesha *180*
Dashamadesha/Gopakshetra style *182*
Dattatreya temple, Chattarki (Karnataka) *188*
Deccan, the 23, 24, 25, 29, 85, 93, 96, 98, 118, 124, 134, 135, 151, 158, 163, 182, 190, 213, 234
Deccani sultanate 238
Delhi, sack of (1398) 234
Delhi Sultanate 25
Deogarh (MP) *116*, 175
   gavaksha *160*
   ghata-pallava pillars *154*
   Gupta temple (Dash-Avatara) *108*, 108, *144*, 145, *153*, 168, *168*
   ruined superstructure 168, *169*

proto-Latina pattern 168
   Vishnu temple *58*
Desai, Devangana 59
'Descent of the Ganges' relief 208
Deva, Krishna 21
Devalana (Maharashtra) *61*
devanagari alphabet 56
Dhaky, MA 21, 177, 182
Dhamnar (MP): Dharmanatha temple *114*
Dhank (Gujarat) 173
   Surya temple *173*
dharma (duty) 61n14
Dharmanatha temple, Dhamnar (MP) *114*
Dharmaraja: *ratha* 208, *209*
Dhobini, Dakshina Koshala (now Chhatisgarh): Shiva temple *173*
   stellate plans *172*
differentiation 66
dikpalas (guardians of the directions of space) *180*
Dilwara: multi-shrine enclosure *237*
diminution 142
Dodda Gaddavalli (Karnataka): Lakshmidevi temple *135*
Doddabasappa, Dambal (northern Karnataka) *133*, 225
domes
   corbelled *94*, 158, 235
   half-domes 158
   kuta 171
   octagonal 215
   quarter-domes 158
Doric capital 153
double *venukosha* 113, 175, *175*, *179*
Draupadi: *ratha* 208
Dravida
   architecture 14, 60, *66*, 74, 80, 83, 87, *107*, 113, 134, 148, 197, 222
   barrel-roofed pavilion 69
   language 14, 125, 134, 148, 161, 215, 235
   mode 14
   order 14
   pyramidal outline 16
   shrine model 64
   shrines *see vimana*
   style 14
   talas 16
   temples 15, 39, 43, 134
   type 14
Dravida temples 15, 39, 43, 134, 147, 239
   see also early Dravida temples; great 8th-century Dravida temples; Karnata Dravida tradition

continued; temples of the Cholas and their contemporaries
Dravida Valabhi 199
Duladeva, Khajuraho (MP) *93*, 185
Dulhinganj (Bihar): Shiva temple *240*
Durga (goddess) 51
Durga temple, Aihole (Karnataka) *18*, 207
   Durga Maishasuramardini (Slayer of the Buffalo Demon) *51*
Durga temple, Baideshvara *196*
dynamism
   of the Baroque 37
   and fusion 66, 67, 69
   in Hinduism 38
   Kandariya Mahadeva temple, Khajuraho (MP) *41*, 43
   in Shekhari temples 16
   Teli-ka Mandir, Gwalior (MP) 39, *39*
   in temple architecture 16, *17*, 38, *41*

Early Chalukya dynasty 15, 85, 92, 111, 135, 207, 222, 223
early Dravida temples 206-9
early medieval period 25-28
early modern period 25
early Nagara temples
   early aedicular Nagara 170-71, *172*, 173, *173*
   Phamsana 169, *170*, *171*
   proto-Latina 168-69, *168*
Early Western Chalukyas of Vatapi (Badami) 207, 210
east-west orientation 86
Eastern Chalukyas of Vengi 222
eave-dormers 113
eaves 15, 109-10, 112
   cornice *see kapotas*
Ekalinga, cult of, Eklingji 32
Elephanta (near Mumbai): Shiva cave *73*, 86
elevations 142
Eliade, Micea 17
Ellora (Maharashtra) 29, 82
   Cave 10 (Vishvakarma), *gavakshas* *161*
   Cave 14 (Ravana-k-Khai) *87*
   Cave 16 (Kailasa) 87, 176, 210, *214*, 215
   Cave 21 (Rameshvara) *85*, *86*, 96
   Cave 23
      Sapta-matrikas (Seven Mothers) *36*
      Shiva Nataraja shrine *36*
   Caves 11 and 12 ('Don Thal' and 'Tin Thal') 83
   Grishneshvara temple *233*, *241*
   Jain Cave 32 (Indrasabha) *152*

Chota ('Little') Kailasa 215
Dravida *gavakshas* *164*
Sarvatobhadra shrine *91*, 215, *215*
emanation 53, 60
emergence 69
emission 50-51, 53
Encyclopaedia of Indian Temple Architecture 165
English Perpendicular 159
enlightenment 11-12, 23, *74*, 170, 192
Erakeshvara temple, Pillamarri (AP) *189*
erotic sculpture 60-61, *60*
essentialism 19, *20*
Eurocentrism 19
evolution 69, *69*, 70, *70*, 140, 177
expanding repetition *38*, 42, 43, 67, 69, 214, 215
expansion 69
extended gnomon diagram 138, *138*, 141, 158
extended star octagon 141

female principle 49-50, 160, 235
Fergusson, James 10, 14, 19-20, *20*
  'Indian and Eastern Architecture' 20
feudalism 25, 32
finials *108*, *113*, *125*, *161*
'five Ms' 50, 51
'five *rathas*' *208*, 209-10
'five-shrine' plan (*panch-ayatana*) *100*, 101
Fletcher, Banister 20
four quarters, conquest of the (*digvijaya*) 24, 29
fragmentation 66, 67, 163
fronton (*shuka-nasa*) ('parrot's beak') *92*, *97*, *114*, *120*, *135*, 215, *223*
fusion *64*, 66-69, *66*, 80, 173, 177, 215, *224*, 225
Futurist movement 39

Gadag (Karnataka)
  Rameshvara *164*
  Someshvara temple 227, *228*
  Trikuteshvara *146*
Gajasamhara *217*
gajatalus ('elephants' palettes') 158
gala (recess) 146
Galaganatha temple, Pattadakal (Karnataka) 40-41, *40*, 109, 174-75
Galateshvara temple, Sarnel (Gujarata) *191*
Gandhara 80-81, 126
  relief *81*
  shrine types *80*
Ganesha 52, 58

Ganesha shrine, Sundareshvara temple complex, Nangavaram (Tamil Nadu) *127*
Ganeshvarpura 198, *198*
Ganga rulers 32, 193
Ganga-Yamuna (Ganges-Jumna) Doab 25
Gangaikondacholapuram (Tamil Nadu) 139, 221
  Brihadeshvara temple 31, *31*, 143n12, *220*
Gangaikondacholishvara 31
Gangetic Basin, northern India 22, 24
garbha-griha ('womb chamber') 16, 52, 59, 90, 93, 127
Garbhagriha 38
Gaudar Gudi, Aihole (Karnataka) *98*, 207
Gauri temple, Bhuvaneshvara 198
gavakshas (horseshoe arch motifs) 39, *60*, 66, 68, 69, 78, *107*, 112, 113, *113*, 114, 142, 151, 160-65, 195, *222*, *228*
  birth of the Nagara *gavaksha* 161
  bush-eared, second-class 190
  cascade *40*, 41, *42*, 43, *43*, 169, *183*, *224*
  ceases to be a focus for invention 165
  Darsanadesha style *165*
  dormer *107*, *130*, 169
  double *132*
  Dravida (*nasis*) *163*, *164*
  floppy wasp 199
  gavaksha nets (*jalas*) 164, *165*, 190, 194, 199, 203
  half-*gavakshas* 43, *107*, 109, *161*
  Karnata Nagata style *165*
  loss of depth 164
  mainstream *162*, *163*, *163*, *164*
  major *163*
  Nagara 163, 190
  onion 189, 190, *191*, 198
  Orissan *164*, *164*
  overlapped *172*, *175*, 176, *176*, *178*
  paired 218
  'Pala' 203
  part-*gavakshas* 164
  'pipal leaf' ('moonstone') 190, *190*
  shapes 161-63
  'standard' 174
  unfolding patterns 163-65
  varieties of typical patterns *165*
gender divisions 27
geometry 136-43, 157, *230*
  elevations 142
  gavakshas *162*, 164
  orientation, the extended gnomon

diagram and the circle-and-square sequence 137-38
  orthogonal plans 138-40
  roof plan *238*
  stellate plans 140-42, 176
  Type 5 Shekhari shrine roof plan *236*
Germanic art historical tradition 66
Ghanerav (Rajasthan): Mahavira *98*
ghanta (ribbed bell) 120
Ghantashala 76
ghata (cushion capital) 152, *153*
ghata-pallava ('sprouting vase') 154, *185*, 194
gnomon (*shanku-yantra*) 137, 158
goddess, the 51, *51*
gods
  carved in a temple superstructure 59-60
  entertainment of 29
  placement in the iconographic scheme 62
Gondeshvara temple, Sinnar (Maharashtra) *100*, *101*, 188
  Bhumija shrine *145*
Gop (Saurashtra)
  temple
    gavaksha 160
  Phamsarma 111, *111*, 120
Gopakshetra (northern MP) 176
gopuras (gateways) 103, 105, *105*, 112, 128, 221, 236, *236*, *241*
Gothic architecture 10, 20, 66, 69
Granoff, Phyllis 17, 18
grasa-mukha (monster face) 119, *145*
Great River 33
Great Stupa (Stupa 1), Sanchi (MP) *74*, 76
Greeks
  Doric temples 69
  first arrival in the subcontinent 23
grids 138, 139, 140, 142, *158*, 162, *164*, *165*
Grishneshvara temple, Ellora (Maharashtra) *233*, *241*
griva (recess) 146
griva gala (horizontal recesses) *222*
gudha-mandapa 93, *230*
Guhilas of Mewar 32
guilds 28, 63, 223, 235
Gujarat 174, 182, 184, 185, 188, 235, 238, 239, 240
Gupta dynasty 12, 21, 24, *24*, 25, 48, 49, 82, 97, 101, *108*, 110, 114, 150, 154, 161, 168, 174, 192
Gupta temple (Dash-Avatara), Deogarh (MP) *144*, *153*, 168, *168*, *169*
Gurjara Pratihara dynasty 29, 174
Gurjaradesha: Maha-Maru style 177,

182
Gwalior (MP) 176
  Sas-Bahu temple 96
  Teli-ka Mandir 39-40, *39*, 176, *177*
Gyaraspur: Maladevi (MP) *153*

Halebid (Karnataka)
  Hoysaleshvara temple 20, *20*, 227
  stellate shrine 227
half-*bhadras* 184-85, 187n5
half-roundels 151
Hampi (Vijayanagara) (Karnataka):
  Vitthala temple *235*
haras see under pavilions
Hardy, Dr. Adam 18
Hare Krishna movement 235
Harihara Temple 1, Osian (Rajasthan) *179*
Harihara Temple 3, Osian (Rajasthan) *97*
harmika (railed platform) *74*
harmyas (mansions) 111, 125
Harsha 25, 174
heaven 17, 29
Hegelianism 19
Hellenistic world 80
Henn, Walter 57
Hindu reform movements 238
Hinduism
  devotional worship through sculpted images 12
  dynamic view of life 38
  early orthodox form 11
  Hindu diaspora 235
  Hindu pantheon 12, 24, 27
  predomination of 13
  theistic cults as its forbears 23
  western understanding of 48
Hirapur (Orissa): Circular temple of the 64 Yoginis *50*
Hirehadgalli: Katteshvara temple *226*
historiography 19-21
horned lions (*vyalas*, *shardhulas*) 200
Hoysalas 68, *134*, 189, 227, *229*
  Hoysala diagonal *gavaksha* 164
  temples 227
Hoysaleshvara temple, Halebid (Karnataka) 20, *20*, 227
Huli (Karnataka): Panchalingeshvara *100*
human body: connection with temples 36-37, 44, 148

iconographic programme 58-61, 62
Inden, Ronald 30
Indian circle method 137
Indian Museum, Kolkat *76*
'Indo-Islamic' architectures 235

INDEX **249**

Indor (MP): Shiva temple *142*, 176, *176*
Indus Valley civilisation 11, 74
interpenetration 66, 67
Iranian world 80
Iravataneshvara temple, Kanchipuram (Tamil Nadu) 210, *210*
irrigation 24, 28, 32
Irrukuvel dynasty 216
Ishana 58
Ishvara temple, Arsikere *230*
Islam 15, 235
  see also Islamic rulers; Muslims
Islamic rulers
  adoption of feudal structures 25
  mosque-building 25
  see also Islam; Muslims
Ittagi (Karnataka): Mahadeva temple 66, *224*
  kuta-stambha 225

jagamohana 199
Jagannatha, cult of 32, 193
Jagannatha, Lord 234
Jagannatha temple, Puri 31, 202
Jagat (Rajasthan)
  Ambika temple *93*
    ceiling *157*
    central projection *183*
    hall *183*
    shrine *184*
    southern view *183*
jagati (moulded platform) 97, *99*, *100*, 144, *146*, *179*, *218*, *227*, *231*
Jageshvara 111
Jainism
  and architecture 239, 240
  flourishes 13, 23
  founder of 192
  a great renunciatory religion 46
  Jain diaspora 235
  and Shekhari temples 182
  temple enclosures of western India 103
  tenets of 11-12
  texts 17
Jaipur: Jawahar Kala Kendra 57
jalas see under gavakshas
Jambulingeshvara temple, Badami 98
jangha 145
Jarkhand 113, 192
Jasmalnatha Mahadeva temple, Asoda (Gujarat) *186*
Javari temple, Khajuraho 187n5
Jawahar Kala Kendra, Jaipur 57
Jejakabhukti 182
Jhalarapatan (Rajasthan): Surya temple *191*

Jodu-Kalashada temple, Sudi (Karnataka) 33, 64, *224*
Jung, CG 17

K-P-S-P-K pattern 214, *214*, 218, 221
K-S-K scheme 214, 217
Kacchapaghatas of Dashamadesha 182
Kachchh (western Gujarat) 184
Kadwaha (MP): Temple 1, Khimivala Group *59*
Kailasa, Ellora (Maharashtra) 87, 176, 210, *214*
Kailasa temple, Kanchipuram (Tamil Nadu) *104*
Kailasanatha ('Lord of Mount Kailasa') temple, Kanchipuram (Tamil Nadu) 30, 31, 103, *104*, *105*, *128*, 210, *211*, *212*, *213*, 216
  central shrines *212*
  Mahendravarmeshvara shrine *128*, *212*
Kakatiyas 154, 189, 227
kaksh-asana (racked back) *179*, *185*, *188*
Kalachuris of Dahala 182, *191*
kalasha (a cushion moulding) 144, 145, 146, 174, 197, *197*, 199, 203
Kali (goddess) 50, 51
Kalinga 193
Kalleshvara, Bagali (Karnataka) *152*
Kalleshvara, Kukkanur (Karnataka) 93
Kalugumalai (Tamil Nadu)
  Dravida *gavaksha* 164
  Vetuvankovil *215*
Kalyani 189, 190, 223
kama (sensual love) 61
kama-kutas (corner-pavilions) 107
Kambadahalli (Karnataka) 222
Kameshvara temple, Auwa (Rajasthan) *122*
Kanauj (ancient Kanyakubja) 25, 29, 174
Kanchipuram (Tamil Nadu) 29, 30, 31, 210
  Iravataneshvara temple 210, *210*
  Kailasa temple *104*
  Kailasanatha ('Lord of Mount Kailasa') temple 30, *104*, *128*, 210, *211*, *212*, *213*, 216
  Mahendravarmeshvara shrine, Kailasanatha temple *128*, *212*, *213*
Kandariya Mahadeva temple, Khajuraho (MP) *41*, *42*, *43*, 59, 69-70, 117
  ceiling *158*

kuta-stambha on sub-base (*pitha*) *186*
  southern view *186*
Kanganhalli (Karnataka) 76
Kanichipuram: Vaikuntha Perumal (temple of Vishnu's heaven) *151*, 212-13
Kapalikas ('skull men') 50, 52
Kapila (a sage) 47
kapota-prati-vedika 146
kapotali 84, 145, 146, 180, 197
kapotas (eave cornice) 15, *43*, 84, *130*, 146, 147, *147*, 169, 198, 212, 214, 220, 222, 227
Karle (Maharashtra)
  chaitya hall 76, *77*, *78*, 79
  makara-torano 79
  pilasters 152
karma (ritual action) 48
Karnata Dravida 198, 213, 222, 226-27, 228
  mainstream style 222, 223
  schools 125, *228*
  shrines *135*
  temples *42*, *43*, 64, 69, 125, 231
  tradition 215, 236
  tradition continued 222-31
  unfolding of 223, 225
Karnata masons 207
Karnataka 25, 43, 60, 64, 92, 111, 124, 129, 134, *134*, 135, *135*, 154, 176-77, 182, 189, 197, 214, 223, 227, 231
  Dravida *gavakshas* 164
  early Dravida temples 207
Karrali 217
Karttikeya 52, 58
Kashivishveshvara temple, Lakkundi (Karnataka) *43*, *223*, 226-27
Kashivishveshvara temple, Pattadakal (Karnataka) *178*, *214*
Kashmir 15, 49, 111
Kashmir Shaiva traditions 52
Katteshvara temple, Hirehadgalli *226*
'Kaula' ('clan') cults 50, 51
Kautilya: Artha Shastra 24
Kerala 15, 156
Keshava temple, Somnathpur (Karnataka) *99*, *229*
Khajuraho (MP) *122*, 182
  Chitradurga *93*
  Duladeva *93*, 185
  ghata-pallava pillars 155
  Javari temple 187n5
  Kandariya Mahadeva temple *41*, *42*, *43*, 59, 69-70, 117
  kuta-stambha on sub-base (*pitha*) *186*

lobed ceiling 158
  southern view *186*
  Lakshmana temple 59, *99*, *100*, 183, *184*, *186*
  Phamsanas 123
  temple complex 32
  Vamana temple 181
  Vishvanatha temple *60*, 185, *186*
Khakara *196*, 198
Khiching 196
Khimivala Group, Kadwaha (MP) *59*
khura-kumbha 145, *146*, 188, 189
Khyber, the 23
Kilayapatti (Tamil Nadu) *127*
Kilayur (Tamil Nadu): Agastishvara temple *130*, 216
kingship
  Brahminic rituals of 24
  royal temples 28
kinkinika-mala (band of swags) 145
Kiradu (Rajasthan)
  Shiva Temple 1 *117*
  Someshvara 185
  Type 4 shrines 185
kirti-mukha (face of glory) 145, 154, 163
Kisukad 70 district 43
Kodumbalur: Muvarkovil (Tamil Nadu) 216-18
  southern shrine *217*
  three-storey *shala* aedicule in central shrine 217, *217*
kolas ('boars'; cusped lobes) 158
Kolkata: Indian Museum 76
Konarak
  aedicule *202*
  Surya temple 31, 114, 202
Kondane: *chaitya* hall 78
Koranganatha, Srinivasanallur (Tamil Nadu) *151*
Koravangala (Karnataka): Bucheshvara *100*
Kramrisch, Stella 17, 20, 38, 57, 58, 135n1, 160-61
Krishna 53, 54
Krishna I 210
Krishna-Gopala, cult of 53
Kshatriyas (warrior nobles) 22
Kukkanur (Karnataka)
  Kalleshvara 93
  Navalinga temple 222
Kullotunga III 221
Kumara Brahma temple, Alampur (AP) *98*
Kumbakonam: Srangapani temple 164
kumbha 145, 146
kumbha-kalasha-kapotali sequence 145

Kumbhariya (Gujarat)
  Mahavira temple *3*
    main ceiling *159*
    multi-shrine enclosure *237*
  Shantinatha Jain temple *105*
kumbhas-panjaras 221
kumuda 146, 152
Kuntaladesha 124, 223
Kuppatur (Karnataka) 64
Kushana period 80, 81
Kushanas 23
kuta-stambha (pillar/pilaster with *kuta* on top) 16, *60*, 115, *116*, 117, 118, 119, 123, 129, *132*, 139, 140, *145*, 155, *182*, *184*, *184*, *185*, *186*, *187*, *188*, *189*, 190, *190*, 191, *191*, *197*, 200, 201, 202, 203n12, *223*, *224*, *227*, *229*, *230*, 237, *239*
kutas (crowning pavilions) 16, 76, *80*, 81, *85*, *87*, 115, 120, 126, 127, *128*, 129, *129*, *130*, 132, 135n1, *169*, 190, 206, 207, 208, 214, 217, *226*

Lad Khan, Aihole 207
Lakkundi (Karnataka) 222, 223
  Kashivishveshvara temple *43*
Lakshmana temple, Khajuraho (MP) *59*, *99*, *100*, *183*, *184*, *186*
Lakshmana temple, Sirpur (Chhatisgarh) 171, *172*
  aedicules *172*
  gavaksha 160
Lakshmeshvara: Someshvara temple 227, *228*
Lakshmi (goddess) 51
Lakshmi-Narasimha temple, Bhadravati (Karnataka) *143*
Lakshmidevi temple, Dodda Gaddavalli (Karnataka) *135*
Lakulisha (a sage) 52
Lalitaditya, lost temple of 29, 30
lasuna 153
'late Chola' models 240
late medieval period 25
Later Chalukyas 32, 182, 188-89, 222, 223
Latina mode *13*, 39, 40, *40*, 42, *60*, 67, 68, *69*, 90, 108-10, 113-15, 135, 141, 165, 184, *186*, 189, 194, 196, 226
Latina and related Valabhi temples 174-81
  8th-century Latina and Valabhi temples 176-77, *178*
  the 9th century and later 179-81
  the Nagara 'Mainstream' of the 7th century 174-76
Latina mode, *see also under* early Nagara temples
Latina shrine, Rameshvara Mahadeva temple (MP) *145*
linearity 69
linga (phallic emblem of Shiva) 37, *42*, 52, 53, *53*, 221
Lingaraja temple, Bhuvaneshvara (Orissa) 31, 201, *201*
lingas
  chatur-mukha-linga (four-faced), Nachna 52, *53*
  ekha-mukha-linga (one-faced), Cave 1, Udayagiri (MP) 52, *53*
  Kalyanpur (Rajasthan) 53, *53*
  pancha-mukha (five-faced) 52, 53, *53*
  plain, Nand Chand 52, *53*
Lingodbhava 37, *42*, 49
Lokamahadevi 31
Lokeshvara temple *see* Virupaksha temple, Pattadakal
Lomas Rishi cave, Barabar Hills near Gaya (Bihar) 77, 161
Lord of Mount Kailasa 52
Lower Shivalaya, Badami (Karnataka) *11*

Madhya Pradesh (MP) 173, 174
Madhyadesha (now UP) 168, 174, 179
Madkheda: Surya temple *139*, *180*
Magadha (southern Bihar) 23, 24, 110, *116*, 192, 194
Magadha tradition 170
Maha Devi 51
Maha-Gurjara style *162*, *165*, 177, *178*, 182-83, *183*
maha-mandapa (main hall) *60*, 98, 120, *184*
Maha-Maru style *165*, 177, *179*, 181, 182, 184, 185
Mahabalipuram (Mamallapuram) (Tamil Nadu) 126, 208, *208*
  Shore temple 212-13
Mahabalipuram (Tamil Nadu): Mahishasuramardini cave: Vishnu Anantashayin *54*
Mahabharata 48, 54, 55, 209n3
Mahabodi temple, Bodhgaya (Bihar) 170, *171*, 194
Mahadeva, General *224*
Mahadeva temple, Bileshvara (Gujarat) 169
  Phamsana shrine *171*
Mahadeva temple, Ittagi (Karnataka) *66*, *224*
Mahakaleshvara 2 (MP) *190*
Mahakuta, near Badami (Karnataka) *107*, 207
  Mahakuteshvara temple *13*, *98*, *207*
  Sangameshvara temple *13*, *175*
Maharashtra 25, 152, 153, 182, 189, 215, 223, 238
Mahavira 192
Mahavira, Ghanerav (Rajasthan) *98*
Mahavira temple, Kumbhariya (Gujarat) *3*
  main ceiling *159*
Mahavira temple, Osian (Rajasthan) 129
  carved ceiling *157*
Mahayana ('Greater Vehicle') Buddhism 12, 68
Mahayana pantheon 83
Mahendravarmeshvara shrine, Kailasanatha temple, Kanchipuram (Tamil Nadu) *128*, *212*, 213
Mahesha (Great Lord) 53, *53*
Maheshvara (Shiva) *86*
Mahishasuramardini cave, Mahabalipuram (Tamil Nadu): Vishnu Anantashayin *54*
Mahua (MP): Shiva Temple 2 *175*
makara-torano (archway) 79
makaras (crocodile monsters) *43*, *79*, 190, *197*, 198
mala (pearl swag) 153, 154
Maladevi, Gyaraspur (MP) *153*, 184
Malava (Malwa, western MP) 188, 189, 190
Malaval temple, Alirajpur (MP) *190*
male principle 49-50
Malegitti Shivalaya, Badami (Karnataka) *11*, 207-8, *208*
Mallikarjuna temple, Kuruvatti (Karnataka) *231*
Mallikarjuna temple, Pattadakal (Karnataka) 31, *146*, 205, *210*, 214, *214*
  west view *214*
Mallikarjuna temple, Sudi (Karnataka) 32, *32*, 42
Malwa (Malava) (western MP) 118
Mamallapuram (Tamil Nadu): 'Arjuna's Penance'/'Descent of the Ganges' *126*
manas (mind) 47
manchika 180
'mandala' plans 17, 82, 93, 101
mandapas (halls) 16, *25*, 60, 61, *61*, 87, 90-97, 98, *102*, 103, *103*, 106, 111, *114*, *116*, 120, 155, *155*, 157, *183*, 199
  closed 96, *99*, 123
  open (*ranga-mandapa*) 96, *96*, *97*, *99*, *100*, *103*, 105
  Samvarana *123*, 185
Mandapika shrines 169
mantras 53, 68
maps
  India, selected Buddhist sites and rock-cut cave temples, *c* 300 BC–AD 800 *6*
  India, showing modern states *6*
  India, temple sites mentioned in the book *7*
  India, with names of ancient and medieval kingdoms *6*
Marathas 234, 237, 238
Markandeyesvara 196
Maru-Gurjara 182, 185, *185*, *186*, *187*, *191*, 240
Marudesha: Maha-Gurjara style 177, 182
Masavadi 140 district 32
Masrur (Himachal Pradesh)
  monolithic temple 29, *29*
  rock-cut temple *100*, 101
Mata-ka-Mandir, Nareshara (MP) 176, *176*
Mathura 23, 81
  early *gavakshas 160*
  relief *150*
Mauryan bell pillar, Vaisali (Bihar) *150*
Mauryan empire 12, 23, 24, 74, 150, *173*, 192, 193
Maya 76
maya (undifferentiated subtle matter) 52
medhi (circular platform) 74
medieval era 21
  early period 25-28
meditation 12, 36, 49
Megheshvara temple, Bhuvaneshvara 202, *202*
Meguti temple, Aihole 90, *146*, 207
Meister, Michael W. *100*, 101, 138
  'Early Architecture and its Transformations: New Evidence for Vernacular Origins for the Indian Temple' 76
Melai-Kkadambur Melaikkadambur, Amritaghateshvara 221, *221*
Menon, AGK 239
Meroli (Delhi) 150
mishraka (hybrid) temples 191, 226
Modhera (Gujarat), Surya temple *102*, *104*, 105, 153, 154, *187*
moksha (release) 28, 48, 61n14
monasteries 12, 33, 74
  Bhaja (Maharashtra) 77

INDEX **251**

building materials 13-14
Cave 3 (Gautamiputra), Nasik *79*
role in the state 24
support from dynasties 28
vihara plan 82
monasticism 12
mosques 25, 159, 235
mouldings 15, 63, 74, *126*, 144-47
cushion *144*, *146*, 147
double eave (*kapota*) 198
Dravida *146*, 206
eave 123, *135*, 142, *144*, *145*, *146*, 147, 159, 168, *170*, *171*, *178*, *180*, 212, 218, *222*, 227
eave-cornice 115
floor (*prati*) 43, *127*, *129*, *146*, 147, 190, *197*, 198, 215, *222*, 225
foot *144*, 147, *188*
hood-mouldings 169
kalasha ('pot'/'vase') *144*, *180*, *197*
kapotali ('abode of doves') *144*, *180*, *197*
kumbha ('pot'/'vase') *144*
lotus 153
Nagara *144*, 145
pillar 120, 181
railing (*vedika*) *145*, *146*, 147, 171, *172*, *180*, 198, *207*
roof *129*, 147
tula-pitha *145*, *146*, *180*
Mount Meru 49
movement in architecture
discussion of 37
expanding repetition 42, *43*
expressing movement in Indian temples 37, *38*
linga myth 37
split pilaster *42*, *43*
MP *see* Madhya Pradesh
Mudhol: Siddheshvara: Dravida *gavakshas* *164*
Mughal empire 234, 235
Muhammad of Gaur 234
mukha-lingas ('face *lingas*') 52
Mukhalingam (AP) 196, 203n5
Mukhteshvara temple, Bhuvaneshvara (Orissa) *102*, 198, 201
central cluster *198*
meandering *gavaksha* *164*
mula-prasada *199*
pediment *200*
mula-manjari 118
mula-prasada (main shrine of a Nagara temple) *41*, *60*, 61, 90, 98, *102*, 105, 184, *186*, *199*
multi-centricity 24, 26
mural paintings *24*
Musée Guimet, Paris 37

Muslims
conquests 25
temple destruction 30
see also Islam; Islamic rulers
Muttaraiyar dynasty 216
Muvarkovil, Kodumbalur (Tamil Nadu) 216-18
southern shrine *217*
three-storey *shala* aedicule in central shrine 217, *217*

nabhi-chchanda 158
Nachna (MP): *chatur-mukha-linga* (four-faced) *53*
nadas (energy channels) 47
Naga tank, Sudi (Karnataka) 33, 35, *35*
Nagadeva, General 33, *35*, 64
Nagara
aedicular components of later Nagara temples *116*
architecture 14, *64*, 74, *80*, 87, *107*, 134, 148, 194
combining with Dravida 226-27
early aedicular Nagara traditions 110
language 14, 110, 111, 134, 148, 161, 176, 235
mainstream 163
modes 14, 106, 108, 111
order 14
Shekhari mode *15*, 16
shrines 13, 14
style 14
type 14
Nagara shrines *13*, 90, 106-23
Bhumija 118-20
birth of the Latina 108-10
early aedicular Ngara traditions 110
five Nagara modes 106-8
late Phamsana forms 120-23
Latina 113-15
Phamsana 111
Shekhari 115-18
shrine model *64*
Valabhi 112-13
Nagara temples *see* Bhumija temples; early Nagara temples; Latina and related Valabhi temples; Shekhari temples; temples of Eastern India
nagas (snake spirits) *157*, 197
Nagda (Rajasthan)
Sas-Bahu complex *15*, 16, *43*
Vamana shrine *15*, 16, 184
Nageshvara 33
Nakula-Sahadevas: *ratha* 208, *209*, *209*

Nalanda (Bihar) 174
characteristic types of *gavaksha* 163
kuta projecting from brick stupa *169*
small *stupa*, *amalaka* shrine depicted *168*
Stupa 3 *193*
Temple 2: *gavaksha* *162*
Valabhi-fronted *stupas* *163*
Nalanda university 192
Nanchna (MP): temple *98*
Nand Chand (MP): plain *linga* 52, *53*
Nandi (bull) 103, *129*, 215
Nandi-Potavarma 30
Narasimha (man-lion) 43, 53
Narasimha Pota-Varma 31
Narasimhavarma II Rajasimha 210
Narayana 53, 54
Nareshara: Mata-ka-Mandir (MP) 176, *176*
Narttamalai (Tamil Nadu)
moulded temple base *218*
temple *129*
Vijayalaya-Cholishvara temple *130*
Nasik (Maharashtra)
Cave 3 (Gautamiputra) *79*, 151
Cave 17 *79*
chaitya hall, Cave 18 *79*
monastery (*vihara*) *79*, *150*
Natesha *217*
Nava Adinatha temple, Adishvara Tuk, Mount Shatrunjaya (Palitana) (Gujarat) *237*, *238*, *239*
Navalakha temple, Sejakpur (Gujarat) *96*, *145*, 185, *185*
Navalinga temple, Kukkanur *222*
nave-and-aisles
cross section *92*
image *81*
Navi Adinatha temple, Adisvara Tuk, Mount Shatrunjaya 237
Nayakas 234, 236, 240
Nayanars 54
Nelliappar temple, Tirunelveli: Dravida *gavaksha* *164*
Nemawar (MP) 190
neo-Platonism 48
Nepal 49
New Delhi: Chhattarpur complex 239
niches *64*, *91*, 113, *127*, *161*, 191, *217*
aedicular 179, 218
blind 226
Nilakantha Mahadeva temple, Sunak (Gujarata) *96*, 185
Nimiyaheda (UP): brick temple 142, *181*
Niralgi (Karnataka): Siddharameshvara 151
Nirvana 74

Nolambas of Hemavati at Nandi (Karnataka) 222
nomadic pastoralists 22
Nuggihalli (Karnataka) 191

orientation 137
Orissa 175, 234
cult of Jagannatha 32
early influence of mainstream Nagara 163
formation of 193
gavakshas 164, *164*
heartland 193, 197, 203n5
masons of 182, 201
temples 39, 192, 193, 195, 199-203
Valabhi aedicules 113
orthogonal plans 138-40, 158, *158*
Osian (Rajasthan)
ghata-pallava pillars 155
Harihara Temple 1 *179*
Harihara Temple 3: open *mandapa* interior *97*
Maha-Maru style 177
Mahavira temple 120
Sachinya Mata temple 120
overdoors *170*
overlap 163

Padhaoli (Paraoli) (MP) 25
padma-shilas 156
Pagan, Burma 173
Paharpur (Bangladesh): *stupa* court 101
Pakistan 80
Pala domains 113
Pala period *113*, 163, *163*, 192, 194-95, *194*
Pala sculpture 192
'Pala' tradition 202
Palamet: Ramappa temple (AP) *231*
Palari, Dakshina Koshala (now Chhatisgarh): Siddheshvara temple 173, *173*
stellate plans *172*
Pallavas 30, 85, 208, 210, 216
panch-ayatana ('five-shrine' plan) *100*, 101, 103, *179*, 198
Pancha Pandava *Rathas* 209n3
Panchalingeshvara, Huli (Karnataka) *100*
Pancharatra sect 30
Pancharatra tradition 54-55, 59
Pandava brothers 209n3
Pandya dynasty 85, 215, 216
panjara (Dravida pavilion) 76, *130*, *132*, *146*, 226
panjara-stambha *132*, 198, 221, *224*, *230*

pantheism 12
Papanatha temple, Pattadakal (Karnataka) *177*
Para Shiva 53
Paramara clan 31, 188, *196*
Parasurameshvara temple, Bhuvabeshvara (Orissa) 59-60, 175-76, 195, *195*
Parasurameshvara type 195-99
Parel, near Mumbai: stele *17*
parinama (emanation, evolution) 47
Parsvanatha temple, Ranakpur (Rajasthan) 236, *237*, 238
Parthenon, Athens 20
Parvati 52, 58
Parvati (Devi) temple, Ramgarh (Rajasthan) *191*
Pashupatas 52
Pataliputra (Patna, Bihar) 192
Pattadakal (Karnataka) 29, 32, 174, 175
  Galaganatha temple 40-41, *40*, 109, 174-75
  Jain temple *98*, *222*, 223
  Kashivishveshvara temple *178*, *214*
  Mallikarjuna temple (previously Trailoleshvara) 31, *146*, *205*, 210, 214, *214*
    west view *214*
  Papanatha temple *177*
  Sangameshvara *151*, 213, *213*
  Virupaksha temple (previously Lokeshvara) 31, 92, *92*, *127*, 210, 213, *213*, *214*
    Dravida *gavakshas 164*
pattika (fillet) 145
pavilions
  Buddha-housing barrel-roofed 84
  corner (*kama-kutas*) *107*, 108-9, 110, 114, *117*, *122*, 169, 174, 176
  crowning *130*
  Dravida-karma 188
  haras (chains of) 16, 84, 87, *117*, *126*, 128, 132, 147, 208, 209
  kuta 209, 210
  linked 129, 132
  miniature *126*, 190-91
  new 235
  Phamsana 120, 123
  shala 207, 209, 212, 213
  thatched roof forms 125-26
  Valabhi *191*
peasants 26
pediments 181, *200*
  niche *190*
  triangular 80
pendants (*lumas*) 159

Perennial Philosophy 20
performing arts 13, 29
Persian empire 23
phalaka (bearing plate) 153, 189
phalaka-padma 153
Phamsana 108, 111, *111*, 112, *114*, 135, *135*, 168, 169, 184, 188, 194
  kuta 223
  late Phamsana forms 120, *122*, 123
  multiple *186*
  tiered-roofed 182
Phamsana shrine, Mahadeva temple, Bileshvara (Gujarat) *171*
Phamsana temple, Badami (Karnataka) *94*
philosophical schools 47-48
Pichard, Pierre *105*, *220*
Pidha Deul *122*, 123, 199
pilasters 97, *107*, 109, 132, 148, *161*, *222*
  Corinthian *81*
  corner 170
  cushion-type *79*, *87*, 171, *178*, 189, 197, 206
  Dravida *151*, 152
  paired 171
  split *42*, 43, 103, 209, *217*
  sprouting vase type (*ghata-pallava*) *87*, 194, 196
  thick 115, 149
Pillamarri (AP): Erakeshvara temple 189
pillars *116*, 148-55
  bell type 150, *150*
  bharana 154, 155, *155*, *185*
  blocks and roundels 150-51, *151*
  cross section 149
  cushion *151*, 152-54, 155, *155*, 209
  cushion-type *87*
  designs 82
  double 155
  ghata-pallava 153, 154-55
  Indo-Gangetic 154
  Indo-Persepolitan 150
  Persepolitan 150
  sprouting vase type (*ghata-pallava*) *87*
'pipal leaf' ('moonstone') motif *190*
pitha (sub-base) 144, *145*, *186*, 188, *189*, 200, *202*
polycentricity 26, 35n10, 44, 156
Popper, Karl: *The Poverty of Historicism* 19
porches 90, 92, 96, 106, 199, 209, 215
  false 98
  Valabhi *182*
post-colonialism 19

Post-Modernism 19
Prachi, Saurashtra: Bhim-Deval temple 184
pradakshina see circumambulation
pradakshina-patha (ambulatory path) 97, 98, *98*, *99*, 183
Pradyumna 55
prakara (enclosure) *99*, *102*, *103*, *104*
prakriti (manifestation) 47, 68, 160
prasada (palace; Nagara shrine) 90, 98
prati (floor moulding) 43, *127*, *129*, *146*, *190*, *197*, 198, 215, 222, 225
prati-bhadra (intermediate projection) 187, 202, 224
prati-kantha (plank-recess') 146
prati-lata 113, *175*, *178*
Pratihara period *180*
pratoli (gatehouse) 103
progressive multiplication 67, 69, 157, 169, 209, 212
'projected manifestations' concept 58, 59
projections 37, *37*, 66, 69, 90, *91*, 112, 114, 115, 117, *117*, *120*, 128-29, 133, *178*, 179, *179*, *180*, 183, 184, 187, *187*, 190, 191, 195, 203, 214, *214*, 220-21, *229*, 237
proliferation 66-67, 69, 111, 163, 164, *178*
proto-Shekhari *122*, 184, *185*, *187*, 187n5
puja (acts of worship) 28
Pullamangai: Brahmapurishvara temple 218, 220
  panjara aedicule 218
Puranas 17, 48, 49, 51, 52, 55
Puri: Jagannatha temple 31, 114, 202
purna-ghata ('brimming vase') 154
purusha 23, 45, 47, 53
Purusha Suktra ('Hymn of Man') 22-23
pyramid, inverted stepped 74

quarter-*shringas* (*prati-angas*) 118, 139, 140, 185, 187, 236-37, 238

Raghurajpur (Orissa): village goddess 51
Rajaraja I 31, *31*, 33
Rajarajeshvara temple, Tanjavur *see* Brihadeshvara temple, Tanjavur
Rajarani temple, Bhuvaneshvara (Orissa) 57, 199-200, *200*
Rajasimeshvara 31
Rajasimha 112, 213
Rajasimheshvara ('Lord [Shiva] of

Rajasimha or Lion King') temple *see* Kailasanatha, Kanchipuram
Rajasthan 174, 182, 188
Rajendra Choli 31, *31*, *220*, 221
Rajim (Chhatisgarh): Rajivalochana temple 110, *110*, 171
Rajivalochana temple, Rajim (Chhatisgarh) 110, *110*
Rajputs 27, 174, 234
  palaces 235
Ramanathpura: Rameshvara temple 230
Ramappa temple, Palampet (AP) *231*
Ramayana 48
Rameshvara, Gadag: Dravida *gavaksha 164*
Rameshvara Mahadeva temple, Amrol (MP) *139*, *175*
  Latina shrine 145
Rameshvara temple, Ramanathpura 230
Ramgarh (Rajasthan): Parvati (Devi) temple *191*
Ranakpur (Rajasthan)
  Adinatha temple 237, *237*
  Jain temple complex 236
  Parsvanatha temple 236, *237*, 238
  Surya temple 191n7
Ranch museum (Jharkhand) 113
ranga-mandapa (Samvarana open hall) 96, *185*, 230
Ranipur-Jharial (Orissa): temple 173, *173*
Rashtrakutas 87, 210, 214, 222
rathas ('chariots', 'vehicles') *91*, 126, 208-9, *208*, 216
Rauravottar Agama 58
Ravana Phadi cave, Aihole (Karnataka) 87, 126, *126*
  alpa vimana 206, 207, *207*
reabsorption 49, 51, 52, 53, 60
regional centres 25-26
'Rekha Deul' 114, 173, 198, *199*
relief carvings 14
remission of sins 28
Renaissance 66
Rig Veda 23
rock-cut architecture
  Buddhist 82-84
  later 82-87
  mythological panels 84-85
  pillar designs 82
Roda (Gujarat)
  Maha-Gurjara style 177, *178*
  mainstream *gavaksha 162*
  Temple 3 *178*, *179*
  Temple 4 *178*
Roman world 23, 80

INDEX **253**

roofs
 'bangaldar' 241
 flat 93, 97, *104*, 169, *214*
 mandapa 200
 'nave and aisles' 93
 'pent roof' 111, *111*, *122*, 169
 Phamsana *223*
 pyramidal 96
 Samvarana 123, *123*, *145*
 tiered 199
 Type 5 Shekhari shrine roof plan *236*
roundels 150-51, *190*
Royal Institute of British Architects 20
Rudra (god of storms) 48
Ruskin, John 20, 64

Sachdev, Vibhuti 57
Sachiya Mata temple, Osian (Rajasthan) 120
sacrifice
 blood 50
 Brahminic emphasis on 11, 45
 and chiefs'/kings' legitimacy 22
 and rituals of temple foundation 28
 Vedic 23, 45, *107*
 horse (*ashvamedha*) 24
Sadashiva 52, 53, *53*, 58
Sadyojata 53, 58
Sakegaon (Maharashtra) *120*
Salt Range 114
salvation 17, 18
samantachakra (circle of tributary princes) 26
Samarangana Sutradhara 62
Samel (Gujarat): Galateshvara temple *191*
Samhitas (Vaishnava Tantras) 55
Samhkya school 46, 47, 54
Samiddheshvara temple, Chittor (Rajasthan) *119*, 187
Samkarshana 55
Samvarana 123, 134
 halls 182, *185*, *187*
Sanchi (MP)
 Great Stupa (Stupa 1) *74*, 76
 Gupta shrines 168
 Temple 1 *150*
Sander (Gujarat): Sanderi Mata temple *185*
Sanderi Mata temple (Type 2), Sander (Gujarat) 185, *185*
sandhara 100, 129, 207
 plans 97-98, *98*, 184, *206*
Sangameshvara temple, Mahakuta, near Badama (Karnataka) *13*
Sangameshvara temple (previously Vijayeshvara), Pattadakal *151*, 213, *213*

Sanskrit 24
Sapta-matrikas (Seven Mothers), Ellora (Cave 23) (Maharashtra) *36*
Saraswati (goddess) 235
Sarnath (UP) 150
 Buddhist temple 169
 kuta 169
 pavilion from overdoor *170*
Sarnel (Gujarat) 191
 Galateshvara temple 191
Sarvatobhadra shrine, Cave 32 (Indrasabhe), Ellora (Maharashtra) *91*, 215, *215*
Sas-Bahu temple, Gwalior 96
Sas-Bahu temple complex, Nagda (Rajasthan): Vamana shrine *15*, *16*, 184
Saunshi (Karnataka) shrine model *133*
Saurashtra style 182
Saurashtra (western Gujarat) 111, *111*, 169, 184
screens
 pierced *99*
 traceried 97
segmentary state 26-27, 32
Sejakpur (Gujarat): Navalakha temple 96, *145*, 185, *185*
semi-stellate plans 173, 191, *229*, 231
Seunadesha (north-west Maharashtra) 118, 188, 189, 190
Shah, Sultan Ibrahim Adil 235
Shailodbhavas 193
Shaiva (worshippers of Shiva) 12, 82
Shaiva Siddhanta 52, 55, 59
Shaivism 52-53
Shaka era 32
shakas (bands) 144
Shakta cults 51
shaktis (energies) 51
shala-stambhas 227
shalas (barrel-roofed pavilions) 16, *42*, 43, 76, *85*, *125*, 126, *127*, *128*, 129, *130*, 206, 208, 215, 217, *222*
 apsidal *219*
 double-staggered *42*, 43, *43*, 69, 70, 132, *132*
 precursors of 83, 84
 single-staggered *42*, 43, 69
 staggered *43*, 70, *87*, 129, 132, *132*, *207*
Shamka (an architect) 64
Shankara 47
Shankaracharyas 51
Shantinatha Jain temple, Kumbharia (Gujarat) *105*

Sharma, RC: 'The Feudal Mind' 22
Shatavahana empire 23
Shekhari mode 15, 16, *16*, 42, *43*, 58, 64, 67, 68, 106, 111, 115, 117-18, *118*, *119*, 134, 139, *140*, 140, *141*, 155, 165, 181, 226, 236, *237*, 238
Shekhari shrine roof plan *236*
Shekhari temples 68, 115, *116*, 140, 140, *141*, 165, 182-89
shikhara (tower/spire of Nagara temple) 16, 40-41, *40*, 58, *109*, 110, 113-14, 115, *116*, 142, *145*, *146*, 168, *173*, 174, 175, 176, 184, 195, 199, 201, *202*, 203
 half-*shikharas* 42
 Latina 117, 119, 142, *201*
 quarter-*shikharas* 42
shilpins (sculptors) 63
Shiva *17*, 210
 and dynasties 28
 ferocious form of (Bhairava) 50
 lower series of his manifestations 58
 manifestations of *217*
 many names and aspects 52
 palace mountain of Shiva, Kailasa temple, Kanchipura *104*
 paramount kings' devotion to 30
 phallic emblem (*linga*) 37, *42*, 52, 53, *53*, 221
 in shrines 12
 supreme god 48
 and Tantric ideas 51
Shiva cave, Elephanta (near Mumbai) *73*, *86*
Shiva Nataraja (Lord of the Dance)
 cult of, at Chidambaram 32
 Ellora (Cave 23) (Maharashtra) 32
Shiva temple, Bahulara 202-3
Shiva temple, Bhavanipur (Rajasthan) *181*
Shiva temple, Dhobini (Chhatisgarh): Dakshina Koshala *173*
 stellate plans *172*
Shiva temple, Dulhinganj (Bihar) *240*
Shiva temple, Indor (MP) *142*, 176, *176*
Shiva Temple 1, Kiradu (Rajasthan) *117*
Shiva Temple 2, Mahua (MP) *175*
Shore temple, Mahabalipuram 212
shri chakra 51
Shri (goddess) 51
Shri Vidya 51
Shri Yantra *49*, 51, 57
'Shrine of the Double-Headed Eagle', Sirkap, Taxilka (Pakistan) *81*

shrines 90
 amalaka 108, *108*, 109, *109*, 168
 Anekandaka (multi-limbed) 115, *115*
 apsidal 207
 bhadra 231
 Bhumija 64, 106, 118-20
 Buddhist 82
 Chola 31
 circular/elliptical/apsidal 134
 countryside 27
 Dravida *see* vimana
 five-projection 128
 'five-shrine' plan 101
 four-projection 128
 free-standing 83
 Gandhara *80*
 image-housing 11, 14
 inner sanctum 12, 16, 90
 Karnata Dravida 189-90
 kuta 81
 Latina 68, 106, 108-10, 112-15, *113*, *114*, 141, 176, 198
 main directions of movement *36*, 38
 Mandapika 169
 miniature, free-standing reliefs 81
 multiple 98, *100*, 101
 Nagara *see* Nagara shrines
 octagonal 134
 Phamsana *60*, 84, 93, 106, 111, *111*, *113*, *171*, 176
 plans *91*
 proto-Shekhari 115
 Samvarana 93
 Sarvatobhadra 91
 Shekhari 16, *16*, 58, 106, 113, 115, 117-18, 139, 155, 200, 228, 237
 five principal types 117-18, 184
 Type 1 117, 184, 187
 Type 2 117, 184, 185, *185*, 187
 Type 3 117, 185, *185*
 Type 4 117-18, *117*, 185, *185*, *186*, 187
 Type 5 117, 118, *186*, 187, *187*
 square 128, 134
 stellate 128, 132-33, *190*, 225, 227, *230*
 three-projection 128, 179
 Valabhi 39-40, *39*, 76, 106, *108*, 112-13, *112*, *113*, 120, 132, 176, 190, *190*, 195, *196*, *199*
 Vesara 134
 village/roadside 15
 votive 126
Shrivasti *81*
Shudras (slaves and labourers) 22
shuka-nasas ('parrot's beak') (frontons) 92, 97, 113, *114*, *120*, 132, *135*, *177*, 213, 215, *223*

Siddharameshvara, Niralgi (Karnataka) *151*
   Dravida *gavakshas 164*
Siddheshvara, Haveri (Karnataka) *96*
Siddheshvara, Mudhol: Dravida *gavakshas 164*
Siddhesvara temple, Palari, Dakshina Koshala (now Chhatisgarh) 173, *173*
   stellate plans: *172*
siddhis (magical powers) 49
Sikh *gurudwaras* 235
Sinan, Mimar 157
Sinnar (Maharashtra): Gondeshvara temple *100*, *101*, 188
Sirkap, Taxilka (Pakistan)
   'Shrine of the Double-Headed Eagle' *81*
   stupa base 80
Sirpur (Chhattisgarh) 197
   Lakshmana temple 171, *172*
   gavaksha 160
Sirval (northern Karnataka) 222
Sisireshvara temple, Bhuvaneshvara *167*, 196, 197, *197*
Sivunur 33
'Solanki' models 240
Solankis 182
Somavamshis 193, 196
Someshvara (a Brahmin votary) 33
Someshvara, Kiradu (Rajasthan) 185, 227
Someshvara temple, Gadag (Karnataka) 227, *228*
Someshvara temple, Lakshmeshvara 227, *228*
Somnatha Patan (Gujarat) *154*
Somnathpur (Karnataka): Keshava temple *99*, *229*
Sompura caste 239
South-east Asia 15, 32, 192, 216
splitting *37*, 38, 67, 69
Srangapani temple, Kumbakonam: Dravida *gavaksha 164*
Sri Lanka 216
Sri Venkateshvara temple of the United Kingdom, Oldbury (West Midlands, UK) 240
Srinivasanallur (Tamil Nadu): Koranganatha *151*
staggering *37*, 67, 69, 90, 154, 213-14, 222-23, 225
stambhas (pillars) 16, *145*, 197
Stein, Burton 32
stele *17*
stellate plans 140-42, *172*, 173, 191, 225
stoboscopic photographs 39

Stravana Belagola 222
stucco work *210*, 221, 236
stupa courts 101, 103
stupas 12, 17, 74, *74*, *76*, *77*, *78*, *79*, 83
   Gandharan 80, *81*
   lack of an entrance 101
   miniature 81
   railings 150
   Valabhi-fronted *153*, *163*
   votive 194
sub-bases 144-45
sub-mouldings 144, *146*
subhadra (a projection) 138-39
Sudi (Karnataka) 32
   Akkeshvara temple (now Mallikarjuna) 32, *42*
   Jodu-Kalashada temple 33, 64, *223*, *224*
   Naga (snake spirit) tank 33, 35, *35*
Sul (goddess at Bath) 51
Sulba Sutras 136
Summerson, John: 'Heavenly Mansions' 10
Sunak (Gujarat): Nilakantha Mahadeva temple *96*, *185*
Sundareshvara temple complex, Nangavaram (Tamil Nadu): Ganesha shrine *127*
sunya (the void) 68
Survaya (MP): small shrine on roof of monastery *182*
Surya shrine, Kashivishveshvara temple, Lakkundi *223*
Surya temple, Dhank (Gujarat) *173*
Surya temple, Jhalarapatan (Rajasthan) *191*
Surya temple, Konarak 31, 114, 202
Surya temple, Madkheda *139*, *180*
Surya temple, Modhera (Gujurat) *103*, *104*, 105, *153*, *154*, *187*
Surya temple, Ranakpur (Rajasthan) 1917
Surya temple, Umri *139*, *180*
Surya (the sun) 48, *180*
sutra-grahin ('drawer of the thread') 63

Taj Mahal *116*, 235
Takht-i-Bahi 81
   Court of the Stupa *80*
takshaka (stone-cutter) 63
talas (tiers) 16, 127, 128, 133, *146*, 147, 157, 207, 209, 216, 220, 222, 223
Tamil culture 25
Tamil Nadu 25, 26, 31, 153, 208
   architects 239, 240

canonical texts 134
cave temples 85
Dravida temples 39, 43, 124, 125
multiple shrines 101
Shaiva Siddhanta 52
Tamil temples 125
Tamil tradition 222
Tanjavur (Tanjore)
   Brihadeshvara (Brihadishvara) temple 31, *31*, 32, 42, 105, *105*, *219*, 220-21
   Brihadeshvara temple, *vimana 139*, *219*
tanks 11, *103*, 105
Tantra 27-28, 49-51, 57
   Kashmiri 51
   Tantric erotic sculpture 61
   Vajrayana 49
   Vaishnava 55
Tantras 49
Taranga (Gujarat): Ajitanatha temple *64*, 187, *187*
Tarappa Basappa, Aihole (Karnakata) *93*
Tatpunsha 58
tattvas ('thatnesses') 47
Telangana (north-west AP) 189, 231
Telangana, schools of (north-west AP) 227
Teli-ka Mandir, Gwalior (MP) 39-40, *39*, 176, *177*
temples
   and the arts 13
   Bhumija 113, *116*, 133, 143n11, 154, *163*, 188-91, *228*, 241
   Chola 139
   connection with the body 36-37, 44, 148
   construction 13, 27, 106, 223
   contemporary 238-41
   desecration 30
   design/making as a collective enterprise 63
   Doric 69
   Dravida *see* Dravida temples
   dynamism in temple architecture 16, *17*, *41*
   expressing movement
      an animation of the basic axial organisation of the temple 38
      bursting of boundaries 38, *38*
      expanding repetition 38, 42
      projection 37, *37*
      splitting *37*, 38
      staggering *37*
   foundation and endowment of 13
   great age of medieval temples (AD 600–1300) 25

   guilds' patronage 28
   Gupta 97
   Hoysala *229*, 231, *231*
   important economic institutions 13
   Jain 14, 90, 96
   Kakatiya 231
   Karnata Dravida *42*, *43*, *64*, *69*, 189
   mishraka 191
   Nagara 15, 39, 134, 135, 138, 147, 207
   nirandhara 97
   Pallava 209
   Phamsana 135, 189
   pyramidal 22
   in recent years 234-35
   rock-cut cave temples 24
   royal 27, 28
   sandhara 97-98, *183*
   Shekhari *see* Shekhari temples
   social and educational centres 13
   Tamil 125
   Valabhi 112-13
   'Vesara' 135
   village 27
   wooden 14-15
temples of the Cholas and their contemporaries 216-21
temples of Eastern India 192-203
   fresh Nagara contacts 199-200
   an influx of early aedicular Nagara 196
   later Orissan temples 201-2
   meanwhile in Bengal 202-3
   the Parasurameshvara and early Orissan Latina 195-96
   a southern wave 196-99
   temple architecture of Bihar, Jarkhand and Bengal 194-95
Ter (Maharashtra)
   alpa vimanas 126
   brick shrine 206
theistic cults 23
theology 45
Theravada ('Hinayana') Buddhism 83
Tibet 49, 192
Tigawa (MP): Gupta shrines 168
Timur 234
Tirthankaras (Jain teachers) 12
Tirunelveli: Nelliappar temple: Dravida *gavaksha 164*
Tiruvannamalai (Tamil Nadu): Arunachaleshvara temple *236*
Tollotson, Giles 57
Tondainadu 216
toranas (gateways, archways) *42*, 43, *74*, *76*, *81*, *102*, *105*, *113*, 155, 194, 198
tortoise (*kurma*) 58

INDEX   **255**

Torugare 60 district 32
torus 144, *145*
trade
    contraction of long-distance trade 26
    developments in 32
    trade routes 23, 74
Trailokamahadavi 31
Trailokeshvara temple *see* Mallikarjuna temple, Pattadakal
transcendence 49
trefoil 161, *164*, 194
tribal areas, integration of 27
tribal states 22, 23
Tribhuvanam 221
Trikuteshvara temple, Gadag (Karnataka) *146*
Trimbakesvara temple, Trimbak (Maharashtra) 237-38, *240*
tula-pitha 145, *146*, *180*
Turuvekere (Karnataka) 191

Udaka province 30
Udayaditya, King 188
Udayagiri (MP) 82
    Cave 1: *ekha-mukha-linga* (one-faced) *53*
    Cave 7: carved lotus ceiling *156*
Udayapur (MP): Udayeshvara temple 188, *188*
Udayeshvara temple, Udayapur (MP) 188, *188*, 190
udgamas (niche 'pediments') 113
Umri: Surya temple *139*, *180*
unfolding 69-70, *69*, *158*, *159*
'unfolding cosmos' idea 17
universe
    as an unfolding of phenomena from formlessness to form 45
    created by Brahma 54
    as a layered topography of worlds and heavens 45
UP *see* Uttar Pradesh
upana (plain plinth courses) 146
Upanishads 46, 47
upapitha (sub-base) 144, *145*, *219*, *220*
upper Indus Valley 114
Upper Shivalaya, Badami (Karnataka) *11*, *206*, 207, *207*
    Dravida *gavakshas* *164*
urah-shringas (half-spires) 58, 115, 117, 118, *122*, 123, *139*, 140, 184, *186*, 187, 201, *228*, 236, 237

Vaikuntha Perumal, Kanchipuram *151*, 212-13

Vaisali (Bihar): Mauryan bell pillar *150*
Vaishnava (worshippers of Vishnu) 12, 24, 82
Vaishnava temple, Anwa (Maharashtra) *155*
Vaishnavism 53-55, 193
Vaishyas (traders and free peasants) 22
Vaital Deul shrine, Bhuvaneshvara *112*, 113, *167*, 196, *196*, *197*
Vakataka dynasty 24, *24*, 82
Valabhi 81, 112-13
    aedicule 41
    cascade *122*, *183*, *186*
    gables 113, 197
    porch *182*
    projections 123
Valabhi shrine form 39-40, *39*, 76, 161, 169, 176
Vamadeva 58
Vamana shrine, Sas-Bahu complex, Nagda (Rajasthan) *15*, *16*, 184
Vamana temple, Khajuraho 181
Varaguna 217
Varaha (boar) 53
Varahi temple, Chaurasi *197*
Varanasi 238
varandika (cornice zone) 145, *175*, 179, 201
vardhaki ('fitter') 63
varnas (estates) 22
vase-finial (*stupi, kalasha*) 146
vastu-purusha-mandala ('diagram of the spirit of the site') 56-57, *138*, 242
vastu-shastra texts 58, 62
Vastushastra of Vishvakarman 58
Vasuveda 53, 55
Vatapi (now Badami) 207, 210
Vatsyayan, Kapila 18
Vedanta 47, 59
Vedas 45, 54
vedibandha (moulded base) 144, *144*, *145*, *146*, *176*, *180*, *188*
Vedic ritual 23
vedika (rail moulding) *145*, *146*, 147, 171, *172*, *180*, 198, *207*, *218*
verandas 96
Vesara 134, 135, 222, 223, 226
Vetuvankovil, Kalugumalai (Tamil Nadu) *215*
Vidisha: Bijamandal 188
viharas see monasteries
Vijayaditya (Chalukya king) 213
Vijayalaya-Cholishvara temple, Narttamalai (Tamil Nadu) *130*
Vijayanagara (Karnataka) 234, 236
Vijayawada (AP): Akkanna-Madanna caves 87

Vikramaditya II ('Son of Valour') 30-31, 210, 213
Vikramaditya V 32
Vimala Vasahi, Dilwara (Mount Abu) (Rajasthan): Jain temple *94*
vimana (Dravida shrine) 9, 13, 14, *15*, 16, *42*, 43, *43*, 90, 97, 98, *99*, *103*, *105*, 124-35, 139, *207*, *211*, *212*, 214, *214*, 215, *215*, 216, 218, *219*, 221, 226, 236, *241*
    alpa vimanas: the simplest Dravida shrines 126-27
    analysis 228
    the Dravida language and early wooden buildings 125-26
    Dravida modes and 'Vesara' 134-35
    lateral *230*
    multi-aedicular vimana designs 127-32
    stellate *vimanas* 132-33
Vira-Narayana temple, Belavadi (Karnataka) 9, *43*
    ceiling *158*
    north-east shrine *229*
Vireshvara 217
Virupaksha temple (previously Lokeshvara), Pattadakal (Karnataka) 31, 92, *92*, 127, 210, 213-14, *213*, *214*
    Dravida *gavakshas* *164*
Vishnu
    avataras of 53
    city of 17
    and dynasties 28
    forms of 213
    fusion with non-Vedic deities 48
    and Gupta elite 192
    linga myth 37
    Pancharatra cult of 30
    in shrines 12
    solar energy 48
    supreme god 48, 53
    and Tantric ideas 51
    as *vishva-rupa* ('universe-form') 54
Vishnu Anantashayin 49
    Mahishasuramardini cave, Mahabalipuram (Tamil Nadu) *54*
Vishnu temple, Deogath (MP) *58*
Vishnuvardhana 189
Vishvanatha temple, Khajuraho (MP) *60*, 185, *186*
Vitruvius 148
Vitthala temple, Hampi (Vijayanagara) (Karnataka) *235*
Volwahsen, Andreas 57
vyuhas (emanations) 55

West Bengal 192, 202
Western Gangas of Talkad 222
Western Ghats (Maharashtra) 76
Wölfflin, Heinrich 37, 66
worship halls 13-14

Yadava dynasty (Seuna) 182, 188, 238
yajamana (performer of a sacrifice, founder of a temple) 23
yantras (sacred diagrams) 49, 51, 57
Yashovarman, emperor 174, 176
Yellama Gudi, Badami (Karnataka) *11*, *96*, 224
Yoga 37, 47, 49
Yoga Sutra of Patanjali 47
Yoga Sutras 68
Yoginis 51

Zimmer, Heinrich 37-38, *39*